Teacher Resource Manual

to Accompany

GLENCOE

INTRODUCTION TO Web Design

Using Dreamweaver®

Mark A. Evans   Michael Hamm

WebDesignDW.glencoe.com

New York, New York   Columbus, Ohio   Chicago, Illinois   Peoria, Illinois   Woodland Hills, California

The McGraw·Hill Companies

Copyright © by Glencoe/McGraw-Hill, a division of the McGraw-Hill Companies. All rights reserved. Permission is granted to reproduce the material contained herein on the condition that such material be reproduced only for classroom use; be provided to students, teachers, and families without charge; and be used solely in conjunction with *Introduction to Web Design Using Dreamweaver*. Any other reproduction, for sale or other use, is expressly prohibited.

Macromedia, Dreamweaver, and all other Macromedia names and logos are registered trademarks of Macromedia Corporation and are used with permission.

All brand names and product names are trademarks or registered trademarks of their respective companies.

ExamView® is a registered trademark of FSCreations, Inc.

Between the time that Web site information is gathered and published, it is not unusual for some sites to have closed. URLs will be updated in reprints when possible.

Printed in the United States of America.

Send all inquiries to:
Glencoe/McGraw-Hill
21600 Oxnard Street, Suite 500
Woodland Hills, CA 91367

ISBN-13: 978-0-07-873686-5
ISBN-10: 0-07-873686-2

2 3 4 5 6 7 8 9   079   11 10 09 08 07 06

TABLE OF CONTENTS

PART 1: TEACHER RESOURCES

Introduction 2
    The Importance of a Web Design Course 2
    Goals of This Book 2
    Course Philosophy 3

National Standards 4
    SCANS Competencies 4
        Connect Skills, School, and Careers 4
        SCANS Correlations 5
    ISTE and Technology Standards 6
        NETS-S Technology Standards for Students 6
        NETS-S Technology Performance Indicators for Students 8
        NETS-S Correlations 9
        NETS-T Educational Technology Performance Profiles for Teachers 10

Program Components 12
    Student Textbook 12
    Student Workbook 13
    Teacher Resource Manual 13
    Teacher Resource CD 14
    Web Site 14

Organization and Content 16
    Teaching with the Student Textbook 16
        How to Use the Unit Opener 16
        How to Use the Chapter Opener 17
        How to Use the Sections 18
        How to Use the Chapter Review 20
    Using the Teacher Resource Manual 22

Course Planning 26
    Guidelines for a Successful Course 26
    Planning a Course and Suggested Course Pacing Charts 28
        How to Develop a Pacing Chart 28
        Suggested Course Pacing Charts 28

TABLE OF CONTENTS

Writing a Course Outline.. 31
    Suggested Course Outline 32
Guidelines for the Technology Classroom 34
    Using the Internet 34
    Acceptable Use Policies 34
    Downloading Files 34
    Copyright Guidelines.. 34
    Suggested Classroom Resources.. 35
    Publishing Web Sites.. 35
    Using the Student Data Files 36
    Recommended Hardware and Software... 38
    Using Equipment 38
    Saving Student Work.. 38

Tools for Professional Development... **39**
    Checklist for Class Preparation 39
        Teaching Tips 39
        Record Keeping 41
    General Classroom Guidelines 41
        The Student's Role... 41
        The Teacher's Role 42
        Instruction Style Guidelines.. 43
        The Teacher's Attitude 44
    Learning-Strategy Guidelines 45
        Helping Improve Study Habits and Time Management 45
        Developing Critical Thinking Skills in Students 46
        Improving Basic Skills 48
    Course Enrichment Guidelines 52
        Integrating Real World Connections.. 52
        Integrating Ethics 53
    Classroom Management Guidelines... 54
        Attendance Problems.. 54
        Problems with Incomplete Work... 54
        Attitude Problems 55
        Behavior Problems 56
        Participation Problems 57

TABLE OF CONTENTS

Creating a Learner-Centered Environment 59
    Cooperative Learning 59
        The Basic Elements of Cooperative Learning 59
        The Benefits of Cooperative Learning Groups 60
        Preparation for Cooperative Learning 60
        Create Heterogeneous Teams 61
        Teacher and Student Responsibilities 61
        Results of Cooperative Learning 62
    Cultural Diversity 62
        The Diverse Classroom 62
        Supporting Diversity 62
        Teaching Tips for the Diverse Classroom 63
        Tips for Working with Diverse Students 64
    Meeting Special Needs 65
        Students with Special Needs 66
        Meeting Individual Needs and Learning Styles 66
        Teaching Students with Special Needs 66
        Preparing for Special Needs 67
        Modifying Your Teaching Style 67
        Tips for Teaching Students with Special Needs 68
        Special Needs Information and Resources 70
        Different Learning Styles 74

Assessment and Evaluation 78
    Student Performance Assessment 78
        Assessment Strategies 78
        Performance Assessment 78
        Skills Development 79
        Project Assessment Rubric 79
        Portfolio Assessment 81
    Determining Assessment Strategies 81
    Course Assessment and Evaluation 84
        Assessment of Teachers 84
        Student Assessments of Course 84
        Assessment of Outcomes 85
        Student Advisory Committee 85

TABLE OF CONTENTS

PART 2: CHAPTER LESSON PLANS AND ANSWER KEYS

Unit 1 Fundamentals of Web Design 89
- Chapter 1 Web Basics 90
- Chapter 2 Computer Basics 112
- Chapter 3 Online Basics 130
- Chapter 4 HTML Basics 154

Unit 2 Designing Web Sites 179
- Chapter 5 Planning a Web Site 180
- Chapter 6 Developing Content and Layout 200
- Chapter 7 Selecting Design and Color 222

Unit 3 Enhancing a Web Site 245
- Chapter 8 Using Web Graphics 246
- Chapter 9 Adding Multimedia to a Web Site 264
- Chapter 10 Adding Interactivity to a Web Site 286

Unit 4 The Web Site Development Process 309
- Chapter 11 Project Planning 310
- Chapter 12 Developing a Web Site 328
- Chapter 13 Adding Web Site Functionality 350
- Chapter 14 Publishing a Web Site 374
- Chapter 15 Maintaining a Web Site 398

Unit 5 Advanced HTML 419
- Chapter 16 HTML Tables and Frames 420
- Chapter 17 HTML, Scripting, and Interactivity 440

PART 3: REPRODUCIBLES AND VISUAL AIDS

Graphic Organizers 457
- What Are Graphic Organizers? 458
- Why Use Graphic Organizers? 458
  - Using the Reading Strategy Organizers in the Classroom 459
  - Using Graphic Organizers Effectively 459

TABLE OF CONTENTS

Graphic Organizer Library... **460**
    Graphic Organizer Library Overview 460
    Graphic Organizer 1: Main Idea Chart 465
    Graphic Organizer 2: K-W-L-H Chart...466
    Graphic Organizer 3: Web Diagram..467
    Graphic Organizer 4: Tree Diagram 468
    Graphic Organizer 5: Venn Diagram...469
    Graphic Organizer 6: Matrix..470
    Graphic Organizer 7: Table..471
    Graphic Organizer 8: Pyramid Table..472
    Graphic Organizer 9: Fishbone Diagram 473
    Graphic Organizer 10: Horizontal Time Line 474
    Graphic Organizer 11: Problem-Solution Chart 475
    Graphic Organizer 12: Cause-Effect Chart (Option 1)...........................476
    Graphic Organizer 13: Cause-Effect Chart (Option 2)...........................477
    Graphic Organizer 14: Chain-of-Events or Flowchart............................478

PART 4: POWERTEACH PRESENTATIONS, *EXAMVIEW*®, and TechSIM™ Interactive Tutorials

PowerTeach Guide... **480**
    PowerTeach Presentation Information 480
        Using Presentations in the Classroom 480
    Installation and Startup Instructions...481
        Setting Up Your Equipment 481
        Loading the Presentations...482
        Running a Presentation with PowerPoint.......................................482
        Running a Presentation with PowerPoint Viewer 483
        Customizing a Presentation..483
        Troubleshooting Tips 483

TABLE OF CONTENTS

ExamView User Guide **484**
 ExamView Pro Test Generator Software Information 484
  Site License 484
  Using the Testbank 484
  Software Support Hotline 484
 ExamView Components. 484
  Test Builder 485
  Question Bank Editor 485
  Online Testing (LAN-based versus Internet) 485
 Installation and Startup Instructions. 487
  System Requirements 487
  Installation Instructions. 488
  Startup Instructions 489
  Using the Help System 489

TechSIM™ Interactive Tutorials User Guide **490**

PART 5: COMPLETE CORRELATIONS TO STANDARDS

ISTE NETS-S Correlations. **492**
 National Technology Standards for Students 492
 NETS-S Correlations to Textbook. 493

SCANS Correlations **505**
 SCANS Competencies for Students. 505
 SCANS Correlations to Textbook 506

PART 1

Teacher Resources

Introduction 2
National Standards 4
Program Components 12
Organization and Content 16
Course Planning 26
Tools for Professional Development 41
Creating a Learner-Centered Environment 59
Assessment and Evaluation 78

INTRODUCTION

THE IMPORTANCE OF A WEB DESIGN COURSE

The ability to use technology effectively, productively, and ethically has become an essential skill in almost every aspect of society whether at home, at school, at work, or at play. *Introduction to Web Design Using Dreamweaver*® is a valuable teaching tool to help students learn about Web design, understand the fundamental principles for creating and maintaining Web pages, and practice creating complete Web sites.

COURSE PHILOSOPHY

Introduction to Web Design Using Dreamweaver addresses the real-world needs of students and teachers. The approach is student-centered with reliance upon teacher guidance and facilitation.

Standards-Based Learning The planning and structure of the course is designed to meet state and national standards while exploring the range of Web design technologies.

Project-Based Learning The course promotes a project-based learning environment so that students learn concepts and practice skills in a real-world context.

Guided Step-by-Step Activities The text is written and designed to be used with the whole class and with individual students.

- Activities can be completed as a whole class (with the teacher guiding students through the steps). You may wish to walk students through activity steps before they complete them on their own.
- Students can complete activities independently as self-guided exercises.
- Collaborative projects also provide students with the real-world experience of working with others.

Assessment and Evaluation The text includes traditional assessment strategies and also relies on evaluation techniques through competency-based projects.

- Section assessments are provided throughout the textbook to check student progress.
- Complete reviews and assessments are also provided at the end of every Chapter and Unit.
- In addition, the text includes feature articles that encourage students to explore the impact of technology on society and the workplace along with associated ethical and legal issues.

Reteaching and Enrichment Activities A variety of additional activities are provided on the book Online Learning Center and in this Teacher Resource Manual. These are designed to extend learning opportunities for students who may need additional review and for those students who need enrichment.

COURSE OBJECTIVES

Introduction to Web Design Using Dreamweaver sets the following objectives for students:

Key Concepts

- Explain Web design and identify types of Web sites and URLs.
- Demonstrate an understanding of how society interacts with the Web.
- Learn how to protect your privacy online.
- Describe specific careers in Web development.
- Define and explain the various stages of a Web design project.
- Describe the roles, job responsibilities, and educational backgrounds for members of a Web design team.
- Identify types of computers, input and output devices, memory and storage devices, and networks.
- Describe Web development applications and hardware.
- Understand the principles of good Web design.
- Explain how to download and use files ethically, how to cite sources properly, and how to follow copyright and fair use guidelines.
- Explain online privacy policies and Web site security measures.
- Summarize guidelines for developing e-commerce Web sites.
- Identify current technology trends and emerging technologies.

Application Skills

- Access the Internet safely for communication and research.
- Search the Internet effectively and evaluate Web sites for reliability.
- Use Dreamweaver to create Web sites.
- Plan and storyboard a Web site.
- Evaluate and create Web content.
- Use hyperlinks, graphics, Web-safe colors, and multimedia elements in a Web site.
- Create, crop, resize, and resample graphics.
- Create an image map with hotspots.
- Create a form.
- Debug and test a Web page.
- Publish and update a Web site.
- Use HTML tags and attributes.

NATIONAL STANDARDS

SCANS COMPETENCIES

In 1990 the Secretary of Labor appointed the Secretary's Commission on Achieving Necessary Skills (SCANS). It identified the competencies and skills necessary to achieve success in the workplace. As an educator, your task is to help your students connect school with job success. *Introduction to Web Design Using Dreamweaver* echoes the message SCANS gave to educators.

SCANS identifies **Foundation Skills** essential for job success:

1. **Basic Skills** Reading, writing, arithmetic, mathematics, and listening and speaking skills.
2. **Thinking Skills** Creative thinking, critical thinking, and problem-solving skills.
3. **Personal Qualities** Responsibility, self-esteem, sociability, self-management, integrity, and honesty.

SCANS also identifies important **Workplace Skills:**

4. **Interpersonal Skills** The ability to work on teams, teach others, serve customers, exercise leadership, negotiate, and work with cultural diversity.
5. **Information** The ability to acquire, evaluate, organize, maintain, interpret, communicate, and use computers to process information.
6. **Systems** The ability to understand, monitor, correct, improve, and design systems.
7. **Resources** The ability to manage time, money, materials, facilities, and human resources.
8. **Technology** The ability to select, apply, maintain, and troubleshoot technology.

Connect Skills, School, and Careers

SCANS skills and competencies apply to various jobs in many different occupations. Becoming productive members of the workforce demands that students acquire the appropriate skills and knowledge to compete in a technologically evolving economy.

Successful students are motivated students who know how to connect their school experiences with success in their careers. They realize that what they learn in school correlates directly with finding, keeping, and succeeding in their chosen career. Learning how to succeed in school will serve as a model for working effectively within a business organization. Connecting education and skills development to career pursuits helps students become employable decision-makers and problem-solvers.

NATIONAL STANDARDS

Connections Between Skills, School, and Careers

Skills	School	Career
Basic skills	Foundation for schoolwork	Foundation for work tasks
Motivation	Motivated to attend classes	Motivated to excel at work
Thinking skills	Solve case studies, equations	Solve work problems
Creativity	Creative experiments	Creative work solutions
Control of time	Homework first	Work priorities in order
Control of money	Personal budget	Departmental budgets
Writing	Writing papers	Writing reports, memos
Speeches	Classroom speeches	Presentations
Test taking	Tests in class	Performance reviews
Information	Selecting class information	Selecting work information
Learning	Learning for class	Learning job skills
Systems	Learning school systems	Learning organization systems
Resources	Using school resources	Using work resources
Technology	Using computers for papers or assignments	Using computers for work

SCANS Correlations

A variety of student text features provide opportunities for your students to improve foundation and workplace skills identified by the U.S. Department of Labor Secretary's Commission on Achieving Necessary Skills. The Commission's fundamental purpose is to encourage a high-performance economy characterized by high-skill, high-wage employment. SCANS competencies include both Foundation Skills and Workplace Competencies.

Easy-to-use SCANS correlations are provided for your convenience in the following locations:

◆ Each Chapter Planning Guide in Part 2 of this Manual includes at-a-glance SCANS correlations. Use the guide to quickly locate activities and projects that meet specific SCANS in the chapter you are teaching.

◆ Complete SCANS Correlations are also provided in Part 5 of this Teacher Resource Manual. **See pages 505–519 to find all the activities and projects throughout the student textbook that relate to SCANS.**

NATIONAL STANDARDS

ISTE AND TECHNOLOGY STANDARDS

To live, learn, and work successfully in an increasingly complex and information-rich society, students must be able to use technology effectively. To provide guidelines for effective technology skills, the International Society for Technology in Education (ISTE) has developed National Technology Standards for Students (NETS-S).

NETS-S Technology Standards for Students

The ISTE National Technology Standards for Students (NETS-S) describe what students should know about and be able to do with technology.

The technology foundation standards for students are divided into six broad categories. Standards within each category are to be introduced, reinforced, and mastered by students. These categories provide a framework for linking performance indicators to the standards.

Activities in the book are specifically designed to meet the standards within each category. Teachers can use these standards as guidelines for planning technology-based activities in which students can achieve success in learning, communication, and life skills.

1. **Basic operations and concepts**
   - Students demonstrate a sound understanding of the nature and operation of technology systems.
   - Students are proficient in the use of technology.

2. **Social, ethical, and human issues**
   - Students understand the ethical, cultural, and societal issues related to technology.
   - Students practice responsible use of technology systems, information, and software.
   - Students develop positive attitudes toward technology uses that support lifelong learning, collaboration, personal pursuits, and productivity.

3. **Technology productivity tools**
   - Students use technology tools to enhance learning, increase productivity, and promote creativity.
   - Students use productivity tools to collaborate in constructing technology-enhanced models, prepare publications, and produce other creative works.

4. **Technology communications tools**
   - Students use telecommunications to collaborate, publish, and interact with peers, experts, and other audiences.
   - Students use a variety of media and formats to communicate information and ideas effectively to multiple audiences.

5. **Technology research tools**
    - Students use technology to locate, evaluate, and collect information from a variety of sources.
    - Students use technology tools to process data and report results.
    - Students evaluate and select new information resources and technological innovations based on the appropriateness of specific tasks.

6. **Technology problem-solving and decision-making tools**
    - Students use technology resources for solving problems and making informed decisions.
    - Students employ technology in the development of strategies for solving problems in the real world.

NATIONAL STANDARDS

NETS-S Technology Performance Indicators for Students

In this text, all students have opportunities to demonstrate the following performance indicators for technological literacy. Each performance indicator refers to the NETS-S Technology Standards category or categories (listed on pages 6–7) to which the performance is linked.

Performance Indicators	NETS-S Standards
1. Identify capabilities and limitations of contemporary and emerging technology resources and assess the potential of these systems and services to address personal, lifelong learning, and workplace needs.	(2) Social, ethical, and human issues
2. Make informed choices among technology systems, resources, and services.	(1) Basic operations and concepts (2) Social, ethical, and human issues
3. Analyze advantages and disadvantages of widespread use and reliance on technology in the workplace and in society as a whole.	(2) Social, ethical, and human issues
4. Demonstrate and advocate for legal and ethical behaviors among peers, family, and community regarding the use of technology and information.	(2) Social, ethical, and human issues
5. Use technology tools and resources for managing and communicating personal/professional information (e.g. finances, schedules, addresses, purchases, correspondence).	(3) Technology productivity tools (4) Technology communications tools
6. Evaluate technology-based options, including distance and distributed education, for lifelong learning.	(5) Technology research tools

Performance Indicators	NETS-S Standards
7. Routinely and efficiently use online information resources to meet needs for collaboration, research, publications, communications, and productivity.	(4) Technology communications tools (5) Technology research tools (6) Technology problem-solving and decision-making tools
8. Select and apply technology tools for research, information analysis, problem-solving, and decision-making in content learning.	(4) Technology communications tools (5) Technology research tools
9. Investigate and apply expert systems, intelligent agents, and simulations in real-world situations.	(3) Technology productivity tools (5) Technology research tools (6) Technology problem-solving and decision-making tools
10. Collaborate with peers, experts, and others to contribute to content-related knowledge base by using technology to compile, synthesize, produce, and disseminate information, models, and other creative works.	(4) Technology communications tools (5) Technology research tools (6) Technology problem-solving and decision-making tools

Reprinted with permission from *National Education Technology Standards for Students—Connecting Curriculum and Technology,* copyright © 2000, ISTE (International Society for Technology in Education), 800.336.5191 (U.S. & Canada) or 541.302.3777 (Int'l). iste@iste.org. All Rights Reserved. Permission does not constitute an endorsement by ISTE.

NETS-S Correlations

The student textbook has been written with the NETS-S in mind. Activities and projects are designed to follow the NETS foundation standards and performance indicators.

Easy-to-use NETS-S correlations are provided for your convenience in the following locations:

◆ Every Chapter Planning Guide in Part 2 of this manual includes at-a-glance NETS-S correlations. Use the guide to quickly locate activities and projects that meet specific NETS-S in the chapter you are teaching.

◆ Complete NETS-S correlations are also provided in Part 5 of this Teacher Resource Manual. **See pages 492–504 to find all the activities and projects throughout the student textbook that relate to NETS-S.**

NATIONAL STANDARDS

NETS-T Educational Technology Performance Profiles for Teachers

Building on the NETS for Students, the NETS for Teachers (NETS-T) define the fundamental concepts, knowledge, skills, and attitudes for applying technology in educational settings. The student textbook and this Teacher Resource Manual are written with these NETS for Teachers in mind. The six standards areas with performance indicators listed below are designed by ISTE to provide guidelines for teachers in the classroom.

1. **Technology Operations and Concepts**
   A. Teachers demonstrate introductory knowledge, skills, and understanding of concepts related to technology.
   B. Teachers demonstrate continual growth in technology knowledge and skills to stay abreast of current and emerging technologies.

2. **Planning and Designing Learning Environments and Experiences**
   A. Teachers design developmentally appropriate learning opportunities that apply technology-enhanced instructional strategies to support the diverse needs of learners.
   B. Teachers apply current research on teaching and learning with technology when planning learning environments and experiences.
   C. Teachers identify and locate technology resources and evaluate them for accuracy and suitability.
   D. Teachers plan for the management of technology resources within the context of learning activities.
   E. Teachers plan strategies to manage student learning in a technology-enhanced environment.

3. **Teaching, Learning, and the Curriculum**
   A. Teachers facilitate technology-enhanced experiences that address content standards and student technology standards.
   B. Teachers use technology to support learner-centered strategies that address the diverse needs of students.
   C. Teachers apply technology to develop students' higher order skills and creativity.
   D. Teachers manage student learning activities in a technology-enhanced environment.

4. **Assessment and Evaluation**
    A. Teachers apply technology in assessing student learning of subject matter using a variety of assessment techniques.
    B. Teachers use technology resources to collect and analyze data, interpret results, and communicate findings to improve instructional practice and maximize student learning.
    C. Teachers apply multiple methods of evaluation to determine students' appropriate use of technology resources for learning, communication, and productivity.

5. **Productivity and Professional Practice**
    A. Teachers use technology resources to engage in ongoing professional development and lifelong learning.
    B. Teachers continually evaluate and reflect on professional practice to make informed decisions regarding the use of technology in support of student learning.
    C. Teachers apply technology to increase productivity.
    D. Teachers use technology to communicate and collaborate with peers, parents, and the larger community in order to nurture student learning.

6. **Social, Ethical, Legal, and Human issues**
    A. Teachers model and teach legal and ethical practice related to technology use.
    B. Teachers apply technology resources to enable and empower learners with diverse backgrounds, characteristics, and abilities.
    C. Teachers identify and use technology resources that affirm diversity.
    D. Teachers promote safe and healthy use of technology resources.
    E. Teachers facilitate equitable access to technology resources for all students.

PROGRAM COMPONENTS

STUDENT TEXTBOOK

Introduction to Web Design Using Dreamweaver is organized to help students learn fundamental Web design concepts and to allow opportunities to apply knowledge and skills. The following features have been designed to help students master Web design knowledge and skills:

- **Technology Handbook** articles at the front of the textbook highlight important Internet and computer skills in an easy to reference format.
- **Chapter Objectives** help students set a purpose for reading.
- **Think About It** activities let students connect their knowledge to new topics.
- **Quick Write Activities** provide writing practice while encouraging independent thinking.
- **Before and After Reading Strategies** help students increase reading comprehension in this course and in all subject areas.
- **You Try It Activities** provide hands-on Dreamweaver practice through step-by-step directions.
- **Go Online Activities** can be found on the book Web site. Use these activities to explore chapter topics in more depth.
- **Focus on Reading Guides** highlight each section's main ideas and key terms, and suggest a reading strategy graphic organizer to help students visualize new concepts.
- **Reading Focus** questions encourage students to read more carefully.
- **Reading Check** questions check for comprehension and help students retain knowledge.
- **Section Assessments** check comprehension and critical thinking skills.
- **Feature Articles** emphasize ethics, career opportunities, real-world uses of technology, and emerging technologies.
- **Chapter Reviews** test student knowledge of vocabulary and main ideas, and allow students to demonstrate their critical thinking skills.
- **Web Design Activities and Projects** let students independently apply their Web design skills and create Web page components and Web sites.
- **Building 21st Century Skills** projects emphasize career skills and professional presentation techniques.
- **Building Your Portfolio** projects guide students in building a professional portfolio to use for class evaluations or for job interviews.

STUDENT WORKBOOK

If you have chosen to purchase the optional student workbook, you can use it to reinforce important concepts and skills from the student textbook.

- **Guided Reading** activities allow students to check their understanding of main ideas and key concepts for each textbook chapter.
- **Web Design Projects** provide additional hands-on practice with essential Web design skills and Dreamweaver software.
- **Workbook Answer Key** is provided for the activities in this workbook on the Teacher Resource CD and at the Online Learning Center under the password-protected Teacher Resources section.

TEACHER RESOURCE MANUAL

This Teacher Resource Manual (TRM) is designed to facilitate effective teaching. It is organized to clarify concepts, to give suggestions for presenting material, and to suggest ways for dealing with difficult students. The manual is divided into the following five parts:

- **Part 1 Teacher Resources** includes course planning resources and professional development tools for successful teaching.
- **Part 2 Lesson Plans and Answer Keys** provide the following materials:
  - Chapter planning guide
  - NETS-S and SCANS correlations to chapter activities and projects
  - Chapter objectives, Internet and CD resources, and teaching strategies
  - Answers to all chapter activities and projects
- **Part 3 Reproducibles and Visual Aids** include blank blackline masters of graphic organizers that you can customize.
- **Part 4 PowerTeach Presentations, *ExamView*®, and TechSIM™ Interactive Tutorials** explain how to use the ready-made presentations and tests for each textbook chapter. Suggestions are also provided for using the TechSIM™ Interactive Tutorials with the textbook.
- **Part 5 Complete Correlations to Standards** provides SCANS and ISTE NETS-S correlations for activities and projects in all chapters of the textbook.

INCLUSION IN THE COMPUTER TECHNOLOGY CLASSROOM BOOKLET

Practical information on how to help special needs students succeed in the computer applications classroom is presented in this booklet for the teacher. Case studies give a real-life look at how special needs students think and feel.

PROGRAM COMPONENTS

TEACHER RESOURCE CD

The Teacher Resource Manual also includes a CD packed with valuable tools:

- **PowerTeach Presentations** provide lecture aids for every chapter in the textbook that can be used to introduce the chapters or as chapter reviews. Students can also use the presentations for independent study.

- **Student Data Files** allow students to quickly complete activities and projects. Whenever you see the Student Data File icon, be sure to locate the correct files to complete the activity.

- **Solution Files** are provided for You Try It activities in the textbook. Before students begin the exercise, you may wish to display the corresponding solution file on a projection screen as a model for student work. If a student did not complete an exercise, then the solution file for that activity may be used as a starting point for the next activity.

- **Reading Strategy Organizers** are provided to help students complete the Reading Strategy found at the beginning of each section. Simply reproduce the organizers for Reading Strategies you want students to complete.

EXAMVIEW CD

The optional *ExamView* **Pro Test Generator CD** contains software and testbanks that allow teachers to create their own or print out ready-made tests for each unit, complete with answer keys. Each test includes true/false, multiple choice, fill in the blank, and short answer questions.

TechSIM™ INTERACTIVE TUTORIALS CD

Interactive Tutorials are provided on a separate CD and on the book Web site. The tutorials let students follow guided step-by-steps to complete exercises similar to those in the textbook, but through an interactive, hands-on interface.

- **TechSIM A: File Management**
- **TechSIM B: E-mail and Microsoft Outlook**
- **TechSIM C: System Settings and the Control Panel**

Simulations may be particularly useful if your lab uses computers with different operating systems and software, or if network settings prevent students from using Microsoft Outlook or from changing system settings.

STUDY-TO-GO™

Practice makes perfect: Your students can now put that fact into action with a new, portable self-test and review tool. Download practice quizzes and vocabulary flashcards onto your Personal Digital Assistant (PDA) with Study-to-Go™. You will find the Study-to-Go logo on the Online Learning Center at **www.WebDesignDW.glencoe.com**. Click on it for download instructions.

PROGRAM COMPONENTS

ONLINE LEARNING CENTER WEB SITE

An accompanying Web site provides additional projects, assessments, and resources. Note that all the materials provided on the Teacher Resource CD are also available on the Web site for easy student and teacher access.

> Visit the *Introduction to Web Design Using Dreamweaver* Web site
> **WebDesignDW.glencoe.com**

Student Online Learning Center Students can access the following materials:

- **Unit Activities** allow students to explore important topics such as the soft skills needed by Web design team members.
- **Online Self Check** exercises allow students to test their own knowledge of Web design vocabulary and concepts.
- **PowerTeach Presentations** for every textbook chapter are also provided on the Web site for easy student access.
- **Go Online Activities** allow students to use the Internet to expand knowledge of topics presented in the student text.
- **Student Data Files** are also available online for quick or remote access.
- **Reading Strategy Organizers** are provided as blackline masters for easy download and printing.
- **Additional Web Design Resources** allow students to find helpful Web design sites over the Internet quickly.
- **TechSIM™ Interactive Tutorials** use an interactive, hands-on interface to teach students basic computer skills such as how to manage files, how to adjust system settings and use the control panel, and how to use e-mail.
- **Study-to-Go™** allows students to download practice quizzes and flashcards onto a Personal Digital Assistant (PDA).

Teacher Online Learning Center This portion of the site is password protected so that only teachers have access. Visit the Teacher Online Learning Center for username and password information (registration is *not* required).

- **Key Terms Online** include a list of key terms and an additional activity for every section in the textbook.
- **Solution Files** are provided as answer keys for You Try It activities.
- **Unit and Go Online Activities and Workbook Answer Keys**
- **Additional Step-By-Step Activities** are provided online for teachers.
- **Teacher Support Materials** include suggested course outline, pacing charts, and grading rubrics.
- **National Standards Correlations** includes chapter correlations for SCANS and NETS-S (ISTE National Technology Standards for Students).

Part 1—Teacher Resources 15

ORGANIZATION AND CONTENT

TEACHING WITH THE STUDENT TEXTBOOK

It has been shown that students who use their textbooks effectively learn the content more easily and more quickly than students who do not understand the author's design in writing the book. The student textbook has been specifically designed with a variety of features that can help students increase comprehension and recall information.

1. Use the following pages to familiarize yourself with the textbook features.
2. When you give students their textbooks, take a few minutes to introduce them to the textbook features so they can get the most out of their reading.
3. Have students complete the fun Scavenger Hunt activity at the front of their textbooks (on pages xviii–xix) to familiarize them with their textbook.

How to Use the Unit Opener

The student textbook is divided into units. Use the unit opener to jump start student thinking about new topics.

Think About It
Each Think About It activity helps students connect what they already know to new unit topics.

Visit Glencoe Online
Students can visit **WebDesignDW.glencoe.com** to learn how to use the Internet and the book Online Learning Center effectively.

Photos
Each photo has been carefully selected to help students visualize unit topics more clearly.

16 Teacher Resource Manual—*Introduction to Web Design Using Dreamweaver*

ORGANIZATION AND CONTENT

How to Use the Chapter Opener

Every chapter opener prepares students to read the chapter and to complete its accompanying activities.

You Will Learn To
Reviewing the chapter objectives helps students set a purpose for reading and make predictions as they read.

What You Will Do
Students can identify the skills they will learn by previewing the activities and projects they will complete in the chapter.

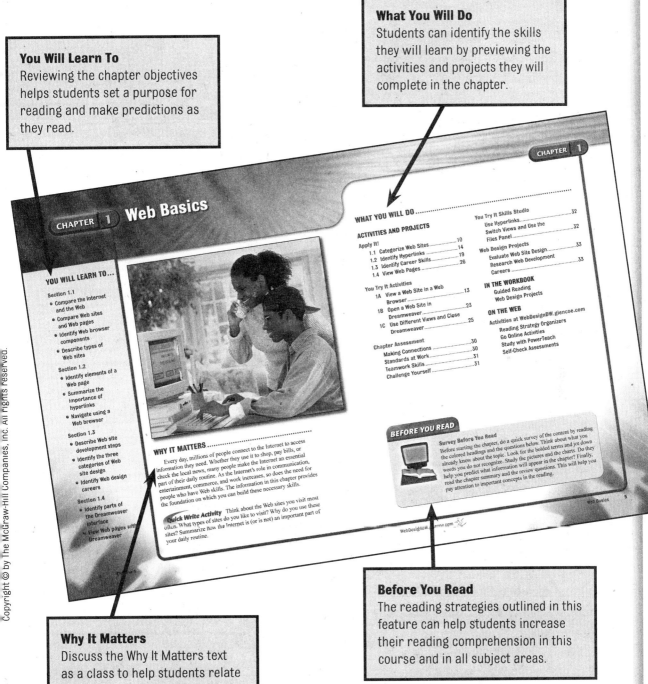

Why It Matters
Discuss the Why It Matters text as a class to help students relate to chapter topics by drawing on their previous knowledge.

Before You Read
The reading strategies outlined in this feature can help students increase their reading comprehension in this course and in all subject areas.

Part 1—Teacher Resources 17

ORGANIZATION AND CONTENT

How to Use the Sections

Each chapter is divided into sections to help further focus attention on main ideas and vocabulary.

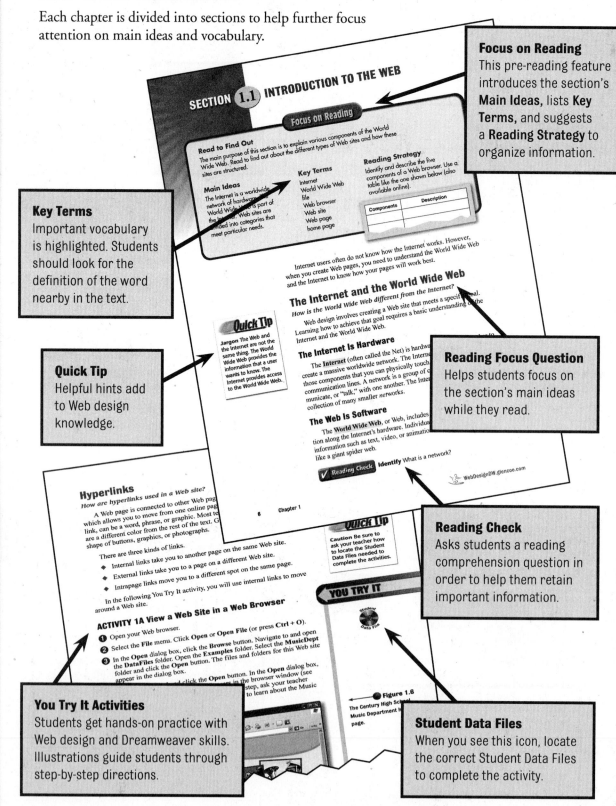

Focus on Reading
This pre-reading feature introduces the section's **Main Ideas**, lists **Key Terms**, and suggests a **Reading Strategy** to organize information.

Key Terms
Important vocabulary is highlighted. Students should look for the definition of the word nearby in the text.

Quick Tip
Helpful hints add to Web design knowledge.

Reading Focus Question
Helps students focus on the section's main ideas while they read.

Reading Check
Asks students a reading comprehension question in order to help them retain important information.

You Try It Activities
Students get hands-on practice with Web design and Dreamweaver skills. Illustrations guide students through step-by-step directions.

Student Data Files
When you see this icon, locate the correct Student Data Files to complete the activity.

ORGANIZATION AND CONTENT

Plan Ahead
Gives students suggestions to help them improve their planning and organizational skills.

Go Online Activities
Students can explore selected topics in more depth. Students complete these activities directly from the book's Online Learning Center and then either print their answers or e-mail them to their teacher.

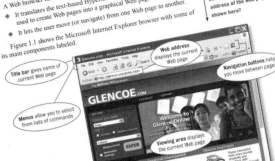

How the Web Works
How is a Web page different from a Web site?
The basic component of a Web page is a text document. A text document contains words, letters, numbers, and other unique characters. Special software called a **Web browser** interprets these files to display Web pages on your computer screen.

Web Sites versus Web Pages
The terms Web site and Web page do not refer to the same thing.
- A **Web site** is a group of related files organized around a common topic.
- A **Web page** is a single file within a Web site, which has a unique name.

A Web site's main page is typically called the home page. The **home page** usually contains general information about the Web site.

Browser Functions
A Web browser has two important functions.
- It translates the text-based Hypertext Markup Language (HTML) used to create Web pages into a graphical Web page.
- It lets the user move (or navigate) from one Web page to another.

Figure 1.1 shows the Microsoft Internet Explorer browser with some of its main components labeled.

● **Figure 1.1**
Web browsers such as Internet Explorer make it easy to move from one Web site to another. How can you determine the address of the Web page shown here?

PLAN AHEAD
Design The home page is almost always the first page a user sees when visiting a Web site, so it is important for it to give a good first impression.

Reading Check Identify What is a Web page?

Educational Sites
Educational sites often provide information
- School and university sites provide gene class schedules and courses offered.
- Distance learning sites offer Web-based
- Museum sites provide information abou

Personal Sites
Personal Web sites allow people to share the others. All individuals should be careful when p on the Internet. Online information is available connection, and posting personal information ca these guidelines when creating a personal site.

Use a personal site to:
- share news with your family and friends
- share your interests and hobbies.
- display a portfolio or résumé.

On your personal site:
- do not post personal contact information.
- do not describe how you look or where you live.
- do not post personal information about other people.

Reading Check Evaluate What type of Web site would you use to learn more about a local news story?

Activity 1.1 Identify Web Sites Visit various categories of Web sites by connecting to the links available at WebDesignDW.glencoe.com.

Figures and Tables
Check student comprehension of main ideas and concepts with the short captions and questions.

Section 1.1 Assessment

Reading Summary
- Web design focuses on creating Web sites that meet specific goals.
- The World Wide Web is the software that allows users to access information stored on the Internet.
- Web browsers interpret and display information found on Web sites.
- Web sites can be placed into particular categories based on their main purpose.

What Did You Learn?
1. Define Internet, World Wide Web, file, Web browser, Web site, Web page, home page.
2. Summarize the difference between the Internet and the World Wide Web.
3. Explain the functions of a Web browser.

Critical Thinking
4. Compare and Contrast How is a portal site different from an educational site?
5. Draw Conclusions What are the advantages and disadvantages of personal Web sites? Why should you be careful when posting personal information?

 **Apply It!**
Categorize Web Sites Make a list of five Web sites that you have visited recently. Beside each site, write the category to which you think this site belongs.

WebDesignDW.glencoe.com

Section Assessments
Post-reading questions assess student understanding and critical thinking skills.

ORGANIZATION AND CONTENT

How to Use the Chapter Review

Comprehensive Chapter Reviews provide additional opportunities for review and assessment.

Reading Review
Quick reference of all chapter key terms and main ideas. Use the page numbers to find definitions quickly.

Web Design Activities
Students apply their knowledge of Web design with these practical, hands-on activities.

Review and Assessment
Test student knowledge of vocabulary and basic Web design concepts.

Teacher Resource Manual—*Introduction to Web Design Using Dreamweaver*

ORGANIZATION AND CONTENT

You Try It Skills Studio
Students demonstrate their Web design skills as they complete these exercises independently.

Web Design Projects
Students apply Web design tools to create Web page components and Web sites.

Building Your Portfolio
Students can build a professional portfolio to use in class for evaluation, or they can use these with real-world clients or potential employers.

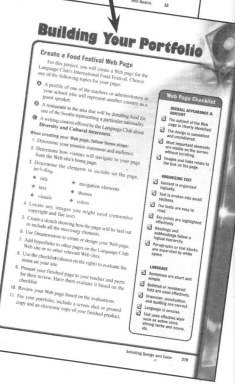

Building 21st Century Skills
Featured projects at the end of each unit allow students to apply Web design concepts and skills in real-world contexts. Projects emphasize career skills and professional presentation.

Part 1—Teacher Resources 21

ORGANIZATION AND CONTENT

USING THE TEACHER RESOURCE MANUAL
How to Use the Chapter Lesson Plans and Answer Keys

Part 2 of this Teacher Resource Manual provides suggestions for how to teach each chapter in the student edition. Answer keys are also provided for all activities and exercises in the student textbook. These teaching suggestions for each chapter follow the Focus, Teach, Assess, and Close format.

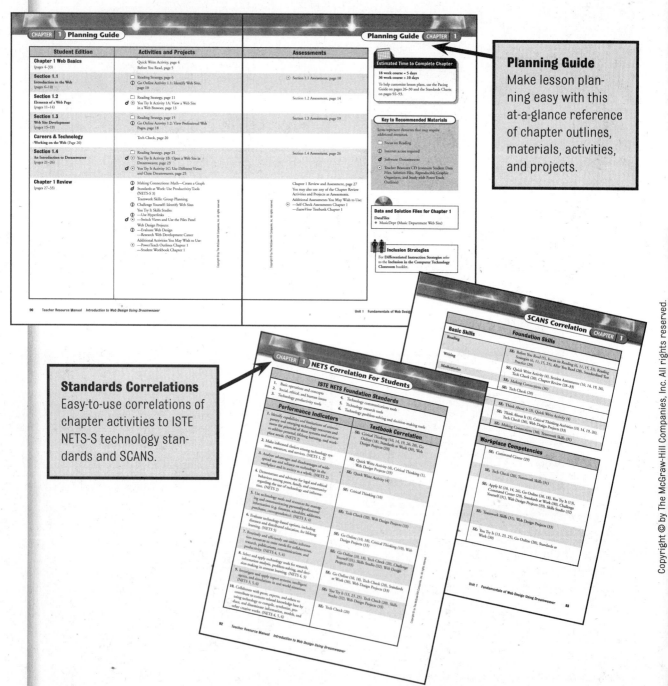

Planning Guide
Make lesson planning easy with this at-a-glance reference of chapter outlines, materials, activities, and projects.

Standards Correlations
Easy-to-use correlations of chapter activities to ISTE NETS-S technology standards and SCANS.

22 Teacher Resource Manual—*Introduction to Web Design Using Dreamweaver*

ORGANIZATION AND CONTENT

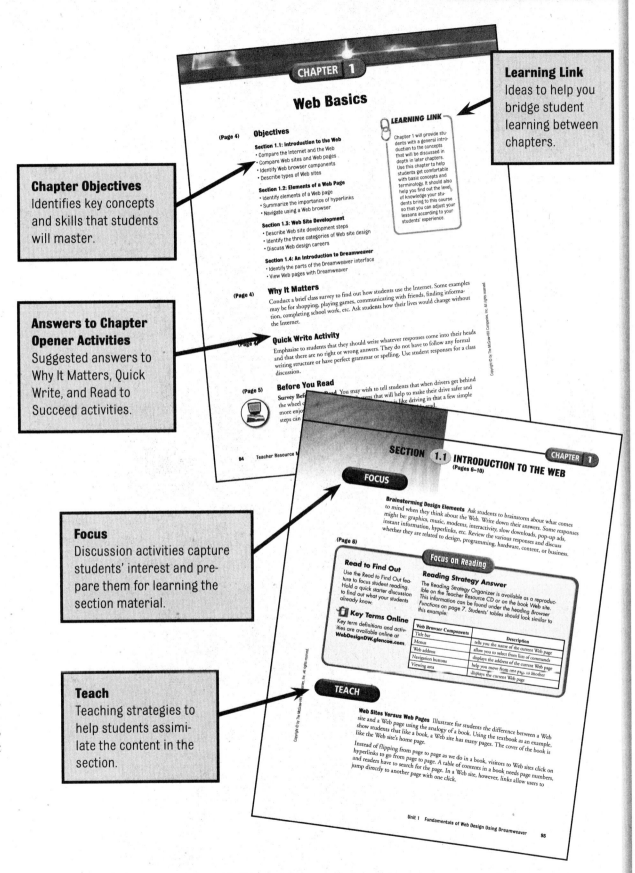

Chapter Objectives
Identifies key concepts and skills that students will master.

Answers to Chapter Opener Activities
Suggested answers to Why It Matters, Quick Write, and Read to Succeed activities.

Learning Link
Ideas to help you bridge student learning between chapters.

Focus
Discussion activities capture students' interest and prepare them for learning the section material.

Teach
Teaching strategies to help students assimilate the content in the section.

Part 1—Teacher Resources 23

ORGANIZATION AND CONTENT

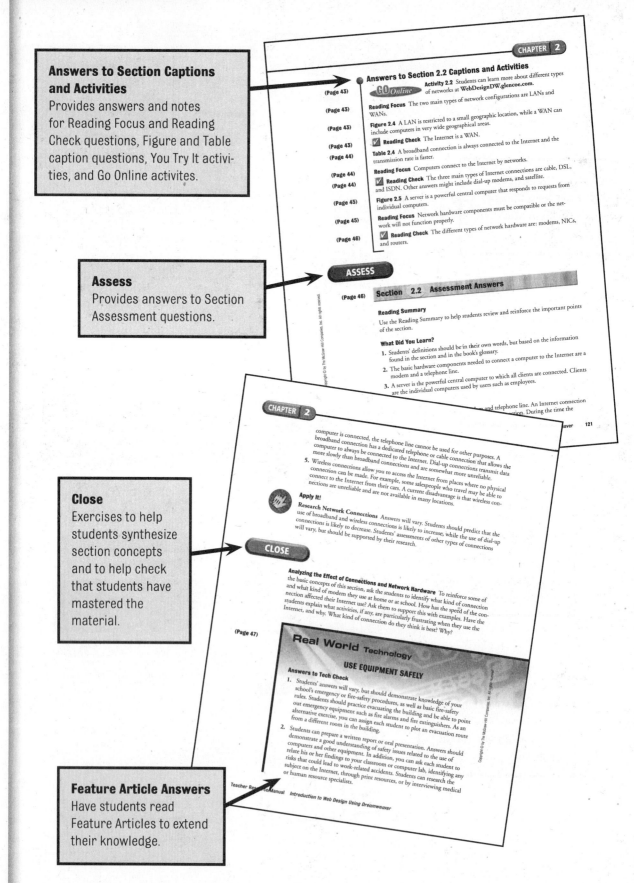

Answers to Section Captions and Activities
Provides answers and notes for Reading Focus and Reading Check questions, Figure and Table caption questions, You Try It activities, and Go Online activites.

Assess
Provides answers to Section Assessment questions.

Close
Exercises to help students synthesize section concepts and to help check that students have mastered the material.

Feature Article Answers
Have students read Feature Articles to extend their knowledge.

24 Teacher Resource Manual—*Introduction to Web Design Using Dreamweaver*

ORGANIZATION AND CONTENT

CHAPTER 3 Answers to Chapter Review

The Chapter Review covers a wide range of student knowledge. Due to time constraints, students may not be able to complete every activity in the Chapter Review. Select the activities that are appropriate for your class needs and resources.

(Page 90) After You Read

Reading Speed Metacognition—the art of knowing what you know and what you do not know—is critically important to the reading process. Too often students complain that they read the chapter, but did not understand the material. This can lead to great frustration. Students who use metacognition strategies are less likely to have this problem. Having students note which paragraphs or sections they had difficulty reading can help develop their metacognition skills. Answer any questions they have about the sections that they may still be having trouble comprehending.

(Page 90) Reviewing Key Terms

1. HTML
2. The Internet is accessible to everyone and uses a number of different protocols to transmit information. An intranet is privately owned and, often, can only be accessed by employees of an organization. The World Wide Web is a part of the Internet that relies on Web browsers to display information in specially formatted documents using HTML.
3. URL stands for Uniform Resource Locator.
4. In the URL **www.uiowa.edu**, the .edu portion of the domain name is the domain name extension.
5. Search engines catalog individual Web pages, while Web directories catalog Web sites (not pages) by topic or category.
6. The applications required to create Web pages themselves, and the applications required to create individual Web page components, such as graphics, video, and audio.
7. A Boolean search specifies how the search engine should use keywords to locate specific pages. You use operators such as AND, OR, and NOT to perform more precise searches.
8. WYSIWYG stands for "what you see is what you get."

Understanding Main Ideas

9. TCP/IP contains the specific inf...
10. An FTP site is...

CHAPTER 3 Answers to Chapter Review

YOU TRY IT Skills Studio

(Page 94)

1. **Search for Information Online** A Boolean search using the **AND** operator and the keywords "famous people," "birthday," and the student's actual birthday should bring up many sites that offer the requested information. For instance, "famous people" **AND** "birthday" **AND** "April 8" led to finding that Harry Truman, Betty Ford, and Mary Pickford all shared this birthday. Using any of these names, the Boolean operator **AND**, and keywords such as "biographical information," should lead a student to informative sites about that person.
A URL that may be useful for this exercise is Those Were the Days, found at **http://www.440.com/twtd/archives**. The History Channel's Web site also contains a database of events that students may find useful.
In Step C, students will cite each URL they have located. Information gathered in this exercise will be used for You Try It Skills Studio Exercise 2.

2. **Create a Web Page with External Links** Students use the information they learned from the search in the activity above to create a Web page in Dreamweaver. In addition to the headings, the students create a hyperlink for each person to the site found in the activity above. Students also include two or three sentences about each person. Then they add a copyright notice at the bottom of the page.

Web Design Projects

(Page 95)

1. **Use Online Resources** Some of the important dates and events in the history of the Internet and Web are discussed in this chapter under the heading *Origins of the Internet*. Ask the students to use search engines or Web directories to find new, additional information, and have them include it in their reports or presentations. Using the example of online privacy, it may be noted that users sometimes have their identity stolen, or may be harassed by someone who has found out personal information such as where they live. Potential solutions include informing users about the danger of offering personal information online, and creating and enforcing laws to prosecute those who use personal information in unethical ways.

2. **Evaluate Software** Students' tables will vary, but should note system requirements, features, and the price of each application.
In predicting which applications might be chosen by individuals or organizations, students may note that a cheaper price and less demanding system requirements might be favored by individuals on a tight budget with older computers. Businesses, on the other hand, have more money to spend and need up-to-date features to remain competitive. They would likely choose the best software available.

Answers to Chapter Review
Complete answers to end-of-chapter questions, activities, and projects.

Part 1—Teacher Resources 25

COURSE PLANNING

GUIDELINES FOR A SUCCESSFUL COURSE

To facilitate the success of the course and the progress of your students, follow these general guidelines:

- **Review course philosophy, theme, and purpose.** Review your philosophy and goals for the course. Has your philosophy of teaching and learning changed over the years? Review the philosophy, goals, and themes of the book. Write the course purpose in your own words. What do you want students to learn from this class?

- **Identify course objectives and goals for students.** Write your objectives and goals for the course. Review your purpose for each class period. Writing your objectives helps you clarify your methods, communicate expectations, and evaluate your success. It is often helpful for students to see your class objective(s) written on the blackboard for each class period.

- **Encourage critical thinking.** Students need to learn how to solve problems, make decisions, and think through issues rationally. Help students use critical thinking skills during class discussions.

- **Make learning personal.** Each chapter presents exercises to help students develop and demonstrate their skills. Ask students to assess their progress and clarify personal and professional goals as they build knowledge and experience. When possible, link concepts to students' everyday experiences.

- **Educate the whole student.** Make certain you stress essential personal qualities throughout the course. Civility, character, integrity, and ethics can be woven throughout the course by asking students to share with the class situations from their jobs (if applicable), their personal lives, and articles from newspapers. Be sure to collect some positive stories and examples as well and acknowledge positive attitudes in your students.

- **Link school and job success.** The instructor must highlight the usefulness and insight gained by studying this subject. Reinforce the idea that success in this course will enhance students' potential for job success.

- **Preview assignments.** Preview assignments with students to clarify your expectations. Previewing chapters helps students prepare, and it can also be a tool for showing how new information relates to what they have just studied and to their everyday work. Before you preview the chapter, review and summarize the previous chapter and discuss what students have learned.

- **Emphasize commitment.** Stress that commitment to study and consistent practice produce results. Real learning is based on positive habits.

- **Encourage attendance and participation.** Take attendance each class period and meet with students who miss twice. Even if this course is not graded, attendance is important. Point out that the course experience is built on classroom participation and exercises. Poor attendance or tardiness results in confusion, low motivation, and resentment from students who attend and are well-prepared and punctual. Full participation means preparation, commitment, and involvement.

The underlying principles that support the preceding guidelines are as follows:

- **Students are responsible for both the academic and social aspects of their education.** It is important that students plan and take charge of their courses and careers. Remind them that blaming others for their circumstances does not empower them to take charge of their lives. Blaming themselves is also a waste of time. Stress that empowerment is facing a problem directly, solving it, and performing the strategies that produce positive results.

- **Effort and commitment to excellence are essential.** To make the most of school and work, students must be willing to put in the time and effort required. Vague wishes, desires, half-hearted attempts, and hopes do not produce results. A commitment to make school a top priority is a key factor for success. Remind students that adopting strategies and turning them into daily habits are important both in school and at work.

- **Cooperative learning promotes interdependence.** Working in small groups is a key factor in getting students involved in their own learning and in the learning of other group members. Group exercises provide application of ideas and strategies. Interaction, interpersonal communication, and teamwork each play a powerful role in student success.

- **Expressing ideas effectively increases self-confidence and self-esteem.** Practicing public speaking skills is fundamental for students to improve their presentations. Group work encourages critical thinking, creative problem-solving, and respect for diversity. Listening to others and keeping an open mind helps reduce misunderstandings and celebrate the valuable experience of working with different kinds of people.

- **Learning how to learn best is important.** Attending school for many years does not guarantee that students know how they learn best. Give students the opportunity, space, and techniques to assess and discover how they learn best. Knowing how to learn and having the willingness to be a lifelong learner are essential to job success.

- **Successful people are positive, resourceful, and motivated.** The most productive, positive, flexible, and courteous people in school and at work are people who are emotionally mature and have developed strong personal qualities. Attitude affects relationships, work habits, and results.

PLANNING A COURSE AND SUGGESTED COURSE PACING CHARTS

Planning a course from the bottom up can be an exciting experience, and it can also be a daunting experience. Preparing to teach requires careful planning as you consider the various assignments, tests, student dynamics, and instructional interactions. Creating a pacing framework that takes all of these elements into account can help make your course progress smoothly.

How to Develop a Pacing Chart

Developing an accurate estimate of how much time it takes to teach the content of the chapters of a text and assess the students' knowledge of that content is not an exact science. Determining how long to spend covering course content and completing student activities and projects requires that teachers consider the amount of actual class time, the abilities of the students, and how motivated and prepared students generally are.

Suggested Course Pacing Charts

Suggested pacing charts are provided in the following pages. These charts suggest how the textbook may be used to teach both a semester-long course (18 weeks) and a year-long course (36 weeks).

The first column of each chart notes which chapters from the student textbook might be taught during the indicated week. Should you choose to use the student workbook in your course, the second column of each chart notes which workbook chapters might complement your lesson plans for that week. Note that using the student workbook is optional.

During the course, take time to develop your own pacing chart and utilize that schedule the next time you teach the course. Depending on your students' knowledge and needs, you may want to spend more or less time covering specific material, such as:

- the basic information about what the Web is and how it works (Chapter 1).
- information about basic computer hardware and software (Chapter 2).
- advanced HTML skills (Unit 5).

Adjust the pacing charts as needed to meet your course's particular requirements.

Suggested Course Pacing Chart

		18-Week Course	
		Textbook	Student Workbook (Optional)
WEEKS	Week 1	Ch 1	Ch 1
	Week 2	Ch 2, Ch 3	Ch 2, Ch 3
	Week 3	Ch 3, Ch 4	Ch 3, Ch 4
	Week 4	Ch 4, Unit 1 Review	Ch 4
	Week 5	Ch 5	Ch 5
	Week 6	Ch 6	Ch 6
	Week 7	Ch 6, Ch 7	Ch 6, Ch 7
	Week 8	Ch 7, Unit 2 Review	Ch 7
	Week 9	Ch 8	Ch 8
	Week 10	Ch 9, Ch 10	Ch 9, Ch 10
	Week 11	Ch 10, Unit 3 Review	Ch 10
	Week 12	Ch 11, Ch 12	Ch 11, Ch 12
	Week 13	Ch 12, Ch 13	Ch 12, Ch 13
	Week 14	Ch 13	Ch 13
	Week 15	Ch 14, Ch 15	Ch 14, Ch 15
	Week 16	Ch 15, Unit 4 Review	Ch 15
	Week 17	Ch 16	Ch 16
	Week 18	Ch 17, Unit 5 Review	Ch 17

Suggested Course Pacing Chart (continued)

WEEKS	36-Week Course	
	Textbook	**Student Workbook (Optional)**
Week 1	Ch 1	Ch 1
Week 2	Ch 1	Ch 1
Week 3	Ch 2	Ch 2
Week 4	Ch 2	Ch 2
Week 5	Ch 3	Ch 3
Week 6	Ch 3	Ch 3
Week 7	Ch 3, Unit 1 Review	Ch 3
Week 8	Ch 4	Ch 4
Week 9	Ch 4	Ch 4
Week 10	Ch 5	Ch 5
Week 11	Ch 5	Ch 5
Week 12	Ch 6	Ch 6
Week 13	Ch 6	Ch 6
Week 14	Ch 7	Ch 7
Week 15	Ch 7	Ch 7
Week 16	Unit 2 Review	Ch 7
Week 17	Ch 8	Ch 8
Week 18	Ch 8	Ch 8
Week 19	Ch 9	Ch 9
Week 20	Ch 9	Ch 9
Week 21	Ch 10	Ch 10
Week 22	Ch 10	Ch 10
Week 23	Unit 3 Review	Ch 10
Week 24	Ch 11	Ch 11
Week 25	Ch 11, Ch 12	Ch 11, Ch 12
Week 26	Ch 12	Ch 12
Week 27	Ch 13	Ch 13
Week 28	Ch 13	Ch 13
Week 29	Ch 14	Ch 14
Week 30	Ch 14, Ch 15	Ch 14, Ch 15
Week 31	Ch 15	Ch 15
Week 32	Unit 4 Review	Ch 15
Week 33	Ch 16	Ch 16
Week 34	Ch 16	Ch 16
Week 35	Ch 17	Ch 17
Week 36	Ch 17, Unit 5 Review	Ch 17

WRITING A COURSE OUTLINE

A course outline adds order and organization to your course. Students want to know what to expect, so it is important to have a detailed written guide for them to follow and refer to throughout the semester. The course outline could include:

- Teacher's name
- Location of class (include building number, classroom number, etc.)
- Day(s) and time(s) the class meets
- Required textbooks and resources
- Course purpose and objectives
- Learning climate or teaching method
- Course requirements and expectations
- Daily outline
- Evaluation or grading methods

The example on the following page has been structured to follow the textbook. You can adapt this suggested course outline and student expectation guide to the specific needs of the class. Tell students that the course outline is a guide and that you may change the order of topics, exercises, and assignments when it is appropriate.

Before developing a course outline, you may want to write down some of your own expectations for the course.

Course Expectations _____
_____
_____
_____
_____
_____
_____
_____
_____
_____
_____
_____

COURSE PLANNING

Suggested Course Outline for *Introduction to Web Design Using Dreamweaver*

Course Outline

Required Textbook

Introduction to Web Design Using Dreamweaver, by Mark Evans and Michael Hamm, Glencoe/McGraw Hill.

Course Description

Introduction to Web Design Using Dreamweaver is an introductory course to the fast growing industry of Web site design and development. The materials in this course will provide you with a solid understanding of the entire Web site development process. You will learn to use Dreamweaver to design and publish Web sites. Throughout this course, you are encouraged to seek outside resources, including the Internet and Web design professionals in your area, to aid you in the learning process.

Course Purpose

The purpose of this course is to help you develop the necessary skills and knowledge to succeed in a career in Web design. The skills you learn here will help you find success both in school, and in the professional Web design world, should you choose a career in this field.

Course Objectives

After completing this course, you will be able to:

- Identify different types of Web sites and URLs
- Describe Web site development stages and project team responsibilities
- Describe Web design career paths
- Compare and contrast the Internet and the Web
- Describe Web development applications and hardware
- Explain how to download and use files ethically
- Learn how to protect your privacy online
- Use Dreamweaver to create Web sites
- Plan and storyboard a Web site
- Identify and apply principles of good Web site design
- Identify and select appropriate navigation schemes
- Evaluate and create Web content
- Create a custom page template
- Use Web-safe colors
- Use hyperlinks, graphics, and multimedia elements in a Web site
- Create, crop, resize, and resample graphics
- Create an image map with hotspots
- Describe scripting languages and apply DHTML behaviors
- Create a form
- Summarize guidelines for developing e-commerce Web sites

- Explain privacy policies and Web site security measures
- Debug and test a Web page
- Publish and update a Web site
- Identify techniques for publicizing sites and increasing Web site traffic
- Use HTML tags and attributes

Learning Climate

Cooperative and experiential learning are based on two key concepts.

1. **You are responsible for your learning and for helping each other.** You will have opportunities to interact with other students and other Web design professionals to gain knowledge and work through difficult Web design concepts and activities. Learning to work with and gain knowledge from others is an important step to becoming a productive member of a Web design project team.
2. **Learning is cooperative and experiential.** You are expected to participate in class and in the exercises, and to apply the concepts to your experiences. Throughout this course you will be asked to think of examples from your own experiences and apply them to basic concepts you will be learning. Active and creative thinking will aid you in understanding the difficult concepts.

Course Requirements and Expectations

- **Attendance** You are expected to attend each class and be on time.
- **Participation** You are expected to participate in class and complete all assignments.
- **Critical Thinking** You are expected to use critical thinking and creative problem solving to complete exercises and to apply these concepts to the activities and projects you will complete in this course.
- **Web Design Skills** Frequent challenges appear throughout the course. You are expected to apply the skills you have learned to come up with creative, effective solutions to the problems presented.

Assessment

Assessments will be based on attendance, participation, and successful completion of various assignments and projects throughout this course. Quizzes and tests will be given periodically to test your knowledge and skills.

Grading

The following is an example of grading guidelines and a grading scale:

Grading Guidelines		Grading Scale
Attendance	= 25%	A = 90–100%
Quizzes/Tests	= 25%	B = 80–89%
Assignments	= 50%	C = 70–79%
		D = 60–69%
Total	= 100%	F = Less than 60%

GUIDELINES FOR THE TECHNOLOGY CLASSROOM

Students will use technology throughout the course. Use the following guidelines to help students use technology responsibly.

Using the Internet

Students are often instructed to access Web sites to complete activities and projects. Where possible, suggested Web sites are provided in the student textbook and in this Teacher Resource Manual. Although suggested live sites have been reviewed, they are not under the control of Glencoe/McGraw Hill. Site content and URLs may also change over time. We therefore strongly encourage teachers to preview these sites before assigning their students individual activities. Teachers may also want to let parents know that students will be using the Internet to complete activities and assignments for the class.

Acceptable Use Policies

Teachers should also check with their schools to learn about their district's acceptable use policy (AUP). Most AUPs provide a statement of responsibilities of educators, parents, and students for using the Internet, guidelines for appropriate online behavior, and a description of consequences should the school district's AUP be violated. Teachers, parents, guardians, and students should all be familiar with their school's AUP before any Internet activities are assigned. Once online, teachers should continue to monitor student's Internet time and watch for objectionable content or for irresponsible computer use.

Publishing Web Sites

Students will be instructed to publish Web sites both locally and remotely. Please review the options available at your school for publishing Web sites. Because of the potential legal ramifications of students publishing Web sites under the school's name and auspices, it is critical that the students understand their responsibility to avoid any content that is controversial. You may want to review appropriate and inappropriate content guidelines with students before they publish any sites.

Copyright Guidelines

When necessary, students should include copyright information and credit lines on their pages to acknowledge their sources. You can use the Technology Handbook in the Student Edition to review basic copyright guidelines with students.

Downloading Files

Students are sometimes instructed to locate and download files to complete activities and projects. Review your school's policies on downloading files from the Internet. If students will not have that capability, supply appropriate files and let students know where to find them. Students should always review a Web site's Terms of Use before downloading and using any files.

MANAGING STUDENT FILES

Depending on your school, students may either work on a local computer or on a networked computer. The following are some guidelines for how to manage student files. It can be a good idea to consult with a technology coordinator to determine the best method for managing and saving files at your specific school.

1. Students can create a general folder and then store individual Web sites in separate subfolders within this general folder. This allows a student's work to be stored in one place, but also keeps the files for individual Web sites organized.

2. When developing each Web site in Dreamweaver, students will need to create a root folder that will contain all of that site's files (HTML files, image files, etc.). Each student should create their own root folder and this root folder should have a unique name (for instance, a name that contains the student's initials and other necessary information). Students will need to reference their site's root folder when they define a site in Dreamweaver. (Note: students will need to create a different root folder for each separate Web site.)

3. When using Student Data Files or files from other sources, it is a good idea to make copies of the original files so they can be used by multiple students. A *copy* of the file (an image file, a text file, or an entire sample Web site) can be placed in each student's root folder. Students can then work on their own Web sites without fear of overwriting the work of other students, or of altering the only copy of an existing file.

SAVING STUDENT WORK

While working with Dreamweaver or other applications, students will need to save their work often.

- Identify where students should save their work before they begin working.
- Remind students to double check that they save to the correct location. Otherwise, they may not be able to find their work later. Should a student's site contain broken links or missing graphics, make sure they have saved their site's files in the correct folder.

Using the Student Data Files

To complete some activities and projects in this book, Student Data Files are required.

- When you see the Student Data File icon, locate needed files *before* beginning the activity.
- Student Data Files are available on the Teacher Resource CD and on the book Web site at **WebDesignDW.glencoe.com**.

Teachers might choose to distribute the files in the following ways:

1. Saving the files in a folder on the school network
2. Posting the files on the teacher's course Web site
3. Saving the files to the hard drive of each computer with read-only access (students can resave file to their location as a writeable file)

A chart outlining each data file and where it is used in the textbook is included on the following pages.

USING THE SOLUTION FILES

Solution Files are provided for the You Try It activities. The files are available on the Teacher Resource CD and online at **WebDesignDW.glencoe.com** under the password-protected Teacher Resources section.

Solution Files are identified by the name of the You Try It activity or activities that they cover. Where possible, solutions have been provided for each individual You Try It activity. In chapters where students develop a Web site that contains multiple files and folders, one solution has been provided for each section in the chapter. For example, the solution for section 8.2 is named SF_YTI_8ABC. This solution can be used for activities 8A, 8B, and 8C. A Solution File that contains the finished version of each unit's major Web site project has also been provided.

NOTE: All of the files and folders related to a Web site must be saved in that site's root folder. Failure to do this may result in broken images and links.

Teachers might choose to use the Solution Files in the following ways:

1. Some You Try It activities require students to continue working on files created in previous activities. If a student did not complete an activity, then the Solution File for that activity may be used as a starting point for the next activity. New students can define a new Web site in Dreamweaver using the files for the activity or section just prior to where the student will be starting.
2. Display an activity's Solution File on a projection screen before students begin the activity as a model for student work and as they complete their work so they can check their progress.

An outline of each Solution File and where it corresponds to the textbook is included on the following pages.

For You Try It activities that have students entering HTML code, you can open the HTML solution file in your browser and select **View>Source** to see the Solution File's coding.

COURSE PLANNING

Student Data Files

Chapter	Files	Path	Activity	Page
1	MusicDept	DataFiles\Examples\MusicDept	YTI 1A	13
	MusicDept	DataFiles\Examples\MusicDept	YTI 1B	23
	MusicDept	DataFiles\Examples\MusicDept	YTI 1C	25
2	camera.gif	DataFiles\Ch02\Images	YTI 2C	52
	cd-rom.gif	DataFiles\Ch02\Images	YTI 2C	52
	scanner.gif	DataFiles\Ch02\Images	YTI 2C	52
	festival.gif	DataFiles\Ch02\Images	Skills Studio #2	62
3	MusicDept	DataFiles\Examples\MusicDept	YTI 3A	74
4	p_border.gif	DataFiles\Ch04\Images	YTI 4A	102
	p_border.gif	DataFiles\Ch04\Images	YTI 4K	120
	movies.gif	DataFiles\Ch04\Images	Skills Studio #1	128
5	MusicDept	DataFiles\Examples\MusicDept	YTI 5B	143
6	MusicDept	DataFiles\Examples\MusicDept	YTI 6B	169
	background_stripes.gif	DataFiles\Ch06\Images	YTI 6C	172
	lc_logo.gif	DataFiles\Ch06\Images	YTI 6D	174
	nav_home_blue.gif	DataFiles\Ch06\Images	YTI 6D	178
	nav_home_red.gif	DataFiles\Ch06\Images	YTI 6F	178
	nav_about_blue.gif	DataFiles\Ch06\Images	YTI 6F	178
	nav_about_red.gif	DataFiles\Ch06\Images	YTI 6F	178
	nav_events_blue.gif	DataFiles\Ch06\Images	YTI 6F	178
	nav_events_red.gif	DataFiles\Ch06\Images	YTI 6F	178
	nav_contact_blue.gif	DataFiles\Ch06\Images	YTI 6F	178
	nav_contact_red.gif	DataFiles\Ch06\Images	YTI 6F	178
7	hdr_welcome.gif	DataFiles\Ch07\Images	YTI 7C	196
	hdr_aboutus.gif	DataFiles\Ch07\Images	YTI 7C	196
	hdr_events.gif	DataFiles\Ch07\Images	YTI 7C	196
	hdr_contactus.gif	DataFiles\Ch07\Images	YTI 7C	196
	photo_members.jpg	DataFiles\Ch07\Images	YTI 7D	199
	hdr_fundraiser.gif	DataFiles\Ch07\Images	Web Design Projects #1	217
	Events.doc	DataFiles\Ch07\Text	Web Design Projects #1	217
8	BikeHike	DataFiles\Ch08\WebExamples	YTI 8A	230
	bike.jpg	DataFiles\Ch08\Images	YTI 8A	230
	image_map.gif	DataFiles\Ch08\Images	YTI 8D	238
	Photos	DataFiles\Ch08\Images	YTI 8E	240
9	sound.swf	DataFiles\Ch09\Multimedia	YTI 9A	260
	bike.swf	DataFiles\Ch09\Multimedia	YTI 9B	262
	title_animate.gif	DataFiles\Ch09\Multimedia	YTI 9C	266
	registration.doc	DataFiles\Ch09\Text	YTI 9D	267
10	banner_01.gif	DataFiles\Ch10\Images	YTI 10A	284
	banner_02.gif	DataFiles\Ch10\Images	YTI 10A	284
	button_funds.gif	DataFiles\Ch10\Images	YTI 10D	288
	button_resale.gif	DataFiles\Ch10\Images	YTI 10D	288
	quotes.html	DataFiles\Ch10\Multimedia	21st Century Skills #1	306
11	proposal.doc	DataFiles\Ch11\Text	YTI 11C	325

COURSE PLANNING

Student Data Files (continued)

Chapter	Files	Path	Activity	Page
12	MyDiskDesigns mydiskdesigns.css hdr_privacy.gif privacy.doc	DataFiles\Ch12\WebExamples DataFiles\Ch12\CSS DataFiles\Ch12\Images DataFiles\Ch12\Text	YTI 12A YTI 12C YTI 12H YTI 12H	337 339 349 349
13	hdr_guestbook.gif logo_mydiskdesigns.gif frames_privacy.doc	DataFiles\Ch13\Images DataFiles\Ch13\Images DataFiles\Ch13\Text	YTI 13B YTI 13C YTI 13C	377 382 382
14	No student data files			
15	No student data files			
16	stylesheet.html	DataFiles\Ch16\HTML	YTI 16C	464
17	birds.wav button1.gif button2.gif	DataFiles\Ch17\Multimedia DataFiles\Ch17\Images DataFiles\Ch17\Images	YTI 17A YTI 17G YTI 17G	476 484 484

Solution Files

Chapter	Files	Path	Activity	Page
1	No solution files			
2	SF_YTI_2A.html SF_YTI_2B.html SF_YTI_2C SF_YTI_2D	SolutionFiles\Ch02\YTI_2A SolutionFiles\Ch02\YTI_2B SolutionFiles\Ch02\YTI_2C SolutionFiles\Ch02\YTI_2D	YTI 2A YTI 2B YTI 2C YTI 2D	49 51 52 55
3	SF_YTI_3C SF_YTI_3D	SolutionFiles\Ch03\YTI_3C SolutionFiles\Ch03\YTI_3D	YTI 3C YTI 3D	81 86
4	SF_YTI_4B.html SF_YTI_4C.html SF_YTI_4D.html SF_YTI_4F SF_YTI_4G SF_YTI_4I.html SF_YTI_4J.html SF_YTI_4K SF_Hardware_Devices_html SF_Hardware_Devices_Dreamweaver	SolutionFiles\Ch04\YTI_4B SolutionFiles\Ch04\YTI_4C SolutionFiles\Ch04\YTI_4D SolutionFiles\Ch04\YTI_4F SolutionFiles\Ch04\YTI_4G SolutionFiles\Ch04\YTI_4I SolutionFiles\Ch04\YTI_4J SolutionFiles\Ch04\YTI_4K SolutionFiles\FinalSites SolutionFiles\FinalSites	YTI 4B YTI 4C YTI 4D YTI 4F YTI 4G YTI 4I YTI 4J YTI 4K	104 106 107 110 112 117 118 120
5	No solution files			
6	SF_YTI_6CDE SF_YTI_6CDE SF_YTI_6CDE SF_YTI_6FGHI SF_YTI_6FGHI SF_YTI_6FGHI SF_YTI_6FGHI	SolutionFiles\Ch06\YTI_6CDE SolutionFiles\Ch06\YTI_6CDE SolutionFiles\Ch06\YTI_6CDE SolutionFiles\Ch06\YTI_6FGHI SolutionFiles\Ch06\YTI_6FGHI SolutionFiles\Ch06\YTI_6FGHI SolutionFiles\Ch06\YTI_6FGHI	YTI 6C YTI 6D YTI 6E YTI 6F YTI 6G YTI 6H YTI 6I	172 174 175 178 179 180 181

Solution Files (continued)

Chapter	Files	Path	Activity	Page
7	SF_YTI_7ABC	SolutionFiles\Ch07\YTI_7ABC	YTI 7A	193
	SF_YTI_7ABC	SolutionFiles\Ch07\YTI_7B	YTI 7B	195
	SF_YTI_7ABC	SolutionFiles\Ch07\YTI_7ABC	YTI 7C	196
	SF_YTI_7D	SolutionFiles\Ch07\YTI_7D	YTI 7D	199
	SF_YTI_7E	SolutionFiles\Ch07\YTI_7E	YTI 7E	208
	SF_Language_Club	SolutionFiles\FinalSites		
8	SF_YTI_8ABC	SolutionFiles\Ch08\YTI_8ABC	YTI 8A	230
	SF_YTI_8ABC	SolutionFiles\Ch08\YTI_8ABC	YTI 8B	233
	SF_YTI_8ABC	SolutionFiles\Ch08\YTI_8ABC	YTI 8C	234
	SF_YTI_8DE	SolutionFiles\Ch08\YTI_8DE	YTI 8D	238
	SF_YTI_8DE	SolutionFiles\Ch08\YTI_8DE	YTI 8E	240
9	SF_YTI_9AB	SolutionFiles\Ch09\YTI_9AB	YTI 9A	260
	SF_YTI_9AB	SolutionFiles\Ch09\YTI_9AB	YTI 9B	262
	SF_YTI_9CD	SolutionFiles\Ch09\YTI_9CD	YTI 9C	266
	SF_YTI_9CD	SolutionFiles\Ch09\YTI_9CD	YTI 9D	267
10	SF_YTI_10ABCD	SolutionFiles\Ch10\YTI_10ABCD	YTI 10A	284
	SF_YTI_10ABCD	SolutionFiles\Ch10\YTI_10ABCD	YTI 10B	285
	SF_YTI_10ABCD	SolutionFiles\Ch10\YTI_10ABCD	YTI 10C	286
	SF_YTI_10ABCD	SolutionFiles\Ch10\YTI_10ABCD	YTI 10D	288
	SF_YTI_10EF	SolutionFiles\Ch10\YTI_10EF	YTI 10E	293
	SF_YTI_10EF	SolutionFiles\Ch10\YTI_10EF	YTI 10F	297
	SF_Bike_Hike	SolutionFiles\FinalSites		
11	No solution files			
12	SF_YTI_12B	SolutionFiles\Ch12\YTI_12B	YTI 12B	338
	SF_YTI_12CD	SolutionFiles\Ch12\YTI_12CD	YTI 12C	339
	SF_YTI_12CD	SolutionFiles\Ch12\YTI_12CD	YTI 12D	340
	SF_YTI_12EFG	SolutionFiles\Ch12\YTI_12EFG	YTI 12E	343
	SF_YTI_12EFG	SolutionFiles\Ch12\YTI_12EFG	YTI 12F	344
	SF_YTI_12EFG	SolutionFiles\Ch12\YTI_12EFG	YTI 12G	345
	SF_YTI_12H	SolutionFiles\Ch12\YTI_12H	YTI 12H	349
13	SF_YTI_13A	SolutionFiles\Ch13\YTI_13A	YTI 13A	373
	SF_YTI_13B	SolutionFiles\Ch13\YTI_13B	YTI 13B	377
	SF_YTI_13C	SolutionFiles\Ch13\YTI_13C	YTI 13C	382
	SF_MyDiskDesigns	SolutionFiles\FinalSites		
14	No solution files			
15	SF_YTI_15C	SolutionFiles\Ch15\YTI_15C	YTI 15C	434
16	SF_YTI_16A	SolutionFiles\Ch16\YTI_16A	YTI 16A	453
	SF_YTI_16B	SolutionFiles\Ch16\YTI_16B	YTI 16B	459
	SF_YTI_16C	SolutionFiles\Ch16\YTI_16C	YTI 16C	464
	SF_YTI_16D	SolutionFiles\Ch16\YTI_16D	YTI 16D	465
17	SF_YTI_17A	SolutionFiles\Ch17\YTI_17A	YTI 17A	476
	SF_YTI_17B	SolutionFiles\Ch17\YTI_17B	YTI 17B	477
	SF_YTI_17C	SolutionFiles\Ch17\YTI_17C	YTI 17C	478
	SF_YTI_17D	SolutionFiles\Ch17\YTI_17D	YTI 17D	479
	SF_YTI_17E	SolutionFiles\Ch17\YTI_17E	YTI 17E	480
	SF_YTI_17F	SolutionFiles\Ch17\YTI_17F	YTI 17F	480
	SF_YTI_17G	SolutionFiles\Ch17\YTI_17G	YTI 17G	484

RECOMMENDED HARDWARE AND SOFTWARE

The activities in the textbook can be easily completed using Dreamweaver MX, MX 2004, or 8. Differences between the versions are noted in Appendix A in the student textbook and at the Online Learning Center at **www.WebDesignDW.glencoe.com**.

Access to Dreamweaver and an Internet browser are required for this course. While access to the Internet is *not* required, it is suggested.

Equipment and Software Needs for Dreamweaver MX 2004

	Hardware	Software
Required	**Windows:** 600 MHz Intel Pentium III processor or equivalent **Macintosh:** 500 MHz Power PC G3 processor 128 MB RAM (256 MB recommended) 275 MB available disk space Color monitor (Make sure your equipment meets the minimum system requirements of your software.)	Dreamweaver Microsoft Notepad or other text editor Microsoft Windows XP, 2000, or 98 Mac OS X 10.2.6 +
Recommended	CD or DVD drive CD burner or other storage drive Printer Scanner Microphone Video camera Digital camera Audio/video editing equipment	Internet access software Flash® Fireworks® Word processing software Presentation software Spreadsheet software Graphics software Multimedia player or editing software Image-editing software

Using Equipment

Review the operating procedures for any technology tools that you have available in the classroom, and make sure that students understand how to use this equipment responsibly. Also, consider posting operating instructions or user manuals for hardware and software in a convenient location for easy reference. (Visit the Online Learning Center at **www.WebDesignDW.glencoe.com** for a chart that lists the differences in operating systems compatibility.)

TOOLS FOR PROFESSIONAL DEVELOPMENT

GENERAL CLASSROOM GUIDELINES

Both students and teachers have a role in creating an effective classroom.

Teaching Tips

The following tips and recommendations from experienced teachers can help you achieve your optimum teaching level and will encourage your students to learn at the rate of their full potential.

1. **Be prepared and organized.**
   - Order books.
   - Write a course outline and student expectation guide.
   - Review files of past classes.
   - Meet with other teachers.
   - Meet with administrators about expectations.
   - Keep an idea file.

2. **Clarify expectations with students.**
   - Review attendance policy.
   - Review course outline.
   - Review expectations of class.
   - Answer students' questions.
   - Set high standards.
   - Reward good work.

The Student's Role

The student's role is changing in today's classroom. Students are expected to be active learners, not passive receivers. The best learning methods incorporate reading and listening to lectures with active student participation. Be sure to review the following general classroom guidelines with your students:

- **Be prepared.** Have students come to class prepared with reading assignments and homework. If students are not prepared, they are less likely to participate and to grasp concepts during the lecture. Stress the importance of completing assigned exercises and coming to class prepared to discuss them. You may want students to complete certain assignments outside class so that classroom time can be devoted to discussion and review. Many of the exercises work well when they are discussed in small groups and others work best when they are completed and reviewed in class.

- **Review objectives.** Read the chapter objectives at the beginning of each class so that the students know the class expectations. Review the instructions of the exercises out loud as students follow in their books so that everyone is on the same track, questions can be clarified, and everyone is ready to start on time.

Part 1—Teacher Resources 41

- **Bring books to class.** Students should bring their books to each class period unless otherwise instructed.
- **Encourage responsibility.** Stress that students should take responsibility for their education by participating in class, looking for innovative solutions, and clarifying course expectations. Their teachers and advisors cannot tell them about all academic regulations. They must be aware of deadlines and procedures, and understand how the system works.
- **Encourage support groups.** Students need support from other students, teachers, advisors, and academic support groups. Encourage them to take responsibility for creating support groups. Point out that learning time management tips can help students in their careers. Discuss with them the value of gaining the support of family members, co-workers, and supervisors.

The Teacher's Role

A teacher must often exhibit a range of skills. In addition to understanding the course material, you must be able to communicate clearly and draw out important concepts from student questions and discussions.

- **Acknowledge the whole of intelligence.** Encourage students to use the whole of their intelligence. IQ is only one indicator of intelligence. Emotional maturity is also fundamental to school and job success. Students who have emotional control, have developed the ability to work well with others, have integrity and character, and have developed the tools to relate to others courteously can greatly increase their effectiveness.
- **Create a supportive climate.** Students will get involved in the exercises if they see that you are enthusiastic, interested, and value the assignments. Walk around while students do the exercises and check their progress, but do not help individuals or join teams. Give students lots of examples and reinforce the material.
- **Establish ground rules early.** Stress that not only is attendance required, but coming to class on time and prepared is also necessary. If students miss five or ten minutes, they have missed the introduction and review, and must interrupt to ask questions. You can always ease the schedule after students demonstrate that they are responsible and take charge of their own learning. Decide how long you need to spend on exercises, class discussions, and lectures.
- **Create diverse teams.** Students can learn from those who offer different perspectives, and diverse groups can foster understanding and respect for differences. Arrange groups to be diverse in age, gender, culture, interests, and so on. Many teachers like to have permanent teams throughout the course to add continuity, increase team skills, and build friendships.
- **Create classwide participation.** Encourage all students to participate. You may want to rotate the role of leader to encourage shy students to participate and learn leadership skills. Shift the location of teams so that those in the back of the classroom can respond more readily.

- **Emphasize communication skills.** Stress the importance of public speaking and interpersonal communication skills. One of the best communication skills is the ability to present short summaries of projects, exercises, or activities. Tell students that you will call on one of them to give a concise and brief summary of the main points covered in the last class meeting. This will not only encourage them to be prepared, but it will increase their public speaking skills and liven up the class as well. A summary also serves as a reminder and review of previous material. You can also add to the student's summary and connect it to the current lecture.
- **Make time for questions.** Have a set time when any topic is allowed, perhaps at the end of the class or once a week during an extended break.
- **Incorporate peer teaching.** Peer teachers and advisors are effective because they are able to relate to one another and they feel encouraged by working together. Students also have a chance to explain concepts in their own words. Peer teachers do not have to be the students with the best grades to be successful. Average students and struggling students can choose a topic and explain it effectively to others. Incorporate peer teaching throughout the course.
- **Make connections.** Education will be more relevant and meaningful if students see the connection between school and work. Throughout the course emphasize these connections:
    - Student to student
    - Student to teacher
    - School to work
    - Theory to practice
- **Encourage students to be open to new perspectives.** Sometimes students have set values and mind-sets. Discuss the value of seeing problems from a fresh perspective.
- **Be aware of other demands on students' time.** Many students have work, family, and community obligations that demand their time. Offer understanding but also discuss the necessity of backup plans. Have students discuss their many roles and concerns.

Instruction Style Guidelines

Students benefit from a variety of teacher input: introduction of new concepts and procedures through oral explanation, demonstration of new procedures and applications, and encouragement and immediate feedback on performance.

Building on Topics

Students need to know where they are headed, where they have been, and how the topics they are learning fit together.

- Always review old learning to be sure students are ready to move on to a new topic.

TOOLS FOR PROFESSIONAL DEVELOPMENT

- Demonstrate new concepts and procedures to the class. Students learn many of their skills by following teacher demonstrations and solving relevant assignment materials.
- Relate new and advanced learning to the students' growing competency with overall skills. Explain how new skills reinforce and build on earlier skills.

Effective Questioning

Questioning is one way to stimulate student participation in class sessions to assess the extent of the learning that has taken place. The following are suggestions for effective questioning practices.

- Ask precise questions that require exact responses when principles or procedures are involved.
- Ask questions that are relevant only to the subject matter.
- Direct your questions to the class as a whole. After a slight pause, call on one student for a reply.
- Ask questions that can be answered by the students to whom they are addressed, with special regard for each student's ability.
- Ask enough questions to reach everyone in the class during the period or during the week.
- Avoid questions that require simple yes or no responses. Ask why, how, and when to encourage students to show that they really understand the material.
- Plan your questions to cover the chapter content as indicated by the chapter objectives.
- Invite your students to ask questions. Have other class members attempt to answer these questions before you do. As you know, students can often explain things to one another very clearly if they are given the opportunity to do so.
- Take note of the questions that most often provoke discussion or are raised frequently. Include them in future quizzes and tests.
- Include some grade or mark for class participation in your overall appraisal of each student.

The Teacher's Attitude

Learning is a process centered around beliefs, attitude, and experience. Build a supportive environment as you create a learning community. As the teacher, you are key in creating this supportive classroom climate. Genuine interest and supportiveness should be shown daily and may be enhanced by the following:

- Listen carefully to student comments and take notes when necessary.
- Respond seriously to students' questions and concerns. Be enthusiastic and positive and show that you enjoy teaching this class.
- Be available to meet with students if necessary.

- As the teacher, try to be seen as an open, supportive member of the team, as well as a coach and facilitator. Student discussion is important to a supportive learning climate.
- Encouraging students to discover that their own answers can help facilitate class discussion.

Managing a classroom takes considerable interpersonal and management skills. When you feel discouraged or fatigued, try the following techniques for renewal:

- Talk with other teachers and share ideas.
- Take students on field trips.
- Find your own style of teaching.
- Focus on your strengths.
- Build a supportive learning environment.
- Be a mentor.
- Express your concerns and expectations to the class.
- Invite stimulating guest speakers to class.

LEARNING-STRATEGY GUIDELINES

The two most common reasons that students fail are poor study habits and lack of time management skills.

Helping Improve Study Habits and Time Management

Follow these guidelines to help students improve their study habits and time-management skills.

- Post reminders of due dates for homework, projects, and tests. Encourage students to break assignments into smaller tasks. They can work backward from the due date, planning all the steps necessary to complete the assignment. Students will be less prone to procrastinate, will find inspiration in completing smaller tasks, and will feel more in control.
- Encourage students to learn how to contact at least two students in their class. They can take notes for each other in an emergency, share information, and study together.
- Encourage study groups. Students will be most effective when they learn to use the skills and talents of others.
- Encourage students to get in touch with you as soon as they have a question or problem. Emphasize that they should not wait until the night before an exam to ask for clarification.
- Return phone calls and e-mails promptly.

TOOLS FOR PROFESSIONAL DEVELOPMENT

Developing Critical Thinking Skills in Students

As your students enter the world of work, they will be required to process, analyze, interpret, and communicate information. Successful employees possess the ability to make insightful decisions, solve problems creatively, and interact with diverse groups.

Basic Elements of Critical Thinking

Critical thinking is the process of logically deciding on a course of action or a conclusion to a question or scenario. It involves the ability to:

- Compare and contrast
- Solve problems and make decisions
- Analyze and evaluate
- Synthesize and transfer knowledge

Benefits of Critical Thinking

- Helps students investigate their own methods for solving problems.
- Leads students to investigations that compare and contrast knowns and unknowns.
- Allows students to make decisions about their own learning.
- Makes students aware of their own learning processes.

Problem-Solving Strategies

1. **Define the problem.** Instruct students to work through the following question: What is the situation or the context of the problem? To define the problem clearly, state the problem in one or two sentences.

2. **Gather information and facts.** Next, students should make sure that they have all the necessary information about the situation. Ask questions and observe.

3. **Go from the general to the specific.** Encourage students to look at the big picture as they gain a general understanding of the context of the problem. Break down the problem into its smaller parts.

4. **Develop a plan.** Problem solvers formulate a potential plan of action based on the information gathered. Students should outline their plan step-by-step and evaluate how the problem will be affected if their plan is enacted.

5. **Make connections.** If students can learn to connect what they have learned in other classes to the problem at hand, they will become successful problem solvers.

6. **Be flexible and creative.** Problems often have a variety of acceptable outcomes. Students should approach the situation from different viewpoints and directions, exploring options. Speculation, intuition, and estimation are important in this process.

How to Teach Critical Thinking

All educational disciplines strive to teach critical thinking skills. Today's business environment is highly competitive and demands skilled employees who can make insightful decisions and solve problems creatively. Your students will need to apply critical thinking skills to make important personal and professional plans and decisions in their own lives now and in the future. When you teach your students critical thinking, you are equipping them with skills that are essential to success.

Since all learning requires thinking, your students will benefit from exposure to a variety of thinking exercises. Benjamin Bloom's Taxonomy of the Cognitive Domain is widely recognized for its schema of levels of thinking. Each of Bloom's cognitive categories includes a list of thinking skills and indicates the kinds of behavior students are expected to demonstrate when performing specific learning tasks. Here are some examples:

Bloom's Cognitive Categories

Thinking Skill	Behaviors Required
Knowledge	define, recognize, recall, identify, label, understand, examine, show, collect
Comprehension	translate, interpret, explain, describe, summarize, extrapolate
Application	apply, solve, experiment, show, predict
Analysis	connect, relate, differentiate, classify, arrange, check, group, distinguish, organize, categorize, detect, compare, infer
Synthesis	produce, propose, design, plan, combine, formulate, compose, hypothesize, construct
Evaluation	appraise, judge, criticize, decide

Integrating Critical Thinking Skills

The student text and the Teacher Resource Manual provide you with a variety of activities and guidelines to help you incorporate and integrate critical thinking and problem-solving skills into your daily plans. The following are some guidelines for integrating and teaching these skills:

◆ Let students know they are engaging in aspects of critical thinking. Explain to students that finding solutions to problems is an example of analyzing and evaluating information. Extend these applications of critical thinking skills into your students' lives. Point out that they constantly analyze and evaluate music, conversations with friends, magazine or newspaper articles, and television programs. This will help demonstrate to students that they have had experience in using these skills.

TOOLS FOR PROFESSIONAL DEVELOPMENT

- Stress the importance of critical thinking in daily life. Students should learn to focus on sound decision-making processes, not snap judgments.

- Use activities that focus on open-ended problems to foster greater growth for creative problem-solving. Discuss how people use different thought processes to solve problems. When possible, have students share their ideas and discuss how they arrived at their solutions.

- Organize students in cooperative learning groups so they can see how others solve problems, give each other feedback, and try out new ideas. Divide students into small discussion groups to think in a cooperative setting.

- Use assessments that measure students' growth and performance. Challenge students to reflect on chapter concepts and apply their knowledge. Ask students to apply their analytical skills to solve a problem.

- Provide feedback and encourage students to feel comfortable experimenting with new ideas and new ways to solve problems.

Improving Basic Skills

As your students progress through their academic education, basic skills in reading, writing, listening, and math continue to evolve and expand. In the classroom there are many opportunities to expose students to activities and exercises that not only contribute to their understanding of the subject matter, but also strengthen basic skills.

Developing Active Reading Strategies for Students

How well do your students read? Do they understand what they read? Are they active readers or passive readers? By applying various strategies for reading, you can help your students understand difficult concepts and theories.

To begin, have your students analyze their reading skills. Are they good at reading factual material? Is it easy or difficult for them to read and interpret data? Do they have a good vocabulary? Then discuss with your students the different skills needed when reading factual material as opposed to recreational material. In order to get the most from reading, your students need to learn how to become active readers, getting involved with and responding to the material. Active readers are effective readers.

Active reading requires focus and concentration. Becoming actively engaged in reading can mean employing a variety of techniques: taking notes, previewing, outlining main points, jotting down key words, finding definitions, looking for patterns, and summarizing information in written or verbal forms.

Using SQ3R. "SQ3R" is known as one of the most successful and efficient study methods used by students. The initials stand for the five steps in the study process: Survey, Question, Read, Recite, and Review. At first, your students may find that the SQ3R method is difficult to master. Putting the steps into practice requires deliberate effort and active involvement. If your students find that they re-read information in order to absorb it, use of this study method will save them time and frustration.

A Reading/Study System The following method should be used by your students on a section-by-section basis for each chapter of the text.

S = SURVEY

Students survey the piece of writing to establish its purpose and to prepare themselves for the main ideas. Students should do the following:

- Read the titles and section headings.
- Read the objectives, instructions, and/or summary to understand how each chapter fits the author's purpose.
- Notice each boldface heading and subheading. Recognize the text's organization before starting to read. Build a structure for the thought and details to come.
- Notice any graphics (charts, maps, diagrams). They are presented to make a point.
- Notice reading aids like italics, highlighting, boldface print, chapter objectives, and margin notations. They are presented to help the reader sort, comprehend, and remember the ideas of the chapter.

Q = QUESTION

As students are surveying the piece, a good way to decide what they will be reading is to question as they survey. Writing down questions keeps students alert and focused on their work. Students should do the following:

- Divide a sheet of paper in half lengthwise.
- On the left half, write questions as they are surveying the section of writing.
- Turn the boldface headings into as many questions as they think will be answered in that section. The better the questions, the better their comprehension is likely to be. Students may always add further questions as they proceed. When their minds are actively searching for answers to questions, they become engaged in learning.

R1 = READ

As students read, they should also actively seek answers to their questions. Students should do the following:

- Read each section (one at a time) with their questions in mind. Look for the answers and write them down on the right side of the sheet of paper.
- Take notes on additional concepts that were not covered in their questions.
- Notice whether they need to make up some new questions and add them to their list.

R2 = RECITE

After students have read and answered all of their questions, it is helpful to recite the questions and their answers.

Students should do the following:

- Recite each question out loud, one at a time.
- Answer each question verbally according to the answer they have written down on the right side of the paper.
- Create flashcards for difficult concepts or procedures.
- After each section, stop, recall their questions, and see if they can answer them from memory. If not, look back again, but do not go on to the next section until they can recite the answers.

R3 = REVIEW

Once students finish the entire chapter using these steps, they should review all the questions from the headings. They should do the following:

- Using their notes, questions, and answers, mentally go over the material within 24 hours of covering it.
- Review again after one week.
- Review approximately once a month until their exam.
- Be sure they can still answer all of the questions they posed in the Question phase of their study process. If not, look back and refresh their memory.

Remember to stress that reading is not a passive activity. Students must train their minds to actively learn.

GRID FOR SQ3R

Students can use the following grid to help them use the SQ3R system.

S = SURVEY: Survey the piece of writing to establish its purpose.	
Titles, Headings, and Subheadings	List chapter, sections, etc.
Objectives/Instructions/Terms	List the major objectives, instructions, and terms used in the text.
Graphics/Visuals	List graphics/visuals in text.
Reading Aids	Objectives, section questions, bolded terms, etc., are all designed to emphasize important information.
Q = QUESTION: Question as you survey the materials.	
Ask questions based on main headings and titles.	For example: What are the different types of multimedia presentations?
R1 = READ: As you read, actively seek answers to your questions. Write them down as you find the answers in your reading.	
What are the different types of multimedia presentations?	Multimedia presentations can be slide show presentations, simulations, Web pages, games, advertisements, etc.

TOOLS FOR PROFESSIONAL DEVELOPMENT

Writing for Success

Effective writing skills are essential for communicating information. Emphasize these four basic steps to students as they attempt to communicate in writing:

1. **Prepare** Emphasize the importance of generating and focusing ideas through brainstorming, research, and observation.
2. **Organize** Review the importance of organizing an outline so students can keep focused on the theme, format, and ideas they want to express.
3. **Write** It is vital that students learn how to develop their main topic and supporting points. Encourage students to prepare a timetable for completing a written assignment and to use this schedule to meet a deadline.
4. **Edit** Emphasize the importance of revising their written work. Ask students how they think editing may help improve their grades.

Listening with Intent

Although attending lectures, taking notes, and gathering information are a daily part of your students' lives, they may not have devoted the proper attention to becoming effective listeners. Professionals in the world of business attend meetings, follow directions, work with clients and customers, take notes, and give and receive feedback. In order to successfully participate in these activities, students must learn to be fully attentive with an intent to understand the topics presented. Active listening must include a desire to listen, a willingness to learn, the postponement of judgment of the teacher or speaker, a mindful approach, a respectful viewpoint, an observant mind-set, and an ability to ask questions. It is important for the listener to invest energy in the act of listening, to reduce distractions, and to be quiet while the speaker is delivering a message.

Strengthening Arithmetic/Mathematics Skills

Basic arithmetic computations are performed on a daily basis in the lives of your students when they compute percentages, keep track of their bank accounts, or calculate their wages after deductions. Draw upon these life experiences to strengthen math skills. Remind students that they can perform basic computations and approach practical problems by choosing appropriately from a variety of mathematical techniques.

Thinking Algebraically

Algebraic thinking recognizes various types of patterns and functional relationships and uses symbolic forms to represent and analyze mathematical situations and structures. Many life and work experiences can be expressed in algebraic terms. Your students' life experiences should provide a broad base of real-world ties that can be readily linked to the concepts of equation, function, and graphs. Use logic puzzles, tables and graphs, and concepts centered on equations to help build algebraic thinking.

TOOLS FOR PROFESSIONAL DEVELOPMENT

COURSE ENRICHMENT GUIDELINES

The following guidelines will help students recognize the value of their efforts and attitudes toward promoting their social, ethical, and cultural awareness as it applies to the course.

Integrating Real-World Connections

Students want to see the relevance of what they are studying. Stress how the course brings them closer to reaching their personal and professional goals. Use practical applications when possible. Make certain that your examples are relevant to students and that you ask them for examples that illustrate concepts.

Value Students' Experiences

Students have a wealth of experience. Have them integrate course concepts with their experiences. Discuss their viewpoints and encourage classroom discussions.

Discuss School and Community Resources That Can Help Students

You can use many resources on campus and in the community to help in teaching. Some campuses have faculty development coordinators, special workshops, and speakers.

Invite Guest Speakers to Your Class

Guest speakers can be an important addition to your class because:

- They are experts in their area.
- They add variety.
- They help students see the resources available.
- They help students see the value of networking and contacts.

You should give your guest speaker this information:

- Purpose of the class
- Description of the students
- Purpose of the presentation
- Topic and what you would like to see covered
- Appropriate amount of time to talk
- Time, place, and directions to the classroom

Ask the speaker for a brief description of his or her background, how he or she would like to be introduced, and if he or she has questions for the students to answer. Remember to send a thank-you note and comments from students.

Evaluate guest speakers for your records by filling in this form:

Guest Speaker Form

Date: _____

Guest speaker: _____

Topic: _____

Students' reaction: _____

Teacher's assessment: _____

Possible alternatives for speakers in this area: _____

_____

_____

Integrating Ethics

As your students engage in business transactions and act as employees and managers, they will encounter ethical dilemmas requiring sound decision-making skills. Students should understand that unethical behavior is often perceived as unethical only after the action or decision has been taken or made.

The purpose of introducing ethics into your instruction is to help your students integrate ethical considerations and basic values into their decision-making process. Students are directed to develop a process for considering both the business and the ethical ramifications of a decision before that decision is made. Even though basic values are set in childhood, people do make different decisions as they gain knowledge and insight.

Teaching Ethics

Educational instruction of ethics as a discipline is an aspect of teaching that is commonly ignored. Yet, you do know how to make decisions and most likely have personal experiences with decisions involving ethical ramifications. You need not be an ethics theorist to incorporate discussions of ethical actions into your instruction.

The Ethical Decision-Making Model

This ethical decision-making model will help your students analyze a situation, evaluate alternatives, consider ramifications of each decision, and choose among the alternatives. The five-step model described on the next page is one possible approach to making an ethical decision.

- What are the ethical issues?
- What are the alternatives?
- Who are the affected parties?
- How do the alternatives affect the parties?
- What would you do?

CLASSROOM MANAGEMENT GUIDELINES

Even the most experienced teacher can have problems in the classroom. The following strategies are designed to help you handle the more common problems encountered by educators. Should you encounter situations that require stronger discipline than what is discussed here, contact your supervisor to learn your institution's guidelines concerning student disciplinary procedures.

Attendance Problems

Sometimes students do not understand how important it is to attend every class. Here are some tips for handling attendance problems:

- **Expect regular attendance.** From the first day of class, announce that attendance, participation, and team cooperation will be graded. Stress that assessing the students' strengths, weaknesses, needs, and motivational levels is important for completing assignments and evaluating progress. Point out that when students miss class, they disappoint their teams. If a student misses class without telling you in advance, talk with the student in private and ask for a commitment.
- **Grade attendance.** Remind students that attendance and participation are large parts of their grade. Prompt attendance is important to a class, students, and teams, and promotes positive habits for the workplace.

Problems with Incomplete Work

You may have some students who are not turning in assignments. Here are some teaching tips to encourage students to complete their work:

- **Communicate expectations.** Explain the guidelines and expectations for receiving a good grade or credit for the course. Discuss what students want to learn from the course and what that means in terms of attendance, assignments, and participation. As suggested earlier, you may want to have students turn in note cards with their name, phone number, the grade they expect to earn, what they hope to learn from the course, and the areas they most want to work on. This is an excellent time to review their goals.
- **Contact students.** Call or e-mail students when they miss class, do not participate, or fail to turn in assignments. After this contact, it is up to students to produce results. Show your concern but avoid rescuing them. They need to be responsible for their behavior.

Attitude Problems

A few students may be unsure of what is expected or skeptical of the value of the course. Dealing with different attitude problems is an important part of classroom management.

Negative Attitude

Occasionally, you may have a student who is negative, argumentative, and refuses to participate in team activities or contribute to class discussions. A negative attitude may indicate a feeling of discomfort or fear. Here are some teaching tips for handling negative attitudes:

- **Expect responsibility.** Stress that students are responsible for their attitudes. Coaching and encouragement often inspire the negative student. Remind students they are responsible for motivating themselves and creating a resourceful state of mind. They cannot blame others and empower themselves at the same time.
- **Isolate the problem student.** Meet with the disruptive student. Indicate that students who are disruptive during team exercises or class discussion will be asked to leave. Indicate that students with negative attitudes affect the entire class. If students complain or are uncooperative, have them answer this question: What can I do to correct this situation?

Unmotivated Students

Increasing motivation is a major factor in helping students to try new strategies, perform the required work, and attend all classes. Here are some teaching tips for handling unmotivated students:

- **Review strategies.** As a group, discuss how students can cope with low motivation. Invite a guest speaker to address motivation and attitude.
- **Make learning active.** When energy is low (and it often is around midterm), you may want to go on a field trip. You could also vary the assignments or discuss students' solutions for increasing motivation and creating a more positive attitude.
- **Model enthusiasm.** When you are excited and enthusiastic about class, students are more likely to be motivated. Enjoy what you are doing and do not get discouraged by a lack of motivation.

Personality Conflicts

At times you may feel that students do not like you. Here are some teaching tips for avoiding personality conflicts:

- **Do not take it personally.** Some students want to appear cool or tough and will not let anyone get close to them. Other students may be especially shy or unresponsive. These behaviors are rarely directed at you alone.
- **Clarify perceptions.** Perhaps there is a misunderstanding or students are unclear about expectations. Be open to listening and trying to improve communication.

TOOLS FOR PROFESSIONAL DEVELOPMENT

- **Discuss learning styles.** Discuss different learning and relating styles. Explain to students that they will have many different kinds of teachers and employers, and it is important to be able to relate and communicate with all kinds of people. Sometimes people are uncomfortable with a teacher because he or she has a different teaching/learning style.
- **Be yourself.** Be confident, approachable, supportive, and a good listener. Your goal is to support students in being successful both inside and outside the classroom.

Behavior Problems

Behavior problems can disrupt the classroom and make it difficult for students to learn. Use the following guidelines to deal with common classroom disruptions.

Class Interruptions

Here are some teaching tips for avoiding interruptions:

- **Expect good manners.** The point of listening until others are finished talking should be stressed from the first day of class. Emphasize how important civility and business etiquette are in the workplace.
- **Model respect.** Show respect to students by modeling good listening skills. Discuss periodically the importance of listening in teams, classes, and relationships.

Too Much Socializing

Sometimes students seem to be having so much fun socializing in class that they do not complete their assignments. Here are some teaching tips for reducing student socializing:

- **Time exercises.** Set a certain amount of time for group and class discussions and exercises. This time limit helps students focus on the task at hand. You can always extend the time if necessary.
- **Do first things first.** Go over the first rule of time management: Do first things first. Set priorities, follow through, and then have fun. Tell students that they will gain confidence when they learn this important habit.

Side Talking in Class

Inappropriate side talking is disruptive and distracting. Side talking is especially common when friends sit in the back of the classroom. Here are some teaching tips to cut down side talking:

- **Encourage courtesy.** Restate your expectations and rules for the class and be consistent. Encourage students to be respectful of all speakers.
- **Illustrate the disruption.** Often students think that because they are in the back of the classroom, the teacher does not see or hear them. Demonstrate the effects of side talking on a speaker and the class. Choose a student to

speak in front of the classroom. Have a few other students talk among themselves. Ask the speaker what it was like to try and speak over conversations. Stress that public speaking and giving presentations are already difficult without distractions or rude behavior.

- **Clarify your feelings.** Use the "I" message to communicate how you feel: "I feel that what I am saying is being ignored when students side talk."

Participation Problems

Active learning simply requires students to participate in class and to interact with classmates. Anticipating students who are reluctant to participate will help you adjust your teaching style to accomodate unequal participation in class.

Lack of Class Participation

Class participation helps you learn more about your students and encourages them to keep up with assignments. You will have some students who are not willing to participate or talk. Here are some teaching tips that will help increase class participation:

- **Talk about the benefits of cooperative learning.** Tell students that organizations are run by teams and require employees to participate.
- **Review expectations.** Announce the first day of the class and several times thereafter that teamwork and participation are important factors in this course and essential in the working world. People who are successful learn to work with various types of people, regardless of whether they like them.
- **Emphasize that students be prepared.** If students do not keep up with assignments, then they cannot contribute to the rest of the class.
- **Get involved.** Indicate that participation and team sharing make the class much more effective and enjoyable. Some students may feel more comfortable talking and participating in a small group. You may want to have teams of four or five students discuss exercises and then spend a few minutes discussing the topic with the class. Teamwork brings out participation even with shy students.

Unequal Participation

Often it is only assertive students who lead the discussions. Here are some teaching tips for getting all students to participate:

- **Encourage all class members.** It is important for you to stress that this course depends on the participation of all class members. Occasionally call on the quieter members of the class. Sometimes this makes it easier for them to participate.
- **Encourage listening.** Listening is not only vital for healthy relationships; it is also an important job skill. Encourage students to listen and to monitor how much time they speak in groups. Communication is always enhanced when people listen and contribute.

Part 1—Teacher Resources 57

TOOLS FOR PROFESSIONAL DEVELOPMENT

Shy Students

You will always have some students who are shy and do not contribute as much as the more outgoing students. Here are some teaching tips for encouraging shy students:

- **Integrate learning styles.** Discuss the different learning styles with students. Point out that some people are more extroverted than others.

- **Take a risk.** If students are shy, ask them to reach out and be more involved. Extroverted students should listen more to draw out the shyer students. Encourage your outgoing students to be supportive, to listen, and to help others express their views. You might want to shift the seating about every four weeks so that shy students sit up front during some of the sessions.

- **Stress class participation.** Acknowledge that many students are shy but are often more comfortable working in small teams.

- **Give positive reinforcement.** Call on students who do not participate much, but who are otherwise doing well in class. If they get a positive response to their contributions, they may become less reluctant to talk in class.

CREATING A LEARNER-CENTERED ENVIRONMENT

COOPERATIVE LEARNING

Studies show that students learn faster and retain more information when they are actively involved in the learning process. Studies also show that in a classroom setting, students often learn more from each other about subject matter than from a traditional teacher-led lecture and discussion. Cooperative learning is one method that gets students actively involved in learning and at the same time allows for peer teaching.

Cooperative learning helps students acquire the interaction skills that are increasingly necessary in today's team-oriented workplaces. Working in teams is so much a part of the workplace that many employers give prospective employees inventories and assessments to determine their ability to function within a team framework. Through the use of cooperative learning, the teacher can emphasize the collaborative skills of team-building and team decision-making, and social skills such as how to listen, respond, agree, disagree, clarify, encourage, and evaluate.

The Basic Elements of Cooperative Learning

In traditional educational settings, students tend to work on their own and compete with one another. In the cooperative learning environment, students work in teams and contribute to each other's learning. Cooperative learning is structured for small group learning, which meets the basic needs for interpersonal relationships, personal growth, and enhanced learning. All members of the group benefit from each other's efforts, backgrounds, experiences, and viewpoints. Cooperative learning can provide invigorating classroom dynamics; increase respect for diversity; and encourage skills in effective listening and speaking, leadership, decision-making, and conflict resolution.

Cooperative learning involves assigning students to small groups to work together within a classroom setting. This learning structure is especially effective for more difficult learning tasks, such as problem-solving, critical thinking, and conceptual learning. Cooperative learning requires a supportive, student-centered, and non-competitive climate. It supplements rather than replaces traditional approaches, including lectures.

Cooperative learning groups emphasize:

- Supporting mutual goals rather than individual competition and achievement.
- Completing structured tasks where each team member contributes.
- Sharing equal responsibility for accomplishing group goals.
- Learning social skills.
- Rotating interdependent roles (discussion leaders, recorders, observers, listeners, and speakers).

CREATING A LEARNER-CENTERED ENVIRONMENT

- Maintaining equal participation.
- Encouraging individual responsibility.

The Benefits of Cooperative Learning Groups

Cooperative learning offers many benefits:

- Students are drawn into learning situations that require them to be directly involved. Each student must make a contribution as well as accept input from others.
- Students discover how to work with people of all types. Schools with racially or ethnically mixed populations often improve interracial and multicultural relationships between students.
- Students improve communication skills.
- Students learn valuable social and problem-solving skills that transfer to real-world occupations and work environments.
- Students learn to work through conflicts.

Preparation for Cooperative Learning

Before assigning a cooperative learning activity, prepare your students for the cooperative learning process. The following tips will help you set the stage for effective cooperative learning.

- **Classroom Arrangement** Move the furniture in the room so that students can face each other.
- **Group Size** Decide on the size of the group. Groups work best when composed of two to five students.
- **Group Assignments** Assign students to groups. Each group should be mixed racially, socially, ethnically, and by gender and range of ability.
- **Rotation of Group Members** Change groups periodically. For example, you can change the groups every four to six weeks, every quarter, every semester, or for every new chapter or section.
- **Student Preparation** Prepare students for cooperation. Students will work with each other to accomplish the same goal, but each student will be individually accountable for learning.
- **Initial Activities** Start small. It is not necessary to incorporate all the characteristics of cooperative learning into the first activity. Some ideas will be easy to adapt while others may be more difficult.
- **Group Roles** Explain group roles. Students need to learn the cooperative skills that are fundamental to each role before they begin interacting in cooperative activities. Their roles should be introduced to students one at a time so the students can learn the differences between them.

Create Heterogeneous Teams

Within the first or second class meeting, place students in four- or five-member teams. You can create heterogeneous class teams by mixing characteristics:

- Learning abilities
- Genders
- Cultures
- Ethnicities

Teachers and team members should assess their team's effectiveness and reflect on the learning process and outcomes. Is the team effective? Does everyone contribute? How can the team be more effective?

Teachers can ascertain how teams interact by completing a chapter exercise each class period. By starting the class with an exercise, you emphasize skills acquisition. Students get the opportunity to become acquainted with each other and exchange ideas.

Teacher and Student Responsibilities

The success of the cooperative learning groups depends largely on the teacher's ability to coach each of the groups and on the students' abilities to accomplish a goal as a team.

The Teacher:

- Creates the learning environment.
- Structures and guides the process of learning.
- Motivates students to learn.
- States the goals of the instruction.
- Teaches the fundamental concepts.
- Interacts with and guides the work of many groups.
- Acts as a resource to the groups as needed.
- Monitors student behavior.
- Evaluates the group process.

The Students:

- Work toward group goals, yet understand that individual responsibility is expected.
- Contribute their own ideas.
- Understand that they are responsible for one another's learning as well as their own.
- Draw upon their own creativity and on the strengths of their teammates.

- Communicate effectively with one another.
- Recognize that the differences among team members are a form of enrichment, not a deficit.

Results of Cooperative Learning

In most classrooms, only a few outspoken and articulate students actively participate. However, one of the goals of cooperative learning is to get all members of the class to share ideas, express opinions, and participate in group exercises. Emphasize the value of inclusive participation and the responsibility of outspoken students to encourage less talkative students to express their views. Stress the importance of listening and taking turns to talk.

CULTURAL DIVERSITY

High schools are becoming increasingly diverse environments. Diversity includes factors such as gender, race, age, sexual orientation, ethnicity, physical ability, social and economic background, and religion.

The Diverse Classroom

Your class may include students who have learning disabilities; students who want more career direction; students who are very goal-oriented and career-directed; transfer students; students on probation; athletes; students of different races, cultures, and religions; and students who are physically impaired. Each of these students will have different needs and problems. The more you know about each individual, the more you will be able to use various strategies, learning methods, examples, and approaches to meet their specific needs.

Emphasize that we can all learn from each other by being open and sharing different views, values, ideas, and goals. Encourage all students to get to know people from different races, cultures, backgrounds, and religions. As contributing members of society, ask your students to assess their assumptions, judgments, prejudices, and stereotypes. Discuss how critical thinking can lead to changes in beliefs and attitudes.

Examine your own concerns, fears, prejudices, and assumptions. Avoid generalizations and make certain your lectures are sensitive to the needs and views of all your students. Be a model for tolerance and understanding, and increase your awareness of other cultures or ethnic groups.

Supporting Diversity

The population of the United States is becoming increasingly diverse. As students from many backgrounds enter our schools, it is becoming evident that versatility is the key for learning. The traditional delivery mode of the teacher lecturing to passive, inexperienced students is no longer relevant. Varied learning approaches and students' active involvement are necessary if students are to make meaningful connections to their classes and to the world of work.

Help prepare students to work with and celebrate differences between co-workers in the business world. Have students discuss situations in which they felt different because they were younger, older, of a different religion or culture, or a minority of some other type.

Explore the available resources in the school and community that support diversity. Post lists of noted speakers, events, and opportunities promoting increased awareness and understanding. Bring in speakers who discuss how to celebrate and promote diversity. Encourage students from different cultures to participate and assume leadership roles.

Teaching Tips for the Diverse Classroom

Here are some teaching tips that may help students learn to value and understand diversity:

- **Be inviting.** Students need to feel that they belong. Make your classroom and office inviting. Be personable, get to know students, and welcome them to your office. Ask questions about how they are adjusting and show that you are interested.
- **Invite outside speakers.** Bring in speakers from different cultural backgrounds.
- **Use peer facilitators.** Hire peer facilitators or tutors from different cultural backgrounds.
- **Plan outside events.** Investigate resources on campus and in the community. Have students attend different cultural events or take a field trip as part of the class experience.
- **Discuss resources.** Have a list of resources available for various cultural groups.
- **Encourage class discussions.** Encourage all students to discuss their viewpoints. Point out how people see things differently. Understanding and respecting differences are the foundations of building common bonds.
- **Encourage creativity and flexibility.** Stress that people can speak and act differently in different situations. Being flexible and relating to diverse people in the work, home, and school environments both expand options and build relationships. Relating to different people does not mean students are rejecting their own culture. They are expanding their communication and relationship skills.

Tips for Working with Diverse Students

High-Risk Students

The term "high-risk student" is often used today to describe students who are at risk of dropping out of school. Emphasize that everyone has some risk factors, and that the more students assess their strengths and weaknesses, the more likely they are to ask for help and thus succeed. Stress to students that the key is to take responsibility for who they are, where they are, and where they want to be.

Transfer Students

Transfer students are often most concerned with what credits are transferred and are acceptable for meeting the school's requirements. It is critical that transfer students see an advisor and plan their educational program. Transfer students may think they already know the rules. Stress that every campus is different and students should not assume that the procedures are the same.

Student Athletes

Athletes have the same issues that other students have, plus they have a large commitment of time for sports practice and the additional stresses of competition, risk of injury, and the need to stay energized and focused on winning.

Here are some teaching tips for student athletes:

◆ **Clarify expectations.** Stress that attending and participating in all classes is important. Athletes' top priority should be school and not sports.

◆ **Help students clarify their goals.** Talk about their academic and career goals. What do they want to do when they finish school? How can this course help them reach their goals? What personal qualities and skills have they gained by playing sports?

◆ **Emphasize planning.** Show students the importance of planning and time management. Have them keep a time log so they can set their priorities and keep their commitments.

Students on Academic Probation

Many students do not understand how easy it is to fall behind and find themselves on academic probation. You may want to invite the principal or another administrator to discuss what "probation" and "disqualified" mean and how students can stay in good standing academically. At some schools a student will be placed on academic probation when his or her overall grade average falls below a C average.

Here are some teaching tips for students on academic probation:

- **Take fewer units.** Students on probation are advised to not take more than 12 units.
- **Compute GPA.** Show students how to compute their grade point average.
- **Talk to teachers.** Stress the importance of meeting with each of their teachers and obtaining regular progress reports or grades.
- **Meet with an advisor.** Students on probation need special attention. Stress the importance of students meeting with their advisors.

International Students

The number of international students is increasing dramatically at many schools. The adjustment to a new culture, language, and climate is tremendous.

Here are some teaching tips for international students:

- **Stress involvement.** Encourage students to form supportive relationships with various types of people by getting involved in campus or community activities.
- **Explore resources.** Learn what resources are available both on and off campus for international students.
- **Encourage mentoring.** Many campuses have a mentoring program. Connect the international student with a student who has been on campus for at least a year.
- **Speak clearly.** If the student's primary language is not English, speak clearly and slowly, avoid slang, and explain the meaning of common expressions and phrases.
- **Clarify assignments.** Make sure students understand what is expected of them. Put important information in writing. It is important that you do not come across as condescending, which can make the students feel uncomfortable.
- **Be warm and friendly.** International students need to see a friendly face. Smile and be welcoming.
- **Integrate learning styles.** As with all students, international students can benefit from seeing, hearing, doing, and utilizing information.
- **Learn about other cultures.** Cultural differences in body language, attitudes toward time, slang, and eye contact may be dramatic. Ask questions and be respectful.
- **Encourage students to talk.** All students can benefit from hearing the experiences of international students. Ask them to explain their customs, country, and background.

MEETING SPECIAL NEEDS

Your classroom contains learners who possess their own unique set of abilities, perceptions, and needs. In order to meet the special needs of students with physical or learning challenges, you may need to utilize more than one approach to teaching. Auditory, visual, or physical difficulties may interfere with an individual's ability to learn in the same way as other students, yet these special needs students have the same educational, social, emotional, and personality development goals. This manual provides a variety of teaching strategies to help you modify and creatively support the concepts that students need to learn.

There are many definitions of what constitutes a learning disability. All of us have certain deficiencies and strengths. The point is to encourage all students to assess their strengths and to seek extra help when they need it.

Special needs and disabilities may be visible or invisible. Some students are deficient in certain skills. Other students may have learning disabilities and have difficulty processing information. This difficulty may interfere with their abilities to take tests, write, read, solve math problems, or comprehend information. Other students may have physical or health disabilities.

The Americans with Disabilities Act stipulates that students are entitled access to public education. Students should investigate the available resources at their campuses. Many schools have a disabled student support services office. Public campuses provide accessibility to classrooms, labs, and the library.

Meeting Individual Needs and Learning Styles

One of your greatest challenges as a teacher is to provide a positive learning environment for all students in your classroom. Because each student is unique, their learning styles and physical abilities may vary widely.

Improve your teaching effectiveness by understanding how students learn and by integrating different learning styles. Students can improve their learning by discovering how they learn best. This understanding can empower them to take control of their learning.

Teaching Students with Special Needs

Students may have orthopedic impairments, hearing or vision impairments, learning disabilities, or behavior disorders — all of which may interfere with their ability to learn. The learning styles of students may also vary. Some students may be visual learners, while others learn more effectively through hands-on activities. Some students may work well independently, while others need interaction. Students may come from a variety of cultural backgrounds, and some may be second-language learners.

CREATING A LEARNER-CENTERED ENVIRONMENT

Once you determine the special needs of your students, you can identify the areas in the curriculum that may present barriers to them. In order to remove those barriers, you may need to modify your teaching methods.

Preparing for Special Needs

In your classroom, you may encounter students who have special needs. A Special Needs Information and Resources chart (pages 70–73) describes some of those special needs and identifies sources of information. Also provided are tips for modifying your teaching style to accommodate the special needs of your students.

The Different Learning Styles chart (pages 74–77) will help you identify your students' learning styles, provides a description of each type of learner, the likes of each type, what each type is good at, and how each type learns best. Famous learners within each type are also listed.

As you prepare for the special learning needs of your students, follow these general guidelines:

- Identify the special needs of your students.
- Identify areas in the curriculum that may present barriers to some students.
- Define ways to remove any impediments to their learning.
- Modify your teaching methods to meet your students' needs.
- Consult with your school professionals about students with special needs.

Modifying Your Teaching Style

Learning can occur in a variety of ways and at different speeds. To maximize their learning experience, it is important to recognize how each of your students learns best. You can meet their various needs by offering activities, resources, and experiences that will help them learn effectively. This will help students reduce frustration, focus on their strengths, and achieve an understanding of the concepts.

Vary the way in which you present material so that you are appealing to all of the different learning styles. If you have traditionally relied on a lecture-question format, consider incorporating more visual aids into your instruction. Instead of explaining a concept only verbally, integrate the use of transparencies, handouts, or charts.

- **For visual learners:** Use visual aids, such as PowerPoint presentations, the board, and transparency masters.
- **For auditory learners:** Present lectures, use small group discussion, and repeat important material.
- **For kinesthetic learners:** Use field trips, student presentations, role-playing, case studies, and activities.

Part 1—Teacher Resources **67**

CREATING A LEARNER-CENTERED ENVIRONMENT

Assign class time for different activities. Use student speakers to add interest and information to the class. As you make adjustments for the benefit of your special needs students, it is important to avoid calling attention to these modifications. By developing good relationships with your special needs students, you can address their specific challenges and offer encouragement.

Another challenge in dealing with special needs learners is how to have them relay to you their understanding of the course material. Methods of assessment may have to be altered in order to fairly apply the same standards to all students. For example, a student who has difficulty writing may have to take a test orally or use a computer. A student who deals with physical challenges may not be equipped to participate in some group activities and may be better evaluated using a project designed for an individual.

Encourage special needs students to take leadership roles just as other students do. They should understand that they offer unique skills, talents, and perspectives to the activities and concepts they are learning.

Tips for Teaching Students with Special Needs

Here are some tips for teaching students with special needs:

- **Be aware of physical requirements.** When an activity requires students to write on a chalkboard or marker board, students who use wheelchairs may require that the board be lowered, or they may use an overhead projector. For students with visual impairments, an oral response is appropriate.
- **Encourage responsibility.** The student is responsible for documenting a disability and requesting accommodations and assistance. Encourage students to communicate what they need to be successful. Encourage them to take responsibility for their learning. Have students find resources available on campus and in the community.
- **Learn about the Americans with Disabilities Act (ADA).** As a teacher, you will want to know about guidelines and resources. Find out what resources are available to support students with disabilities.
- **See the whole student.** Do not allow disabilities to create a faulty perception of a student's talents, effort, and abilities.
- **Use various learning styles.** Use visual, auditory, and hands-on learning techniques. Have students discover how they learn and relate best. Knowing how they learn, process information, and relate to others is an essential tool that students can use for school and job success. Have students integrate different learning styles.
- **Use success tips and strategies.** Studying in teams, previewing chapters, sitting in the front row, attending all classes, actively participating in class, making learning active, taping lectures, planning daily schedules, and getting organized are just a few tips that can help students succeed.

CREATING A LEARNER-CENTERED ENVIRONMENT

- **Encourage students to meet with teachers and advisors.** One of the best tips is to encourage students to meet with each of their teachers and their advisors. Students should review course expectations, plan a course of study, and seek feedback.

- **Encourage students to use available resources.** Have students explore campus resources. For example, many schools have tutors, learning centers, free workshops, and study guides. Encourage students to seek tutors, and to ask teachers for extra help, more classroom discussions, explanations, alternative methods for completing projects or testing, and extended time for tests. Being assertive involves speaking calmly, concisely, directly, and courteously. Students do not need to be pushy or aggressive to ask for what they need.

- **Use individualized projects.** Students who are assigned to individual projects are free to progress at their own pace. You may ask your students to use tutorial software that allows learners to advance at their own pace.

CREATING A LEARNER-CENTERED ENVIRONMENT

Special Needs Information and Resources

The following table contains information and resources that may help teachers who have students with special needs. Teachers should always consult campus professionals when working with students who have special needs.

Subject	Description	Sources of Information
Students with Limited English Proficiencies	Multicultural and/or bilingual individuals often speak English as a second language. The customs and behavior of people in the majority culture may be confusing to these individuals. Cultural values may inhibit some of these students from full participation.	◆ Teaching English as a Second Language ◆ Mainstreaming and the Minority Child ◆ Children with Limited English: Teaching Strategies for the Regular Classroom ◆ Educational Services to Handicapped Students with Limited English Proficiency: A California Statewide Study/ PBN B621
Students with Behavior Disorders	Individuals with behavior disorders deviate from standards or expectations of behavior and impair the functioning of others and themselves. These learners may also be gifted or learning disabled.	◆ Exceptional Children ◆ Journal of Special Education ◆ Educating Students with Behavior Disorders
Students with Orthopedic Impairments	Individuals who have orthopedic impairments have restricted use of one or more limbs and require the assistance of wheelchairs, crutches, or braces. Other impairments may require the use of respirators or other medical equipment.	◆ The Source Book for the Disabled ◆ Teaching Exceptional Children ◆ Vocational Preparation and Employment of Students with Physical and Multiple Disabilities

CREATING A LEARNER-CENTERED ENVIRONMENT

Tips for Instruction

- Remember that students' ability to speak English does not reflect their academic ability.
- Try to incorporate students' cultural experiences into your instruction. The help of a bilingual aide may be effective.
- Include information about different cultures in your curriculum to help build students' self-image.
- Avoid cultural stereotypes.
- Encourage students to share their cultures in the classroom.

- Provide a clearly structured environment with regard to scheduling, rules, room arrangement, and safety.
- Clearly outline objectives and how you will help students obtain objectives.
- Work for long-term improvement; do not expect immediate success.
- Model appropriate behavior for students and reinforce it.
- Adjust group requirements for individual needs.

- Discuss with the student when you should offer aid.
- Help students and staff understand orthopedic impairments.
- Invite all students to participate in activities including field trips, special events, and projects.
- Learn more about special orthopedic devices; be aware of any special safety precautions needed.

continued on next page

CREATING A LEARNER-CENTERED ENVIRONMENT

Subject	Description	Sources of Information
Students with Visual Impairments	The visually disabled have partial or total loss of sight. Individuals with visual impairments are not significantly different from their sighted peers in ability range or personality. However, blindness may affect cognitive, motor, and social development, especially if early intervention is lacking.	◆ Journal of Visual Impairment and Blindness ◆ Education of the Visually Handicapped ◆ American Foundation for the Blind
Students with Hearing Impairments	Partial or total loss of hearing may affect an individual's cognitive, motor, social, and speech development if early intervention did not occur. The ability range or personality of the hearing impaired is not significantly different from the hearing student.	◆ American Annals of the Deaf ◆ Journal of Speech and Hearing Research ◆ National Association of the Deaf
Students with Learning Disabilities	All learning-disabled students have an academic problem in one or more areas, such as academic learning, language, perception, social-emotional adjustment, memory, or ability to pay attention.	◆ Journal of Learning Disabilities ◆ The ABCs of Learning Disabilities ◆ Learning Disability Quarterly
Gifted Students	Gifted students are often described as those having above-average ability, task commitment, and creativity. Gifted students rank in the top five percent of their class. They usually finish work more quickly than others and are capable of divergent thinking.	◆ Journal for the Education of the Gifted ◆ The National Research Center on the Gifted and Talented

CREATING A LEARNER-CENTERED ENVIRONMENT

Tips for Instruction

- Help students become independent. Modify assignments as needed.
- Provide tactile models whenever possible.
- Team the students with sighted peers.
- Teach classmates to serve as guides.
- Tape lectures and reading assignments.

- Seat students where they can see your lip movements easily.
- Avoid verbal directions.
- Avoid standing with your back to the window or to a light source.
- Use an overhead projector to help you maintain eye contact while writing.
- Write all assignments on the board, or hand out written instructions.

- Create a classroom environment that leads to success.
- Provide assistance and direction; clearly define rules, assignments, and duties.
- Allow for peer interaction during class time; utilize peer helpers.
- Practice skills frequently.
- Use games and drills to help maintain interest.
- Allow students to record answers on tape, and allow extra time to complete tests and assignments.
- Provide outlines or tape lecture materials.

- Emphasize concepts, theories, relationships, ideas, and generalizations.
- Let students express themselves in a variety of ways including drawing, creative writing, or acting.
- Make arrangements for students to work on independent projects.
- Make arrangements for students to advance to selected subjects early.
- Utilize public services and resources, such as agencies providing free and inexpensive materials, community services and programs, and people in the community with specific expertise.

Part 1—Teacher Resources

CREATING A LEARNER-CENTERED ENVIRONMENT

Different Learning Styles

Students often have different learning styles. Knowing how a particular student learns can be the key to academic success.

Type	Description	Likes to...
Verbal/Linguistic Learner	Intelligence is related to words and language, written and spoken.	read, write, tell stories, play word games, and tell jokes and riddles.
Logical/Mathematical Learner	Intelligence deals with inductive and deductive thinking and reasoning, numbers, and abstractions.	perform experiments, solve puzzles, work with numbers, ask questions, and explore patterns and relationships.
Visual/Spatial Learner	Intelligence relies on the sense of sight and being able to visualize an object, including the ability to create mental images.	draw, build, design, and create things; daydream; do jigsaw puzzles and mazes; watch videos; look at photos; and draw maps and charts.
Naturalistic Learner	Intelligence involves observing, understanding, and organizing patterns in the natural environment.	spend time outdoors and work with plants, animals, and other parts of the natural environment; good at identifying plants and animals and at hearing and seeing connections to nature.

CREATING A LEARNER-CENTERED ENVIRONMENT

Is Good at...	Learns Best by...	Famous Learners...
memorizing names, dates, places, and trivia; spelling; using descriptive language; and creating imaginary worlds.	saying, hearing, and seeing words.	◆ Maya Angelou—poet ◆ Abraham Lincoln—U.S. President and statesman ◆ Jerry Seinfeld—comedian
math, reasoning, logic, problem solving, computing numbers, moving from concrete to abstract, and thinking conceptually.	categorizing, classifying, and working with abstract patterns and relationships.	◆ Stephen Hawking—physicist ◆ Albert Einstein—theoretical physicist ◆ Alexa Canady—neurosurgeon
understanding the use of space and how to get around in it, thinking in three-dimensional terms, and imagining things in clear visual images.	visualizing, dreaming, using the mind's eye, and working with colors and pictures.	◆ Pablo Picasso—artist ◆ Maria Martinez—artist ◆ I.M. Pei—architect
measuring, charting, mapping, observing plants and animals, keeping journals, collecting, classifying, and participating in outdoor activities.	visualizing, performing hands-on activities, bringing outdoors into the classroom, and relating home/classroom to the natural world.	◆ George Washington Carver—agricultural chemist ◆ Rachel Carson—scientific writer ◆ Charles Darwin—scientist

continued on next page

CREATING A LEARNER-CENTERED ENVIRONMENT

Type	Description	Likes to…
Musical/Rhythmic Learner	Intelligence is based on recognition of tonal patterns, including various environmental sounds, and on sensitivity to rhythm and beats.	sing and hum, listen to music, play an instrument, move body when music is playing, and make up songs.
Bodily/Kinesthetic Learner	Intelligence is related to physical movement and the brain's motor cortex, which controls bodily motion.	learn by hands-on methods, demonstrate skill in crafts, tinker, perform, display physical endurance, and challenge self physically.
Interpersonal Learner	Intelligence operates primarily through person-to-person relationships and communication.	have lots of friends, talk to people, join groups, play cooperative games, solve problems as part of a group, and volunteer help when others need it.
Intrapersonal Learner	Intelligence is related to inner states of being, self-reflection, metacognition, and awareness of spiritual realities.	work alone, pursue own interests, daydream, keep a personal diary or journal, and think about starting own business.

CREATING A LEARNER-CENTERED ENVIRONMENT

Is Good at...	Learns Best by...	Famous Learners...
remembering melodies; keeping time; mimicking beat and rhythm; noticing pitches, rhythms, and background and environmental sounds.	rhythm, melody, and music.	◆ Henry Mancini—composer ◆ Marian Anderson—opera singer ◆ Paul McCartney—singer, songwriter, musician
physical activities such as sports, dancing, acting, and crafts.	touching, moving, interacting with space, and processing knowledge through bodily sensations.	◆ Jackie Joyner-Kersey—Olympic gold medalist ◆ Katherine Dunham—modern dancer ◆ Dr. Christian Barnard—surgical pioneer
understanding people and their feelings, leading others, organizing, communicating, and mediating conflicts.	sharing, comparing, relating, cooperating, and interviewing.	◆ Jimmy Carter—U.S. President, statesman, winner of Nobel Peace Prize ◆ Eleanor Roosevelt—humanitarian ◆ Lee Iacocca—former president of Chrysler Corporation
understanding self, focusing inward on feelings/dreams, following instincts, pursuing interests, and being original.	working alone, doing individualized projects, and engaging in self-paced instruction.	◆ Marva Collins—educator ◆ Mara Montessori—educator and physician ◆ Sigmund Freud—psychotherapist

Part 1—Teacher Resources

ASSESSMENT AND EVALUATION

STUDENT PERFORMANCE ASSESSMENT

Assessing the level of understanding that your students have gained is both an administrative necessity and a useful tool for motivating students. When grading, promote a positive attitude. Grades should provide positive reinforcement of your assessment of students' performance. Grades can also help students feel proud of their accomplishments and motivate them to work at improving their overall performance.

Vary your grading standards according to time and purpose. For example, you may be lenient at the beginning of the course to help students develop feelings of success and confidence. Later, when your expectations are higher, your standards may be more rigid.

Quizzes and tests should be scored and ranked but not necessarily graded. Sometimes percentage grades may be misleading or even confusing. Since many quizzes and some tests, especially short tests, cannot be scored on the basis of 100 percent, many teachers maintain a cumulative record of points earned and make no association with letter grades or percentages.

In determining a student's final grade, do not depend entirely on a mathematical average. Also give consideration to the general quality of the student's homework, the quantity and quality of the student's class participation, and evidence of improvement in skills, knowledge, habits, and attitudes.

As the teacher for this course, you may want to consider the purpose of assessment:

- What is it you want to evaluate and why?
- What are your goals for the course?
- How do you meet your goals and objectives?

Assessment Strategies

You may need a variety of ways to assess what your students have learned. One traditional method of measuring student progress is the written test that evaluates recall of subject content. This program offers students assessment opportunities at the section, chapter, and unit levels. Use *ExamView* Pro Test Generator Software to evaluate and assess student progress. The *Introduction to Web Design Using Dreamweaver* Web site also offers self-assessment exercises for your students.

Performance Assessment

It is important to assess more than students' rote learning skills. Performance assessment gives you the opportunity to evaluate whether or not a student has learned to analyze and plan under different sets of circumstances. A traditional paper-and-pencil test will not demonstrate your students' skills in these areas.

ASSESSMENT AND EVALUATION

The assessment process for this course is designed to be multidimensional and provides you with many activities, projects, and situations that create opportunities for performance assessment. Cooperative learning, discussion activities, and research projects provide opportunities for students to practice new skills and to apply what they have learned to hands-on projects.

Skills Development

Skills development is the application of learning. It is the concept that skills can be taught and that practice of those skills improves learning. The assumptions underlying skills development accept that students:

- Are responsible for their learning, their behavior, and their actions.
- Must be active participants in the learning process.
- Must participate in cooperative and experiential learning.
- Must be open and willing to experiment and to learn new ideas, information, and skills.

Ask students to complete the following questions at the end of each chapter or at the end of each week:

- What is the most important thing I learned in class this week?
- How can I apply what I learned to my other classes?
- How can I apply what I learned to the workplace?

Project Assessment Rubric

The rubric on the following page may be used to assess Web design projects, research assignments, and class presentations. You may wish to work with individual students to set more specific goals and use those goals to assess student work. Using this rubric, a student can receive a maximum score of 20 points. The point grade can be assessed as letter grade following the information below:

Total Possible Points = 20

Score		Grade
18–20	=	A
15–17	=	B
10–14	=	C
5–9	=	D
0–4	=	F

ASSESSMENT AND EVALUATION

Project Assessment Rubric

	1	2	3	4
Technical Requirements Has the student met the technical requirements of the project as assigned?	No technical requirements have been met.	The student has met some of the technical requirements.	The student has met the technical requirements.	The student has exceeded the technical requirements.
Content Does the project contain the required content as assigned?	No content requirements of the project have been met.	The student has met some of the content requirements.	The student has met the content requirements of the project.	The student has exceeded the content requirements of the project.
Organization Is the information in the project well organized and appropriate to the goals of the project?	The information in the project is not understandable.	The organization of information can be followed with difficulty but is not appropriate to the goals.	The organization of information is adequate and appropriate to the goals.	The organization is logical and interesting; the goals are met in creative ways.
Design Is the design understandable and appropriate to the goals of the project?	The design detracts from the clarity of the project.	The design is somewhat understandable but is not appropriate to the goals.	The design is clear and adequate to the goals.	The design is compelling and creative and serves the goals.
Mechanics Is the text or the speech (for oral presentations) grammatically correct?	The text has more than ten grammatical errors. The student has great difficulty speaking clearly and correctly.	The text has six to nine grammatical errors. The student has some difficulty speaking clearly and correctly.	The text has two to five grammatical errors. The student has little difficulty speaking clearly and correctly.	The text has no grammatical errors. The student's speaking is clear and correct.

Portfolio Assessment

If they are used, student portfolios can also provide assessment. Have students include in their portfolios:

- Work that reflects an achievement of SCANS skills and competencies.
- Work that reflects growth as a critical thinker.
- Work that demonstrates presentation skills.
- Work that shows interdisciplinary thinking.
- Something that reflects growth in professional behavior.
- Something that shows application of logical reasoning.
- Something that shows application of scientific reasoning.
- Work that shows an ability to effectively communicate.
- Something that shows an aesthetic analysis or evaluation of artwork.
- Something from an extracurricular activity that reflects personal or professional growth or understanding.

DETERMINING ASSESSMENT STRATEGIES

The chart below can help you determine which assessment strategies will work best for you and your students.

Assessment Strategies	Advantages	Disadvantages
Objective Measures Multiple choice Matching Item sets True/False	◆ Reliable, easy to validate ◆ Objective, if designed effectively ◆ Low cost, efficient ◆ Automated administration ◆ Lends to equating	◆ Measures cognitive knowledge effectively, but is limited on other measures ◆ Not a good measure of overall performance

continued on next page

ASSESSMENT AND EVALUATION

Assessment Strategies	Advantages	Disadvantages
Written Measures Essays Restricted response Written simulations Case analysis Problem-solving exercises	◆ Face validity (real life) ◆ In-depth assessment ◆ Measures writing skills and higher level skills ◆ Reasonable developmental costs and time	◆ Subjective scoring ◆ Time consuming and expensive to score ◆ Limited breadth ◆ Difficult to equate ◆ Moderate reliability
Oral Measures Oral examinations Interviews	◆ Measures communications and interpersonal skills ◆ In-depth assessment with varied stimulus materials ◆ Learner involvement	◆ Costly and time consuming ◆ Limited reliability ◆ Narrow sample of content ◆ Scoring difficult, need multiple raters
Simulated Activities In-basket Computer simulations	◆ Moderate reliability ◆ Performance-based measure	◆ Costly and time consuming ◆ Difficult to score, administer, and develop
Portfolios and Product Analysis Work samples Projects Work diaries and logs Achievement records	◆ Provides information not normally available ◆ Learner involvement ◆ Face validity (real life) ◆ Easy to collect information	◆ Costly to administer ◆ Labor and paper intensive ◆ Difficult to validate or equate ◆ Biased toward best samples or outstanding qualities

continued on next page

ASSESSMENT AND EVALUATION

Assessment Strategies	Advantages	Disadvantages
Performance Measures Demonstrations Presentations Performances Production work Observation	◆ Job-related ◆ Relatively easy to administer ◆ In-depth assessment ◆ Face validity (real life)	◆ Rater training required ◆ Hard to equate ◆ Subjective scoring ◆ Time consuming if breadth is needed
Performance Records References Performance rating forms Parental rating	◆ Efficient ◆ Low cost ◆ Easy to administer	◆ Low reliability ◆ Subjective ◆ Hard to equate ◆ Rater judgment
Self-Evaluation	◆ Learner involvement and empowerment ◆ Learner responsibility ◆ Measures dimensions not available otherwise	◆ May be biased or unrealistic

ASSESSMENT AND EVALUATION

COURSE ASSESSMENT AND EVALUATION

The first place to start in the evaluation process is to examine goals and objectives against outcomes.

Assessment of Teachers

The point of giving teacher and course evaluations is to receive comments from students concerning their opinions of the course and the teacher's teaching. Students can use many standard evaluation forms to evaluate teachers. You may also want to have students give you verbal or written suggestions.

Teacher Self-Assessment

A good place to start when designing your own instructional assessment plan is to review your goals. Give some thought to what it is you want to accomplish. You may have a long list. Review your list carefully and choose the goals that are most important.

- What were the goals and objectives of the class?
- Did the course meet these goals and objectives?
- Did students make connections to other courses?
- Did students make connections to the workplace?
- Did students use critical thinking and creative problem solving?
- Did students learn how to learn?
- Did lectures integrate learning styles?
- Did students understand the value of cooperative learning?
- How can you make the class more experiential and active?
- Were guest speakers effective?
- What topics did students enjoy most?

Student Assessments of Course

Alternatively, teachers may want students to evaluate the course. Students can answer the same questions listed above under teacher self-assessment. Teachers may also want students to complete an evaluation form. You will probably want to formulate specific questions to help students focus on particular topics and concerns.

Assessment of Outcomes

You may want to gather data and work with staff in research and development to measure outcomes. Compare students who took the class with those who did not. Investigate:

- The retention rates of students over several years
- GPAs
- Graduation rates

You may also want to look at other factors considered important in the success of the class. For example:

- The class is limited to 25 students.
- The class is taught by experienced teachers.
- The class includes peer teachers.
- The textbook is new and required.
- The course is offered at a reasonable time.
- The teachers are given training and support.

Student Advisory Committee

You may want to suggest that a student advisory committee be established to collect data, set goals, and assess the success of the program. This committee may be composed of teachers, administrators, and staff interested in student success and retention. It should be stressed that data not be used punitively, and there should also be multiple measures. The data should be a basis for ongoing conversations. This committee may want to:

- Develop a historical database.
- Set goals and objectives.
- Monitor results and outcomes.
- Meet with employers.
- Analyze student performance.
- Integrate data and goals into strategic planning and budget procedures.
- Collect data for program review and accreditation.

Notes

PART 2

Lesson Plans and Answer Keys

Unit 1 Fundamentals of Web Design **89**
Chapter 1 Web Basics 90
Chapter 2 Computer Basics 112
Chapter 3 Online Basics 130
Chapter 4 HTML Basics 154

Unit 2 Designing Web Sites **179**
Chapter 5 Planning a Web Site 180
Chapter 6 Developing Content and Layout 200
Chapter 7 Selecting Design and Color 222

Unit 3 Enhancing a Web Site **245**
Chapter 8 Using Web Graphics 246
Chapter 9 Adding Multimedia to a Web Site 264
Chapter 10 Adding Interactivity to a Web Site ... 286

Unit 4 The Web Site Development Process **309**
Chapter 11 Project Planning 310
Chapter 12 Developing a Web Site 328
Chapter 13 Adding Web Site Functionality 350
Chapter 14 Publishing a Web Site 374
Chapter 15 Maintaining a Web Site 398

Unit 5 Advanced HTML **419**
Chapter 16 HTML Tables and Frames 420
Chapter 17 HTML, Scripting, and Interactivity .. 440

UNIT 1
Fundamentals of Web Design

(Page 2)

 **Visit** *Glencoe Online*

Introduce students to the resources that are available online at **WebDesignDW.glencoe.com.** Have students select **Unit Activities > Unit 1 Internet Scavenger Hunt.** The four-question scavenger hunt will help them learn more about how to use this Web site and how to use the Internet safely. Students simply key their answers into the online form. Let students know if you want them to print their answers or e-mail their responses to you.

The Internet Scavenger Hunt will introduce students to several helpful parts of the book Web site: Web Design Resources, Go Online Activities, and Study with PowerTeach Outlines. Point out that the Web Design Resources links and Go Online links take students to Web sites that are not part of the book Web site. Therefore, they should carefully evaluate the information on these sites. We encourage you to preview any external links before students access them; the information on these sites is not under the control of Glencoe/McGraw-Hill.

Complete answers to each Unit Activity are available on the book Web site in the password-protected Teacher Center portion of the site.

(Page 3)

Think About It

Use the Think About It activity to get students thinking about the topics you will be discussing in the unit. Students can start by thinking about the steps they take to complete a particular task such as writing a research paper or preparing for a trip. Common steps may include the following: thinking about what steps need to be done to complete the activity; creating a checklist that identifies these steps and the order in which they should be completed; identifying when the activity must be finished (determining a schedule); identifying what resources are needed to complete the activity; gathering the resources needed to complete the activity; and completing the steps. Students can then suggest steps specific to creating a Web site. They can use their experience as Web site creators or users to identify what kind of tasks may need to be completed by a Web designer (for example, deciding how pages will relate to each other, determining what the site will look like, and so on).

CHAPTER 1 Planning Guide

Student Edition	Activities and Projects
Chapter 1 Web Basics (pages 4–33)	Quick Write Activity, page 4 Before You Read, page 5
Section 1.1 Introduction to the Web (pages 6–10)	▫ Reading Strategy, page 6 ⓘ Go Online Activity 1.1: Identify Web Sites, page 10
Section 1.2 Elements of a Web Page (pages 11–14)	▫ Reading Strategy, page 11 **d** ⊙ You Try It Activity 1A: View a Web Site in a Web Browser, page 13
Section 1.3 Web Site Development (pages 15–19)	▫ Reading Strategy, page 15 ⓘ Go Online Activity 1.2: View Professional Web Pages, page 18
Careers & Technology Working on the Web (Page 20)	Tech Check, page 20
Section 1.4 An Introduction to Dreamweaver (pages 21–26)	▫ Reading Strategy, page 21 **d** ⊙ You Try It Activity 1B: Open a Web Site in Dreamweaver, page 23 **d** ⊙ You Try It Activity 1C: Use Different Views and Close Dreamweaver, page 25
Chapter 1 Review (pages 27–33)	ⓘ Making Connections: Math—Create a Graph **d** Standards at Work: Use Productivity Tools (NETS-S 3) Teamwork Skills: Group Planning ⓘ Challenge Yourself: Identify Web Sites You Try It Skills Studio: ⓘ —Use Hyperlinks **d** ⊙ —Switch Views and Use the Files Panel Web Design Projects: ⓘ —Evaluate Web Design —Research Web Development Career Additional Activities You May Wish to Use: ⊙ —PowerTeach Outlines Chapter 1 —Student Workbook Chapter 1

Planning Guide — CHAPTER 1

Assessments

⊙ Section 1.1 Assessment, page 10

Section 1.2 Assessment, page 14

Section 1.3 Assessment, page 19

Section 1.4 Assessment, page 26

Chapter 1 Review and Assessment, page 27
You may also use any of the Chapter Review Activities and Projects as Assessments.
Additional Assessments You May Wish to Use:
⊙ —Self-Check Assessments Chapter 1
—*ExamView* Testbank Chapter 1

Estimated Time to Complete Chapter

18 week course = 5 days
36 week course = 10 days

To help customize lesson plans, use the Pacing Guide on pages 26–30 and the Standards Charts on pages 92–93.

Key to Recommended Materials

Icons represent elements that may require additional resources.

☐ Focus on Reading

ⓘ Internet access required

♪ Software: Dreamweaver

⊙ Teacher Resource CD (contains Student Data Files, Solution Files, Reproducible Graphic Organizers, and Study with PowerTeach Outlines)

Data and Solution Files for Chapter 1

DataFiles
◆ MusicDept (Music Department Web Site)

Inclusion Strategies

For **Differentiated Instruction Strategies** refer to the **Inclusion in the Computer Technology Classroom** booklet.

Unit 1 Fundamentals of Web Design Using Dreamweaver

CHAPTER 1 — NETS Correlation For Students

ISTE NETS Foundation Standards

1. Basic operations and concepts
2. Social, ethical, and human issues
3. Technology productivity tools
4. Technology communications tools
5. Technology research tools
6. Technology problem-solving and decision-making tools

Performance Indicators	Textbook Correlation
1. Identify capabilities and limitations of contemporary and emerging technology resources and assess the potential of these systems and services to address personal, lifelong learning, and workplace needs. (NETS 2)	**SE:** Critical Thinking (10, 14, 19, 26, 28), Go Online (18), Standards at Work (30), Web Design Projects (33)
2. Make informed choices among technology systems, resources, and services. (NETS 1, 2)	**SE:** Quick Write Activity (4), Critical Thinking (1), Web Design Projects (33)
3. Analyze advantages and disadvantages of widespread use and reliance on technology in the workplace and in society as a whole. (NETS 2)	**SE:** Quick Write Activity (4)
4. Demonstrate and advocate for legal and ethical behaviors among peers, family, and community regarding the use of technology and information. (NETS 2)	**SE:** Critical Thinking (10)
5. Use technology tools and resources for managing and communicating personal/professional information (e.g. finances, schedules, addresses, purchases, correspondence). (NETS 3, 4)	**SE:** Tech Check (20), Web Design Projects (33)
6. Evaluate technology-based options, including distance and distributed education, for lifelong learning. (NETS 5)	**SE:** Go Online (10, 18), Critical Thinking (10), Web Design Projects (33)
7. Routinely and efficiently use online information resources to meet needs for collaboration, research, publications, communications, and productivity. (NETS 4, 5, 6)	**SE:** Go Online (10, 18), Tech Check (20), Challenge Yourself (31), Skills Studio (32), Web Design Projects (33)
8. Select and apply technology tools for research, information analysis, problem-solving, and decision-making in content learning. (NETS 4, 5)	**SE:** Go Online (10, 18), Tech Check (20), Standards at Work (30), Web Design Projects (33)
9. Investigate and apply expert systems, intelligent agents, and simulations in real-world situations. (NETS 3, 5, 6)	**SE:** You Try It (13, 23, 25), Tech Check (20), Skills Studio (32), Web Design Projects (33)
10. Collaborate with peers, experts, and others to contribute to content-related knowledge base by using technology to compile, synthesize, produce, and disseminate information, models, and other creative works. (NETS 4, 5, 6)	**SE:** Tech Check (20)

SCANS Correlation — CHAPTER 1

Foundation Skills

Basic Skills

Reading	**SE:** Before You Read (5), Focus on Reading (6, 11, 15, 21), Reading Strategies (6, 11, 15, 21), After You Read (28), Standardized Test Practice (29)
Writing	**SE:** Quick Write Activity (4), Section Assessments (10, 14, 19, 26), Tech Check (20), Chapter Review (28–33)
Mathematics	**SE:** Making Connections (30)
Listening and Speaking	**SE:** Tech Check (20)

Thinking Skills

Creative Thinking	**SE:** Think About It (3), Quick Write Activity (4)
Critical Thinking	**SE:** Think About It (3), Critical Thinking Activities (10, 14, 19, 26), Tech Check (20), Web Design Projects (33)
Problem Solving	**SE:** Making Connections (30), Teamwork Skills (31)

Workplace Competencies

Resources Manage time, money, materials, facilities, human resources	**SE:** Command Center (29)
Interpersonal Work on teams, teach others	**SE:** Tech Check (20), Teamwork Skills (31)
Information Acquire, evaluate, organize, maintain, interpret, communicate and use computers to process information	**SE:** Apply It! (10, 14, 26), Go Online (10, 18), You Try It (13), Command Center (29), Standards at Work (30), Challenge Yourself (31), Web Design Projects (33), Skills Studio (32)
Systems Understand, monitor, correct, improve, design systems	**SE:** Teamwork Skills (31), Web Design Projects (33)
Technology Select, apply, maintain, and troubleshoot technology.	**SE:** You Try It (13, 23, 25), Go Online (20), Standards at Work (30)

CHAPTER 1

Web Basics

(Page 4) ### Objectives

Section 1.1: Introduction to the Web
- Compare the Internet and the Web
- Compare Web sites and Web pages
- Identify Web browser components
- Describe types of Web sites

Section 1.2: Elements of a Web Page
- Identify elements of a Web page
- Summarize the importance of hyperlinks
- Navigate using a Web browser

Section 1.3: Web Site Development
- Describe Web site development steps
- Identify the three categories of Web site design
- Discuss Web design careers

Section 1.4: An Introduction to Dreamweaver
- Identify the parts of the Dreamweaver interface
- View Web pages with Dreamweaver

LEARNING LINK

Chapter 1 will provide students with a general introduction to the concepts that will be discussed in depth in later chapters. Use this chapter to help students get comfortable with basic concepts and terminology. It should also help you find out the level of knowledge your students bring to this course so that you can adjust your lessons according to your students' experience.

(Page 4) ### Why It Matters

Conduct a brief class survey to find out how students use the Internet. Some examples may be for shopping, playing games, communicating with friends, finding information, completing school work, etc. Ask students how their lives would change without the Internet.

(Page 4) ### Quick Write Activity

Emphasize to students that they should write whatever responses come into their heads and that there are no right or wrong answers. They do not have to follow any formal writing structure or have perfect grammar or spelling. Use student responses for a class discussion.

(Page 5) ### Before You Read

Survey Before You Read You may wish to tell students that when drivers get behind the wheel of a car, they go through steps that will help to make their drive safer and more enjoyable. Suggest to students that reading is like driving in that a few simple steps can prepare the reader for a more effective and enjoyable read.

94 Teacher Resource Manual *Introduction to Web Design Using Dreamweaver*

CHAPTER 1

SECTION 1.1 INTRODUCTION TO THE WEB
(Pages 6–10)

FOCUS

Brainstorming Design Elements Ask students to brainstorm about what comes to mind when they think about the Web. Write down their answers. Some responses might be: graphics, music, modems, interactivity, slow downloads, pop-up ads, instant information, hyperlinks, etc. Review the various responses and discuss whether they are related to design, programming, hardware, content, or business.

(Page 6)

Focus on Reading

Read to Find Out
Use the Read to Find Out feature to focus student reading. Hold a quick starter discussion to find out what your students already know.

 Key Terms Online
Key term definitions and activities are available online at **WebDesignDW.glencoe.com**.

Reading Strategy Answer
The Reading Strategy Organizer is available as a reproducible on the Teacher Resource CD or on the book Web site. This information can be found under the heading *Browser Functions* on page 7. Students' tables should look similar to this example:

Web Browser Components	Description
Title bar	tells you the name of the current Web page
Menus	allow you to select from lists of commands
Web address	displays the address of the current Web page
Navigation buttons	help you move from one page to another
Viewing area	displays the current Web page

TEACH

Web Sites Versus Web Pages Illustrate for students the difference between a Web site and a Web page using the analogy of a book. Using the textbook as an example, show students that like a book, a Web site has many pages. The cover of the book is like the Web site's home page.

Instead of flipping from page to page as we do in a book, visitors to Web sites click on hyperlinks to go from page to page. A table of contents in a book needs page numbers, and readers have to search for the page. In a Web site, however, links allow users to jump directly to another page with one click.

Unit 1 Fundamentals of Web Design Using Dreamweaver   95

CHAPTER 1

Answers to Section 1.1 Captions and Activities

(Page 6) **Reading Focus** The Internet is the hardware components that connect computers around the world. The World Wide Web consists of the software needed to access information stored on the Internet.

(Page 6) ✓ **Reading Check** A network is a group of computers connected together.

(Page 7) **Reading Focus** A Web site is a group of related files organized around a common topic. A Web page is a single file within a Web site.

(Page 7) **Figure 1.1** The address appears in the Web address box of the browser.

(Page 7) ✓ **Reading Check** A Web page is a single file within a Web site, which has a unique name.

(Page 8) **Reading Focus** Most Web sites are categorized by their main purpose.

(Page 8) **Figure 1.2** An educational site provides information about a school or university.

(Page 9) **Figure 1.3** Answers may include news, business information, search engine, maps, sports scores, stocks, telephone directories, and weather information.

(Page 9) **Table 1.1** A government site would be used to locate information about applying for a driver's license.

(Page 10) **Go Online** **Activity 1.1** Students can learn more about different types of Web sites at **WebDesignDW.glencoe.com**. Tell students whether you want them to print or e-mail their answers to you. Go Online answers can be found under Teacher Resources on the book Web site.

> **Teaching Tip**
> Have students bookmark the book's Web site at **WebDesignDW.glencoe.com** so they can easily return to the site to complete each of this book's Go Online activities.

(Page 10) ✓ **Reading Check** To learn more about a local news story you should use an informational site, such as a news site.

ASSESS

(Page 10) ### Section 1.1 Assessment Answers

Reading Summary

Use the Reading Summary to help students review and reinforce the important points of the section.

What Did You Learn?

1. Students' definitions should be in their own words, but based on the information found in the section and in the book's glossary.

2. The Internet is the hardware components that connect computers around the world. The World Wide Web consists of the software needed to access information stored on the Internet.

3. A browser lets you navigate easily from page to page and to view the HTML code in a graphical manner.

Critical Thinking

4. A portal site is different from an educational site because a portal site provides a variety of services that people use everyday, and an educational site provides information about a school, university, museum, and interactive tutorials such as provided in distance learning.

5. The advantage of a personal Web site is that it allows people to share information, news, interests, and hobbies with others. The disadvantages are that posting personal information can be dangerous, because information is available to everyone. You should be careful posting personal information such as contact information, what you look like, and where you live, or information about other people, because this information is available to everyone once it is on the Internet.

Apply It!

Categorize Web Sites Students list and categorize five Web sites they have recently visited in class or at home. Encourage them to specify a specific subcategory for each site they choose. Do some sites fit into more than one category? Students should provide the name of sites they have visited (e.g., Lands' End) and the URL if possible (**landsend.com**). If students need to look for new examples, you can make the following suggestions and have students classify them.

Commercial	Portal	Informational	Educational	Personal
Lands' End **www.landsend.com**	Google **www.google.com**	CNN **www.cnn.com**	The Smithsonian **www.si.edu**	Examples are up to your discretion. Teachers' Web sites from your school would probably be the best (and safest) examples.
Travelocity **www.travelocity.com**	Yahoo **www.yahoo.com**	U.S. Senate **www.senate.gov**	W3 School's Online Tutorials **www.w3schools.com**	
Microsoft **www.ms.com**	Excite **www.excite.com**	Library Spot **www.libraryspot.com**	Your own school site	

CLOSE

Assessing Student Understanding Have students write down a question that they still have about the Internet. Choose five questions to read aloud and see if members of the class can answer them. If not, respond with one or more of the following options:

◆ Provide the answer yourself.
◆ Tell students where they will find the answer in the textbook.
◆ Have students find out the answer by doing research.

Read through all the questions yourself to see what students are interested in and what they may or may not understand.

CHAPTER 1

SECTION 1.2 ELEMENTS OF A WEB PAGE
(Pages 11–14)

FOCUS

Identifying Web Page Elements Have students look at Figure 1.4 (on page 11 of the student textbook) showing the NASA Web page. Have them point out the various graphics, text, hyperlinks, and other elements that they can identify in the illustration. Then, if possible, log onto the actual NASA Web site (**www.nasa.gov**). Have students identify elements and talk about where the hyperlinks take users.

(Page 11)

Focus on Reading

Read to Find Out
Use the Read to Find Out feature to focus student reading. Hold a quick starter discussion to find out what your students already know.

 Key Terms Online
Key term definitions and activities are available online at **WebDesignDW.glencoe.com**.

Reading Strategy Answer
Students can find information about internal and external hyperlinks under the heading *Hyperlinks* on page 13. Students' diagrams should look similar to this example:

- **Internal Links** Connects to other parts of the current Web site
- **Both** Moves user from place to place
- **External Links** Connects to other, related Web sites

TEACH

Web Page Elements Access specific Web pages for students or have them find Web pages that contain interesting examples of text, graphics, multimedia, and animation as well as internal, external, and intrapage hyperlinks. Have students predict where the link will take them and see if their prediction was correct. Discuss the different ways the same element might be used on different Web pages. For example, text might be descriptive, instructive, or used as a hyperlink.

Some Web sites you might use to provide interesting examples are: National Oceanic and Atmospheric Administration (NOAA) Satellites and Information (**www.goes.noaa.gov**), Nickelodeon TV, (**www.nick.com**), Getty Museum, (**www.getty.edu/art/collections**), and CNN News, (**www.cnn.com**).

CHAPTER 1

Answers to Section 1.2 Captions and Activities

(Page 11) **Reading Focus** Individually created elements, such as text, graphics, multimedia, and hyperlinks, are combined to form a completed Web page.

(Page 11) **Figure 1.4** Answers may include graphics, links, or a multimedia component such as an animation.

(Page 11) ✓ **Reading Check** Text, graphics, multimedia, and hyperlinks.

(Page 12) **Reading Focus** Text, graphics, and multimedia are included to make a Web page appealing and easy-to-use.

(Page 12) **Table 1.2** Graphics are included to make a Web page appealing and easy-to-use. Including graphics on a Web page is important because they illustrate information, attract viewers' attention, provide visual interest, and act as navigation buttons.

(Page 12) **Figure 1.5** Answers may include live radio feeds, commentary, or sound clips.

(Page 12) ✓ **Reading Check** Graphics are still images and video refers to live or recorded moving images.

(Page 13) **Reading Focus** Hyperlinks are often used in a Web site to move from one online page to another.

(Page 13) **You Try It** **Activity 1A View a Web Site in a Web Browser** Students will explore the Century High School Music Department Web site in a browser. Use the Student Data File noted in this chapter's Planning Guide.

Teaching Tip
You Try It activities give students hands-on opportunities to try out the skills discussed in the chapter. If students need extra time to complete an activity, arrange time for students to use school computers.

(Page 14) ✓ **Reading Check** An internal hyperlink moves the user to another Web page within the same Web site.

ASSESS

(Page 14) **Section 1.2 Assessment Answers**

Reading Summary
Use the Reading Summary to help students review and reinforce the important points of the section.

What Did You Learn?
1. Students' definitions should be in their own words, but based on the information found in the section and in the book's glossary.

CHAPTER 1

2. Web page elements can include text, graphics, audio, animation, video, and hyperlinks.

3. In a Web browser, you click on the navigation buttons or hyperlinks to move from page to page and site to site.

Critical Thinking

4. Answers will vary, but should note how the various Web elements (text, graphics, multimedia, and hyperlinks) are used on each site.

5. Hyperlinks allow you to move from place to place in a Web site, skipping pages or moving to specific locations as needed.

Apply It!

Identify Hyperlinks Students should identify an internal and external link on the site. They should write down the URL of the page the link takes them to. The URL for the internal link should indicate a different place in the same site, while the URL for the external link should move the user to a different site. Some Web pages that contain both internal and external links are:

- Dictionary.com: **http://dictionary.reference.com/others**
- City of Los Angeles: **http://www.lacity.org/lacity73.htm**

CLOSE

Reviewing Hyperlinks Discuss with students how hyperlinks are used on Web sites they visited in this chapter.

- What kind of links are usually on the home page? (Internal links, but one of those might link to a page with external links.)
- How are internal and external links distinguished from each other on the page? (They are often placed on a different part of the page or use different text styles.)
- Can students think of Web sites that would only have internal links? (Retail sites for specific stores would have only internal links because they want shoppers to stay there and buy from them.)
- When would it be useful to have external links? (Some retail sites link to a number of vendors, information sites might link to outside resources, etc.)

CHAPTER 1

SECTION 1.3 WEB SITE DEVELOPMENT
(Pages 15–19)

FOCUS

Identifying the Steps for Creating Web Sites Discuss the steps of building a house and who and what is involved in each stage. Students might come up with a sequence such as: 1) The customer needs the house, 2) The customer plans the house with the architect and contractor (Where should it be located, how big should it be, what features will it need, how shall it be financed, how much time do you have?), 3) The architect designs the house, 4) The contractor builds the house, 5) The customer lives in the house. Using the house example for comparison, have students come up with the steps for creating a Web site, and who creates what.

(Page 15)

Focus on Reading

Read To Find Out
Use the Read to Find Out feature to focus student reading. Hold a quick starter discussion to find out what your students already know.

 Key Terms Online
Key term definitions and activities are available online at **WebDesignDW.glencoe.com**.

Reading Strategy Answer
Students can find descriptions of the tasks that are performed in Web site development under the heading *Web Site Development Careers* on page 18. Students' diagrams should look similar to this example:

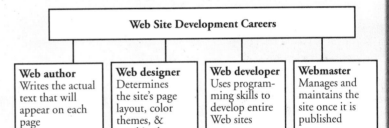

TEACH

Using Go Online Activities Use the Go Onlines to find supplementary material for student projects or independent study activities for students who want to learn more about specific topics in the chapter. The Go Online Activity 1.2 (page 18) provides useful examples of Web pages that save you the trouble of finding them and checking them yourself. Unlike browsing the Internet, where students may access questionable material, Go Onlines present material which is safe and up-to-date.

CHAPTER 1

Answers to Section 1.3 Captions and Activities

(Page 15) **Reading Focus** There are five steps in the Web site development process.

(Page 15) **Figure 1.8** Students ideas will vary. They should be able to identify smaller parts of studying for the exam such as reviewing the material for each chapter, taking notes, studying with a classmate, getting a good night's sleep.

(Page 16) **Figure 1.9** It shows the basic content and structure of the site, just like an outline shows basic structure and content of the report.

(Page 17) **Table 1.3** Presentation design

(Page 17) ✓ **Reading Check** A Web design program, such as Dreamweaver, Microsoft FrontPage, or Adobe GoLive.

(Page 18) **Reading Focus** Writing skills, design skills, and programming skills are needed to pursue a career in Web site development.

(Page 18) **Go Online Activity 1.2** As a class, have students analyze some of the Web page examples for Activity 1.2 at the **WebDesignDW.glencoe.com** site. When they look at these examples, can they answer the questions about determining a site's purpose and goals on page 16?

(Page 18) **Figure 1.10** Web authors, Web designers, Web developers, Webmasters

(Page 19) ✓ **Reading Check** Answers will vary, but might note that a Web designer should have artistic skills, creativity, knowledge of graphics software and some programming.

ASSESS

(Page 19) ### Section 1.3 Assessment Answers

Reading Summary

Use the Reading Summary to help students review and reinforce the important points of the section.

What Did You Learn?

1. Students' definitions should be in their own words, but based on the information found in the section and in the book's glossary.

2. Interaction design focuses on site navigation. Information design focuses on content. Presentation design focuses on the physical appearance of the site.

3. Steps include determining the purpose and goals for the site, designing and implementing the site, evaluating and testing the site, publishing the site, and maintaining the site.

CHAPTER 1

Critical Thinking

4. A Web author writes the text that appears on the site, while a Web designer creates the physical appearance for the site. A Webmaster manages and maintains a Web site.

5. The three design processes work together to allow the user to find information quickly and efficiently and to encourage the user to return to the site.

Apply It!

Identify Career Skills Discuss results in class. Students might include the following: Web designer (artistic skills, creativity, adept at using graphics software, basic knowledge of programming, communications skills for teamwork); Web developer (creativity, knowledge of Web programming, basics of Web design, problem solving skills, communication skills with customers and team, time and budget management skills); Web author (writing, communication skills for teamwork, time management skills); Webmaster (knowledge of Web hardware and software, basic programming skills, communication skills, management skills).

CLOSE

Reviewing the Steps in Web Site Development Go back to the list you and your students created in the Section 1.3 Student Focus activity about the steps in Web site development. Review the original list with students. Discuss any steps that were missing or added.

(Page 20)

Real World Technology

WORKING ON THE WEB

Answers to Tech Check

1. Students' answers should demonstrate an understanding of the need for goal-setting and targeting a job search and résumé. Students can create a career map or résumé (print or electronic) that illustrates their skills, education, and career goals. They should use online or printed employment ads, course descriptions in college catalogs, or interviews with professionals to get specific information about particular Web careers, their educational requirements, and educational institutions.

2. This activity should make students interact on a professional basis with one another or with prospective employers in your community. Students may complete this school-to-work activity by attending a job fair, a day of mentoring spent with a Web professional, or a simulated job interview in the classroom. Students' reports should describe ways in which the student benefited from the experience. Encourage students to be creative. They may also write up an event that they would like to organize.

CHAPTER 1

SECTION 1.4 AN INTRODUCTION TO DREAMWEAVER
(Pages 21–26)

FOCUS

Compare Software Tools Compare the toolbars and menus in Dreamweaver to those in Microsoft Word. Show students that if they know how to use Word, they should understand how to use many of the features in Dreamweaver. Have students look at the illustration in Figure 1.10 (on page 22). See if they can identify toolbar buttons that are the same as those in Word. What elements look the same in the two programs?

> **Teaching Tip**
> Use the PowerTeach Outline to give students an overview of the subjects that will be discussed in a section. There is no need to explain concepts in detail, but give examples from this section.

(Page 21)

Focus on Reading

Read to Find Out
Use the Read to Find Out feature to focus student reading. Hold a quick starter discussion to find out what your students already know.

 Key Terms Online
Key term definitions and activities are available online at **WebDesignDW.glencoe.com**.

Reading Strategy
Students can find information about the Dreamweaver interface under the heading *Main Dreamweaver Interface Elements* on page 22. Students' diagrams should look similar to this example:

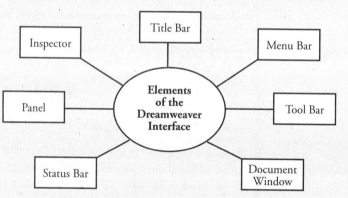

TEACH

Comparing versions of Dreamweaver If you are using a different version of Dreamweaver than Dreamweaver MX 2004, discuss the differences with the class. Tell them to go to the Glencoe Web site (**WebDesignDW.glencoe.com**) to find information about the features in various versions. Go over the figures and activities in this chapter to make sure that students understand how they might differ from the version of Dreamweaver that they are using.

104 Teacher Resource Manual *Introduction to Web Design Using Dreamweaver*

CHAPTER 1

Answers to Section 1.4 Captions and Activities

(Page 21) **Reading Focus** The main elements of the Dreamweaver interface are: Title bar, Menu bar, Toolbar, Document window, Status bar, Panel, and Inspector.

(Page 21) **Figure 1.11** Answers may vary. The three options available on the Start page are: Open a recent item, create new, and create from samples.

(Page 22) **Figure 1.12** Answers may include elements such as drop-down menus with buttons, toolbars, and Document window.

(Page 22) **Reading Check** Information to help manage and navigate the files and folders in a Web site.

(Page 23) **Reading Focus** To open a site's home page in Dreamweaver, double-click the Web site's index.html or default.html file in the Files panel.

(Page 23) **You Try It** **Activity 1B Open a Web Site in Dreamweaver** Students learn how to open Dreamweaver and the Music Department Web site. They also access the Navigation panel and use the Toggle Panel button to access the Folder List. Use the Student Data Files noted in this chapter's Planning Guide.

Teaching Tip
Some students may have difficulty launching the **Start** page. If the **Start** page does not appear, students may need to choose **Edit** on the **Menu bar**, select **Preferences**, and check the box next to **Show start page**. Have students click **OK** and exit Dreamweaver. Dreamweaver should now open with the **Start** page.

(Page 25) **You Try It** **Activity 1C Use Different Views and Close Dreamweaver** Students see how the Music Department Web site is displayed in the Preview, Code, Split, and Design views. Use the Student Data Files noted in this chapter's Planning Guide.

(Page 26) **Reading Check** The file name index.html identifies the homepage.

ASSESS

(Page 26) **Section 1.4 Assessment Answers**

Reading Summary

Use the Reading Summary to help students review and reinforce the important points of the section.

What Did You Learn?

1. Students' definitions should be in their own words, but based on the information found in the section and in the book's glossary.

Unit 1 Fundamentals of Web Design Using Dreamweaver 105

CHAPTER 1

2. Toolbars, task panes, folder list, navigation pane.
3. Students' answers will vary but should identify at least one of the following:
   - The Files panel opens by default once a Web site has been defined in Dreamweaver.
   - The F8 shortcut command opens and closes the Files panel in Dreamweaver.

Critical Thinking

4. If there is a problem with the Web page, Code (HTML) view allows users to examine the HTML code and make changes to correct the problem.
5. Web developers need to be able to identify how small changes in the HTML code affect the way the Web page displays and works.

Apply It!

View Web Pages Students identify the title of three pages in the Code view. They should notice how the HTML code identifies the titles with <TITLE></TITLE>.

CLOSE

Comparing Dreamweaver and HTML Discuss with students the advantages and disadvantages of creating a Web site using a program like Dreamweaver versus creating a Web site using HTML.

Answers to Chapter Review — CHAPTER 1

The Chapter Review covers a wide range of student knowledge. Due to time constraints, students may not be able to complete every activity in the Chapter Review. Select the activities that are appropriate for your class needs and resources.

(Page 28) ## After You Read

Survey Skills Complete the first section with students, and then have them outline the rest of the chapter, based on the headings and subheadings. Encourage students to share aloud the facts they wrote down to stimulate memories and additional background knowledge. Students can use this survey and outlining strategy with each chapter to build study and comprehension skills.

(Page 28) ## Reviewing Key Terms

1. Web browser
2. panel
3. focus on the physical appearance of the site
4. home page
5. World Wide Web
6. hyperlink
7. network

(Page 28) ## Understanding Main Ideas

8. audio, video, animation
9. internal, external, intrapage
10. Answers may include reading the site's content carefully, making certain the text is clearly written, checking the spelling and grammar of the text, verifying that the site's look and feel meet your design goals.
11. A Webmaster manages Web sites that have been designed, developed, and published. A Web author works during Web site design and development to write the text that appears on each page.
12. Dreamweaver has scroll bars, menus, toolbars, and task panes similar to other software applications.
13. Students should use their own words from the section *Main Dreamweaver Interface Elements*. The parts are: Title bar, Menu bar, Toolbar, Document window, Status bar, Panel, and Inspector.
14. A Web site contains one or more Web pages. The pages of a Web site are linked by internal links that allow the user to navigate through the site. A Web page is a single page that may be part of a Web site or may function as a Web site.
15. Answers may include: determine site's purpose; determine site's goals; determine tools to reach your goals; determine site's audience; and determine the hardware or software used by visitors to your site.
16. Categories are: interaction design, information design, and presentation design. Functions are:
    - Interaction design — To determine how hyperlinks will help the user navigate through the site.
    - Information design — To determine the content that will appear on each page.
    - Presentation design — To determine the physical appearance of the site's pages.

CHAPTER 1 Answers to Chapter Review

(Page 28) **Critical Thinking**

17. In Dreamweaver, Code view lets you examine the HTML code and make changes. Design view lets you see how the page will look in a browser. In Split view, the top half of the screen shows the HTML code while the bottom half shows the page in Design view.

18. Students should note that the calendar and pictures of recent events will need to be updated regularly to keep the site relevant. All links should be checked regularly to make sure that they still work.

19. Answers include convenience, selection of merchandise, ability to examine the merchandise, methods of payment, shipping fees, and delivery time. Students may discover that the benefits from buying from a local merchant is better service, while the benefits from buying from e-commerce would be a better price.

20. The second sentence (B) is easier to read, because it is short, precise, and all the words are easy to understand. In the first sentence, it is difficult to find the essential information that the reader needs to know.

(Page 29) **Command Center**

21. Ctrl + O = Opens file
22. F12 = Preview a Web site in a browser
23. Ctrl + W = Close an open Web page

Standardized Test Practice

The correct answer is C. As students review the paragraph describing the four main types of Web design professionals and the possible answers, make sure they pay close attention to words such as "always" and "never." Noting these words may help to eliminate incorrect answer choices such as answers A and B.

e-Review

Have students use the book's Web site **WebDesignDW.glencoe.com**.

♦ **Study with PowerTeach** Encourage your students to use the Chapter 1 PowerTeach Outline to review the chapter before they have a test.

♦ **Online Self Check** These quick five-question assessments may be used as an in-class activity, a homework assignment, or test review.

Answers to Chapter Review — CHAPTER 1

(Page 30) **Making Connections**

Math—Create Graph Students should not count words in menus, recurring features and headers, or advertisements. They should only look at the changing, constantly updated text in articles, article titles, and summaries. If students are not sure which text to count, they should at least try to be consistent about the type of text they count from one Web site to the next.

Students should analyze patterns such as use of various sizes of type, use of lists, hyperlinks, and how text is grouped. Students may use productivity tools such as Microsoft Excel to create their graphs. If there are time restrictions, this can be done as a class project, where each student chooses a different news site and adds the result to a class graph and average calculations.

Following is an example of a bar graph using the following word number counts:

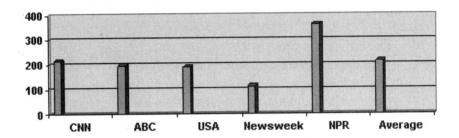

(Page 30) **Standards at Work**

NETS-S 3 Use Productivity Tools Students might use help to explore topics such as the use of task panes, use of the Navigation Pane, adding hyperlinks, finding and opening Web sites, using Page View options, etc. If you prefer, have students look for topics that they may want to use when creating their own personal Web pages, such as importing graphics or audio, or using animation. Students' charts will vary, but may look similar to the partial example below:

Feature	How to Access the Feature	Why I Want to Use It
Opening a Web site	Click the File menu. Select Open. Choose the folder where the Web site is saved.	To access Web sites that I am working on.
Seeing the HTML code for a Web page	In open Web site, click the Preview button. Then click the Code button.	Allows me to view the code and make changes in the code, if necessary.

CHAPTER 1 Answers to Chapter Review

(Page 31) ## Teamwork Skills

Group Planning Encourage students to select a national park in their state or one that a member of the group has visited. The group's summary should clearly state the purpose and goals of the Web page. It also should reference relevant hyperlinks (both internal and external) and describe the look and feel of the page. Evaluate the sketches for consistency with the purpose and goals of the page. Have the groups share their Web page plans and sketches with the rest of the class. Students should provide feedback to each other.

(Page 31) ## Challenge Yourself

Identify Web Sites For this project, encourage students to find sites that do not fit neatly into one category or another. For example, many informational sites can also be commercial. (CNET, **www.cnet.com**, for example, offers reviews and articles about technology, as well as shopping opportunities.)

Students should briefly describe the two Web sites and the category they both fit into. They should then create a chart to compare and contrast the features of the two sites. From this, they should conclude how these sites should be specifically classified. This project can be a written report, poster, or presentation.

> ⚠ **Troubleshooting**
>
> If students need help finding Web pages, refer to the list of Web Sites examples found in Teacher's Resources at **WebDesignDW.glencoe.com**.

Answers to Chapter Review — CHAPTER 1

You Try It — Skills Studio

(Page 32)

1. **Use Hyperlinks** Students should go to one of the following suggested sites or one of your choosing: USA Today (**www.usatoday.com**), New York Times (**www.nytimes.com**), Chicago Tribune (**www.chicagotribune.com**), Los Angeles Times (**www.latimes.com**). Have them write down the name of the site they choose and its URL. Students may need help finding the link to travel news or vacation listings.

2. **Switch Views and Use the Files Panel** Students will learn to switch views and use the Files panels. Students will notice that Design view shows the way the page should look in a browser, and that Code view shows the HTML markup that produces the structure and presentation of the Web page.

Web Design Projects

(Page 33)

1. **Evaluate Web Site Design** Students' charts should look similar to the example in their book, but if they prefer they can create their own chart. They should also use their own words when evaluating their sites. Check the printouts of the five home pages to see if the information in the chart is accurate and clearly evaluates category, purpose, audience, and elements in the chosen sites.

   This activity can also be done as a group activity. For examples of Web sites, see the suggestions in *Section 1.1 Apply It!* (page 10). Students must be supervised when using the Web.

2. **Research Web Development Careers** Students' reports should provide accurate information about the chosen career. They can research by searching the Web or print resources, looking at online or print classified ads, or conducting interviews with professionals in the field.

   Students should try to find out the following details:

   ◆ **Specialized skills:** Does the professional need to know programming, have an artistic background, have experience using a variety of Web authoring tools?

   ◆ **Leadership skills:** Would the professional need experience creating schedules or budgets? Would they need to work with management, employees, or customers? Which 21st Century Skills or SCANS would this professional need?

   ◆ **Preparations:** What kinds of college degrees or certifications are needed for this career?

   ◆ **Job Responsibilities:** Students might find this information in classified ads.

CHAPTER 2 Planning Guide

Student Edition	Activities and Projects
Chapter 2 Computer Basics (Pages 34–63)	Quick Write Activity, page 34 Before You Read, page 35
Section 2.1 Computer Hardware and Software (Pages 36–42)	📁 Reading Strategy, page 36 ⓘ TechSIM: System Settings, page 38 ⓘ Go Online Activity 2.1: Investigate Storage Devices, page 39
Section 2.2 Networks (Pages 43–46)	📁 Reading Strategy, page 43 ⓘ Go Online Activity 2.2: Explore Networks, page 43
Real World Technology Use Equipment Safely (Pages 47)	Tech Focus, page 47
Section 2.3 Creating a Basic Web Site (Pages 48–56)	📁 Reading Strategy, page 48 ⓘ TechSIM: File Management, page 48 𝒅 You Try It 2A: Create a One-Page Web site, page 49 𝒅 You Try It 2B: Insert and Format Text, page 51 𝒅 ⊙ You Try It 2C: Insert Graphics, page 52 𝒅 You Try It 2D: Creating Subpages, page 55
Chapter 2 Review (Pages 57–63)	ⓘ Making Connections: Language Arts—Write a Report ⓘ Standards at Work: Evaluate Scanners (NETS-S 5) Teamwork Skills: Understand Computer Skills Challenge Yourself: Explore Networks You Try It Skills Studio: 𝒅 —Format Text 𝒅 ⊙ —Add Graphics and a List to a Web Site Web Design Projects: —Create Inventory Sheets —Prepare a Presentation Additional Activities You May Wish to Use: ⊙ ⓘ —PowerTeach Outlines Chapter 2 —Student Workbook Chapter 2

Planning Guide — CHAPTER 2

Assessments

Section 2.1 Assessment, page 42

ⓘ Section 2.2 Assessment, page 46

Section 2.3 Assessment, page 56

Chapter 2 Review and Assessment, page 57
You may also use any of the Chapter Review Activities and Projects as Assessments.
Additional Assessments You May Wish to Use:
ⓘ —Self-Check Assessments Chapter 2
—*ExamView* Testbank Chapter 2

Estimated Time to Complete Chapter

18 week course = 2–3 days
36 week course = 10 days

To help customize lesson plans, use the Pacing Guide on pages 26–30 and the Standards Charts on pages 114–115.

Key to Recommended Materials

Icons represent elements that may require additional resources.

☐ Focus on Reading

ⓘ Internet access required

𝒹 Software: Dreamweaver

⊙ Teacher Resource CD (contains Student Data Files, Solution Files, Reproducible Graphic Organizers, and Study with PowerTeach Outlines)

Data and Solution Files for Chapter 2

DataFiles
- camera.gif
- cd-rom.gif
- scanner.gif
- festival.gif

SolutionFiles
- SF_YTI_2A.html
- SF_YTI_2B.html
- SF_YTI_2C
- SF_YTI_2D

Inclusion Strategies

For **Differentiated Instruction Strategies** refer to the **Inclusion in the Computer Technology Classroom** booklet.

CHAPTER 2 NETS Correlation For Students

ISTE NETS Foundation Standards

1. Basic operations and concepts
2. Social, ethical, and human issues
3. Technology productivity tools
4. Technology communications tools
5. Technology research tools
6. Technology problem-solving and decision-making tools

Performance Indicators	Textbook Correlation
1. Identify capabilities and limitations of contemporary and emerging technology resources and assess the potential of these systems and services to address personal, lifelong learning, and workplace needs. (NETS 2)	**SE:** Critical Thinking (42, 46, 58), Go Online (39, 43), Apply It! (46), Making Connections (60), Standards at Work (60), Challenge Yourself (61)
2. Make informed choices among technology systems, resources, and services. (NETS 1, 2)	**SE:** Apply It! (42), Critical Thinking (42, 46, 58, 59), Standardized Test Practice (59), Standards at Work (60)
3. Analyze advantages and disadvantages of widespread use and reliance on technology in the workplace and in society as a whole. (NETS 2)	**SE:** Quick Write Activity (34)
4. Demonstrate and advocate for legal and ethical behaviors among peers, family, and community regarding the use of technology and information. (NETS 2)	**SE:** Challenge Yourself (61)
5. Use technology tools and resources for managing and communicating personal/professional information (e.g. finances, schedules, addresses, purchases, correspondence). (NETS 3, 4)	**SE:** You Try It (49, 51, 52, 55), Critical Thinking (59), Web Design Projects (63)
6. Evaluate technology-based options, including distance and distributed education, for lifelong learning. (NETS 5)	**SE:** Go Online (39, 43)
7. Routinely and efficiently use online information resources to meet needs for collaboration, research, publications, communications, and productivity. (NETS 4, 5, 6)	**SE:** Go Online (39, 43), Apply It! (46), Making Connections (60), Standards at Work (60), Teamwork Skills (61)
8. Select and apply technology tools for research, information analysis, problem-solving, and decision-making in content learning. (NETS 4, 5)	**SE:** Apply It! (42), Making Connections (60), Standards at Work (60), Web Design Projects (63)
9. Investigate and apply expert systems, intelligent agents, and simulations in real-world situations. (NETS 3, 5, 6)	**SE:** Skills Studio (62), Web Design Projects (63)
10. Collaborate with peers, experts, and others to contribute to content-related knowledge base by using technology to compile, synthesize, produce, and disseminate information, models, and other creative works. (NETS 4, 5, 6)	**SE:** Tech Check (47), Teamwork Skills (61), Web Design Projects (63)

SCANS Correlation — CHAPTER 2

Foundation Skills	
Basic Skills	
Reading	**SE:** Before You Read (35), Focus on Reading (36, 43, 48), Reading Strategies (36, 43, 48), After You Read (58)
Writing	**SE:** Quick Write Activity (34), Section Assessments (42, 46, 56), Chapter Review (58–63), Making Connections (60)
Mathematics	**SE:** Apply It! (42), Standardized Test Practice (59)
Listening and Speaking	**SE:** Tech Check (47), After You Read (86), Challenge Yourself (61), Web Design Projects (63)
Thinking Skills	
Creative Thinking	**SE:** Quick Write Activity (34)
Critical Thinking	**SE:** Critical Thinking (42, 46, 56, 58, 59), Tech Check (47), Standards at Work (60), Challenge Yourself (61), Web Design Projects (63)
Problem Solving	**SE:** Apply It! (42), Tech Check (47), Standards at Work (60), Web Design Projects (63)

Workplace Competencies	
Resources — Manage time, money, materials, facilities, human resources	**SE:** Apply It! (42), Command Center (59), Standards at Work (60)
Interpersonal — Work on teams, teach others	**SE:** After You Read (58), Teamwork Skills (61), Web Design Projects (63)
Information — Acquire, evaluate, organize, maintain, interpret, communicate and use computers to process information	**SE:** Go Online (39, 43), Apply It! (42, 46, 56), Tech Check (47), You Try It (49, 51, 52, 55), Command Center (59), Teamwork Skills (61), Skills Studio (62), Web Design Projects (63)
Systems — Understand, monitor, correct, improve, design systems	**SE:** Tech Check (47), Skills Studio (62), Web Design Projects (63)
Technology — Select, apply, maintain, and troubleshoot technology.	**SE:** Go Online (39, 43), You Try It (49, 51, 52, 55), Apply It! (42, 46, 56), Standards at Work (60), Skills Studio (62), Web Design Projects (63)

CHAPTER 2

Computer Basics

(Page 34) ## Objectives

Section 2.1: Computer Hardware and Software
- Identify hardware
- Describe processing components
- Compare and contrast input and output devices
- Compare and contrast storage devices
- Identify and describe operating system software
- Identify and describe application software
- Summarize cross-platform issues

Section 2.2: Networks
- Identify types of networks
- Examine types of network connections
- Identify network hardware and software

Section 2.3: Creating a Basic Web Site
- Create a new Web site
- Save a Web site
- Format text
- Insert a graphic
- Create subpages

LEARNING LINK

Chapter 1 provided an introduction to basic Web concepts and terminology. Use Chapter 2 to explain the components and devices that make up computer systems and to present the software, networks, and connections that allow us to use them.

(Page 34) ## Why It Matters

Lead a brief discussion about different ways your students use computers. Discuss the benefits as well as the potential problems of computers. For example, what might be the effects of relying too much on computers for spelling and grammar help, or for calculating the change due to customers?

(Page 34) ## Quick Write Activity

Have students think about the days before computers, when students used typewriters or wrote reports by hand. To help students appreciate the time saved by using a computer's word processing application, have them write about what they would need to do to change the sentence order or add examples in a handwritten report.

(Page 35) ## Before You Read

Key Terms Word maps help students expand word meanings and think proactively about important concepts. This strategy is also effective as a paired activity.

CHAPTER 2

SECTION 2.1 COMPUTER HARDWARE AND SOFTWARE
(Pages 36–42)

FOCUS

Identifying Examples of Computer Hardware and Software To relate the concepts in this section to a situation the students are already familiar with, ask them to name various computer games or programs they especially like. Ask them if these would be examples of computer hardware or software. Then ask them if they know the system requirements for their favorite game or program. Do they know what these requirements refer to? (Do they refer to the amount of temporary memory (RAM), a particular version of Windows, available disk space, or to something else?) Ask students to identify which of these requirements relate to hardware and which relate to software.

(Page 36)

Focus on Reading

Read to Find Out
Use the Read to Find Out feature to focus student reading. Hold a quick starter discussion to find out what your students already know.

 Key Terms Online
Key term definitions and activities are available online at **WebDesignDW.glencoe.com**.

Reading Strategy Answer
In this activity, students will list facts about the four types of computer hardware. This information can be found by looking at the section *Computers and the Computer System* on page 36. Students' diagrams should look similar to this example:

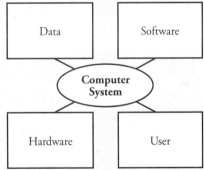

TEACH

Using Auto Save to Prevent Data Loss Although the students' text notes the importance of saving data frequently, you should emphasize how critical this can be. People have lost hours of work in a moment. You can also teach students how to use the auto save feature on their computers (**Tools>Options>Save**). Show them how to change the number of minutes between auto-saves of their work.

Unit 1 Fundamentals of Web Design Using Dreamweaver 117

CHAPTER 2

Answers to Section 2.1 Captions and Activities

(Page 36) **Reading Focus** Data, software, hardware, and the user are the parts of a computer system.

(Page 36) **Figure 2.1** The CPU is where data is processed.

(Page 36) ✓ **Reading Check** A user is 'in charge' of everything the computer does, including simply turning it on.

(Page 37) **Reading Focus** The CPU is like the brain of the computer and is located on the computer's motherboard. The RAM is where the computer stores the data it is currently processing.

(Page 37) ✓ **Reading Check** RAM is also called primary storage because it is where the computer first processes data.

(Page 38) **Reading Focus** There are at least six ways to input data into a computer: keyboard, mouse, joysticks and controllers, scanner, digital camera, and microphone.

(Page 38) **Table 2.1** Microphones are used to input audio files into a computer.

(Page 38) ✓ **Reading Check** Three common output devices are monitors, printers, and speakers.

(Page 39) **Reading Focus** The best way to store data long term is with a secondary storage device such as a CD.

(Page 39) **Activity 2.1** Students can learn more about storage devices in the Go Online activities at **WebDesignDW.glencoe.com**. Go Online answers can be found under Teacher Resources on the Web site.

(Page 39) **Table 2.2** Examples of removable storage devices include CDs, DVDs, Floppy disks, Zip disks, and Flash drives.

(Page 39) ✓ **Reading Check** A hard drive is fixed hardware inside of a computer while removable storage devices allow you to take data with you.

(Page 40) **Reading Focus** An operating system controls all of the other software programs on a computer, is responsible for task and memory management, keeps track of input devices, and sends output to the appropriate hardware.

(Page 40) **Figure 2.3** A GUI allows users to select words, symbols, or graphics from a desktop.

(Page 41) **Table 2.3** Word processing software is the best application choice for newsletters.

(Page 41) ✓ **Reading Check** An operating system (such as Microsoft Windows or Macintosh OS) controls all of the other software programs on a computer. Application software performs specific tasks on the computer.

(Page 42) **Reading Focus** A computer's components must be compatible or the computer will not function properly.

(Page 42) ✓ **Reading Check** Windows and Macintosh computers are incompatible in that their operating systems must only be run on the computers for which they were designed.

ASSESS

(Page 42) **Section 2.1 Assessment Answers**

Reading Summary

Use the Reading Summary to help students review and reinforce the important points of the section.

What Did You Learn?

1. Students' definitions should be in their own words, but based on the information found in the section and in the book's glossary.
2. Students' explanations will vary, but should note that various devices are used to input different types of data. For example, a keyboard is used primarily to input words, while a digital camera is used to input photos.
3. The six types of application software are Web browsers, which are used to visit Web sites; e-mail, which is used to exchange messages and files with other computers; word processing, which is used to create documents like letters, reports, and newsletters; spreadsheet, which is used to work with numbers and calculations, and to create tables, charts, and graphs; database, which is used to organize and retrieve large amounts of information; and presentation, which is used to create a slide presentation.

Critical Thinking

4. Lists will vary, but should reflect information similar to that found in the table on page 39 of the student textbook.
5. Answers will vary. Since the computer is being used for Web development, students might recommend such input devices as a scanner, a digital camera, and a Webcam. Output devices will include a monitor and a printer. Storage devices might include a CD burner, Zip drive, or other drives.

Apply It!

Research Computer Systems You can bring in computer ads or have students team up to check the options at computer retailers. Final recommendations should include the reason for students' choices. They should be aware that the lowest price may not be the best value, once they evaluate storage capacity, memory, speed, etc.

CLOSE

Reviewing Computer Hardware Students may have significant familiarity with most of the input, output, and storage devices discussed in this section. Instead of just asking them to review the general concepts, it may be more interesting to let them discuss the different devices they have worked with, as well as the most current features, capacities, or capabilities of such devices.

CHAPTER 2

SECTION 2.2 NETWORKS
(Pages 43–46)

FOCUS

Understanding the Concept of Networks Students are already familiar with the Internet, so take advantage of their prior knowledge to help explain the concept of networks. The Internet can be thought of as a vast network that effectively allows computers around the world to communicate with each other. Does your school use a local area network? If so, use this as an example of a LAN. Explain what a LAN allows users to do.

(Page 43)

Focus on Reading

Read to Find Out
Use the Read to Find Out feature to focus student reading. Hold a quick starter discussion to find out what your students already know.

Key Terms Online
Key term definitions and activities are available online at **WebDesignDW.glencoe.com**.

Reading Strategy Answer
Students can find information about the three types of network connections under the heading *Types of Connections* on page 44. The students' tables should look similar to this example:

Dial-Up	Broadband	Wireless
Connects by modem	Hardware provided by ISP	Uses infrared waves to connect
Inexpensive to use	Always connected to Internet	Transmission rates vary
Slow transmission rate	More expensive than dial-up	Suited to small areas

TEACH

Explaining and Using LANs If your school uses a LAN, show the students how to use it, who can access it, and what kind of information it allows them to access. Compare it to the information available on the Internet. (The information and resources available through a LAN are limited in amount and in scope compared to the Internet.) Explain why a school would want to use a LAN. (The school has information that is of particular use to its LAN users. It may also not want to share certain information with the general public.)

CHAPTER 2

Answers to Section 2.2 Captions and Activities

(Page 43) **Activity 2.2** Students can learn more about different types of networks at **WebDesignDW.glencoe.com**.

(Page 43) **Reading Focus** The two main types of network configurations are LANs and WANs.

(Page 43) **Figure 2.4** A LAN is restricted to a small geographic location, while a WAN can include computers in very wide geographical areas.

(Page 43) ✓ **Reading Check** The Internet is a WAN.

(Page 44) **Table 2.4** A broadband connection is always connected to the Internet and the transmission rate is faster.

(Page 44) **Reading Focus** Computers connect to the Internet by networks.

(Page 44) ✓ **Reading Check** The three main types of Internet connections are cable, DSL, and ISDN. Other answers might include dial-up modems, and satellite.

(Page 45) **Figure 2.5** A server is a powerful central computer that responds to requests from individual computers.

(Page 45) **Reading Focus** Network hardware components must be compatible or the network will not function properly.

(Page 46) ✓ **Reading Check** The different types of network hardware are: modems, NICs, and routers.

ASSESS

(Page 46) **Section 2.2 Assessment Answers**

Reading Summary

Use the Reading Summary to help students review and reinforce the important points of the section.

What Did You Learn?

1. Students' definitions should be in their own words, but based on the information found in the section and in the book's glossary.
2. The basic hardware components needed to connect a computer to the Internet are a modem and a telephone line.
3. A server is the powerful central computer to which all clients are connected. Clients are the individual computers used by users such as employees.

Critical Thinking

4. Dial-up connections require a modem and telephone line. An Internet connection is established only when the user makes the connection. During the time the

CHAPTER 2

computer is connected, the telephone line cannot be used for other purposes. A broadband connection has a dedicated telephone or cable connection that allows the computer to always be connected to the Internet. Dial-up connections transmit data more slowly than broadband connections and are somewhat more unreliable.

5. Wireless connections allow you to access the Internet from places where no physical connection can be made. For example, some salespeople who travel may be able to connect to the Internet from their cars. A current disadvantage is that wireless connections are unreliable and are not available in many locations.

Apply It!

Research Network Connections Answers will vary. Students should predict that the use of broadband and wireless connections is likely to increase, while the use of dial-up connections is likely to decrease. Students' assessments of other types of connections will vary, but should be supported by their research.

CLOSE

Analyzing the Effect of Connections and Network Hardware To reinforce some of the basic concepts of this section, ask the students to identify what kind of connection and what kind of modem they use at home or at school. How has the speed of the connection affected their Internet use? Ask them to support this with examples. Have the students explain what activities, if any, are particularly frustrating when they use the Internet, and why. What kind of connection do they think is best? Why?

(Page 47)

Real World Technology

USE EQUIPMENT SAFELY

Answers to Tech Check

1. Students' answers will vary, but should demonstrate knowledge of your school's emergency or fire-safety procedures, as well as basic fire-safety rules. Students should practice evacuating the building and be able to point out emergency equipment such as fire alarms and fire extinguishers. As an alternative exercise, you can assign each student to plot an evacuation route from a different room in the building.

2. Students can prepare a written report or oral presentation. Answers should demonstrate a good understanding of safety issues related to the use of computers and other equipment. In addition, you can ask each student to relate his or her findings to your classroom or computer lab, identifying any risks that could lead to work-related accidents. Students can research the subject on the Internet, through print resources, or by interviewing medical or human resource specialists.

CHAPTER 2

SECTION 2.3 CREATING A BASIC WEB SITE
(Pages 48–56)

FOCUS

Planning a Personal Web Site To keep the students' interest, it is important not to inundate them with text. Instead, let them get some hands-on experience in creating Web sites early in the course. Another way to generate interest is to ask them what they would put on a one-page Web site about themselves or a favorite interest of theirs. At the end of the section, you can give students an assignment that asks them to do this.

(Page 48)

Focus on Reading

Read to Find Out
Use the Read to Find Out feature to focus student reading. Hold a quick starter discussion to find out what your students already know.

 Key Terms Online
Key term definitions and activities are available online at **WebDesignDW.glencoe.com**.

Reading Strategy Answer
Students can find the Properties inspector text formatting buttons in You Try It Activity 2B on page 51. Students should become familiar with the purpose of each button. Students' tables may look similar to this example:

Button	Purpose
Text Format	Applies various Heading formats (H1–H6) to text or formats text within paragraph tag sets.
Font	Formats text in various fonts.
Style	Formats text using options specified in a cascading style sheet (CSS).
Font Size	Formats text size using user-specified or user-chosen numeric values.
Font Color	Formats text using user-specified color choices.
Bold	Formats selected text in bold using the <STRONG> tag set.
Italic	Formats selected text in italics using the <EM> tag set.
Indent Options	Indent buttons are used to format paragraphs.
Alignment Options	Formats appearance of paragraphs and blocks of text using Align Right, Align Left, Align Center, and Justify.

TEACH

Explaining How to Save and Store Web Sites One of the most important topics in this chapter is how to actually save and store the Web sites. Every school will have a different method and standards for saving files and folders. Some instructors have

Unit 1 Fundamentals of Web Design Using Dreamweaver 123

CHAPTER 4

students save their work in a hard drive, and others have students save their work on a network. (If available, a network storage method is recommended.) Tell students exactly how you want them to save and store their sites based on your school's policies and procedures.

Answers to Section 2.3 Captions and Activities

(Page 48) **Reading Focus** It is important to stay organized when saving Web pages so you can locate your Web pages easily.

(Page 48) **Figure 2.6** It is important to know where you have saved items so you can easily locate them.

(Page 49) **You Try It** **Activity 2A Create a One-Page Web Site** Students create a simple, one-page Web site, choose a background color, and create a folder to hold their site's images. Use the Solution Files noted in this chapter's Planning Guide.

> **Teaching Tip**
> Make sure students save their files to the correct location. In addition, remind students to save changes to their document frequently using **File>Save** or the shortcut keys of Ctrl + S or Cmd + S.

(Page 50) ✓ **Reading Check** Answers can include using meaningful file names, using the underscore character to separate individual words in a file name (no blank spaces), including one's initials within a file name, and not using prohibited characters in a file name (? \ * " < > / |).

(Page 51) **Reading Focus** Web text is formatted by choosing a font and size.

(Page 51) **You Try It** **Activity 2B Insert and Format Text** Students key text into their one-page Web site and change the style and size of the text. Use the Solution Files noted in this chapter's Planning Guide.

(Page 51) ✓ **Reading Check** Formatting text means specifying how it looks on a page.

(Page 52) **Reading Focus** Graphics enhance a Web page by providing visual interest.

(Page 52) **You Try It** **Activity 2C Insert Graphics** Students insert two graphics into their one-page Web site. Use the Student Data Files and Solution Files noted in this chapter's Planning Guide.

(Page 54) ✓ **Reading Check** The Insert toolbar must be in the Common view.

(Page 55) **Reading Focus** Pages are added to a Web site by creating subpages.

(Page 55) **You Try It** **Activity 2D Create a Subpage** Students practice creating and saving subpages to their one-page Web site. Use the Solution Files noted in this chapter's Planning Guide.

(Page 56) ✓ **Reading Check** A subpage is a page on a Web site inserted below the site's main page.

ASSESS

(Page 56) Section 2.3 Assessment Answers

Reading Summary
Use the Reading Summary to help students review and reinforce the important points of the section.

What Did You Learn?

1. Students' definitions should be in their own words, but based on the information found in the section and in the book's glossary.
2. Answers may vary but should follow the steps outlined in You Try It activity 2D (page 55).
3. A root folder is the main folder that contains all of a site's files and folders.

Critical Thinking

4. When individuals are ready to move the files to a Web server for publishing, they want to be able to easily locate all the files.
5. Changing the font and font size for text headings allows the headings to stand out. It helps users quickly see how the text is organized.

Apply It!

Format Text Students should add text to the Software Applications subpage and experiment with different fonts, sizes, and styles. Students should examine various examples of text formatting and participate in a discussion about when formatting enhances a page's readability, and when it detracts.

CLOSE

Organizing Files and Folders An important concept that students need to understand is the concept of organization. Ask students to describe the organizational structure of the main folder of a Web site. Describe the way that moving a Web site from a local computer to a server takes organization to a higher level. Have students explain where their Web site files are when they originally create and store a Web site folder, the final server storage place where the folder is uploaded or transferred, and the path to the folders from the original to the final storage place.

> **Teaching Tip**
>
> After saving Web site files, if a student cannot locate the files, three places to look are: 1) wherever the default "save" is set for the computer; 2) on the computer desktop; or 3) in the deleted items or trash bin.

CHAPTER 2 Answers to Chapter Review

The Chapter Review covers a wide range of student knowledge. Due to time constraints, students may not be able to complete every activity in the Chapter Review. Select the activities that are appropriate for your class needs and resources.

(Page 58) ## After You Read

Key Term Journal By focusing on a key term definition, the brain creates more neural connections than if the student were merely reading a glossary definition. Doing the *After You Read* activity and discussing results with peers are ways of focusing attention. Ask students to create flow charts of how the terms interrelate, when possible, to help students integrate the material into their own understanding.

(Page 58) ## Reviewing Key Terms

1. The physical components of the computer are hardware (CPU, hard drive, monitor, keyboard, and mouse).
2. A monitor is an example of an output device.
3. The networks are local area network (LAN) and wide area network (WAN).
4. The Internet is considered to be a wide area network (WAN).
5. A Graphical User Interface (GUI) allows users to interact with software by selecting words, symbols, or graphics from the screen.
6. Application software is used to perform different tasks on the computer.
7. The purpose of the server is to respond to requests from individual computers called clients.
8. A subfolder further organizes files. It is always within another folder.

(Page 58) ## Understanding Main Ideas

9. The two main processing components are the central processing unit (CPU) and random-access memory or RAM.
10. Hardware is the physical components of the computer. Software is the instructions that tell the computer what to do.
11. A GUI allows users to select words, symbols, or graphics from a desktop.
12. The two basic categories of networks are local area networks (LAN) and wide area networks (WAN).
13. Answers can include dial-up modem, broadband connection (Cable, DSL, ISDN, T1, T3), wireless, or even satellite connection.
14. The NOS is responsible for managing network resources, controlling who can access different network components, and keeping the network running smoothly.
15. It's important to save work frequently in the event electricity or the computer's hardware or software fails.
16. The four main parts are data, software, hardware, and the user.

Answers to Chapter Review — CHAPTER 2

17. Answers can include Web browsers, e-mail applications, word processing applications, spreadsheet applications, database applications, graphics applications, and presentation applications.

(Page 58) ## Critical Thinking

18. The invention of the graphical user interface made it easier for people to interact with computers because it was the first time users were able to interact with software by selecting words, symbols, or graphics from the screen.

19. Answers will vary. Students should present their reasons for their recommendation. Their focus should be on cost, speed, and efficiency. Since several people need access to the Internet, a broadband connection would be wise. Students can evaluate the estimated time family members will be online against the cost of using a broadband connection to see whether this option would make sense for the family. Students should also take into account the fact that the family members' needs will change as the children get older.

20. Operating systems include Windows, Mac OS, Unix, and Linux. Students should identify the most current versions of these operating systems. Students can use Word or Excel to create a spreadsheet that lists the features of each system.

21. Suggestions for graphics, audio, and video will vary. Students should recommend specific elements that would interest all the people who will likely visit the site. These graphics, audio, and video should be relevant to the information to be communicated to this audience.

(Page 59) ## Command Center

22. **Ctrl + S** = Saves the selected file.
23. **Ctrl + Shift + S** = Opens the Save As dialog box to allow a user to save their file using a different file name.
24. **Ctrl + I** = Places the <EM> tag set around selected text to format it in italics.

Standardized Test Practice

The answer is D. Tell students that they should first separate out the different elements of the assignment: researching, writing, and creating a graph. Then they can use the process of elimination when choosing the best software for each task.

Have students use the book's Web site **WebDesignDW.glencoe.com**.

- **Study with PowerTeach** Encourage your students to use the Chapter 2 PowerTeach Outline to review the chapter before they have a test.

- **Online Self Check** These quick five-question assessments may be used as an in-class activity, a homework assignment, or test review.

CHAPTER 2 Answers to Chapter Review

(Page 60) ## Making Connections

Language Arts—Write a Report Students' reports should summarize their research. The reports should tell the story of a Finnish university student who set out to create an operating system based on Unix that would be available for free. They should continue through the development phase and explain that today Linux is a common operating system on Web servers around the world.

(Page 60) ## Standards at Work

NETS-S 5 Evaluate Scanners Students' recommendations will vary. They should balance features against prices. Their recommendations should include scan resolution capability and model type (flatbed or upright). Students' tables may look similar to the one below. Students might use product reviews from sites like **www.CNET.com**.

Students' tables might look like the one below:

Scanners	Type of scanner	Features (including DPI options)	Where to purchase	Price
Canon CanoScan 9950F	Flatbed scanner	Single-pass scan mode, FireWire interface, 2400 dpi	Buy.com	$342.98
Epson Perfection 3170	Flatbed scanner	Single-pass scan mode, USB interface, 3200 dpi	Staples	$174.99
Microtek ScanMaker i900	Flatbed scanner	Single-pass, Firewire interface, 6400 dpi	PC Connection	$579.00

(Page 61) ## Teamwork Skills

Understand Computer Terms Encourage students to visit Web sites such as **www.webopedia.com** and **www.whatis.com** to find good working definitions of computer terminology. Often the definition of one term uses another term that should be included in the dictionary. Have students notice the hyperlinks at these dictionary Web sites. These can provide additional terms for their dictionaries.

(Page 61) ## Challenge Yourself

Explore Networks If you have several students completing this activity, suggest that they work together to develop a list of questions. Contact the network administrator to arrange for him or her to be available to the students.

Answers to Chapter Review — CHAPTER 2

You Try It Skills Studio

(Page 62)
1. **Format Text** Check students' screens when they have completed Step E. Their screens should look similar to the illustration shown in the You Try It Skills Studio in the student text. Note that the color and image choices available may vary depending on the version of Dreamweaver being used. If necessary, help students print the page.

2. **Add Graphics and a List to a Web Site** Students create a list of local restaurants. They add the list to their Web sites in Step C and format the list in Step D using the Menu List style.

Web Design Projects

(Page 63)
1. **Create Inventory Sheets** Evaluate inventory sheets for accuracy and completeness. If you have a large computer lab, you may assign students specific computers to inventory.

2. **Prepare a Presentation** Students' presentations should be appropriate for adults who are unfamiliar with Web page creation. Students can use software to create posters or a slide show for their presentations. You may provide a specific rubric for students to use as they evaluate each other's presentations. If possible, arrange for the best presentations to be given to members of the school board or parents.

CHAPTER 3 Planning Guide

Student Edition	Activities and Projects
Chapter 3 Online Basics (pages 64–95)	Quick Write Activity, page 64 Before You Read, page 65
Section 3.1 The Internet (pages 66–70)	📁 Reading Strategy, page 66 ⓘ Go Online Activity 3.1: Explore Online History, page 66 ⓘ TechSIM: E-mail
Section 3.2 The Web (pages 71–77)	📁 Reading Strategy, page 71 d ⊙ You Try It Activity 3A: Preview a Web Page, page 74 ⓘ You Try It Activity 3B: Perform a Boolean Search, page 76
Section 3.3 Web Site Development Tools (pages 78–82)	📁 Reading Strategy, page 78 d ⊙ You Try It Activity 3C: Insert External Hyperlinks, page 81
Ethics & Technology Verifying Your Sources (page 83)	Tech Check, page 83
Section 3.4 Social, Ethical, and Legal Issues (pages 84–88)	📁 Reading Strategy, page 84 ⓘ Go Online Activity 3.2: Use Online Resources Ethically, page 84 d You Try It Activity 3D: Add a Copyright Notice, page 86
Chapter 3 Review (pages 89–95)	ⓘ Making Connections: Social Studies–Perform an Online Search Standards at Work: Understand Copyrights and Trademarks (NETS-S2) ⓘ Teamwork Skills: Evaluate Internet Service Providers ⓘ Challenge Yourself: Internet Puzzle You Try It Skills Studio: ⓘ —Search for Information Online d —Create a Web Page with External Links Web Design Projects: —Use Online Resources ⓘ —Evaluate Software Additional Activities You May Wish to Use: ⊙ ⓘ —PowerTeach Outlines Chapter 3 —Student Workbook Chapter 3

Planning Guide — CHAPTER 3

Assessments

Section 3.1 Assessment, page 70

(i) Section 3.2 Assessment, page 77

Section 3.3 Assessment, page 82

(i) Section 3.4 Assessment, page 88

Chapter 3 Review and Assessment, page 89
You may also use any of the Chapter Review Activities and Projects as Assessments.
Additional Assessments You May Wish to Use:
(i) —Self-Check Assessments Chapter 3
—*ExamView* Testbank Chapter 3

Estimated Time to Complete Chapter

18 week course = 4–6 days
36 week course = 12–13 days

To help customize lesson plans, use the Pacing Guide on pages 26–30 and the Standards Charts on pages 132–133.

Key to Recommended Materials

Icons represent elements that may require additional resources.

📁 Focus on Reading

(i) Internet access required

♪ Software: Dreamweaver

⊙ Teacher Resource CD (contains Student Data Files, Solution Files, Reproducible Graphic Organizers, and Study with PowerTeach Outlines)

Data and Solution Files for Chapter 3

DataFiles
◆ MusicDept (Music Department Web Site)

SolutionFiles
◆ SF_YTI_3C
◆ SF_YTI_3D

Inclusion Strategies

For **Differentiated Instruction Strategies** refer to the **Inclusion in the Computer Technology Classroom** booklet.

CHAPTER 3 NETS Correlation For Students

ISTE NETS Foundation Standards

1. Basic operations and concepts
2. Social, ethical, and human issues
3. Technology productivity tools
4. Technology communications tools
5. Technology research tools
6. Technology problem-solving and decision-making tools

Performance Indicators	Textbook Correlation
1. Identify capabilities and limitations of contemporary and emerging technology resources and assess the potential of these systems and services to address personal, lifelong learning, and workplace needs. (NETS 2)	**SE:** Critical Thinking (70, 88, 90, 91), Tech Check (83), Teamwork Skills (93), Web Design Projects (95)
2. Make informed choices among technology systems, resources, and services. (NETS 1, 2)	**SE:** Apply It! (70), Tech Check (83), What Did You Learn? (88), Critical Thinking (91), Teamwork Skills (93), Web Design Projects (95)
3. Analyze advantages and disadvantages of widespread use and reliance on technology in the workplace and in society as a whole. (NETS 2)	**SE:** Tech Check (83), Critical Thinking (88), Web Design Projects (95)
4. Demonstrate and advocate for legal and ethical behaviors among peers, family, and community regarding the use of technology and information. (NETS 2)	**SE:** Quick Write Activity (64), Tech Check (83), Go Online (84), Apply It! (88), Critical Thinking (88, 90), Standards at Work (92)
5. Use technology tools and resources for managing and communicating personal/professional information (e.g. finances, schedules, addresses, purchases, correspondence). (NETS 3, 4)	**SE:** Apply It! (70), You Try It (86), Teamwork Skills (93)
6. Evaluate technology-based options, including distance and distributed education, for lifelong learning. (NETS 5)	**SE:** Go Online (66, 84), Web Design Projects (95)
7. Routinely and efficiently use online information resources to meet needs for collaboration, research, publications, communications, and productivity. (NETS 4, 5, 6)	**SE:** Go Online (66, 84), Tech Check (83), You Try It (76, 81), Apply It! (77, 88), Making Connections (92), Standards at Work (92), Skills Studio (94), Web Design Projects (95)
8. Select and apply technology tools for research, information analysis, problem-solving, and decision-making in content learning. (NETS 4, 5)	**SE:** Tech Check (83), Apply It! (77), Standards at Work (92), Challenge Yourself (93), Web Design Projects (95)
9. Investigate and apply expert systems, intelligent agents, and simulations in real-world situations. (NETS 3, 5, 6)	**SE:** You Try It (74), Apply It! (77), Skills Studio (94), Web Design Projects (95)
10. Collaborate with peers, experts, and others to contribute to content-related knowledge base by using technology to compile, synthesize, produce, and disseminate information, models, and other creative works. (NETS 4, 5, 6)	**SE:** Teamwork Skills (93)

SCANS Correlation — CHAPTER 3

Foundation Skills

Basic Skills

Reading	**SE:** Before You Read (65), Focus on Reading (66, 71, 78, 84), Reading Strategies (66, 71, 78, 84), After You Read (90), Standardized Test Practice (91)
Writing	**SE:** Quick Write Activity (64), Section Assessments (70, 77, 82, 88), Chapter Review (90–95)
Mathematics	**SE:** Teamwork Skills (93), Web Design Projects (95)
Listening and Speaking	**SE:** Teamwork Skills (93), Web Design Projects (95)

Thinking Skills

Creative Thinking	**SE:** Quick Write Activity (64)
Critical Thinking	**SE:** Critical Thinking (70, 77, 82, 88, 90, 91), Tech Check (83), Teamwork Skills (93), Web Design Projects (95)
Problem Solving	**SE:** Challenge Yourself (93), Web Design Projects (95)

Workplace Competencies

Resources — Manage time, money, materials, facilities, human resources	**SE:** Tech Check (83), Command Center (91), Web Design Projects (95)
Interpersonal — Work on teams, teach others	**SE:** Apply It! (70), Teamwork Skills (93)
Information — Acquire, evaluate, organize, maintain, interpret, communicate and use computers to process information	**SE:** Go Online (66, 84), Apply It! (70, 77, 82, 88), Tech Check (83), You Try It (74, 76, 81, 86), Command Center (91), Making Connections (92), Teamwork Skills (93), Challenge Yourself (93), Skills Studio (94), Web Design Projects (95)
Systems — Understand, monitor, correct, improve, design systems	**SE:** Skills Studio (94)
Technology — Select, apply, maintain, and troubleshoot technology.	**SE:** Go Online (66, 84), Apply It! (70, 77, 82, 88), Tech Check (83), You Try It (74, 76, 81, 86), Making Connections (92), Challenge Yourself (93), Skills Studio (94), Web Design Projects (95)

CHAPTER 3

Online Basics

(Page 64) ## Objectives

Section 3.1: The Internet
- Describe Internet hardware and software
- Explain Internet protocols
- Compare intranets, extranets, and the Internet

Section 3.2: The Web
- Identify URL components
- Compare Web browsers
- Use search engines

Section 3.3: Web Site Development Tools
- Describe Web development applications and hardware
- Describe connectivity components
- Insert external hyperlinks

Section 3.4: Social, Ethical, and Legal Issues
- Explain how to download files responsibly
- Summarize copyright and fair use laws
- Cite digital sources
- Evaluate online information

> **LEARNING LINK**
>
> Chapter 2 explained the components and devices that make up computer systems, and the software, networks, and connections that allow us to use them. Use Chapter 3 to show students how computers give us access to the various resources available on the Internet. Also use this chapter to discuss ethical and other issues created by Internet use.

(Page 64) ## Why It Matters

Take a class poll to find out how many students have ever downloaded a music file or swapped music files with friends. Lead a brief discussion about whether it occurred to them that these might not be ethical acts, and who might object to these actions.

(Page 64) ## Quick Write Activity

Students' responses will vary, but may touch on the use of others' text without providing credit to the authors, and unauthorized use of graphics or other materials. Clarify the concept that paying for Internet access does not mean that anything that can be downloaded is available without further monetary or ethical obligation.

(Page 65) ## Before You Read

Adjust Reading Speed Scientific research reveals that monitoring comprehension is one of six proven strategies for improving text comprehension. The other five include using graphic and semantic organizers, answering questions, generating questions, recognizing structure, and summarizing. As you go through each chapter's material with the class, you may have the students generate questions about the subject matter. You can answer these questions or let other students try answering these questions.

CHAPTER 3

SECTION 3.1 THE INTERNET
(Pages 66–70)

FOCUS

Identifying How Students Use the Internet Many students are already using the Internet to create their own Web pages or e-zines, or to talk with friends in chat rooms. Ask your students what kinds of uses they are currently making of the Internet, and list them on the board. Have them discuss their experiences, both positive and negative.

(Page 66)

Focus on Reading

Read to Find Out
Use the Read to Find Out feature to focus student reading. Hold a quick starter discussion to find out what your students already know.

 **Key Terms Online**
Key term definitions and activities are available online at **WebDesignDW.glencoe.com**.

Reading Strategy Answer
In this activity, students will be looking for key events in Internet history, and their corresponding dates. This information can be found under the heading *Origins of the Internet*, below. Students time lines should look similar to this example:

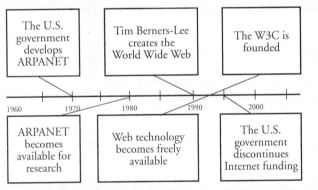

TEACH

Explaining Internet Connections Students may have frequently connected to the Internet, but without ever stopping to think about the steps that had to happen in order to do so. Use one of the school's computers to walk the students through the process, explaining what is occurring at each point along the way, such as the kind of hardware that is allowing the connection, the particular ISP that is providing access to the Internet, and so on. You may choose to first see if the students can explain each step in the process before providing the answer. Listing some common ISPs, such as AOL or Time-Warner, may also help students make the connection between what an ISP is and the services that they may already be using to access the Internet.

Unit 1 Fundamentals of Web Design Using Dreamweaver **135**

CHAPTER 3

Answers to Section 3.1 Captions and Activities

(Page 66) **Reading Focus** The Internet was developed by the government as a way to create a network of computers with various universities and defense contractors.

(Page 66) **GO Online** **Activity 3.1** Students can learn more about the history of the Internet at **WebDesignDW.glencoe.com.**

(Page 66) ✓ **Reading Check** Tim Berners-Lee created the first GUI in 1990.

(Page 67) **Reading Focus** An Internet service provider (ISP) is a business that allows its customers' computers to access the Internet through its own network.

(Page 67) **Figure 3.1** A gateway is an Internet server that allows the network to communicate with the Internet.

(Page 68) **Figure 3.2** IP stands for Internet Protocol.

(Page 68) ✓ **Reading Check** A protocol allows one computer to "talk" to another.

(Page 69) **Reading Focus** Answers will vary, but can include e-mail, listserv, FTP site, newsgroups, chat rooms, Internet relay chat, instant messaging, and online gaming.

(Page 69) **Table 3.1** Answers will vary, but can include the ease of use for many people in different locations, real-time communication between two or more people, the ability of users to share large files, and respond to messages at their convenience.

(Page 69) ✓ **Reading Check** Answers will vary, but students should note two examples from Table 3.1 on page 69 of the student textbook.

(Page 70) **Reading Focus** Other networks allow users to control access to their content.

(Page 70) **Figure 3.3** Intranets and extranets are different from the Internet because they allow companies to control the content and protect their resources.

(Page 70) ✓ **Reading Check** Intranets and extranets are similar in that they both allow users to have more control over their content and resources. They are different in that an Intranet can only be accessed by employees of an organization and an extranet can be accessed by outside or remote users who have authorization.

ASSESS

(Page 70) ### Section 3.1 Assessment Answers

Reading Summary

Use the Reading Summary to help students review and reinforce the important points of the section.

What Did You Learn?

1. Students' definitions should be in their own words, but based on the information found in the section and in the book's glossary.

2. Answers will vary, but students may note the following:
   - **HTTP** interprets hyperlinks to transfer files from a server to a browser.
   - **FTP** provides a standardized method of uploading and downloading large or shared files on the Internet.
   - **Telnet** allows a computer user to access another computer from a remote location. It is often used by colleges and universities to give authorized users access to a larger computer system.
   - **Gopher** uses software applications called Veronica and Jughead to let users search indices of text-based resources on Gopher servers around the world.
   - **WAIS** uses its own protocol to access servers that store specialized databases organized by subject. All WAIS documents are text-based.
3. A **MUD** is a multiuser domain game. Users play games in real time with people in other locations.

Critical Thinking

4. A common set of rules and procedures makes it possible for the many different types of computers on the Internet to share information and resources.
5. The Internet, intranets, and extranets are all networks that provide access to information. All use the same hardware and TCP/IP. Each network can use standard Web browsers and e-mail applications. The differences are the way these networks are used, who owns them, and who is allowed to access them. An intranet is designed to share information within a private organization while protecting this information from outsiders. An extranet is similar to an intranet, but can also be accessed by authorized outside or remote users. The Internet is public and can be accessed by anyone with the required hardware and software.

Apply It!

Communicate on the Internet E-mail is the most common way to communicate over the Internet. The other types of Internet communication covered include listerv, newsgroups or forums, chat rooms, Internet relay chat, and instant messaging. Students should identify which of these methods are available for their classroom use and explain why a user might choose one method over another for a specific task.

CLOSE

Reviewing Internet Resources and Uses Clarify and distinguish important concepts in this section by discussing with students:

- Which Internet service providers they have used (AOL, Earthlink, MSN, etc.).
- Which Internet protocols they have used, once they were allowed access to the Internet by their ISP (TCP/IP, HTTP, etc.).
- What these protocols have allowed them to do on the Internet (Listen to music, play games, visit chat rooms, instant messaging, etc.).

CHAPTER 3

SECTION 3.2 THE WEB
(Pages 71–77)

FOCUS

Locating Information on the Web Students are probably already familiar with the use of URLs. Ask students to name and describe some of their favorite Web sites, and list the appropriate URL on the board. Discuss how they found these sites, and how they would go about finding others they might be interested in. They might mention that often all you have to do is add .com to the end of a company's name.

(Page 71)

Focus on Reading

Read to Find Out
Use the Read to Find Out feature to focus student reading. Hold a quick starter discussion to find out what your students already know.

 Key Terms Online
Key term definitions and activities are available online at **WebDesignDW.glencoe.com**.

Reading Strategy Answer
Students should list the four steps in order. This information can be found under the heading *Retrieving a Web Page* on page 73. Students' charts should look similar to this example:

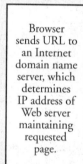

TEACH

Understanding Domain Name Extensions Discuss the domain name extensions of Web sites your students visit regularly. (Answers might include sites that end in .com.) What kind of information is available there? (.com sites often offer information about products or services for sale.) Have students visit other sites with this extension to see if similar kinds of information are offered there. Then have them visit several sites with extensions such as .gov, .edu and .org. Ask students to draw conclusions about the kinds of information that will appear at common domain name extensions. Students can work in groups that each research a different extension.

CHAPTER 3

Answers to Section 3.2 Captions and Activities

(Page 71) **Reading Focus** URLs enable browsers to locate specific files on the Web.

(Page 72) **Figure 3.4** The *www* at the beginning of the URL indicates that the file is part of the World Wide Web.

(Page 72) **Table 3.2** Domain name extensions indicate a type of site—commercial, educational, non-profit, government, etc.

(Page 72) ✅ **Reading Check** The components of a URL are the protocol, address, domain name, domain name extension, directory path, and retrieved file.

(Page 73) **Reading Focus** A Web browser requests and retrieves Web pages, which is essential to viewing them.

(Page 73) **Figure 3.5** The browser is the client that requests a Web page.

(Page 74) **You Try It** **Activity 3A Preview a Web Page** Students use Dreamweaver to open a premade Web page and preview it in more than one Internet browser to compare results. Use the Student Data Files noted in this chapter's Planning Guide.

(Page 75) **Reading Focus** Search tools help users locate online information by providing a portal that responds to keywords and specific instructions.

(Page 76) **Table 3.3** The three most commonly used Boolean operators are AND, OR, and NOT.

(Page 76) **You Try It** **Activity 3B Perform a Boolean Search** Students practice performing Internet Boolean searches in order to locate information and understand the way to get the fewest results with the most specific information.

(Page 77) ✅ **Reading Check** Two different types of searches are a keyword search and a Boolean search.

ASSESS

(Page 77) **Section 3.2 Assessment Answers**

Reading Summary

Use the Reading Summary to help students review and reinforce the important points of the section.

What Did You Learn?

1. Students' definitions should be in their own words, but based on the information found in the section and in the book's glossary.

2. Answers will vary, but may include Microsoft Internet Explorer, Netscape Navigator, Mozilla, Firefox, Opera, Lynx, Safari, and America Online's browser.

3. Text may wrap in different places. In addition, font sizes, colors, margin spacing around page edges, and the appearance of hyperlinks may vary.

Critical Thinking

4. The domain name extension for the official site of the U.S. Supreme Court is .gov.

5. Students' examples will vary but should note that the AND operator will tell the search engine to locate only those pages that contain all keywords entered. For example, if you wanted to find hotels in Miami, it would be better to use *hotels* AND *Miami*. Using *hotels* OR *Miami* would find pages about hotels in any location and information about Miami that had nothing to do with lodging.

Apply It!

Perform a Keyword Search Students should list the sites found on the first page of each of three search engine's results, locate local population information, and summarize which search engine most quickly helped locate their information. Students should use the same keyword search on each search engine.

CLOSE

Using Search Engines To make sure the students have grasped the concept of how to locate information online, have them select several topics they would like to know more about. Write these on the board. Then have the students decide whether they would use a search engine or a Web directory to begin their research. What keywords do they think would help them in their search? Would any Boolean operators be useful? Which ones? Correct any misunderstandings the students have about any of these basic concepts.

CHAPTER 3

SECTION 3.3 WEB SITE DEVELOPMENT TOOLS
(Pages 78–82)

FOCUS

Exploring Web Site Elements Many students may have either created a Web page of their own or thought of creating one. Ask students who have created one to describe their page. Ask those who would like to create one what they would put on their page. This may include graphics, audio or video, in addition to text. Lead a brief discussion to see what, if anything, the students already know about the kinds of software, hardware, and connectivity tools they would need to turn their ideas into actual Web pages.

(Page 78)

Focus on Reading

Read to Find Out

Use the Read to Find Out feature to focus student reading. Hold a quick starter discussion to find out what your students already know.

 Key Terms Online

Key term definitions and activities are available online at **WebDesignDW.glencoe.com**.

Reading Strategy Answer

Students should list the software, hardware, and connectivity tools found under the headings *Software Needs* and *Hardware and Connectivity Needs* on pages 78 and 80. The students' charts should look similar to this example:

Web Site Development Tools		
Software	**Hardware**	**Connectivity**
• text editors	• computer	• computer hard
• Web site	• monitor	drive or network
development	• mouse	server
• text	• any requirements	• Web server
• graphics	by software	
• video/audio		

TEACH

Comparing Hardware and Software Needs Have students compare the hardware and software needs discussed in this section with the actual hardware and software available on the school's computers. Ask them to make a list of any items that differ. Have the students determine whether the lack of any of these items will affect the ability to create a Web site.

Unit 1   Fundamentals of Web Design Using Dreamweaver   **141**

CHAPTER 3

Answers to Section 3.3 Captions and Activities

(Page 78) **Reading Focus** Web pages are created with two types of software tools: applications that create Web pages themselves, and applications that create the individual Web page components.

(Page 79) **Figure 3.9** Web designers use graphic applications to create, edit, resize, crop, change the color of, and otherwise modify graphics to suit their designs.

(Page 79) ✓ **Reading Check** A text editor is a tool that allows the user to manually key HTML commands into a blank document.

(Page 80) **Reading Focus** The basic hardware and connectivity needs of every user are a computer, a monitor, and a mouse.

(Page 80) **Table 3.4** Web design involves many graphics and multimedia files that use video RAM to display.

(Page 80) ✓ **Reading Check** A monitor with a resolution of at least 800 x 600 that is capable of displaying at least 256 colors, a color printer, a scanner and digital camera, and a camcorder, microphone, and speakers are the input and output devices usually used when creating a Web site.

(Page 81) **Reading Focus** Hyperlinks allow a user to quickly jump from page to page, which makes Web navigation easier.

(Page 81) **You Try It** **Activity 3C Insert External Hyperlinks** Students learn how to add external hyperlinks to a Web site. Use the Solution Files provided in this chapter's Planning Guide.

(Page 82) ✓ **Reading Check** An external hyperlink takes users to a page on a different Web site.

ASSESS

(Page 14) **Section 3.3 Assessment Answers**

Reading Summary

Use the Reading Summary to help students review and reinforce the important points of the section.

What Did You Learn?

1. Students' definitions should be in their own words, but based on the information found in the section and in the book's glossary.

2. Answers from students should be in their own words and include information found on page 80 (*Hardware and Connectivity Needs*) of the student textbook. Answers might include a monitor with a resolution of at least 800 × 600 that is

capable of displaying at least 256 colors, a color printer to produce hard copies of Web pages, a scanner and digital camera for graphics, and a camcorder, microphone, and speakers for multimedia.

3. Students' answers should reflect the steps shown in You Try It activity 3C on page 81 of the student textbook.

Critical Thinking

4. Compared to Web site development applications, text editors are simple to learn, relatively inexpensive, and require much less hard drive space, but you must know HTML code to use one. If you would like to add features such as animation or would like help maintaining your Web site, a Web site development application may be a better choice.

5. Answers will vary. Students should choose three external hyperlinks that visitors to their site about Japan would find useful or interesting. These may include links to information about Japanese customs, language, food, leisure activities, or places of special interest. One site they might use is the Japan National Tourist Organization. **(http://www.jnto.go.jp/)**.

Apply It!

Identify Hardware This information is available on Windows by following this route: **Start>Settings>Control Panel>Systems**. Click on the **General** tab for processor type and available RAM. Click on the **Device Manager** tab to see what kinds of devices are being used. Students can also view the amount of memory on the hard drive by right-clicking on **Local Disk (C:)** in **My Computer** and then clicking **Properties**. There are different ways to access this information. Use the method you are most comfortable with and that is appropriate for your operating system. Students should be supervised at all times for this activity.

CLOSE

Reviewing Web Site Development Tools In the Section 3.3 Focus activity, the students discussed the content of Web pages they would like to create. Now have the students explain what software applications they would actually use to create these pages, and why. Also have them explain what hardware requirements would be entailed by the use of this software.

CHAPTER 3

(Page 83)

Ethics & Technology

VERIFYING YOUR SOURCES

Answers to Tech Check

1. One way to carry out this activity is having all students look up the same information on different Web sites. For example, they might all use a search engine to find information about the Battle of Gettysburg. Each student should choose a different site from the search results. As a class, have students come up with a checklist for evaluating the reliability of a site. They should include items such as who the advertisers are on the site, the name of the site's sponsor or creator, the latest site update, the information sources cited, etc. Students should use the checklist to evaluate the information they find online, including its accuracy, relevance, appropriateness, comprehensiveness, and bias. Have them write down the information on their checklist. They can also use screen captures of the site to illustrate their findings. Afterwards, have students compare their sites. Which sites seem most reliable? Which are least reliable? Have students explain how they came to these conclusions.

2. Students may present their findings as a written or oral report. Ask each student to pick a political or social issue in which bias is a common factor. Students should then research various online resources (including Web sites, newsgroups, and others) to find examples of information relating to the issue, which is presented in a clearly biased manner. In presenting their case studies, students should discuss the origins and history of their chosen issue, along with a balanced sampling of views (biased or unbiased) on it. The biased information should be presented against this background of historical fact and well-rounded viewpoint.

CHAPTER 3

SECTION 3.4 SOCIAL, ETHICAL, AND LEGAL ISSUES
(Pages 84–88)

FOCUS

Identifying Issues Involving Internet Use Students are probably familiar with some of the benefits of Internet use, including the availability of games and chat rooms. Ask them if they or their friends have experienced any of the drawbacks, such as not being sure of the identity of someone they are chatting with, or being told by a teacher they have plagiarized when they thought the material on the Internet was "free" or "for everyone's use." Make a list of these issues. Later, at the end of this section, use it to see if the students have a better understanding of some of the social, ethical, and legal issues involving Internet use.

(Page 84)

Focus on Reading

Read to Find Out
Use the Read to Find Out feature to focus student reading. Hold a quick starter discussion to find out what your students already know.

 Key Terms Online
Key term definitions and activities are available online at **WebDesignDW.glencoe.com**.

Reading Strategy Answer
Students should describe how software can be used in a legal way. This information can be found in Table 3.5 on page 85. Students' tables should look similar to this example:

Commercial Software	Shareware	Freeware
Must be purchased. Illegal to copy or sell to others.	Can be downloaded or copied for a small fee to copyright holder.	Can be freely downloaded, copied, and used for any legal purpose.

TEACH

Identifying Plagiarism Because students will frequently use the Internet to create school projects, it is critical that they understand the concept of plagiarism. Visit a Web site such as an online encyclopedia and have the students read some of its text. Give the students examples of what kinds of use of this text would be plagiarism, such as taking the text verbatim, or using the text after making minor changes. Explain why this is plagiarism and give examples of how to use the text in an ethical way.

CHAPTER 3

Answers to Section 3.4 Captions and Activities

(Page 84) **Go Online** **Activity 3.2** Students can learn more about the ethical use of online information at **WebDesignDW.glencoe.com**. Tell students whether you want them to print or e-mail their answers to you. Go Online answers can be found under Teacher Resources on the book Web site.

(Page 84) **Reading Focus** Internet ethics are important because they prevent copyright abuse and protect organizations and individuals.

(Page 85) ✓ **Reading Check** Some common rules in Acceptable Use Policies are checking with an authorized individual before downloading files, understanding which Web sites are authorized for access, and not using the Internet for personal reasons if an organization forbids it.

(Page 85) **Reading Focus** Copyrights exist to protect creators of original work.

(Page 85) **Table 3.5** Shareware can be downloaded and used for free. However, if you continue to use it, you must pay a small fee to the copyright holder. Freeware can be downloaded and used free of charge.

(Page 86) **You Try It** **Activity 3D Add a Copyright Notice** Students learn how to add a copyright notice to a Web page. Use the Solution Files noted in this chapter's Planning Guide.

(Page 87) **Table 3.6** It is important to identify a site's purpose because it may contain a bias, such as a company trying to sell a product or sponsorship by a particular organization.

(Page 88) **Figure 3.14** Information on Web sites may change often. If someone is looking at the site for the information you cited, it may no longer be there.

(Page 88) ✓ **Reading Check** Fair use means that excerpts from copyrighted work can be used under specific circumstances, such as educational purposes.

ASSESS

(Page 88) ### Section 3.4 Assessment Answers

Reading Summary

Use the Reading Summary to help students review and reinforce the important points of the section.

What Did You Learn?

1. Students' definitions should be in their own words, but based on the information found in the section and in the book's glossary.

2. Commercial software is purchased by the user and cannot be copied, sold, or given away by the user. Shareware is freely available for trial and download, but a fee must be paid to the author if the user continues to use it. Freeware is free to the user.

3. Answers will vary, but after reading the information found under the heading *Copyright and Fair Use Laws,* students' answers should indicate that fair use allows small portions of a work to be used for educational purposes. A "small portion" generally means a few paragraphs from a book or a short excerpt from a song or video. Students' answers may include an excerpt from an online news story, four to five lyrics from a song, or two or three screen captures of an online video.

Critical Thinking

4. Internet use may isolate people who spend a lot of time online. Users must protect their privacy since other users may take advantage of personal information. Site owners, including designers, software developers, and authors, must guard against copyright infringements by their site's users.

5. Answers will vary, but after reading this section's material, students may include an assessment of a site's copyright or Terms of Use documentation. Students' answers should indicate they understand that just because something is available does not mean it is available for free. A useful analogy may be that music stores often allow you to play a CD in the store, but that does not mean the CD can be taken home for free.

Apply It!

Cite Digital Sources Students will locate and write citations for three Web sites relating to Antarctica. Such sites are available in abundance by simply entering "Antarctica" into any search engine. Student responses should use the citation method found under the heading *Digital Source Citations* on page 88 of the student textbook. For an example of a site and its citation, you can use:

Brown, Susan. "Documenting Certificates." <u>Middletown Genealogy Information</u>. September 19, 2008. Middletown Genealogy Center. October 20, 2008 <www.middletwn.org/genealogy>

Evaluating Web Site Information Visit a variety of sites with the students, including ones that are likely to reflect bias in the content. Examples might include sites of organizations that might feel not enough is being done to protect the environment, such as Greenpeace (**www.greenpeace.com**), and organizations representing the recording industry, such as IFPI (**www.ifpi.org**), that are concerned about music piracy. Have the students analyze the quality of information on several sites. Students should be able to detect hidden agendas, unsupported claims, and outdated information. Students should also pay attention to the name of the Web site they are visiting, since some sites may redirect visitors to different sites without their knowledge. You may also want to point out to students that visitors may be using similar evaluation guidelines to evaluate the Web sites that students create.

CHAPTER 3 Answers to Chapter Review

The Chapter Review covers a wide range of student knowledge. Due to time constraints, students may not be able to complete every activity in the Chapter Review. Select the activities that are appropriate for your class needs and resources.

(Page 90) ## After You Read

Reading Speed Metacognition—the art of knowing what you know and what you do not know—is critically important to the reading process. Too often students complain that they read the chapter, but did not understand the material. This can lead to great frustration. Students who use metacognition strategies are less likely to have this problem. Having students note which paragraphs or sections they had difficulty reading can help develop their metacognition skills. Answer any questions they have about the sections that they may still be having trouble comprehending.

(Page 90) ## Reviewing Key Terms

1. HTML
2. The Internet is accessible to everyone and uses a number of different protocols to transmit information. An intranet is privately owned and, often, can only be accessed by employees of an organization. The World Wide Web is a part of the Internet that relies on Web browsers to display information in specially formatted documents using HTML.
3. URL stands for Uniform Resource Locator.
4. In the URL **www.uiowa.edu,** the .edu portion of the domain name is the domain name extension.
5. Search engines catalog individual Web pages, while Web directories catalog Web sites (not pages) by topic or category.
6. The applications required to create Web pages themselves, and the applications required to create individual Web page components, such as graphics, video, and audio.
7. A Boolean search specifies how the search engine should use keywords to locate specific pages. You use operators such as AND, OR, and NOT to perform more precise searches.
8. WYSIWYG stands for "what you see is what you get."

Understanding Main Ideas

9. TCP/IP contains the specific information that allows computers to identify each other and exchange data on the Internet.
10. An FTP site is useful if you want to send someone a file that is too large to be transmitted as an e-mail attachment, or if many people need access to the same file. A listserv allows users to post and respond to group messages at their convenience, allowing discussions to continue over long periods of time. A newsgroup allows subscribers to post and read articles for and by other subscribers, and is useful for special topics and searchable news.
11. An IP address is a four-part numeric address specific to each computer on the Internet. A domain name address consists of words, which makes the address easier for most people to remember. Each domain name address is a nickname for an IP address; either one will send you to its site.

Answers to Chapter Review — CHAPTER 3

12. Not all browsers display Web pages in the same way; page formatting may appear very different from one browser to another, with results the designer did not intend.

13. **AND** tells the search engine to locate only Web pages containing both the keyword before and after the **AND** operator. **OR** tells the search engine to locate pages containing one or both of the keywords. **NOT** tells the search engine to locate pages containing the first keyword, but not the keyword that follows the **NOT** operator.

14. Answers may include: guarding access to your personal identity, including your name, address, or information that would allow others to determine your identity; communicating with, and sharing personal information with, only trusted sources via e-mail, chats, newsgroups, or IM; and informing a parent or trusted adult if an individual seeking to communicate with you makes you feel uncomfortable.

15. The components of a URL include:

    http specifies that this page is stored on an HTTP or Web server and the HTTP protocol must be used to access this server.

    www indicates that the server is part of the World Wide Web.

    redcross is the site's domain name, identifying the entity that sponsors the site.

    .org is the domain name extension, telling users what type of organization uses the address. In this case, the extension is that of a non-profit organization.

16. The seven essential elements to be documented when you cite the use of a Web site are: author's name (last name first), title of the article or Web page (in quotes), complete title of the Web site (underline), date of Internet publication or copyright date, name of the organization, date you visited the site, and the site's URL.

(Page 90) ## Critical Thinking

17. Intellectual property is the ownership of creative works by authors, software developers, and musicians. Plagiarism is copying the work of others and presenting it as your own. Copyrights exist to protect creators of original work. A copyright asserts that only the copyright's owner has the right to sell his or her work or to allow someone else to sell it. Fair use allows excerpts from works to be used under specific circumstances (educational purposes).

18. Web pages are often updated, and so information you have cited in a report may be inaccessible at a later date or may have been placed elsewhere in a site.

19. It takes you to the National Oceanic and Atmospheric Administration's home page. The first page of every Web site is located at the domain name address, which ends with the domain name extension. Subsequent pages are placed after a forward slash at the end of the address.

20. Answers will vary, but given the increasing visibility this issue and its prosecution have received in the press, students may reason that the illegal downloading of music will decrease over the next few years.

21. Answers will vary depending on the type of graphics application a user installs or uses. Students should note some of the general system requirements listed under *General System Requirements* on page 80 of the student textbook.

22. Answers will vary but students should note that their graphics software will run very slowly and their computer may freeze.

CHAPTER 3 Answers to Chapter Review

23. Using a text editor may be your best choice if your site is text based or small with low graphics or other multimedia components; if cost is a factor; if you know HTML; if you do not have the time, resources, or desire to learn a Web site development application; if you can troubleshoot and maintain the site yourself; or if your computer has minimal processing power.

24. Knowing the author and/or sponsor allows you to figure out whether the author and/or sponsor has a hidden agenda, and so may not be offering factual information. For example, organizations may be trying to convince you of their political views. Businesses may be trying to sell their products, regardless of quality. Individuals may be giving you "facts" that are actually opinion.

25. Unlike commercial software, shareware allows users to test the software before paying a fee, so that the user can see if the software will be of value to him or her.

(Page 91) ## Command Center

26. Ctrl + Alt + Shift + C = Formats text to align center.
27. Ctrl + End = Moves the insert cursor to the bottom of the page.
28. Ctrl + Q = Closes the application.

Standardized Test Practice

The correct answer is C. As students review the statements, encourage them to go back to the reading section that discusses Internet protocols to determine whether an answer statement is true or false.

e-Review

Have students use the book's Web site **WebDesignDW.glencoe.com**.

- **Study with PowerTeach** Encourage your students to use the Chapter 3 PowerTeach Outline to review the chapter before they have a test.
- **Online Self Check** These quick five-question assessments may be used as an in-class activity, a homework assignment, or test review.

(Page 92) ## Making Connections

Social Studies—Perform an Online Search Students may need practice in choosing the most productive keywords, or Boolean operators. Have students discuss any problems they encountered while trying to locate information for this activity. Students' responses will vary, but may contain the following:

- 1947: AT&T asks the FCC to increase number of frequencies for widespread mobile phone service. FCC limits the frequencies available.
- 1968: FCC allows more frequencies, encouraging research in the new technology.
- 1973: Motorola is the first to use the technology in a portable device. The first call on a portable cell phone is made.
- 1977: AT&T and Bell Labs construct a prototype cellular system.

Answers to Chapter Review — CHAPTER 3

(Page 92) ## Standards at Work

NETS-S 2 Understand Copyrights and Trademarks Many people do not read the Terms of Use page before using a Web site. Encourage students to do so, and use this exercise to point out why it is important. Without reading this, a user might think it was permissible to copy software and give it to a friend. This could infringe on Microsoft's interest in selling its software, and could result in legal action.

(Page 93) ## Teamwork Skills

Evaluate Internet Service Providers Students' charts should provide information about the services and prices of at least three ISPs. Encourage students to contact local ISPs, so that they can compare prices and services to large, national ISPs such as AOL or Earthlink. You may have each group decide which ISP would be best for individuals, and which would be best for businesses, and be prepared to explain their choices to the class.

Students' charts will vary, but may look similar to the table below:

ISP Name	Services for Individuals	Services for Businesses	Prices for Services
Net Zero	Internet connection		$9.95/month
	High Speed Internet		14.95/month
		None listed on site	
Earthlink	Internet connection		21.95/month
	High Speed Internet		49.95/month
	Call waiting		3.95/month
		High Speed DSL	129.00/month
		ISDN	50.00/single channel hr.
		E-commerce pkg.	29.95/month

(Page 93) ## Challenge Yourself

Internet Puzzler Answers to the six scavenger hunt items are: (1) Stone Age, (2) Ecuador, (3) Rojo, (4) Versailles, (5) Euphrates, (6) Rolling Stones. Answer to the riddle: server.

CHAPTER 3 Answers to Chapter Review

You Try It Skills Studio

(Page 94)

1. **Search for Information Online** A Boolean search using the **AND** operator and the keywords "famous people," "birthday," and the student's actual birthday should bring up many sites that offer the requested information. For instance, "famous people" **AND** "birthday" **AND** "April 8" led to finding that Harry Truman, Betty Ford, and Mary Pickford all shared this birthday. Using any of these names, the Boolean operator **AND**, and keywords such as "biographical information," should lead a student to informative sites about that person.

    A URL that may be useful for this exercise is Those Were the Days, found at **http://www.440.com/twtd/archives**. The History Channel's Web site also contains a database of events that students may find useful.

    In Step C, students will cite each URL they have located. Information gathered in this exercise will be used for You Try It Skills Studio Exercise 2.

2. **Create a Web Page with External Links** Students use the information they learned from the search in the activity above to create a Web page in Dreamweaver. In addition to the headings, the students create a hyperlink for each person to the site found in the activity above. Students also include two or three sentences about each person. Then they add a copyright notice at the bottom of the page.

Web Design Projects

(Page 95)

1. **Use Online Resources** Some of the important dates and events in the history of the Internet and Web are discussed in this chapter under the heading *Origins of the Internet*. Ask the students to use search engines or Web directories to find new, additional information, and have them include it in their reports or presentations. Using the example of online privacy, it may be noted that users sometimes have their identity stolen, or may be harassed by someone who has found out personal information such as where they live. Potential solutions include informing users about the danger of offering personal information online, and creating and enforcing laws to prosecute those who use personal information in unethical ways.

2. **Evaluate Software** Students' tables will vary, but should note system requirements, features, and the price of each application.

    In predicting which applications might be chosen by individuals or organizations, students may note that a cheaper price and less demanding system requirements might be favored by individuals on a tight budget with older computers. Businesses, on the other hand, have more money to spend and need up-to-date features to remain competitive. They would likely choose the best software available.

Notes

CHAPTER 4 Planning Guide

Student Edition	Activities and Projects
Chapter 4 HTML Basics (pages 96–129)	Quick Write Activity, p. 96 Before You Read, p. 97
Section 4.1 HTML Coding (pages 98–101)	📁 Reading Strategy, p. 98 ⓘ Go Online 4.1: Use HTML Tutorials, p. 100
Section 4.2 Using a Text Editor (pages 102–108)	📁 Reading Strategy, p. 102 ⊙ YTI 4A: Create Folders to Organize a Site, p. 102 𝒅 YTI 4B: Create and Save an HTML Document, p. 104 𝒅 YTI 4C: Add Color and Format Text Using HTML, p. 106 𝒅 YTI 4D: Create an Unordered List Using HTML, p. 107 𝒅 ⓘ YTI 4E: View HTML in a Browser, p. 108
Section 4.3 Enhancing and Testing Your HTML Page (pages 109–114)	📁 Reading Strategy, p. 109 𝒅 YTI 4F: Insert an Image, p. 110 ⓘ Go Online 4.2: Identify Absolute and Relative Links, p. 111 𝒅 YTI 4G: Insert Absolute Links Using HTML, p 112 𝒅 YTI 4H: Test an HTML Document, p. 113
Emerging Technology Web Languages (page 115)	Tech Check, p. 115
Section 4.4 Dreamweaver versus Notepad (pages 116–122)	📁 Reading Strategy, p. 116 𝒅 YTI 4I: Create and Format a Page in Dreamweaver, p. 117 𝒅 YTI 4J: Add Headings and Unordered Lists in Dreamweaver, p. 118 𝒅 YTI 4K: Insert a Graphic and Links in Dreamweaver, p. 120 𝒅 YTI 4l: Test a Web Page in Dreamweaver, p. 122
Chapter 4 Review (pages 123–129)	ⓘ Making Connections: Social Studies—Perform an Online Search Standards at Work: Create an HTML Quick Reference Table (NETS-S 4) Teamwork Skills: Create Web Design Biographies Challenge Yourself: Create a Table Using HTML YTI Skills Studio: ⓘ —Create a Home Page Using HTML 𝒅 ⊙ —Create a Links Page Using HTML Web Design Projects: 𝒅 —Create a Home Page Using HTML 𝒅 —Add Pages in Dreamweaver Additional Activities You May Wish to Use: ⊙ ⓘ —PowerTeach Outlines Chapter 4 —Student Workbook Chapter 4

Planning Guide CHAPTER 4

Assessments

Section 4.1 Assessment, page 101

ⓘ Section 4.2 Assessment, page 108

Section 4.3 Assessment, page 114

𝒹 ⊙ Section 4.4 Assessment, page 122

Chapter 4 Review and Assessment, page 123
—Building 21st Century Skills
—Building Your Portfolio
You may also use any of the Chapter Review Activities and Projects as Assessments.
Additional Assessments You May Wish to Use:
ⓘ —Self-Check Assessments Chapter 4
⊙ ⓘ —*ExamView* Testbank Chapter 4

Estimated Time to Complete Chapter

18 week course = 4–6 days
36 week course = 10 days

To help customize lesson plans, use the Pacing Guide on pages 26–30 and the Standards Charts on pages 156–157.

Key to Recommended Materials

Icons represent elements that may require additional resources.

▫ Focus on Reading

ⓘ Internet access required

𝒹 Software: Dreamweaver

⊙ Teacher Resource CD (contains Student Data Files, Solution Files, Reproducible Graphic Organizers, and Study with PowerTeach Outlines)

Data and Solution Files for Chapter 4

DataFiles
◆ p_border.gif
◆ movies.gif

SolutionFiles
◆ SF_YTI_4B.html
◆ SF_YTI_4C.html
◆ SF_YTI_4D.html
◆ SF_YTI_4F
◆ SF_YTI_4G
◆ SF_YTI_4I.html
◆ SF_YTI_4J.html
◆ SF_YTI_4K
◆ Hardware_Devices_html
◆ Hardware_Devices_Dreamweaver

Inclusion Strategies

For **Differential Instruction Strategies** refer to the **Inclusion in the Computer Technology Classroom** booklet.

Unit 1 Fundamentals of Web Design Using Dreamweaver

CHAPTER 4 NETS Correlation For Students

ISTE NETS Foundation Standards

1. Basic operations and concepts
2. Social, ethical, and human issues
3. Technology productivity tools
4. Technology communications tools
5. Technology research tools
6. Technology problem-solving and decision-making tools

Performance Indicators	Textbook Correlation
1. Identify capabilities and limitations of contemporary and emerging technology resources and assess the potential of these systems and services to address personal, lifelong learning, and workplace needs. (NETS 2)	**SE:** Critical Thinking (101, 108, 114, 122, 125), Building 21st Century Skills (130)
2. Make informed choices among technology systems, resources, and services. (NETS 1, 2)	**SE:** Critical Thinking (125), Building 21st Century Skills (130), Building Your Portfolio (131)
3. Analyze advantages and disadvantages of widespread use and reliance on technology in the workplace and in society as a whole. (NETS 2)	**SE:** Tech Check (115), Making Connections (126)
4. Demonstrate and advocate for legal and ethical behaviors among peers, family, and community regarding the use of technology and information. (NETS 2)	**SE:** Building Your Portfolio (131)
5. Use technology tools and resources for managing and communicating personal/professional information (e.g. finances, schedules, addresses, purchases, correspondence). (NETS 3, 4)	**SE:** Teamwork Skills (127), Building 21st Century Skills (130)
6. Evaluate technology-based options, including distance and distributed education, for lifelong learning. (NETS 5)	**SE:** Tech Check (115), Building 21st Century Skills (130)
7. Routinely and efficiently use online information resources to meet needs for collaboration, research, publications, communications, and productivity. (NETS 4, 5, 6)	**SE:** Go Online (100, 111), Building 21st Century Skills (130), Building Your Portfolio (131)
8. Select and apply technology tools for research, information analysis, problem-solving, and decision-making in content learning. (NETS 4, 5)	**SE:** You Try It (102, 104, 106, 107, 108, 110, 112, 113, 117, 118, 120, 122), Apply It! (108, 114, 122), Skills Studio (128), Building 21st Century Skills (130), Building Your Portfolio (131)
9. Investigate and apply expert systems, intelligent agents, and simulations in real-world situations. (NETS 3, 5, 6)	**SE:** Quick Write Activity (96), Skills Studio (128), Web Design Projects (129)
10. Collaborate with peers, experts, and others to contribute to content-related knowledge base by using technology to compile, synthesize, produce, and disseminate information, models, and other creative works. (NETS 4, 5, 6)	**SE:** Teamwork Skills (127), Building 21st Century Skills (130)

SCANS Correlation — CHAPTER 4

Foundation Skills

Basic Skills

Reading	SE: Before You Read (97), Focus on Reading (98, 102, 109, 116), Reading Strategies (98, 102, 109, 116), After You Read (124)
Writing	SE: Quick Write Activity (96), Section Assessments (101, 108, 114, 122), Chapter Review (124–129)
Mathematics	SE: Building 21st Century Skills (130)
Listening and Speaking	SE: Teamwork Skills (127)

Thinking Skills

Creative Thinking	SE: Quick Write Activity (96), Building Your Portfolio (131)
Critical Thinking	SE: Critical Thinking (101, 108, 114, 122), Making Connections (127), Teamwork Skills (127), Building 21st Century Skills (130)
Problem Solving	SE: Apply It! (101, 108, 11, 112), Skills Studio (128), Web Design Projects (129-131)

Workplace Competencies

Resources Manage time, money, materials, facilities, human resources	SE: Command Center (125), Building 21st Century Skills (130)
Interpersonal Work on teams, teach others	SE: Teamwork Skills (127), Building 21st Century Skills (130)
Information Acquire, evaluate, organize, maintain, interpret, communicate and use computers to process information	SE: Go Online (100, 111), Tech Check (115), Command Center (125), Making Connections (126), Standards at Work (126), Teamwork Skills (127), Challenge Yourself (127), Skills Studio (128), Web Design Projects (129), Building 21st Century Skills (130), Building Your Portfolio (131)
Systems Understand, monitor, correct, improve, design systems	SE: Web Design Projects (129), Building 21st Century Skills (130), Building Your Portfolio (131)
Technology Select, apply, maintain, and troubleshoot technology.	SE: Go Online (100, 111), You Try It (102, 104, 106, 107, 108, 110, 112, 113), Apply It! (101, 108, 114, 122), Challenge Yourself (127), Skills Studio (128), Web Design Projects (129), Building 21st Century Skills (130), Building Your Portfolio (131)

CHAPTER 4

HTML Basics

(Page 96) ## Objectives

Section 4.1: HTML Coding
- Format HTML tags
- Identify HTML Guidelines

Section 4.2: Using a Text Editor
- Organize Web site files and folder
- Use a text editor
- Use HTML tags and attributes
- Create lists using HTML
- View an HTML document

Section 4.3: Enhancing and Testing Your HTML Page
- Insert images using HTML
- Insert links using HTML
- Debug and test a Web page

Section 4.4: Dreamweaver versus Notepad
- Re-create an existing HTML document in Dreamweaver
- Test a Web page in Dreamweaver

> **LEARNING LINK**
> Chapter 3 showed students how computers give us access to the various resources available on the Internet. Use Chapter 4 to show students how HTML is needed to create these resources, and that knowledge of HTML basics will be helpful to them when they are creating Web pages of their own.

(Page 96) ## Why It Matters

Conduct a brief discussion about the latest improvements in computer programs or games. Encourage students to see that, because computer technology is changing constantly, it will be helpful to them to learn all they can, including the basics of HTML and how to create Web pages.

(Page 96) ## Quick Write Activity

Students might discuss CD players, game playing devices, and cell phones. They will probably not know the internal components of the devices. Suggest that they focus on what they know about the various options that the device offers.

(Page 97) ## Before You Read

Create Memory Tools Developing reliable memory skills was extremely important in the days before paper and printing were common. Mnemonic (nee-MON-c) devices were intended to help remember oral histories. (Mnemosyne was the Greek goddess of memory.) For example, a mnemonic used for remembering the names of the planets in order from the sun is, "My very educated mother just showed us nine planets" (Mercury, Venus, Earth, Mars, Jupiter, Saturn, Uranus, Neptune, Pluto). Ask students to share other mnemonics that they have used successfully to help them remember.

CHAPTER 4

SECTION 4.1 HTML CODING
(Pages 98–101)

FOCUS

Comparing HTML to Other Sets of Rules HTML is a set of rules that must be applied in a particular way in order to be understood by an end user. To drive home the point, and to encourage the students to have fun with it, you may make an analogy to pig Latin. In pig Latin, the rule is to omit the first letter of a word, and add it to the end of the word, along with the letters "ay." "Web" becomes eb-way. In the same way that pig Latin can be applied to encode an existing sentence, HTML can be applied to encode text.

(Page 98)

Focus on Reading

Read to Find Out
Use the Read to Find Out feature to focus student reading. Hold a quick starter discussion to find out what your students already know.

 **Key Terms Online**
Key term definitions and activities are available online at **WebDesignDW.glencoe.com**.

Reading Strategy Answer
Students will be giving an example of each of the four types of tags discussed in the section *HTML Tags* on pages 98–99. Students' examples will vary, but their tables should look similar to this example:

Types of Tags	Example
Starting tag	<STRONG>
Ending tag	</STRONG>
Empty tag	 or <HR> or <IMG>
Nested tag	<P><EM></EM></P>

TEACH

Understanding the Importance of W3C Guidelines To illustrate how differences in encoding rules could lead to problems in understanding, organize the class into two groups. Using the rules that follow, give both groups this sentence to encode: "You can see what occurs if you do not take care to use the proper rules." Group 1's encoding rules are to replace every "o" with a "u," every "t" with an "s," and every "c" with a "d." Group 2's rules are to replace every "us" with an "o," every "t" with an "f," and every "c" with an "m." Then, have the groups give each other the encoded sentence, and work backwards to find the original, using their own code. This will demonstrate how difficult it would be if the same HTML code were not used by everyone.

Unit 1 Fundamentals of Web Design Using Dreamweaver 159

CHAPTER 4

Answers to Section 4.1 Captions and Activities

(Page 98) **Reading Focus** You can create a Web page by inserting HTML tags that tell the Web browser how to display a page's content.

(Page 99) **Figure 4.1** To alter the code, place the tags <STRONG></STRONG> around the italicized word "very" as follows:
<P>It is <STRONG><EM>very</EM></STRONG> important to carefully proofread your <STRONG>HTML</STRONG>code.</P>.

(Page 99) ✓ **Reading Check** Tag sets are pairs of HTML tags; they usually indicate the beginning and end of formatting.

(Page 100) **Reading Focus** It is important to follow W3C specifications because they help ensure that Web designers create pages that can be displayed on any browser or browsing device.

(Page 100) **GO Online** **Activity 4.1** Students can learn more about HTML guidelines and practice with online tutorials at **WebDesignDW.glencoe.com.** Tell students whether you want them to print or e-mail their answers to you. Go Online answers can be found under Teacher Resources on the book Web site.

(Page 100) **Figure 4.2** The text will display as if there were no extra space between the words.

(Page 101) ✓ **Reading Check** The source code allows users to see the HTML tags of any Web page.

ASSESS

(Page 101) ### Section 4.1 Assessment Answers

Reading Summary

Use the Reading Summary to help students review and reinforce the important points of the section.

What Did You Learn?

1. Students' definitions should be in their own words, but based on the information found in the section and in the book's glossary.

2. starting tag (opening tag) – tells Web browser where the specific feature should start
ending tag (closing tag) – tells Web browser where specific feature should end
nested tag – a tag that is enclosed within another set of tags
empty tag – a tag that requires only an opening tag

3. In Dreamweaver you can see the source code by selecting the Code view button in the Document toolbar. Dreamweaver also offers Split view, which allows you to see both the Web page and its source code on the same screen. You can also view either Code or Split by choosing **View>Code** or **View>Code and Design** from the Menu bar.

Critical Thinking

4. Knowing HTML is useful if you need to correct or modify the code used to create your page.

5. An individual must be careful to include all end tags because, if he or she forgets to include an end tag, then the formatting specified by an HTML start tag will continue to the end of the document.

Apply It!

Write HTML Code Students should write the following:

```
<P><STRONG>HTML code</STRONG> allows information to be
displayed in a <EM>Web browser.</EM></P>
```

Understanding HTML Code To review and reinforce the concepts in this section, you may ask the students to write a sentence that includes some italicized words and some words in bold. Then have them exchange sentences with another student and write the HTML code needed to display that sentence. Ask them to identify which of the tags they have written are starting tags, ending tags, and nested tags.

CHAPTER 4

SECTION 4.2 USING A TEXT EDITOR
(Pages 102–108)

FOCUS

Organizing Information Using a text editor requires students to be organized. They must organize files and folders, and also learn to enter HTML tags in an organized way. To illustrate this, take a randomly assorted variety of documents (or pictures), and ask the students to find a particular one. Then, give them an organized set of documents (or pictures) and ask them to find a particular one. Have them compare the experiences to see how being organized will save them effort and frustration.

(Page 102)

Focus on Reading

Read to Find Out
Use the Read to Find Out feature to focus student reading. Hold a quick starter discussion to find out what your students already know.

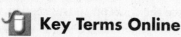
Key Terms Online
Key term definitions and activities are available online at **WebDesignDW.glencoe.com**.

Reading Strategy Answer
Students should compare and contrast ordered and unordered lists using the information found under the heading *Types of Lists* on page 106. Students can also use the HTML Reference Guide found in Appendix B to answer the question.

Ordered List
List items must appear in a certain sequence. Must use a numbered list Use `<OL>` `</OL>`tags.

Both
Use `<LI>` and `</LI>` to begin and end each item in the list.

Unordered List
List items can appear in any order. Can use a bullet list. Use `<UL>` `</UL>`tags.

TEACH

Demonstrating Cause and Effect Create a simple HTML document that contains errors to show students the cause and effect relationship between entering HTML coding improperly and having what appears on the screen be something other than what was intended. You can omit tags or cross them, or enter hexadecimal numbers that are non-existent or incorrect. Ask the students how to change the coding to produce the intended effect.

CHAPTER 4

Answers to Section 4.2 Captions and Activities

(Page 102) **Reading Focus** It is important to organize a Web site's files because it makes it easier to locate files and to add or update HTML information.

(Page 102) **You Try It** **Activity 4A Create Folders to Organize a Site** Students will create a folder and store an image in it. Use the Student Data Files noted in this chapter's Planning Guide.

(Page 102) ✓ **Reading Check** Graphics are stored in a Web site's images folder.

(Page 103) **Reading Focus** The three main parts of an HTML document are the document type definition, the header, and the body.

(Page 103) **Figure 4.3** The <HTML> tag tells the browser to interpret every tag as HTML code until it reaches the closing </HTML> tag.

(Page 104) **You Try It** **Activity 4B Create and Save an HTML Document** Students will create and save an HTML document. Use the Solution Files noted in this chapter's Planning Guide.

(Page 104) ✓ **Reading Check** A DTD specifies what version of HTML is used in a Web page.

(Page 105) **Figure 4.6** The words "grass is greener" would appear in green if the </FONT> tag were moved after the word "greener."

(Page 106) **You Try It** **Activity 4C Add Color and Format Text Using HTML** Students return to the HTML document they created in Activity 4B and add background color and colored headings. Use the Solution Files noted in this chapter's Planning Guide.

(Page 106) ✓ **Reading Check** An attribute is an instruction that further specifies a tag's characteristics.

(Page 106) **Reading Focus** An ordered list displays items that must appear in a particular sequence. An unordered list contains items that can appear in any order.

(Page 106) **Figure 4.7** A bulleted list is an example of an unordered list.

(Page 107) **You Try It** **Activity 4D Create an Unordered List Using HTML** Students create two unordered lists within the document they created in Activity 4B. Use the Solution Files noted in this chapter's Planning Guide.

(Page 107) ✓ **Reading Check** The tags for an ordered list are <OL></OL>. The tags for an unordered list are <UL></UL>.

(Page 108) **Reading Focus** A Web page created in a text editor must be saved as an HTML document and then opened in a browser in order to be viewed.

(Page 108) **You Try It** **Activity 4E View HTML in a Browser** Students view the unordered lists they created in Acitivty 4D in a browser to make sure there are no errors.

(Page 108) ✓ **Reading Check** Web pages created in text editors must be viewed in a browser to make sure the code is accurate and the page is error-free.

Unit 1 Fundamentals of Web Design Using Dreamweaver

CHAPTER 4

ASSESS

(Page 108) Section 4.2 Assessment Answers

Reading Summary

Use the Reading Summary to help students review and reinforce the important points of the section.

What Did You Learn?

1. Students' definitions should be in their own words, but based on the information found in the section and in the book's glossary.

2. Keep file names to eight or fewer characters, since some Web servers cannot recognize longer names. Do not include blank spaces in file names. Use the underscore character in place of a blank space. Use the file name extension .html.

3. Web browsers do not recognize a .txt file name extension, which is the extension automatically assigned to a file when using Notepad.

Critical Thinking

4. Having well-organized files makes it easier to tell a Web browser which file it should access to locate a particular graphic or linked page, and simplifies uploading the site to a Web server.

5. Ordered lists should be used to organize sequential information (such as a recipe), while unordered lists are appropriate for items that can be in any order (such as a list of items to take on a trip).

Apply It!

Create an Ordered List Students create a numbered list of their five favorite books using <OL></OL> tags in Notepad. Students will print out their documents.

CLOSE

Reviewing Section Concepts To test whether the students have begun to integrate the concepts in this section, write several sets of HTML code on the board that specify background color, text color, and text alignments. Ask the students what they would expect to see when viewing the document in a browser. Clarify any misconceptions indicated by the students' answers. Students may be confused about the structure of an HTML document. Re-emphasize the fact that HTML documents only have one header section and one body section. Also emphasize that the page's title is placed in the header section, and that it appears in the Web browser and not on the Web page itself.

CHAPTER 4

SECTION 4.3 ENHANCING AND TESTING YOUR WEB PAGE
(Pages 109–114)

FOCUS

Using Web Page Enhancements Images make Web pages more interesting for readers, and links save readers time if they want more information. To impress the importance of these Web page enhancements, have students read a portion of text that has no graphics. Have them suggest what graphics and links would be interesting and relevant to the text.

(Page 109)

Focus on Reading

Read to Find Out
Use the Read to Find Out feature to focus student reading. Hold a quick starter discussion to find out what your students already know.

 **Key Terms Online**

Key term definitions and activities are available online at **WebDesignDW.glencoe.com**.

Reading Strategy Answer
Students should compare and contrast absolute and relative links using information from the section *Relative versus Absolute Links* on page 111.

Absolute Links	Relative Links
HTML code contains the complete URL or path of the file being linked to.	HTML code contains the name of the file being linked to.
Document being linked to does not have to be in the same folder as document containing link.	Works only if document being linked to is in same folder as document containing link.
External links are often absolute links.	Internal links are often relative links.
If files change location, you need to update the paths in absolute links.	As long as folder structure remains the same, Web browsers will be able to locate files as needed.

TEACH

Comparing Hyperlinks and Absolute/Relative Links Absolute and relative links are a method of writing the HTML coding that tells the browser where an item is located so it can be displayed. Hyperlinks are clicked on to take the user to another place. These terms can be confusing. An image can be written in the code using a relative link to locate where it is displayed, and there can be a `<A href>` hyperlink to allow that image to be clickable in order to take the viewer to another location. But these two items are completely unrelated.

Unit 1   Fundamentals of Web Design Using Dreamweaver   **165**

CHAPTER 4

To illustrate this for students, the code in **bold** on this page are hyperlinks. These hyperlinks can be either text or graphic links. (The ones shown are graphic links.) The sections that are highlighted are the absolute or relative hyperlink samples. For each, the different effect on the page's display and function is indicated.

> **Teaching Tip**
>
> If a page does not work in a browser, suggest that students check the file extensions used for the page and for the page links. Using a combination of .html and .htm extensions may cause some links not to work. When choosing extensions, encourage students to use .html.

This is a graphic link that is relative to another folder location. The reference here does not care what drive letter location the file is in, but only that it is in the listed location. The graphic will work on any drive letter (C: D: W: and so on) and the link will work.

```
<A href="http://www.GoldenEagleCC.com">
<IMG src="web/Student Data Files/screagle.gif" Width="134" height="124"></A>
```

This is the exact same graphic link but with an absolute link. This reference demands that the image be in the G drive only, in this exact folder structure, or it will not show the graphic (but the hyperlink will still work.)

```
<A href="http://www.GoldenEagleCC.com">
<IMG src="G:/web/Student Data Files/screagle.gif" width="134" height="124"></A>
```

This is the exact same graphic link but with a relative link to the image within the exact folder. This reference does not care about drive location or folder structure, and the hyperlink will work.

```
<A href="http://www.GoldenEagleCC.com">
<IMG src="screagle.gif" width="134" height= "124"></A>
```

Answers to Section 4.3 Captions and Activities

(Page 109) **Reading Focus** An image tag tells the computer to locate an image and display it on a Web page in a browser.

(Page 110) **Activity 4F Insert an Image Using HTML** Students take a graphic stored in their Web site's images subfolder and insert it into a document. Use the Solution Files noted in this chapter's Planning Guide. Note that double-clicking the data file name may open the document in the computer's default word processing application, and not in Notepad. Students should open the document in Notepad.

> **Troubleshooting**
>
> Let students know that they are inserting the image file they added to the image folder they created in You Try It activity 4A.

(Page 110) **Reading Check** Five common image tag attributes are `src`, `alt`, `align`, `border`, and `width` and `height`.

(Page 110) **Reading Focus** External, internal, or intrapage hyperlinks can be inserted into a Web page.

(Page 111) **Figure 4.11** In general, graphic links add visual interest to a Web site.

(Page 111) **GO Online** **Activity 4.2** Students who would benefit from additional help with relative and absolute links can find more examples at **WebDesignDW.glencoe.com**.

(Page 112) **You Try It** **Activity 4G Insert Absolute Links Using HTML** Students insert absolute links into their Web page. Use the Solution Files noted in this chapter's Planning Guide.

(Page 112) ✓ **Reading Check** Absolute links contain the complete file or path of the file being linked to. Relative links contain only the name of the file being linked to.

(Page 113) **Reading Focus** It is important to check a Web page to make sure that it displays as designed.

(Page 113) **You Try It** **Activity 4H Test an HTML Document** Students should check their page in several browsers to make sure it displays correctly and links work. They should make any necessary corrections and then retest.

(Page 114) ✓ **Reading Check** Debugging refers to locating and correcting code errors.

> **Teaching Tip**
>
> Students may notice a difference between the MySkills1 site created using HTML and the MySkills2 site created using Dreamweaver. When they insert the image of the border in You Try It activity 4F, it will be aligned left when viewed in a browser. In You Try It activity 4K, the image will be center aligned when it is inserted. Have students add the following coding around the image code: `<P align="center"><IMG....></P>` to center the image.

ASSESS

(Page 114) **Section 4.3 Assessment Answers**

Reading Summary

Use the Reading Summary to help students review and reinforce the important points of the section.

What Did You Learn?

1. Students' definitions should be in their own words, but based on the information found in the section and in the book's glossary.

2. The attributes `src` and `alt` should be used with every `<IMG>` tag. The `src` attribute provides the Web browser information on the name and location of the file, such as its path or URL. The `alt` attribute gives the browser a text message to display if the image is not available.

CHAPTER 4

3. Test a Web site in many different browsers; check to correct any formatting issues including spelling, headings, and images; make certain all links function correctly; and submit your site to an HTML validator in order to check that your code is properly written.

Critical Thinking

4. The HTML command contains a relative link, `<A href="products.html">`. A relative link does not include an entire URL or path name. This file, products.html, would be found at the same folder level as the Web page that references it.

5. Student examples will vary. An absolute link should be used when a Web page includes a link to a different Web site. A relative link is used when linked files are in the same Web site as one another.

Apply It!

Insert an Image Students write the following HTML code:
```
<P align="center"><IMG src= "images/frame.gif" alt= "Frame"></P>
```

CLOSE

Using Relative Links You Try It activity 4G lets students practice inserting absolute links. You can allow students to gain familiarity with relative links by having them create an additional document in the same folder as their Web page, and then inserting a relative link for it. You can also make up a number of examples of relative and absolute links, and ask students to distinguish between the two.

(Page 115)

EMERGING Technology

WEB LANGUAGES

Answers to Tech Check

1. Students should identify current languages, which may include XML, DHTML, XHTML or they may be interested in emerging languages that are still under development. Research can be done on the Internet or print resources such as reference books. (Students should be supervised when using the Internet.) Students may use tables or another type of graphic organizer to compare HTML to at least two other languages. Results may be presented as a written report, a poster, a presentation, or even a multimedia Web page.

2. Students' answers should demonstrate a basic understanding of HTML's capabilities and limitations, and sound critical-thinking skills as they consider ways in which new markup languages "fill the gaps." Encourage students to think of specific examples of technological problems that create a demand for new and better markup languages.

CHAPTER 4

SECTION 4.4 DREAMWEAVER VERSUS NOTEPAD
(Pages 116-122)

FOCUS

Describe Experience with Dreamweaver Some students may have already used Dreamweaver. Generate interest among those who have not by asking students to discuss their experiences with this method of creating a Web page.

(Page 116)

Focus on Reading

Read to Find Out
Use the Read to Find Out feature to focus student reading. Hold a quick starter discussion to find out what your students already know.

 **Key Terms Online**
Key term definitions and activities are available online at **WebDesignDW.glencoe.com**.

Reading Strategy
Students identify the steps involved in testing a Web page found under the heading *Testing a Web Page* on page 122. Students' organizers should look similar to this example:

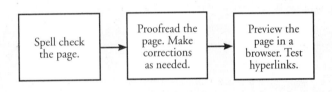

TEACH

Testing a Web Page Using Various Platforms Students should test their pages in more than one browser if possible. It is also beneficial to examine a page on various platforms like Linux and Mac, and using various PCs and even various Windows and IE versions. If any of these options are available to you, test student pages or a page you create on various platforms. If the page displays differently, explain to the students why this occurred.

Unit 1 Fundamentals of Web Design Using Dreamweaver 169

CHAPTER 4

Answers to Section 4.4 Captions and Activities

(Page 116) **Reading Focus** Adding formatting is different in Dreamweaver because it is possible to see approximately how the final page will appear while the user works on it.

(Page 117) **You Try It** **Activity 4I Create and Format a Page in Dreamweaver** Students create an empty Web site and set the background color of a page in that site using Dreamweaver. Use the Solution File noted in this chapter's Planning Guide.

(Page 118) **You Try It** **Activity 4J Add Headings and Unordered Lists in Dreamweaver** Students add headings and unordered bulleted) lists, (using Dreamweaver. Use the Solution File noted in this chapter's Planning Guide.

(Page 119) **Reading Check** To change the background color of a Web page in Dreamweaver, click the Page Properties button on the Properties inspector. In the dialog box that appears, either click the color box to the right of the Background color label or enter a hexadecimal or color name within the input field. Click OK. Save the page.

(Page 120) **Reading Focus** A border enhances a Web site by adding visual interest and separating items on a page.

(Page 120) **You Try It** **Activity 4K Insert a Graphic and Links in Dreamweaver** Students insert graphics and links using Dreamweaver. Use the Student Data File and Solution Files noted in this chapter's Planning Guide.

(Page 121) **Reading Check** A border is a visual break on a Web page.

(Page 122) **Reading Focus** It is important to test a Web page to check for errors or broken links.

(Page 122) **You Try It** **Activity 4L Test a Web Page in Dreamweaver** Students test their Web pages in Dreamweaver. They spell check and proofread, test hyperlinks, and view the page in one or more browsers.

(Page 122) **Reading Check** The Text menu contains the Check Spelling option.

ASSESS

(Page 122) **Section 4.4 Assessment Answers**

Reading Summary

Use the Reading Summary to help students review and reinforce the important points of the section.

What Did You Learn?

1. Students' definitions should be in their own words, but based on the information found in the section and in the book's glossary.

2. Align Left aligns text to the left margin. Align Right aligns text to the right margin. Align Center centers between margins, and Justify aligns text to the left and right margins.

3. To create an unordered list in Dreamweaver, click the Unordered List button on the Properties inspector. Key each item and press Enter to key in the next item. Click the Unordered List button to deselect it when last item has been keyed.

Critical Thinking

4. A hexadecimal number lets you specify a color from a greater variety of colors with a higher degree of precision.

5. Students answers should be in their own words, but they should note that selecting text and entering a link within the Link input field of the Properties inspector creates a hyperlink in Dreamweaver. In Notepad (or other text editor), students must key in all of the anchor tag information as well as the link text. For example:
```
<A href="http://coralvillepubliclibrary.org/">
Coralville Public Libarary<A>
```

Apply It!

Change Colors Students will locate and enter three shades from the hexadecimal equivalent chart into their MySkills2 Web page. They decide which background color looks best and why. Students close the Web page without saving.

CLOSE

Comparing Notepad and Dreamweaver Ask students to compare their experience creating a Web page in Notepad (or other text editor) with their experience creating one in Dreamweaver. Which do they plan to use in the future? Why? Discuss any aspects of each they did not like. If they preferred one experience to the other because of ease of use, remind them that with practice this would change. Those contemplating jobs in Web design would be well advised to be familiar with all methods of creating a Web page.

CHAPTER 4 Answers to Chapter Review

The Chapter Review covers a wide range of student knowledge. Due to time constraints, students may not be able to complete every activity in the Chapter Review. Select the activities that are appropriate for your class needs and resources.

(Page 124) After You Read

Exchange Memory Tools "*SEEN* any HTML tags?" is a memory aid students might use for remembering the four types of HTML tags: **S**tarting tags, **E**nding tags, **E**mpty tags, and **N**ested tags. Let students know that such mnemonics will only work if they are used as memory aids right from the start. Research shows that attempting to attach them later is not as effective.

(Page 124) Reviewing Key Terms

1. `alt` is NOT an HTML tag. It is an attribute.
2. Nested tags are made up of a full set of tags—a starting and ending tag—placed within another set of tags. An empty tag does not have an ending tag.
3. Viewing a Web site's source code refers to looking at the HTML tags that define both the structure and presentation of the page for a Web browser.
4. An attribute can be added to some HTML tags, allowing further refinement of an HTML tag's instructions, such as color, alignment, file source, and so on.
5. The tag sets used to create lists are `<OL></OL>` for ordered lists and `<UL></UL>` for unordered lists.
6. A Web browser uses the anchor tag to create a hyperlink around selected text.
7. Change the sentence to read: When a link statement contains the complete URL of the site being linked to, it will create an absolute link.
8. Testing a Web page involves looking for broken links, missing images, misspellings, grammar errors, as well as making sure the page or site displays normally in a number of available browsers.

(Page 124) Understanding Main Ideas

9. Starting tags define the beginning of a particular HTML tag such as a heading or a paragraph. Ending tags tell the browser where a starting tag ends. It specifies the end of a heading or the end of a paragraph.
10. Having well-organized files makes it easier to add information to your document. When you add graphics and create hyperlinks in an HTML document, you must include instructions that tell the Web browser which file to access and where to find it.
11. A Web browser uses the `<TITLE>` tag to display the Web page's title and refer to that page in bookmarks. The title should be short and descriptive of the Web page, as it will appear in the Web browser's title bar.
12. An ordered list is numbered, indicating list items that must be approached sequentially. An unordered list is bulleted, with list items that may appear in any order.
13. To view a Web page created in a text editor, the file needs to have an .htm or .html extension. Open a Web browser and use the **File>Open** or **File>Open Page** command to locate the file you created. Once located, click **OK**. You can also open a Web browser and drag the HTML file directly into the browser window to view it.

Answers to Chapter Review — CHAPTER 4

14. A Web browser may be unable to display an image, creating a blank space on the page without any explanation. An alt attribute gives the browser alternate text to use in the absence of the image.

15. Answers will vary but should be similar to those shown below:
    - The DTD (Document Type Definition) specifies what version of HTML is used in your page.
    - The `<HEAD>` tag set, or header, provides information to the browser about your page, such as its title and author, as well as keywords used by search engines.
    - The `<BODY>` tag set encloses the code for the content you see displayed in the browser's window.

16. Debugging refers to locating and correcting errors in your Web page as you are building it. Testing involves the formal process of checking your Web pages for completeness and full functionality in a browser before launching it.

Critical Thinking

(Page 124)

17. This statement explains that HTML is used to create most Web pages. HTML codes define a page's structure and elements.

18. Note: Students may use different hexadecimal codes for red and blue.
```
<HTML>
<BODY bgcolor"#99CCFF">
<P>
The American flag is <FONT color="#FF0000">
<STRONG>red</STRONG></FONT>, <FONT
color="#FFFFFF">white</FONT>, and <FONT
color="#0000FF"><STRONG>blue</STRONG></FONT>.
It has <EM>thirteen stripes</EM> and <EM>fifty
stars</EM>.
</P>
</BODY>
</HTML>
```

19. Students will create a two-column table listing the advantages to creating Web pages in either Dreamweaver or Notepad. For example, you do not necessarily need to know HTML to create a Web page in Dreamweaver. Students will then summarize their discoveries in a few sentences.

20. Answers will vary, but students should note the following: If you create a link to an image file that was not stored in the images folder, the browser would typically display a broken image icon on the Web page or an error message indicating the file was missing.

21. Students should use their own words for this answer, however, it should reflect the following: The code used to create a relative link contains the name of the file being linked to. A relative link only works if the document being linked to is in the same Web site folder as the document containing the link. Relative links are useful as internal links because they do not rely on linking to files outside of their file structure or domain name. The code used to create an absolute link contains the complete URL or path of the file being linked to. Absolute links are essential as external links because they are linking to external URLs/files outside of their file structure or domain name.

CHAPTER 4 Answers to Chapter Review

(Page 125) ## Command Center

22. **Shift + >** = Inserts the closing bracket > of an HTML tag.
23. **Shift + <** = Inserts the opening bracket < of an HTML tag.
24. **Ctrl + Shift + S** = Displays the Save As dialog box.

Standardized Test Practice

The correct answer is A. As students review the answer statements, remind them to start with the first HTML tag listed in the table and use the process of elimination to find the answer.

Have students use the book's Web site **WebDesignDW.glencoe.com**.

- **Study with PowerTeach** Encourage your students to use the Chapter 4 PowerTeach Outline to review the chapter before they have a test.
- **Online Self Check** These quick five-question assessments may be used as an in-class activity, a homework assignment, or test review.

(Page 126) ## Making Connections

Social Studies—Perform an Online Search Tim Berners-Lee's work (creating and monitoring the World Wide Web) has changed the world in which we live. Papers should be well organized and use proper grammar and punctuation.

(Page 126) ## Standards at Work

NETS-S 4 Create an HTML Quick Reference Table Students' tables can help them as they create Web pages using HTML. Verify that the examples given are accurate and that opening and closing tags are used as needed. Students can post their work on a classroom bulletin board or, if possible, on the class Web site so that the information is available to a wide audience.

(Page 127) ## Teamwork Skills

Create Web Design Biographies Students create a Web page with biographical information about team members. The same information should be gathered about each team member. The Web page should be well structured and error free. The specifications sheet should match the Web page and should explain all the elements of the page including background color, font color, and placement of rule. Note: some schools restrict a student's name and personal e-mail from being posted online. If that is the case with your school, then omit this information. Students can also collect information but agree not to post it online.

Answers to Chapter Review — CHAPTER 4

(Page 127) **Challenge Yourself**

Create a Table Using HTML Students key the code to create a simple table. They view the results in a browser. Then, students should change the text in the first and third cells (for example, make the text bold or italic), and then view the changes in a browser. Although tables will be covered in more depth later in the book, this activity is designed to help students type HTML code properly and edit code to make changes.

(Page 128) 1. **Create a Home Page Using HTML** A) Students create a Movies_Seen folder. B) Students create an unordered list of movies they have seen. C) Students choose appropriate colors and fonts, and change fonts as needed. D) Students view the page in a browser and make changes as needed. Encourage students to check their changes in a browser. Sometimes one change can have unintended results or create a problem with another part of the page.

2. **Create a Links Page Using HTML** A) Students create a second page that describes more about the movies listed on the home page. B) Students list each movie's title as a heading and type a brief paragraph summarizing each book. They choose appropriate colors for the background and fonts, and change fonts as needed. C) Students add relative links to the links.htm page. D) Students open their work in a browser and test all links, making changes as needed.

(Page 129) 1. **Create a Home Page Using HTML** Students create the home page for the Cross-Cultural Travel Club according to directions. Students can use Dreamweaver as their text editor when creating the page.

2. **Add Pages in Dreamweaver** Students add a meetings page to their Dreamweaver cross-cultural travel site according to directions. Students add links from the home page to the meetings page and external links to a government site for Guatemala (such as **www.guatemala-embassy.org/**) and Taiwan (**www.gio.gov.tw/**).

UNIT 1

(Page 130) BUILDING 21ST CENTURY SKILLS

Project 1 Critical Thinking: Evaluate Technology Resources

Students evaluate the computer needs of a friend, research catalogs on the Web or print catalogs to find products that meet those requirements, prepare a table comparing the resources, and make a recommendation about which computer to buy.

Students should recognize the need for a laptop (notebook) computer that has a fast processing speed, a large hard drive, and can operate in a wireless environment. The friend also wants the assurance of a well-known reliable manufacturer.

If possible, provide catalogs from computer manufacturers such as Dell and Gateway. Also encourage students to research information online. Sites to recommend include **www.dell.com**, **www.gateway.com**, **www.toshibadirect.com**, and **www.panasonic.com**. Encourage students to explore small business computers, not the home products offered at these sites.

Be certain that students use good reasons for their recommendations. Since price is not mentioned as a factor, students might select examples in a variety of price ranges. Reasons may include features available for price, technical support available, warranty offered, reputation of manufacturer, and so on.

Project 2 Use Technology Tools: Create a Web Page Using HTML

Students create a Web page using HTML that includes a page title, a graphic, and an unordered list of three Web sites that they use to research school projects. The list should include a short description of each research site. Descriptions may include what types of subject materials are available, the reliability of information at the site, and the features available to help locate information (table of contents, site map, and so on).

Students select background and font colors that provide good contrast. The graphic may be a border or other Clip Art. Students can search online for free clips. Alternately, you may provide a graphic for students to use. Students will learn more about graphics in Unit 3.

Students proofread and test their page in a browser. The project also recommends a peer review process for Web pages. You may want to provide a checklist or rubric which the reviewer can use. (A sample rubric is provided in Appendix D of the student textbook, or you can search for appropriate rubrics online). Peer reviews help students learn how to critique others' work in a positive way.

UNIT 1

(Page 131) ## BUILDING YOUR PORTFOLIO

The Portfolio projects are ongoing activities that build upon the material in the unit. By the end of the course, the students should have work samples that show every stage of their knowledge development. Explain to students how to save their samples as hard copies, online copies, or personal disks.

Create a Community Web Site

As a class, you may want to brainstorm a list of community and national issues that students could use to build their Web pages. Students should get your final approval of the subject matter before they design the site.

Provide time and resources for students to research the issue, either using library resources or the Internet. If it is a local community issue, students may also conduct interviews with community leaders about the issue. During their research, students should identify links to reliable sources that provide more information about the issue.

Students will use Dreamweaver to create a one-page Web site about the issue. Since space is limited, encourage students to summarize their research in one or two brief paragraphs or short bulleted lists. Students also need to include a list of steps people must take to address the issue, and links to sites with more information. More advanced students might want to add a "Contact Us" link, which links to an e-mail screen.

Since most students' skills in Dreamweaver are limited, focus your evaluation of this site on the quality of the writing, the accuracy of the information, the clarity of the action steps, and the functioning of the hyperlinks.

CAUTION: Using FTP to transfer files to a Web server that has Dreamweaver Server Extensions installed and enabled may disable the extensions. If necessary, please check with your network administrator before publishing sites created in Dreamweaver.

Notes

UNIT 2
Designing Web Sites

(Page 132)

Visit *Glencoe Online*

Introduce students to the resources that are available online at **WebDesignDW.glencoe.com**. Have students select **Unit Activities > Unit 2 Internet Research Tips.** Students can practice skills and strategies that will help them quickly find information on the Internet.

Students can complete this four-question activity to practice searching the Internet using Google or another search engine of your choice. Point out the use of quotes to yield more precise search results. You can also have students practice using the Boolean operators AND, OR, and NOT to further refine searches. Using the special Google searches for images, news, groups, and other features can also help narrow the search field.

Complete answers to each Unit Activity are available on the book Web site, in the password-protected Teacher Center portion of the site.

(Page 133)

Think About It

Student answers will vary. Students will identify the two tasks they have enjoyed the most during the course, and the two tasks they have enjoyed the least. They will then analyze these tasks to see what all four have in common. The goal of the exercise is to help students identify their own strengths and weaknesses as Web designers. Identifying their strengths will encourage students to continue developing these skills and to share their abilities with others in the class. Identifying their weaknesses will help students focus on what they need to learn and encourage them to seek extra assistance and practice to improve these skills.

CHAPTER 5 Planning Guide

Student Edition	Activities and Exercises
Chapter 5 Planning a Web Site (pages 134–159)	Quick Write Activity, page 134 Before You Read, page 135
Section 5.1 Creating a Mission Statement (pages 136–139)	▫ Reading Strategy, page 136 ♪ You Try It Activity 5A: Create a Mission Statement, page 139
Section 5.2 Navigation Schemes (pages 140–145)	▫ Reading Strategy, page 140 ⓘ Go Online Activity 5.1: Explore Navigation Schemes, page 140 ♪⊙ You Try It Activity 5B: View a Web Site in Map View, page 143
Section 5.3 Storyboarding Your Site (pages 146–151)	▫ Reading Strategy, page 146 ⓘ Go Online Activity 5.2: Storyboarding a Web Site, page 146 ♪ You Try It Activity 5C: Chart Navigation Structure, page 147 ♪ You Try It Activity 5D: Specify File Names, page 149 ♪ You Try It Activity 5E: Sketch a Web Page, page 150
Careers & Technology Developing Web Content (page 152)	Tech Check, page 152
Chapter 5 Review (pages 153–159)	▫ Making Connections: Social Studies–Create a Time Line ▫ Standards at Work: Analyze Web Sites (NETS-S 5) Teamwork Skills: Create A Storyboard ▫ Challenge Yourself: Plan a Web Site You Try It Skills Studio: —Create a Mission Statement —Plan a Web Site Web Design Projects: —Create a Storyboard —Create Sketches ⊙ⓘ Additional Activities You May Wish to Use: —PowerTeach Outlines Chapter 5 —Student Workbook Chapter 5

Planning Guide — CHAPTER 5

Activities and Exercises

Section 5.1 Assessment, page 139

Section 5.2 Assessment, page 145

Section 5.3 Assessment, page 151

Chapter 5 Review and Assessment, page 153
You may also use any of the Chapter Review Activities and Projects Assessments.
ⓘ Additional Assessments You May Wish to Use:
— Self-Check Assessments Chapter 5
— *ExamView* Testbank Chapter 5

Estimated Time to Complete Chapter

18 week course = 5 days
36 week course = 10 days

To help customize lesson plans, use the Pacing Guide on pages 26–30 and the Standards Charts on pages 182–183.

Key to Recommended Materials

Icons represent elements that may require additional resources.

📄 Focus on Reading

ⓘ Internet access required

𝒅 Software: Dreamweaver

⊙ Teacher Resource CD (contains Student Data Files, Solution Files, Reproducible Graphic Organizers, and Study with PowerTeach Outlines)

Data and Solution Files for Chapter 5

DataFiles
◆ MusicDept

SolutionFiles
◆ No Solution Files for this chapter.

Inclusion Strategies

For **Differentiated Instruction Strategies** refer to the **Inclusion in the Computer Technology Classroom** booklet.

CHAPTER 5 — NETS Correlation For Students

ISTE NETS Foundation Standards

1. Basic operations and concepts
2. Social, ethical, and human issues
3. Technology productivity tools
4. Technology communications tools
5. Technology research tools
6. Technology problem-solving and decision-making tools

Performance Indicators	Textbook Correlation
1. Identify capabilities and limitations of contemporary and emerging technology resources and assess the potential of these systems and services to address personal, lifelong learning, and workplace needs. (NETS 2)	**SE:** Critical Thinking (139, 145, 154)
2. Make informed choices among technology systems, resources, and services. (NETS 1, 2)	**SE:** Critical Thinking (145, 151, 154), Apply It! (151)
3. Analyze advantages and disadvantages of widespread use and reliance on technology in the workplace and in society as a whole. (NETS 2)	**SE:** Tech Check (152)
4. Demonstrate and advocate for legal and ethical behaviors among peers, family, and community regarding the use of technology and information. (NETS 2)	
5. Use technology tools and resources for managing and communicating personal/professional information (e.g. finances, schedules, addresses, purchases, correspondence). (NETS 3, 4)	**SE:** Quick Write Activity (134), Tech Check (152)
6. Evaluate technology-based options, including distance and distributed education, for lifelong learning. (NETS 5)	**SE:** Go Online (140, 146)
7. Routinely and efficiently use online information resources to meet needs for collaboration, research, publications, communications, and productivity. (NETS 4, 5, 6)	**SE:** Go Online (140, 146), Tech Check (152), Standards at Work (156), Web Design Projects (159)
8. Select and apply technology tools for research, information analysis, problem-solving, and decision-making in content learning. (NETS 4, 5)	**SE:** Go Online (140, 146), You Try It (143), Tech Check (152), Standards at Work (156)
9. Investigate and apply expert systems, intelligent agents, and simulations in real-world situations. (NETS 3, 5, 6)	**SE:** You Try It (139, 147), Apply It! (145), Challenge Yourself (157), Web Design Projects (159)
10. Collaborate with peers, experts, and others to contribute to content-related knowledge base by using technology to compile, synthesize, produce, and disseminate information, models, and other creative works. (NETS 4, 5, 6)	**SE:** Teamwork Skills (157)

SCANS Correlation — CHAPTER 5

Foundation Skills

Basic Skills

Reading	**SE:** Before You Read (135), Focus on Reading (136, 140, 146), Reading Strategies (136, 140, 146), After You Read (154), Standardized Test Practice (155)
Writing	**SE:** Quick Write Activity (134), You Try It (139), Section Assessments (139, 145, 151), Tech Check (152), Chapter Review (154–159)
Mathematics	**SE:** Apply It! (145), Challenge Yourself (157)
Listening and Speaking	**SE:** Teamwork Skills (157)

Thinking Skills

Creative Thinking	**SE:** Think About It (133), Quick Write Activity (134)
Critical Thinking	**SE:** Critical Thinking Activities (139, 145, 151), Standards at Work (156), Teamwork Skills (157), Challenge Yourself (157), Web Design Projects (159)
Problem Solving	**SE:** Teamwork Skills (157), Challenge Yourself (157), Skills Studio (158), Web Design Projects (159)

Workplace Competencies

Resources Manage time, money, materials, facilities, human resources	**SE:** Quick Write Activity (134), Tech Check (152), Command Center (155)
Interpersonal Work on teams, teach others	**SE:** Teamwork Skills (157)
Information Acquire, evaluate, organize, maintain, interpret, communicate and use computers to process information	**SE:** You Try It (139, 143, 147, 149, 150), Apply It! (139, 151), Go Online (140, 146), Command Center (155), Making Connections (156), Standards at Work (156), Teamwork Skills (157), Challenge Yourself (157), Skills Studio (158), Web Design Projects (159)
Systems Understand, monitor, correct, improve, design systems	**SE:** Apply It! (145), You Try It (150), Making Connections (156), Teamwork Skills (157), Challenge Yourself (157), Skills Studio (158), Web Design Projects (159)
Technology Select, apply, maintain, and troubleshoot technology.	**SE:** Go Online (140, 146), You Try It (143)

CHAPTER 5

Web Basics

(Page 134) **Objectives**

Section 5.1: Creating a Mission Statement
- Determine the purpose of your Web site
- Define the target audience for your Web site
- Write a mission statement

Section 5.2: Navigation Schemes
- Describe three types of navigation schemes
- State the advantages and disadvantages of each scheme
- Choose the appropriate navigation scheme for a particular site

Section 5.3: Storyboarding Your Site
- Discuss the advantages of storyboarding a site
- Draw the navigation structure of a site
- Create sketches of a site's pages

> **LEARNING LINK**
>
> Chapter 4 showed students how HTML is needed to create resources available on the Internet, and that knowledge of HTML basics will help them when they are creating Web pages of their own. Now that students understand the basics of creating a Web page, see Chapter 5 to encourage students to see the benefits of planning their Web sites before they actually create them.

(Page 134) **Why It Matters**

Ask students if they have ever had an experience in which doing an activity without planning it first has led to either a poor result (such as a poor grade on a report or getting lost trying to find a place without directions) or the need to go back and do the activity over. Encourage them to see that planning can save them time and can be critical in having their message understood by their audience.

(Page 134) **Quick Write Activity**

Ask your students to write a paragraph about an issue that is important to them (a bigger allowance, the need for a car, an unpopular school policy, and so on). After they have finished, ask them with whom they would speak to change the situation and what points they would need to make to achieve the desired change. Are these considerations addressed in their paragraphs? Probably not. Explain that before starting any project students should know what they hope to accomplish.

(Page 135) **Before You Read**

Reading for a Purpose Encourage students to break their assigned reading into sections or chunks that are comfortable for them. Too often students try to sit down and read a chapter at one sitting. Before they read, have students write down their own purpose for reading. If they set the goals, they are more likely to recognize when they have or have not met those goals. Be sure that students understand that their defined purpose should not be "to pass the course" or "to get good grades." The purpose needs to be a specific, measurable objective, such as "to plan an effective Web site."

CHAPTER 5

SECTION 5.1 CREATING A MISSION STATEMENT
(Pages 136–139)

FOCUS

Comparing Effectiveness in Commercials Ask students to describe "good" and "bad" commercials they have seen on television. What did they like about the good ones? What did they dislike about the bad ones? Select an ad that students thought would encourage them to purchase the product. Explain that, like ads, Web sites should have a clear purpose and target a certain audience to be effective.

(Page 136)

Focus on Reading

Read to Find Out
Use the Read to Find Out feature to focus student reading. Hold a quick starter discussion to find out what your students already know.

 Key Terms Online
Key term definitions and activities are available online at **WebDesignDW.glencoe.com**.

Reading Strategy Answer
In this activity, students will be identifying the steps in planning a Web site. This information can be determined from the main headings in the section. Students' flowcharts should look similar to this example:

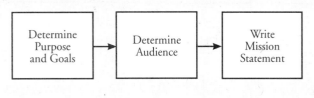

TEACH

Understanding the Target Audience Use the two following paragraphs (or come up with your own) to illustrate how to meet the needs of different audiences. The first paragraph is written like a press release for consumers:

ToughTread, Inc. is committed to offering our customers safe, high-quality tires. Because of recent concerns, we are voluntarily recalling our TS110 model tires and replacing them, free of charge, with our TX440 model tires. The TX440 is a superior grade tire with an unblemished performance record.

This is the same subject written for a shareholder report:

The recent problem with our TS110 tires required prompt action to restore consumer confidence. Therefore, the company voluntarily recalled all TS110 model tires and replaced them with TX440 tires, at a cost of less than twenty million dollars.

Discuss the differences and why they exist. See if students can identify other information that each audience might want. (For example, consumers might want to know where to go to get their free tires, or a number to call if they have questions.)

CHAPTER 5

Answers to Section 5.1 Captions and Activities

(Page 136) **Reading Focus** Possible goals of a Web site are to inform, entertain, serve as a Web portal, address a particular group of people, provide a personality profile, or fill another purpose such as sell a product or service.

(Page 136) ✓ **Reading Check** It is important to define a Web site's purpose because the goals of the Web site serve to define that purpose.

(Page 137) **Reading Focus** The best way to determine a Web site's audience is to answer a series of questions designed to narrow down a demographic. (see Table 5.1)

(Page 137) **Table 5.1** It is important to consider how people will access your site because if your target audience uses dial-up connections, you would want to avoid complex graphics that increase download time.

(Page 137) ✓ **Reading Check** It is important to identify a site's target audience in order to determine the tone, or look and feel, of a site.

(Page 138) **Reading Focus** A mission statement helps the Web designer determine what content is essential to a site.

(Page 138) **Figure 5.1** The mission statement would encourage other schools to participate in contests. The focus would be on promoting advantages of competition.

(Page 139) **You Try It** **Activity 5A Create a Mission Statement** Students use provided information to create a short mission statement. One example might be: The Language Club is aimed at high school students interested in foreign languages. It will include a range of topics, for all levels of knowledge, and also display a calendar showing meetings and events.

(Page 139) ✓ **Reading Check** A mission statement works to remind the Web designer of the purpose of the site during the creation process.

ASSESS

(Page 139) **Section 5.1 Assessment Answers**

Reading Summary

Use the Reading Summary to help students review and reinforce the important points of the section.

What Did You Learn?

1. Students' definitions should be in their own words, but based on the information found in the section and in the book's glossary.
2. If a student's chosen topic is too broad or lacks focus, narrowing that topic will make the site's goal more achievable.
3. Students should know who their target audience is, what that audience already knows about the site's topic, what that audience wants to find out, and how that audience will access the site.

Critical Thinking

4. Student analyses will vary. The site's long-term goals will expand on the immediate goals to encompass the additional knowledge, skills, and requirements of its audience as time goes on.
5. Student answers will vary. A clothing Web site for very young children would be more picture-based and have information for parents. A Web site aimed at teenagers might have more popular jargon and phrases, and might try to construct a "lifestyle" around the clothes that would appeal to teens.

Apply It!

Write a Mission Statement Students will write a mission statement and describe a target audience and site purpose for a Web page about one of their hobbies. Students' audiences and purposes will vary, but should reflect the goals outlined in their mission statements.

Reviewing Chapter Concepts To reinforce the concepts in this section, have students imagine they are creating a Web site to sell their favorite product. Ask for suggestions (like favorite snacks, music, and cars, among others) then choose two or three products that might appeal to different target audiences and lead to different mission statements. Have students identify the purpose of each site and its target audience. Ask them to create a mission statement for each site. In addition, you can change the purpose and ask students how this leads to changes in the mission statement. For example, if the product is a skateboard, the initial site's purpose might be to sell the product, but how might the mission statement change if a page were added about skateboard safety? You might also want to note that mission statements are used to plan a site, but are usually not placed in the actual text of the site itself.

CHAPTER 5

SECTION 5.2 NAVIGATION SCHEMES
(Pages 140–145)

FOCUS

Navigating a Web Site Have the students name some of their favorite Web sites. Go online and visit some of these sites. Let the students note what kind of pages are in the site and how they get to those pages (from a line on the home page, from a different page, and so on). Tell them that after they have finished this section, they will be able to explain the navigation scheme of the site as a Web designer would. (Note: After finishing this section, have them explain the navigation scheme.)

(Page 140)

Focus on Reading

Read to Find Out
Use the Read to Find Out feature to focus student reading. Hold a quick starter discussion to find out what your students already know.

 Key Terms Online
Key term definitions and activities are available online at **WebDesignDW.glencoe.com**.

Reading Strategy Answer
Students should compare and contrast characteristics of hierarchical and linear navigation using information found under the headings *Hierarchical Navigation Scheme* and *Linear Navigation Scheme* on pages 141–142. The students' diagrams should look similar to this example:

Hierarchical
Pages arranged on levels with parent-child relationships; users can choose order to view pages according to their interest

Home page located at topmost, or first, level; used by professional Web designers

Linear
All ages on same level; each page accessed from last page and linked to next; user must navigate one page at a time in a specific order

TEACH

Evaluating Navigation Schemes In your experience using the Internet, you have probably found some sites easier to navigate than others. Use this experience to show students the importance of a good navigation scheme. Visit at least one site that, in your opinion, is easy to navigate, and one that is difficult. Ask students why the less effective one is hard to navigate, and how it could be improved. If possible, have the class create a new navigation scheme for that site.

CHAPTER 5

Answers to Section 5.2 Captions and Activities

(Page 140) **Reading Focus** When choosing a navigation scheme, it is important to consider how visitors will interact with a site.

(Page 140) **Activity 5.1** More information about navigation schemes is available at **WebDesignDW.glencoe.com**.

(Page 141) **Figure 5.2** The site's home page is at the top-most level.

(Page 142) **Figure 5.3** They will enter the site at the home page.

(Page 142) **Reading Check** The three different types of navigation schemes are hierarchical, linear, and random-access.

(Page 143) **Reading Focus** Use the Map view function to view a navigation scheme in Dreamweaver.

(Page 143) **Activity 5B View a Web Site in Map View** Students use Dreamweaver to view the navigation structure of a Web site. They also view the subtree of the Performances page. Use the Student Data Files noted in this chapter's Planning Guide.

(Page 145) **Reading Check** The Music Department uses a hierarchical navigation scheme.

ASSESS

(Page 145) ### Section 5.2 Assessment Answers

Reading Summary

Use the Reading Summary to help students review and reinforce the important points of the section.

What Did You Learn?

1. Students' definitions should be in their own words, but based on the information found in the section and in the book's glossary.

2. Consider what kind of information is presented on the site and how the audience will want to access that information.

Critical Thinking

3. A Web page may be both a parent and a child page. If a page is linked to a preceding page on a level above it, it is a child page. If the same page is also linked to a page one level down, it is that page's parent.

4. Both hierarchical and linear navigation schemes start at the home page level. The hierarchical site then branches off to many levels while the linear site's pages remain on one level. A hierarchical site's pages may be accessed in the user's preferred order, whereas the linear navigation scheme requires the user to access the pages in a specific order.

Unit 2 Designing Web Sites **189**

CHAPTER 5

Apply It!

Create a Hierarchical Chart The hierarchical structure is best represented as an upside-down tree. The main level, or "Movies I Have Seen" home page, should be placed at the top of the chart. The second level contains two pages: "Action-Adventure" and "Comedy." The "Action-Adventure" has four child pages (each page contains one action-adventure movie title). The "Comedy" page has three child pages (each page contains one comedy movie title). Students are asked to include all seven movie titles in their chart.

CLOSE

Analyzing Types of Navigation Schemes Ask students to imagine they are creating a Web site that will consist of multiple pages. The site can be about themselves, a celebrity, or any topic of interest to them, but it should have at least eight pages. Have students decide what the pages would be, and then analyze whether it would be best to use a hierarchical or linear navigation scheme in designing the site. Ask them to explain their decision and to create a chart showing the navigation scheme they have selected.

CHAPTER 5

SECTION 5.3 STORYBOARDING YOUR SITE
(Pages 146–151)

FOCUS

Create a Storyboard Create a storyboard as a class. Tell students to imagine they are directing a short film. Have them come up with a very simple story. (For example, a student who is always late to school learns to run fast and becomes an Olympic track star.) Have them first decide on the proper navigation scheme for that movie (i.e. linear). Then, ask them to suggest the first five scenes in sequential order, that begin to develop the story. (You need not finish it!) Draw simple sketches of the scenes. (Students may have difficulty creating sketches, so you may want to model a sketch so they know what elements to include.) Ask how this compares to Web site storyboarding. Students should understand that in a Web site, the navigation scheme may be linear or hierarchical and the "scenes" are equivalent to the Web site's pages. And just as they decided the general content of each scene, they must decide the general content of each page of their site.

(Page 146)

Focus on Reading

Read To Find Out
Use the Read to Find Out feature to focus student reading. Hold a quick starter discussion to find out what your students already know.

 Key Terms Online
Key term definitions and activities are available online at **WebDesignDW.glencoe.com**.

Reading Strategy Answer
Students can find facts about the two storyboarding processes under the headings *Storyboarding, Drawing a Site's Navigation Structure,* and *Creating Sketches of Individual Pages* on pages 146–149.

```
                    Storyboarding
                    /           \
```

Draw a site's navigation structure— Determine what kind and how many pages (in general) your site will contain. Choose either a linear or hierarchical scheme depending on how your audience needs to access the site's information. Create the particular structure of your site.	Create a brief summary of page content— For each page, create a sketch identifying basic text and graphics plus an idea for placement of these elements.

TEACH

Identifying Storyboarding Problems Create a brief mission statement. Then create a storyboard for it and intentionally insert elements that will create problems. These may include not fulfilling the mission statement, using page names that are nondescriptive and/or confusing, using graphics that are irrelevant or uninteresting, and so on. See if the students can identify and explain all the potential problems with the Web site. If not, describe and explain the problems, and offer ways to correct them.

CHAPTER 5

Answers to Section 5.3 Captions and Activities

(Page 146) **Reading Focus** Storyboarding helps Web designers avoid mistakes by providing a visual of a site and giving an overall idea of the content of the site.

(Page 146) **Go Online** **Activity 5.2** You may have students gain additional experience with various storyboarding methods by having them visit **WebDesignDW.glencoe.com**.

(Page 146) ✓ **Reading Check** Three different ways to approach storyboarding are with formal drawing tools, presentation software, and a paper and pencil.

(Page 147) **Table 5.3** The Language Club and Events pages will likely be parent pages.

(Page 147) **Reading Focus** Charting a Web site's structure helps the designer to organize the basic pages a Web site will contain.

(Page 147) **You Try It** **Activity 5C Chart Navigation Structure** Students create a hierarchical navigation scheme for the Language Club Web site.

(Page 148) **Table 5.4** The page name, also called the page title, is the name you choose to display on the browser's title bar. The file name is the name you choose to save your page as and can be an .html (or .htm) document.

(Page 149) **You Try It** **Activity 5D Specify File Names** Students create a hierarchical navigation scheme for the Language Club Web site.

(Page 149) ✓ **Reading Check** A file name is the name of the HTML document that makes up the Web page itself.

(Page 149) **Reading Focus** A sketch helps a Web designer ensure that all the goals of the Web site are met, provide guidelines for developing Web page content, and is useful for creating the page template.

(Page 150) **You Try It** **Activity 5E Sketch a Web Page** Students create a simple drawing of the About Us page of the Language Club Web site, identify text and graphics they plan to use, and determine the placement of these elements. Then they create a second sketch for the same page, with the same content, but different placement of the elements. They compare and evaluate sketches, and explain the placement they chose.

(Page 150) ✓ **Reading Check** The different elements of the page, including the content and graphics, should be included in a Web page sketch.

(Page 150) **Reading Focus** A checklist helps to plan a Web site because it is a way to keep track of all the planning tasks.

(Page 151) **Figure 5.12** Planning results in a clearly stated purpose and audience for a Web site, as well as a mission statement. This makes it more likely that any potential problems will be identified at this stage, before storyboarding begins.

(Page 151) ✓ **Reading Check** It is important to follow all the planning steps to help identify any potential problems before the site is actually built.

CHAPTER 5

ASSESS

(Page 151) Section 5.3 Assessment Answers

Reading Summary
Use the Reading Summary to help students review and reinforce the important points of the section.

What Did You Learn?
1. Students' definitions should be in their own words, but based on the information found in the section and in the book's glossary.
2. Storyboarding helps you visualize the basic structure of your Web site, illustrates how pages will be linked, and provides a brief look at the contents of each page.
3. A Web page sketch should identify the text and graphics you plan to use, and how you plan to place these elements on the page. These items provide an overview to your Web site, and allow you to determine whether the text and graphics will work together, and whether the site is set up in a logical way.

Critical Thinking
4. Students' answers will vary. The advantage in a particular navigation scheme lies in how the site's designer wants visitors to access information. For example, if information must be accessed sequentially, then a linear scheme works best. If, however, information should be accessed by interest or topic, then a hierarchical scheme might work best.
5. Students' conclusions will vary but should reflect an understanding of the section material. Problems to be avoided include unclear site goals or purpose, information that is inappropriate for the target audience, and an inefficient navigation scheme for the site (making it difficult to access the information desired).

Apply It!
Create a File Name List Students will choose various file names, but the table should be organized similarly to the one below. Students' file names should not include spaces, should be reasonably short, and end with an .html extension.

Page Name	File Name (examples—students' will vary)
Welcome to the Music Department	home.html
Band	band.html
Choir	choir.html
Performances	performances.html
Contact Us	contact_us.html

Unit 2 Designing Web Sites **193**

CHAPTER 5

CLOSE

Planning a Web Site Have students work in small groups and use the steps found in Web Site Planning Checklist on page 151 of the student textbook to plan a Web site of their choosing. They should produce a brief mission statement (clearly indicating the site's purpose, goals, and audience), a chart showing the navigation scheme, including each page's title and file name, and a sketch of the three most important pages of the site. Have them exchange these items with those of another group and get feedback from their peers (who can use the same list as a rubric).

(Page 152)

Careers & Technology

DEVELOPING WEB CONTENT

Answers to Tech Check

1. Students should be supervised when searching for Web sites. They should look for sites that use heavy text or graphic content, such as educational, e-commerce, and informational sites. Large organizations often post job openings on their sites. Even if a student is not particularly interested in this field, have him or her think about the education, training, and experience they might want on a résumé targeted to this type of position. Résumés may be created with word processing, desktop publishing or Web authoring software. They can be published as print documents or Web pages.

2. Students should examine different types of Web sites including informational, educational, commercial, etc. They should look at elements that might require specific content providers such as writers, instructional designers, artists, videographers, etc. The essay should identify the content, discuss the probable provider, and describe why particular content is important for a specific kind of site. Students may also have the option of creating a chart that compares the content elements of the Web sites.

Answers to Chapter Review — CHAPTER 5

The Chapter Review covers a wide range of student knowledge. Due to time constraints, students may not be able to complete every activity in the Chapter Review. Select the activities that are appropriate for your class needs and resources.

(Page 154) After You Read

Review the Purpose In order for "reading for a purpose" to be effective, students should write down their goals (or at least re-read them) just before reading the particular section. The brain is not designed for 'nonstop' learning. The whole point of this activity is to show students how setting discrete measurable goals and purposes aids in comprehension and retention.

(Page 154) Reviewing Key Terms

1. A mission statement is a brief statement that describes the purpose and audience of a Web site.
2. A target audience is all the people that you want to visit your Web site.
3. An oval is NOT a type of navigation scheme.
4. A top-level page is the highest page or level in a Web site's structure. It is typically the home page.
5. Each child page can only have a single parent, whereas a parent page can have many child pages.
6. Two or more child pages with the same parent have a peer-to-peer relationship, also called a "sibling" relationship.
7. The two main items created would be the navigation structure for the site and a brief summary of each page's content.

(Page 154) Understanding Main Ideas

8. Immediate and long-term goals of a Web site are similar in that the long-term goals contain the same information and basic purpose of the initial site design. Long-term goals differ from the immediate goals in that the goals of the Web site have expanded.
9. Understanding what your audience knows helps you determine a Web site's scope—the depth of information to provide the site's audience.
10. A linear navigation scheme does not include navigation to various levels as a hierarchical scheme does.
11. Creating sketches: (1) helps make sure that all the goals of the Web site are met, (2) provides guidelines when it comes time to develop Web page content, and (3) is useful when it comes time to create the template to be used for the pages.
12. The Web site planning checklist can help designers determine whether they have completed every step in the planning process.
13. The page name is the name you choose to display on the browser's title bar and should make sense to the user. The file name is the relatively short name you choose to save your page as an .html document.
14. The advantages of a hierarchical scheme are that visitors can get a site overview quickly by examining the home page; visitors can go directly to the pages that interest them and skip the pages that do not interest them; the freedom to "click around" prevents visitors from becoming overwhelmed by information they do not want; and visitors can keep track of where they are on the site.

CHAPTER 5 Answers to Chapter Review

(Page 154) ## Critical Thinking

15. Students should specify that a linear navigation scheme would work best for a slide show. In a linear navigation scheme, every page exists at the same level. Each Web page in this scheme is accessed from the previous page and then is linked to the next page. Linear navigation schemes are the best choice when pages need to be viewed in a certain order, such as a slide show, story, or step-by-step directions.

16. Students' answers should reflect the following information: Removing the Events page from the Language Club Web site and linking all the pages below it would cause confusion to visitors. The subpages that were under Events would now be linked under the Home page and would therefore have no context. While changing the navigation scheme this way would provide quicker access to these pages that were formerly two levels below the home page, it would cause frustration and may end up driving visitors away.

17. A drawing of a hierarchical scheme is called a tree diagram because it looks like an upside down tree with the home page being the trunk of the tree, and subsequent pages creating its branches. These branches can have branches of their own as well.

18. Students' suggestions will vary but should supply specific examples to accompany those suggestions. For example, the site could create specific areas within the navigation scheme for each type of audience. Other suggestions can include creating a Web site that is accessible to as wide as an audience as possible; providing introductory information about topics rather than in-depth information; creating a Web site that loads into a browser quickly and does not need plug-ins; designing a site that appeals to visitors and regular users alike while keeping the navigation intuitive and easy to use; and providing topics and information that a wide-ranging age group can relate to.

19. To make the About Us page a parent page, the existing home page would have to be moved below About Us to form a hierarchical relationship. Navigation on the About Us page would have to be modified to show the new relationship.

(Page 155) ## Command Center

20. **F8** = View only a site's file structure
21. **Ctrl + Shift + T** = View page titles in a site map
22. **Alt + F8** = View site map and file structure

Standardized Test Practice

The correct answer is C. As students review the paragraph about Web site navigation schemes and each answer statement, remind them to use the process of elimination to find the answer.

Answers to Chapter Review CHAPTER 5

Have students use the book's Web site **WebDesignDW.glencoe.com**.

- **Study with PowerTeach** Encourage your students to use the Chapter 5 PowerTeach Outline to review the chapter before they have a test.
- **Online Self Check** These quick five-question assessments may be used as an in-class activity, a homework assignment, or test review.

(Page 156) ## Making Connections

Social Studies—Create a Time Line Students' time lines will include the dates the printing press was invented and when the Internet was invented, as well as at least three other significant dates in the history of communications (a third date should be when the Web was invented). Note that students may give slightly different dates for events depending on their sources. Encourage students to use only reliable sources such as encyclopedias, government and education Web sites, and so on. Students use their information to create a storyboard with a linear navigation scheme.

(Page 156) ## Standards at Work

NETS-S 5 Analyze Web Sites Students' charts should adequately compare and contrast the two sites. Their analysis should include the sites' purpose, goals, target audience, content, and navigation scheme. Students are asked to use two sites that, though they are in the same category, are very different from each other. For example, two educational sites could be very different if one is intended as a tool for college students, while the other is designed for use by middle school students. For a list of suggested URLs, see the chart in Chapter 1, page 97.

Students' tables may look similar to the one below:

Criteria	www.landsend.com	www.travelocty.com
Category	Commercial	Commercial
Purpose	To sell clothes and home goods	To sell travel-related goods and services
Goal	To increase sales and revenue	To increase sales and revenue
Target Audience	Adults and families	Adults
Target Audience Need	Clothes and home goods	Plane tickets, hotel rooms, rental cars, etc.
Content Readability	Good	Good
Navigation Scheme	Hierarchical	Hierarchical

CHAPTER 5 Answers to Chapter Review

(Page 157) ## Teamwork Skills

Create a Storyboard Groups should present their storyboards for the Services for Seniors Web site to the class. The storyboards should show the navigation scheme and all planned pages with page titles and file names. Have students share their site's mission statement and site goals with the class. Encourage students to compare the results of the various groups and discuss which items will be most useful and most accessible to senior citizens in your community.

(Page 157) ## Challenge Yourself

Plan a Web Site Students' storyboards must contain 20 pages arranged in a hierarchical navigation scheme. The navigation scheme for the aquarium Web site must have four levels of pages that highlight its many activities and exhibitions.

A suggested organization is as follows:

- The home page at the top-most level
- Second level pages for general information, types of exhibitions, special attractions, and information about the aquarium gift shop
- Third level pages that offer more information about specific exhibitions, special attractions, and merchandise available at the gift shop
- Fourth level that allows purchase of gift shop items

Encourage students to share their storyboards and sketches with the class.

Answers to Chapter Review — CHAPTER 5

(Page 158) 1. **Create a Mission Statement** Students create a mission statement for a group, organization, or club to which they belong. You may need to assign an organization to any students who do not participate in organized activities outside the classroom (e.g., "Students for Better Cafeteria Food"). Students also analyze their target audience. Students should recognize the characteristics that all members of the target group have in common.

2. **Plan a Web Site** Students create a storyboard for the group that they wrote a mission statement for in You Try It Skills Studio 1 (you may want to set a minimum and maximum number of pages for the site). The storyboard should indicate navigation structure, page names, and file names. Students also create a sketch of two pages for the site. The storyboard and sketches should have a clear connection to the mission statement.

Web Design Projects

(Page 159) 1. **Create a Storyboard** Groups should present their storyboards to the class. The storyboards show the navigation scheme and all planned pages with page titles and file names. Encourage students to compare the results of the various groups and discuss which items will be most useful and most accessible to fans of the band.

2. **Create Sketches** Students create sketches for the photo gallery page and the first two locations pages. Students should include links to the San Francisco and Grand Canyon photo galleries on the locations pages, and a link to the locations pages on the photo gallery page. Suggest to students that they also may want to include links to Web pages that tell more about both locations, such as **http://www.sfvisitor.org/** and **http://www.nps.gov/grca**.

CHAPTER 6 Planning Guide

Student Edition	Activities and Exercises
Chapter 6 Developing Content and Layout (pages 160–189)	Quick Write Activity, p. 160 Before You Read, p. 161
Section 6.1 Creating Web Site Content (pages 162–165)	📁 Reading Strategy, p. 162 ⓘ Online Activity 6.1: Evaluate Writing Styles, p. 164 YTI Activity 6A: Create Content for a Web Page, p. 165
Real World Technology Using the Web for Learning (page 166)	Tech Check, p. 166
Section 6.2 Placing Items on a Page (pages 167–170)	📁 Reading Strategy, p. 167 ⓘ Go Online Activity 6.2: Evaluate Page Layouts, p. 167 𝑑 ⦿ YTI Activity 6B: View a Page at Various Resolutions, p. 169
Section 6.3 Creating a Page Template (pages 171–176)	📁 Reading Strategy, p. 171 𝑑 ⦿ YTI Activity 6C: Create a Page Template, p. 172 𝑑 ⦿ YTI Activity 6D: Add a Logo, p. 174 𝑑 YTI Activity 6E: Create a Table, p. 175
Section 6.4 Enhancing the Template (pages 177–182)	📁 Reading Strategy, p. 177 𝑑 ⦿ YTI Activity 6F: Add Navigation Buttons, p. 178 𝑑 YTI Activity 6G: Add Footer Information, p. 179 𝑑 YTI Activity 6H: Add Text Links, p. 180 𝑑 YTI Activity 6I: Add a Link to an E-mail Window, p. 181
Chapter 6 Review (pages 183–189)	𝑑 Making Connections: Language Arts—Write Web Text ⓘ Standards at Work: Evaluate Layout (NETS-S 4) 𝑑 Teamwork Skills: Evaluate Content 𝑑 Challenge Yourself: Create a Template You Try It Skills Studio —Create Web Content 𝑑 —Create a Template Web Design Projects: 𝑑 —Develop Content for a Template —Create a Personal Web Site ⦿ ⓘ Additional Activities You May Wish to Use: —PowerTeach Outlines Chapter 6 —Student Workbook Chapter 6

Planning Guide — CHAPTER 6

Activities and Exercises

Section 6.1 Assessment, page 165

Section 6.2 Assessment, page 170

Section 6.3 Assessment, page 176

d Section 6.4 Assessment, page 182

Chapter 6 Review and Assessment, page 183
You may also use any of the Chapter Review Activities and Projects as Assessments. Additional Assessments You May Wish to Use:
(i) —Self-Check Assessments Chapter 6
—*ExamView* Testbank Chapter 6

Estimated Time to Complete Chapter

18 week course = 4–6 days
36 week course = 10 days

To help customize lesson plans, use the Pacing Guide on pages 26–30 and the Standards Charts on pages 202–203.

Key to Recommended Materials

Icons represent elements that may require additional resources.

☐ Focus on Reading

(i) Internet access required

d Software: Dreamweaver

◉ Teacher Resource CD (contains Student Data Files, Solution Files, Reproducible Graphic Organizers, and Study with PowerTeach Outlines)

Data and Solution Files for Chapter 6

DataFiles
- MusicDept
- background_stripes.gif
- lc_logo.gif
- nav_home_blue.gif
- nav_home_red.gif
- nav_about_blue.gif
- nav_about_red.gif
- nav_events_blue.gif
- nav_events_red.gif
- nav_contact_blue.gif
- nav_contact_red.gif

SolutionFiles
- SF_YTI_6CDE
- SF_YTI_6FGHI

Inclusion Strategies

For **Differentiated Instruction Strategies** refer to the **Inclusion in the Computer Technology Classroom** booklet.

Unit 2   Designing Web Sites

CHAPTER 6 NETS Correlation For Students

ISTE NETS Foundation Standards

1. Basic operations and concepts
2. Social, ethical, and human issues
3. Technology productivity tools
4. Technology communications tools
5. Technology research tools
6. Technology problem-solving and decision-making tools

Performance Indicators	Textbook Correlation
1. Identify capabilities and limitations of contemporary and emerging technology resources and assess the potential of these systems and services to address personal, lifelong learning, and workplace needs. (NETS 2)	**SE:** Critical Thinking (165, 170, 176, 182, 184), Tech Check (166)
2. Make informed choices among technology systems, resources, and services. (NETS 1, 2)	**SE:** Critical Thinking (165, 170, 176, 182, 184, 185), You Try It (170), Apply It! (170), Teamwork Skills (187)
3. Analyze advantages and disadvantages of widespread use and reliance on technology in the workplace and in society as a whole. (NETS 2)	**SE:** Quick Write Activity (160), Tech Check (166), Critical Thinking (184)
4. Demonstrate and advocate for legal and ethical behaviors among peers, family, and community regarding the use of technology and information. (NETS 2)	**SE:** Quick Tip (174)
5. Use technology tools and resources for managing and communicating personal/professional information (e.g. finances, schedules, addresses, purchases, correspondence). (NETS 3, 4)	**SE:** Standards at Work (186), Challenge Yourself (187), Skills Studio (188), Web Design Projects (189)
6. Evaluate technology-based options, including distance and distributed education, for lifelong learning. (NETS 5)	**SE:** Quick Write Activity (160), Go Online (164, 167), Tech Check (166)
7. Routinely and efficiently use online information resources to meet needs for collaboration, research, publications, communications, and productivity. (NETS 4, 5, 6)	**SE:** Go Online (164, 167)
8. Select and apply technology tools for research, information analysis, problem-solving, and decision-making in content learning. (NETS 4, 5)	**SE:** Go Online (164, 167), Apply It! (176), Standards at Work (186), Challenge Yourself (187), Skills Studio (188), Web Design Projects (189)
9. Investigate and apply expert systems, intelligent agents, and simulations in real-world situations. (NETS 3, 5, 6)	**SE:** You Try It (172, 174, 175, 178, 179, 180, 181), Web Design Projects (189)
10. Collaborate with peers, experts, and others to contribute to content-related knowledge base by using technology to compile, synthesize, produce, and disseminate information, models, and other creative works. (NETS 4, 5, 6)	**SE:** Standards at Work (186), Teamwork Skills (187)

SCANS Correlation — CHAPTER 6

Foundation Skills

Basic Skills

Reading	**SE:** Before You Read (161), Focus on Reading (162, 167, 171, 177), Reading Strategies (162, 167, 171, 177), After You Read (184), Teamwork Skills (187)
Writing	**SE:** Quick Write Activity (160), Section Assessments (165, 170, 176, 182), You Try It (165), Tech Check (166), Chapter Review (184–189), Making Connections (186)
Mathematics	**SE:** Tech Check (166), Standardized Test Practice (185)
Listening and Speaking	**SE:** Tech Check (166), Teamwork Skills (187)

Thinking Skills

Creative Thinking	**SE:** Quick Write Activity (160), Making Connections (186), Web Design Projects (189)
Critical Thinking	**SE:** Critical Thinking Activities (165, 170, 176, 182), Tech Check (166), Standards at Work (186), Teamwork Skills (187), Web Design Projects (189)
Problem Solving	**SE:** Apply It! (165), Teamwork Skills (187)

Workplace Competencies

Resources Manage time, money, materials, facilities, human resources	**SE:** Tech Check (166), Command Center (185)
Interpersonal Work on teams, teach others	**SE:** Standards at Work (186), Teamwork Skills (187)
Information Acquire, evaluate, organize, maintain, interpret, communicate and use computers to process information	**SE:** You Try It (165, 172, 174, 175, 178, 179, 180, 181), Apply It! (165, 170, 176, 182), Go Online (164, 167), Tech Check (166), Command Center (185), Making Connections (186), Standards at Work (186), Teamwork Skills (187), Challenge Yourself (187), Skills Studio (188), Web Design Projects (189)
Systems Understand, monitor, correct, improve, design systems	**SE:** You Try It (169, 178), Apply It! (170), Standards at Work (186), Teamwork Skills (187), Skills Studio (188)
Technology Select, apply, maintain, and troubleshoot technology.	**SE:** You Try It (169, 172, 174, 175, 178, 179, 180, 181), Go Online (164, 167), Apply It! (170), Standards at Work (186), Challenge Yourself (187), Skills Studio (188), Web Design Projects (189)

CHAPTER 6

Web Basics

(Page 160) **Objectives**

Section 6.1: Creating Web Site Content
- Generate and organize content ideas
- Write and organize Web text

Section 6.2: Placing Items on a Page
- Identify page dimension guidelines
- Determine content placement
- Evaluate page layouts

Section 6.3: Creating a Page Template
- Create a custom page template
- Insert a logo
- Create a table

Section 6.4: Enhancing the Template
- Create navigation buttons
- Add footer information
- Add text links
- Create an e-mail window

> **LEARNING LINK**
>
> Chapter 5 showed students the benefits of planning their Web sites. Use Chapter 6 to explain how students can start using their site plan to create Web content that will sustain a viewer's interest.

(Page 160) **Why It Matters**

Ask students to imagine that they will create a new soft drink company. Ask them how many existing products would be in competition with theirs (e.g. Coke®, Pepsi®, 7-Up®, Gatorade®, and others). Finally, ask them how they would get their target market to pay attention to their ads, considering all the competing advertisements. Draw an analogy between this situation and the one confronting a Web site designer.

(Page 160) **Quick Write Activity**

Have students write a report about what sparks their interest in a particular site. (For example, students may prefer Web sites that offer interactive activities, flashier graphics, or special online promotions.)

(Page 161) **Before You Read**

Stay Engaged Once students understand their purpose for reading, they ask better questions. Have students use section headings to come up with questions about the chapter. Students should not be discouraged if their questions are at first too vague. The important issue is to keep the mind engaged.

CHAPTER 6

SECTION 6.1 CREATING WEB SITE CONTENT
(Pages 162–165)

FOCUS

Analyzing Web Pages Have students locate a Web site of their choosing. Have them quickly scan some of the pages and print out the page they find most interesting and the page they find least interesting (if students cannot print pages, have them note the elements they like and dislike about particular pages). Lead a class discussion about what they think makes some pages effective in drawing and keeping their attention, and what makes others fail. Use the elements discussed in this chapter (i.e. text, layout, graphics, etc.) to guide the discussion. (NOTE: Save the printed pages or bookmark pages that are discussed. You will use them again in the Focus activity for Section 6.2.)

(Page 162)

Focus on Reading

Read to Find Out
Use the Read to Find Out feature to focus student reading. Hold a quick starter discussion to find out what your students already know.

 Key Terms Online
Key term definitions and activities are available online at **WebDesignDW.glencoe.com**.

Reading Strategy Answer
Students can find the information for identifying the steps under the heading *Generating and Organizing* Ideas on page 164. Students' flow diagrams should look similar to this example:

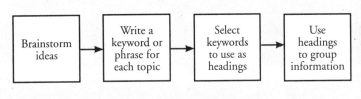

TEACH

Organize Headings Of all the Web text guidelines offered in this section, the one students may have the most trouble grasping is: "Make sure your headings follow a logical and clear hierarchy." The reason for possible confusion is that this guideline assumes a good understanding of organization and the ability to outline. Students may need help with this concept. Have the class come up with a topic for a Web site. Then brainstorm three to five headings. Ask students how the headings might be organized and visually portrayed on a page. If necessary, explain why the suggested organization will not be effective. Repeat the exercise until the class follows the basic principles of organizing information.

CHAPTER 6

Answers to Section 6.1 Captions and Activities

(Page 162) **Reading Focus** Visitors usually scan online text, reading snippets of information that interest them.

(Page 163) **Table 6.1** Bulleted lists summarize information on Web pages.

(Page 163) **Figure 6.1** Headings and subheadings are different sizes to help emphasize the importance of information.

(Page 164) **Figure 6.2** Important information should appear first on a Web page because in this position it can best catch the attention of online readers when they first access the page.

(Page 164) **Reading Check** Effective online text should be structured like an inverted pyramid, with the most important information at the top of the page.

(Page 164) **Reading Focus** Brainstorming is a technique used to generate ideas.

(Page 164) **Activity 6.1** To expose students to the variety of writing styles they will encounter and use when writing for the Web, have them visit **WebDesignDW.glencoe.com**.

(Page 165) **Activity 6A Create Content for a Web Page** Using brainstorming techniques, students create content (no more than 200 words) for the Foods of the World Fundraiser page in the Language Club Web site.

(Page 165) **Reading Check** It is important to identify keywords when creating a Web site, because these words may be used as headings for important information.

ASSESS

(Page 165) ### Section 6.1 Assessment Answers

Reading Summary

Use the Reading Summary to help students review and reinforce the important points of the section.

What Did You Learn?

1. Students' definitions should be in their own words, but based on the information found in the section and in the book's glossary.

2. Web page are not usually read in a linear fashion. Readers of Web text scan text, click links, and are taken to another page or site rather than proceed page by page. Also, reading text online takes approximately 25 percent longer than reading the same text on a printed page.

3. Initial factors to consider when planning your Web page's content include deciding what information to include, what graphics will be informative and visually appealing, and remembering that the page's text needs to be short and easy to read.

Critical Thinking

4. Student answers will vary. It takes longer to read text online so pages that contain too much content may discourage viewers of the Web page. They also have to scroll to read pages with a lot of content.

5. If a keyword serves to call attention to a topic or a group of topics on the page, it can be used as a heading. The keyword that identifies the most important topic or idea should be the first heading and should be placed at the top of the page.

Apply It!

Determine Content Students will write a mission statement and define a target audience for a class Web page. Ideas for content will vary but should reflect the goals outlined in their mission statements. For example, a Web site that lists all the classes being offered might contain links to course descriptions or to homework assignments.

CLOSE

Reviewing Web Text Guidelines Create the text for a Web page, but ignore all Web text guidelines. That is, have multiple ideas in lengthy paragraphs with complex sentence structures, use numbered lists for items that are not a series of steps, and so on. Make sure to use headings that are uninformative and do not follow a hierarchy. Then have the students work in small groups to identify the problems and correct them. As a class, compare several of the students' rewritten versions. Have other students point out whether the changes have improved the readability of the page, and why.

(Page 166)

Real World Technology

USING THE WEB FOR LEARNING

Answers to Tech Check

1. Students may use various resources (the Internet, interviews, print) for their research. Answers will vary, but should reveal an awareness of different cultures and socioeconomic circumstances among the users of distance-learning technologies. Reports may focus on distance learners in rural areas or other countries, while others focus on those who are homebound for health problems or other reasons. Students should understand how distance-learning technologies enhance the lives of their users and how they can affect different cultures. Reports can be written or oral and should demonstrate proper spelling, grammar, punctuation, and communication skills.

2. Students' answers will vary, but should provide detailed information about the schools they find and the offerings available through each. If possible, students should try to find information about a variety of schools, including high schools, technical schools, or colleges. Students should also demonstrate effective information-gathering skills in conducting their research.

CHAPTER 6

SECTION 6.2 PLACING ITEMS ON A PAGE
(Pages 167–170)

FOCUS

Analyzing Ineffective Layouts Many Web pages have confusing or unattractive layouts. Use some of the printed or bookmarked Web pages from the Section 6.1 Focus activity that the students thought looked uninteresting. Ask them what is unappealing about these pages. Then ask them to draw any conclusions they can about what they would want to avoid when designing a page layout. After finishing this section, ask the students to suggest specific strategies that would help the layout of these pages.

(Page 167)

Focus on Reading

Read to Find Out
Use the Read to Find Out feature to focus student reading. Hold a quick starter discussion to find out what your students already know.

 Key Terms Online
Key term definitions and activities are available online at **WebDesignDW.glencoe.com**.

Reading Strategy Answer
Students can find guidelines for Web page layout throughout the section. The students' charts will vary, but should look similar to this example:

Layout/Design Guidelines	How It Helps
640 x 480 pixel page dimension	Provides a "safe area" that most browsers will display without user scrolling
Create visual rest stops	Eases eyestrain; helps frame and draw attention to the content
Eliminate clutter	Allows user to identify and navigate main content of site more easily

TEACH

Applying Layout Guidelines Layout guidelines are just that—guidelines. For example, students must be careful to understand what "clutter" is before trying to eliminate it, and that what is clutter in one situation may be important information in another. Explain that if there is too much necessary information for one page, they should expand the page into a Web site, with separate subpages linked to a home page.

 Answers to Section 6.2 Captions and Activities

(Page 167) **Reading Focus** Eliminating clutter on a Web page makes the most important information stand out, and helps to keep visitors' interest.

(Page 167)  **Activity 6.2** For additional experience with layout guidelines, you may have students visit **WebDesignDW.glencoe.com**.

208 Teacher Resource Manual *Introduction to Web Design Using Dreamweaver*

CHAPTER 6

(Page 168) **Figure 6.3** The title should be the largest item on the page because it is the most important information, and the visitor should read it first.

(Page 168) ☑ **Reading Check** A bigger design emphasizes important content.

(Page 169) **Reading Focus** Different monitors may have different resolutions, which can affect how pages appear.

(Page 169) **You Try It** **Activity 6B View a Page at Various Resolutions** Students learn how to view a page at different screen resolutions. Use the Student Data Files noted in this chapter's Planning Guide.

(Page 170) ☑ **Reading Check** The safe area is the 800 × 600 pixel area that is typical to a computer monitor. It is called the safe area because it displays on every Web browser/system combination.

ASSESS

(Page 170) **Section 6.2 Assessment Answers**

Reading Summary
Use the Reading Summary to help students review and reinforce the important points of the section.

What Did You Learn?
1. Students' definitions should be in their own words, but based on the information found in the section and in the book's glossary.
2. The most important content should be placed at the top and left edge.
3. White space eases eyestrain caused by reading long, unbroken lines of text. It gives the eyes a break and helps frame and draw attention to the page's content.

Critical Thinking
4. Users will set their resolution to a size and display that suit their reading and working needs.
5. Students' explanations will vary but might explain that if visitors do not find information they want, they move on. Clutter can confuse readers or waste their time.

Apply It!
Compare Web Designs Students' comparisons of the two pages should use the information they have learned to select the more effective layout between two pages.

CLOSE

Comparing Layouts Students use content from articles and ads to create a page layout. Have them compare layouts.

Unit 2 Designing Web Sites 209

CHAPTER 6

SECTION 6.3 CREATING A PAGE TEMPLATE
(Pages 171–176)

FOCUS

Understanding the Concept of Templates A template is a model for something that you will want to re-create at least one other time. One way to give students a feeling for the ease and usefulness of templates is to show them how to create memos or letters using word processing templates. Ask them which elements are always present in a memo or a letter. These are the elements that will appear in the template. Ask them what elements they think will always appear on a Web page.

(Page 171)

Focus on Reading

Read to Find Out

Use the Read to Find Out feature to focus student reading. Hold a quick starter discussion to find out what your students already know.

 Key Terms Online

Key term definitions and activities are available online at **WebDesignDW.glencoe.com**.

Reading Strategy Answer

Students should describe the parts of a table. This information can be found under the heading *Tables* on page 175. The students' tables should look similar to this example:

Part	Description
column	the vertical elements of a table
row	the horizontal elements of a table
cell	each individual square within a table
header row	the row that contains the headings for each column
header column	the column that contains the headings for each row

TEACH

Using Tables Have students convert the following information into a table:

Sherman High School had 1200 students enrolled in 2004. In 2005, student enrollment jumped to 1400 students due to Shermanville becoming a more popular place to live for families with school-age children. In 2006, enrollment increased to 1850 after Sherman High was rated as one of the top five high schools in the Midwest. Because the school administration didn't feel that they could keep up the same level of education with the increased student body size, they opened a second, smaller, high school in Shermanville, called Sherman West. In 2007, students were divided between the two schools, and student population of Sherman High School was 1100.

One possible table might look like this:

Year	Student Enrollment	Explanation
2004	1200	
2005	1400	More families moved to area
2006	1850	Sherman High listed as one of top five high schools in area
2007	1100	Students divided between two high schools

Answers to Section 6.3 Captions and Activities

(Page 171) **Reading Focus** Most templates contain a logo, navigation links, a title graphic, body of text, and a footer.

(Page 171) **Figure 6.6** A template is a reusable pattern used to lay out elements on a Web page.

(Page 172) **You Try It** **Activity 6C Create a Page Template** Students use Dreamweaver to begin creating the Language Club Web site's basic template, and to insert the site's background graphic. Use the Student Data Files and Solution Files noted in this chapter's Planning Guide.

(Page 173) **Reading Check** A custom template can help meet site-specific needs.

(Page 174) **Reading Focus** A logo represents an organization, and can link back to the home page.

(Page 174) **You Try It** **Activity 6D Add a Logo** Students add a logo to the template they created in You Try It activity 6C. The logo on each page is linked to the site's home page. Use the Student Data Files and Solution Files noted in this chapter's Planning Guide.

(Page 175) **Reading Focus** Tables can be used to organize and lay out text and graphics on a Web page.

(Page 175) **Figure 6.11** Multiply the number of rows in a table by the number of columns to determine the number of cells.

(Page 175) **You Try It** **Activity 6E Create a Table** Students add a table to the template they created in You Try It activity 6C. Use the Solution Files noted in this chapter's Planning Guide.

(Page 176) **Reading Check** Columns are vertical and rows are horizontal.

Unit 2 Designing Web Sites 211

CHAPTER 6

ASSESS

(Page 176) Section 6.3 Assessment Answers

Reading Summary

Use the Reading Summary to help students review and reinforce the important points of the section.

What Did You Learn?

1. Students' definitions should be in their own words, but based on the information found in the section and in the book's glossary.
2. A custom template is designed by a Web page author to meet the specific needs of his or her Web site. A pre-made template is supplied by the Web design application.
3. Students can choose from many properties: cell height and width, horizontal and vertical alignment of text, cell borders, colors, and background. Students should explain the function of the three properties they choose, using information found in the chapter.

Critical Thinking

4. Student answers will vary. Text that can be categorized and better understood by a row and column heading, such as facts, lists, and data comparisons, should be placed in a table. Text that is meant to be read in a linear way, where a concept is being explained or a story is being told, should be placed in a paragraph.
5. Placing text in the alternative representations box gives the Web browser a message or label to display to the user if the image is unavailable. If this "alt text" is not available, the Web browser will simply display an empty area or small graphic in the image space.

Apply It!

Create a Table Students create a table based on class notes. Remind students that organizing information into a table can be a good way to study. Students might use a word processor or spreadsheet application to create their tables.

CLOSE

Reviewing Web Page Templates Have students create their own template using the skills they have learned in this section. They should select and insert a background graphic, a logo, a title graphic, alternate text, a table, and different colors for the background of the table's columns.

CHAPTER 6

SECTION 6.4 ENHANCING THE TEMPLATE
(Pages 177–182)

FOCUS

Using Navigation Links Ask students if they have ever encountered a site that was hard to navigate, and if so, what made it difficult. (Perhaps there was no link bar, the bar was not in an optimal place, the links were not sufficiently descriptive, there were so many links that it was discouraging, and so on.) See if they can make predictions about how to effectively use navigation links to make a site more user-friendly.

(Page 177)

Focus on Reading

Read To Find Out
Use the Read to Find Out feature to focus student reading. Hold a quick starter discussion to find out what your students already know.

 Key Terms Online
Key term definitions and activities are available online at **WebDesignDW.glencoe.com**.

Reading Strategy
Students will compare buttons and links using information found under the headings *Navigation Buttons* on page 177, and *Text Links* on page 180. The students' diagrams should look similar to this example:

Buttons
Buttons used to navigate to other locations, includes hover buttons and active buttons

Take you to another location; often change color

Text Links
Text that takes you to another location; include nonvisited, visited, and active

TEACH

Identifying Poorly Designed Templates Often, one of the most effective teaching methods is showing students what not to do. Create a template that does not use a link bar, and position numerous links at random points on the page. Make some of the links similar in name. Include a footer with text links, but use colors that blend into the background of the template. Get student feedback on the template, and ask how it could be improved. Show the students how to make any changes that you agree would benefit the page.

Unit 2 Designing Web Sites 213

CHAPTER 6

Answers to Section 6.4 Captions and Activities

(Page 177) **Reading Focus** Navigation buttons are used to link to additional information and to navigate to other Web pages.

(Page 178) **You Try It** **Activity 6F Add Navigation Buttons** Students add five navigation buttons to the Language Club template. If students do not have access to a temporary file to preview their page, they can preview it in a browser. It is important to note in this activity that when the students click on the navigation buttons, they will get an error message. They will create the actual linked pages in Chapter 7. Use the Student Data Files and Solution Files noted in this chapter's Planning Guide.

> ⚠ **Troubleshooting**
>
> Students can search online for images to use as buttons. They can use search words such as rollover buttons, navigation buttons, and link-bar buttons. Make sure that the images are in the public domain, or that the students follow the correct fair use guidelines before downloading the images. As an alternative, you can search and download suitable images to provide to students for activities that require them.

(Page 178) ✓ **Reading Check** A navigation button links to additional information and can navigate to other Web pages.

(Page 179) **Reading Focus** Footer information includes copyright and contact information that is important to have on every page.

(Page 179) **You Try It** **Activity 6G Add Footer Information** Students add footer information to the template. Make sure students proofread their work. Use the Solution Files noted in this chapter's Planning Guide.

(Page 180) **You Try It** **Activity 6H Add Text Links** Students add text links to the template. Use the Solution Files noted in this chapter's Planning Guide.

(Page 181) **You Try It** **Activity 6I Add a Link to an E-mail Window** Students learn how to add a link to an e-mail window (also referred to as an e-mail hyperlink). Make sure students check their work carefully since they will be using this template to build a Web page. Use the Solution Files noted in this chapter's Planning Guide.

(Page 182) ✓ **Reading Check** A Web page's footer usually contains copyright information, contact information, and any text links that are necessary.

ASSESS

(Page 182) **Section 6.4 Assessment Answers**

Reading Summary

Use the Reading Summary to help students review and reinforce the important points of the section.

214 Teacher Resource Manual *Introduction to Web Design Using Dreamweaver*

What Did You Learn?

1. Students' definitions should be in their own words, but based on the information found in the section and in the book's glossary.
2. Students' answers may include touching the mouse pointer on the button or clicking the button.
3. The e-mail window allows users to contact the Webmaster to report a problem on the site, ask a technical question, or offer suggestions or praise for the site's design.

Critical Thinking

4. Interactive buttons let users know an action has taken place, and increase the user-friendliness of the site.
5. Ideas may include adding an e-mail link and text links that change color depending upon their state.

Apply It!

Create a Footer Students add a copyright notice and e-mail contact to the bottom of the MySkills page they created in Chapter 4. If students do not have an e-mail address, you will need to provide one they can use.

Creating a Template Have students create a template for a personal Web site or a site on a topic of their choice. (Or provide a specific topic if you prefer.) The template should include:

- A link bar at the left side of the page, with five navigation links (for pages the students would want to include in their site).
- A footer with text links, copyright information, and a link to an e-mail window. (If students do not have an e-mail address, you will need to provide one they can use.)

CHAPTER 6 Answers to Chapter Review

The Chapter Review covers a wide range of student knowledge. Due to time constraints, students may not be able to complete every activity in the Chapter Review. Select the activities that are appropriate for your class needs and resources.

(Page 184) After You Read

Create a Study Guide Have students review their questions to jog their memory about key points in the chapter. Then have them create brief answers for their questions, which they can use to review important points at a later date, such as for a cumulative test. Their questions and answers together will effectively produce an outline of the chapter material.

(Page 184) Reviewing Key Terms

1. Text and graphics are the items that make up a Web page's content.
2. Use white space to create visual space between images and body text.
3. A pixel is a picture element.
4. The logo should be placed in a page's safe area.
5. The standard screen resolution is 800 × 600.
6. Templates make it easy to create a new Web page or site. Templates use placeholders for basic elements on a page such as navigation, content area, and footer information.
7. False. A table consists of *vertical columns* and *horizontal rows*.
8. Change the sentence to read: *A logo is a symbol used to identify a business or an organization.*

(Page 184) Understanding Main Ideas

9. Size is often used as an indication of an item's importance. If the size of an element is out of proportion to its importance to the site, the user will be misled and confused.
10. An inverted pyramid can serve as a visual aid to remind you how to best organize your content. More attention and space should be given to your most important items and less emphasis and less conspicuous placement should be given to the least important information.
11. As Web pages display differently on different browsers, the most important elements should be placed in a "safe area" of the screen, that is, the 640 × 480 pixel area of the upper-left portion of the page. The most important item should be placed in the top and left edge of the page, as users will be less likely to scroll to items that are below the "fold" of the page.
12. Designers use tables to organize and lay out text and graphics on a Web page.
13. A table is a grid made up of horizontal rows and vertical columns. Table cells are the squares formed when the rows and columns intersect.
14. A link bar acts as a map to the site's main pages and is placed in the same place on each page, making it easy to locate. It also makes links easy to find, since they are in the same order on every page.

Answers to Chapter Review — CHAPTER 6

15. Students will use their own words, however, their answers should reflect the content of those shown below:
    - Use headings and subheadings to break up text.
    - Use headings and subheadings to highlight key points so readers can locate information quickly.
    - Format main headings larger than subheadings to denote importance.
    - Use different colors and typefaces for heading and subheadings to add visual interest and draw attention.

16. Students should create a table that includes four of the answers shown below:

Property	Result of Modification
Split cell in rows or columns command	Breaks one cell into two or more rows or columns
Width	Modifies the width of a cell
Height	Modifies the height of a cell
No wrap	Does not wrap contents of a cell to a second line
Header	Converts a cell into a header cell which provides information about a row or column of content
Background URL of cell command	Inserts a background image into a cell
Background color	Changes the background color of a cell
Border color of cell command	Change the border color around a table cell

(Page 184) ## Critical Thinking

17. An interactive button's appearance might change when a user places the pointer over the button, clicks on the button, or moves the pointer off the button.

18. Students' answers will vary, but should include suggestions such as using an e-mail link to allow visitors to report problems about the Web site to the Webmaster, ask questions about the products or services a Web site offers, provide feedback on the site, or ask support-related questions. Students may suggest a site use text links and graphic links to make the site more accessible to users with assistive technology devices, provide an additional way to navigate through the site, and provide a location for pages and information of lesser importance.

19. Students' answers will vary as they compare their preference for online or printed magazines. Students might mention the interactive components of online magazines, additional media like video and real time interviews, and the ability to quickly access older articles.

20. The rule of function over form means keeping elements that fill a need or do a job, rather than those elements that are merely ornamental. Students will apply this rule when identifying the various elements they would include or not include when designing their favorite movie Web site. For example, if Star Wars is a favorite film, a student may decide to provide links to information about each character instead of placing numerous photos of characters on the home page.

CHAPTER 6 Answers to Chapter Review

21. Situations will vary. A pre-made template may be more appropriate for use for customers with a limited budget, or who want to get their site up and running quickly. Custom templates may be the best choice for customers with a moderate sized budget and special requirements or content they wish to incorporate. A custom designed site can be used for customers with a large budget who want to have a unique presence on the Web, or for customers with content, products, or services that require a high level of customization.

22. Visual cues may include white space, custom link colors, and consistent use of navigation elements such as the site's logo serving as a link to the home page. Any cues that allow users to navigate a site more easily, or process the site's information more efficiently make a site user-friendly.

23. Answers will vary. Answers from students about CNN.com, for example, may include headings (or headlines) that are larger based on the story's importance. Related headlines are grouped under a common title such as Sports. Bullet points may be used to highlight key elements of a story. Images are used to enhance stories and break up text. Navigation is distinct in color and style from the rest of the site's content.

(Page 185) ## Command Center

24. **F4** = Hide Files panel
25. **Ctrl + F3** = Open Properties inspector
26. **Shift + 1** = Key vertical line

Standardized Test Practice

The correct answer is B. Advise students to read the possible answers carefully, and not to make assumptions.

Have students use the book's Web site **WebDesignDW.glencoe.com**.

- **Study with PowerTeach** Encourage your students to use the Chapter 6 PowerTeach Outline to review the chapter before they have a test.

- **Online Self Check** These quick five-question assessments may be used as an in-class activity, a homework assignment, or test review.

Answers to Chapter Review — CHAPTER 6

(Page 186) Making Connections

Language Arts—Write Web Text Students rewrite provided text for use on a Web page, using guidelines recommended in Section 6.1. These guidelines include the use of headings and bulleted lists. Students' rewrites might look similar to this example:

Cape Cod, Massachusetts Cape Cod is a popular vacation destination with activities for all seasons.

Summer
- Swim in the ocean
- Go on whale-watching expeditions
- Walk on the beach at Cape Cod Bay

Fall
- Take nature walks at the National Seashore
- Attend cranberry harvest festivals
- Visit Plymouth Plantation to learn how the pilgrims lived

Winter
- Enjoy the snow
- Attend the holiday festivals

(Page 186) Standards at Work

NETS-S 4 Evaluate Layout Students print out the home page of a Web site they visit often and evaluate the page's layout according to the five questions in the activity. You might use these questions to create a rubric for the students to use in their evaluations for both parts of this activity. Students' tables may look similar to the one below:

PAGE TRAIT	EVALUATION
Important Content	Excellent-easy to read
White Space	Fair-a lot of information on one page
Proximity	Good-important items grouped together
Alignment	Good-all text left aligned, graphics centered

(Page 187) Teamwork Skills

Evaluate Content Students select a Web page they have created and, working in teams of four, receive feedback about their page from the other students on the team. Each Web page should be scanned for no more than ten seconds. Students should all look at the same student Web page at the same time. They should then discuss the page as a group, but the author of the page should at first remain silent and listen to the opinions of the other team members. Emphasize that the point is not to tear down another student's work, but to make constructive comments that suggest how the Web page can be improved. Students make any needed changes to their page, and then share it with the group once more, pointing out how they have improved the page.

CHAPTER 6 Answers to Chapter Review

(Page 187) Challenge Yourself

Create a Template Students create a custom template to be used as a photo gallery. The template includes an area at the top of the screen for a logo and title graphic, a link bar on the left, text links at the bottom, a placeholder for text, and a table with two rows and three columns in which six photos can be placed. Students can then use the template to create a page on a topic of their own choosing.

(Page 188)
1. **Create Web Content** Students plan content for a site for an Italian restaurant. As students plan the site, they should list keywords, content for the home page, and content for the menu page. The home page content should be based on the advertisement shown. The menu page should be based on menu samples from restaurants. Content can include text, graphics, and links.

2. **Create a Template** Students use the content from You Try It Skills Studio #1 to create a template for the site. Students use placeholders for the logo and title. The template should include a footer, and navigation links in the left column to three other pages in the site. The page's content should appear in the right column. Students add a link from "E-mail the Webmaster" in the footer to an e-mail window.

Web Design Projects

(Page 189)
1. **Develop Content for a Template** Students use the storyboard and sketches created in Chapter 5 to create the site for the local band. Students create the template, write the content for the home page, create additional pages (no content), and build navigation for the site.

    This activity can also be done as a group activity. For examples of Web sites, see the suggestions in the Section 1.1 Apply It! answer (on page 97 of this manual). Students must be supervised when using the Web.

2. **Create a Personal Web Site** Students plan and create a personal Web site that includes a home page and at least three other pages. All aspects of planning content and creating a good layout should be employed in planning and executing the site.

Notes

CHAPTER 7 Planning Guide

Student Edition	Activities and Exercises
Chapter 7 Selecting Design and Color (pages 190–219)	Quick Write Activity, page 190 Before You Read, page 191
Section 7.1 Principles of Presentation Design (pages 192–197)	📁 Reading Strategy, page 192 ⓘ Go Online Activity 7.1: Explore Presentation Design, page 192 d You Try It Activity 7A: Use a Template to Create New Pages, page 193 d You Try It Activity 7B: Organize the Site's File Structure, page 195 d ⊙ You Try It Activity 7C: Insert Page Headers, page 196
Section 7.2 Choosing Colors (pages 198–201)	📁 Reading Strategy, page 198 ⓘ Go Online Activity 7.2 Select Color Schemes, page 198 d ⓘ You Try It Activity 7D: Add Content and Color to the Home Page, page 199
Section 7.3 Fonts and Typography (pages 202–209)	Reading Strategy, page 202 d You Try It Activity 7E: Format Text, page 208
Ethics & Technology Respecting Intellectual Property (page 210)	Tech Check, page 210
Chapter 7 Review (pages 211–219)	d Making Connections: Science—Demonstrate Color Difference d Standards at Work: Analyze Text Styles and Color ⓘ Teamwork Skills: Create Web Content Challenge Yourself: Create a Color Scheme d You Try It Skills Studio: d —Format Text in Tables d —Add a Contact Us Page Web Design Projects: d ⓘ —Add Text to a Web Page —Refine Your Personal Web Site Additional Activities You May Wish to Use: ⊙ ⓘ —PowerTeach Outlines Chapter 7 —Student Workbook Chapter 7

Planning Guide — CHAPTER 7

Assessments

Section 7.1 Assessment, page 197

Section 7.2 Assessment, page 201

Section 7.3 Assessment, page 209

Chapter 7 Review and Assessment, page 211
Building 21st Century Skills, page 218
Building Your Portfolio, page 219
You may also use any of the Chapter Review Activities and Projects as Assessments.
Additional Assessments You May Wish to Use:
⦿ ⓘ —Self-Check Assessments Chapter 7
—*ExamView* Testbank Chapter 7

Estimated Time to Complete Chapter

18 week course = 4–6 days
36 week course = 36–30 days

To help customize lesson plans, use the Pacing Guide on pages 26–30 and the Standards Charts on pages 224–225.

Key to Recommended Materials

Icons represent elements that may require additional resources.

📁 Focus on Reading

ⓘ Internet access required

𝒅 Software: Dreamweaver

⦿ Teacher Resource CD (contains Student Data Files, Solution Files, Reproducible Graphic Organizers, and Study with PowerTeach Outlines)

Data and Solution Files for Chapter 7

DataFiles
- hdr_welcome.gif
- hdr_aboutus.gif
- hdr_events.gif
- hdr_contactus.gif
- photo_members.gif
- hdr_fundraiser.gif
- Events.doc

SolutionFiles
- SF_YTI_7ABC
- SF_YTI_7D
- SF_YTI_7E
- SF_Language Club

Inclusion Strategies

For **Differentiated Instruction Strategies** refer to the **Inclusion in the Computer Technology Classroom** booklet.

CHAPTER 7 — NETS Correlation For Students

ISTE NETS Foundation Standards

1. Basic operations and concepts
2. Social, ethical, and human issues
3. Technology productivity tools
4. Technology communications tools
5. Technology research tools
6. Technology problem-solving and decision-making tools

Performance Indicators	Textbook Correlation
1. Identify capabilities and limitations of contemporary and emerging technology resources and assess the potential of these systems and services to address personal, lifelong learning, and workplace needs. (NETS 2)	**SE:** Critical Thinking (200, 209, 212, 213)
2. Make informed choices among technology systems, resources, and services. (NETS 1, 2)	**SE:** You Try It (193, 194, 195, 196, 199, 208), Critical Thinking (201, 209, 213), Apply It! (209)
3. Analyze advantages and disadvantages of widespread use and reliance on technology in the workplace and in society as a whole. (NETS 2)	**SE:** Quick Write Activity (90)
4. Demonstrate and advocate for legal and ethical behaviors among peers, family, and community regarding the use of technology and information. (NETS 2)	**SE:** Tech Check (210)
5. Use technology tools and resources for managing and communicating personal/professional information (e.g. finances, schedules, addresses, purchases, correspondence). (NETS 3, 4)	**SE:** Web Design Projects (217)
6. Evaluate technology-based options, including distance and distributed education, for lifelong learning. (NETS 5)	**SE:** Go Online (192, 198)
7. Routinely and efficiently use online information resources to meet needs for collaboration, research, publications, communications, and productivity. (NETS 4, 5, 6)	**SE:** Go Online (192, 198), Teamwork Skills (215), Building 21st Century Skills (218)
8. Select and apply technology tools for research, information analysis, problem-solving, and decision-making in content learning. (NETS 4, 5)	**SE:** Go Online (192, 198), Making Connections (214), Standards at Work (214), Teamwork Skills (215), Challenge Yourself (215), Skills Studio (216), Web Design Projects (217), Building 21st Century Skills (218), Building Your Portfolio (219)
9. Investigate and apply expert systems, intelligent agents, and simulations in real-world situations. (NETS 3, 5, 6)	**SE:** You Try It (193, 195, 196, 199, 208), Skills Studio (216), Web Design Projects (217), Building 21st Century Skills (218)
10. Collaborate with peers, experts, and others to contribute to content-related knowledge base by using technology to compile, synthesize, produce, and disseminate information, models, and other creative works. (NETS 4, 5, 6)	**SE:** Teamwork Skills (215), Building 21st Century Skills (218), Building Your Portfolio (219)

SCANS Correlation — CHAPTER 7

Foundation Skills

Basic Skills

Reading	**SE:** Before You Read (191), Focus on Reading (192, 198, 202), Reading Strategies (192, 198, 202), After You Read (212), Standardized Test Practice (213)
Writing	**SE:** Quick Write Activity (190), Section Assessments (197, 201, 209), Chapter Review (212–217), Teamwork Skills (215), Building 21st Century Skills (218), Building Your Portfolio (219)
Mathematics	
Listening and Speaking	**SE:** Teamwork Skills (215), Building 21st Century Skills (218), Building Your Portfolio (219)

Thinking Skills

Creative Thinking	**SE:** Quick Write Activity (190), Teamwork Skills (215), Challenge Yourself (215), Web Design Projects (217), Building 21st Century Skills (218), Building Your Portfolio (219)
Critical Thinking	**SE:** Critical Thinking Activities (197, 201, 209, 212, 213), Tech Check (210), Making Connections (214)
Problem Solving	**SE:** Web Design Projects (217)

Workplace Competencies

Resources — Manage time, money, materials, facilities, human resources	**SE:** Command Center (213), Web Design Projects (217)
Interpersonal — Work on teams, teach others	**SE:** After You Read (212), Teamwork Skills (215), Building 21st Century Skills (218)
Information — Acquire, evaluate, organize, maintain, interpret, communicate and use computers to process information	**SE:** Go Online (192, 198), You Try It (193, 195, 196, 199, 208), Apply It! (201, 209), Command Center (213), Standards at Work (214), Teamwork Skills (215), Challenge Yourself (215), Skills Studio (216), Web Design Projects (217), Building 21st Century Skills (218), Building Your Portfolio (219)
Systems — Understand, monitor, correct, improve, design systems	**SE:** You Try It (193, 195, 196, 199, 208), Apply It! (197, 201, 209), Standards at Work (214), Challenge Yourself (215)
Technology — Select, apply, maintain, and troubleshoot technology.	**SE:** Go Online (192, 198), You Try It (193, 195, 196, 199, 208), Apply It! (186, 193), Making Connections (214), Standards at Work (214), Challenge Yourself (215), Skills Studio (216), Web Design Projects (217), Building 21st Century Skills (218), Building Your Portfolio (219)

CHAPTER 7

Selecting Design and Color

(Page 190) **Objectives**

Section 7.1: Principles of Presentation Design
- Identify presentation design principles
- Use a custom template
- Add pages to a navigation structure

Section 7.2: Choosing Colors
- Use color scheme guidelines
- Add colors to a Web site
- Identify Web-safe colors

Section 7.3: Fonts and Typography
- Adjust text properties
- Summarize formatting guidelines
- Format text in Dreamweaver

> **LEARNING LINK**
>
> Chapter 6 explained how students can use their site plan to create Web content that will sustain a viewer's interest. Another aspect of sustaining a viewer's interest has to do with the site's ease of use. Chapter 7 shows students how to design user-friendly Web-sites by applying principles of presentation design and making appropriate color and typography choices.

(Page 190) **Why It Matters**

Just as consistency in road signs helps us drive more safely no matter where we travel in the United States, consistency helps us use computers efficiently. Lead a brief discussion about how students use various search engines. In what ways are all search engines similar? How does this affect the user?

(Page 190) **Quick Write Activity**

Ask students to work in pairs and discuss some of the tools they use every day. Have them create a list of features that make this tool easy to use. Then, have them discuss the difficulties in learning to use the same tool with different features. (Responses may include dial pads on phones, on/off buttons on remote controls, and so on.)

(Page 191) **Before You Read**

Get Creative Teaching students to bring kinesthetic and other sensory learning styles to bear on the reading has been shown to raise comprehension levels. It not only appeals to various strengths that the student may have in other areas, it literally forges additional synapses in the brain that stimulate recall.

CHAPTER 7

SECTION 7.1 PRINCIPLES OF PRESENTATION DESIGN
(Pages 192–197)

FOCUS

Identifying Consistency Lead a discussion applying the ideas of consistency and repetition to something that students are usually interested in: television. Ask them what their favorite shows are, and who the main characters are on these shows. What character traits do they exhibit week after week? Why do students think this is so? Ask why the network that produces this show probably offers similar kinds of shows, particularly on the same night. (Networks usually put similar shows on the same night because they assume that the elements that attract a viewer to one show will also attract that viewer to a similar show.)

(Page 192)

Focus on Reading

Read to Find Out
Use the Read to Find Out feature to focus student reading. Hold a quick starter discussion to find out what your students already know.

 Key Terms Online
Key term definitions and activities are available online at **WebDesignDW.glencoe.com**.

Reading Strategy Answer
In this activity, students will be identifying the five presentation design principles that are found under the heading *Consistency and Repetition* on page 192. Students' Web diagrams should look similar to this example:

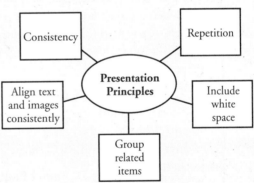

TEACH

Analyzing Ineffective Design Create two or more pages of the Language Club Web site that do not follow presentation design guidelines. Change the order of links on the pages, place them in different locations on different pages, use a different color scheme on some pages or a different visual style, and change the page banners in ways that create confusion. Have the students discuss the design and its likely effect on the user. Let them suggest ways to improve the pages.

Unit 2 Designing Web Sites   227

CHAPTER 7

Answers to Section 7.1 Captions and Activities

(Page 192) **Reading Focus** Web designers use consistency and repetition by creating a Web site that has the same look throughout, and that repeats specific elements on all (or most) of the site's pages.

(Page 192) **GO Online** **Activity 7.1** To give students additional information and experience with presentation design, have them visit **WebDesignDW.glencoe.com**.

(Page 193) **Figure 7.1** When users are comfortable with a Web site, they will visit the site more often.

(Page 193) ✓ **Reading Check** The logo or name of the site, the page title and its location on the page, the navigation options, and a link back to the home page should be on every page on a Web site.

(Page 193) **Reading Focus** Templates help build consistency and repetition into a Web site, and give the site a unified design from page to page.

(Page 193) **You Try It** **Activity 7A Use a Template to Create New Pages** Students should use the Language Club Web site template to create the five main pages of the site. They use the information in Table 7.1 to assign file names and page titles to each of these pages. Remind students to select names that are relevant and appropriate. You may also want to note that a page's title often becomes the name of the link when a visitor adds that page to his or her favorites list. A page title that is too long does not make a good link name. Use the Solution Files noted in this chapter's Planning Guide.

> ✎ **Teaching Tip**
> As students work through Activity 7B, tell them that they can still open a Web site without opening any files by going to **Site>Manage Sites**, choosing a project, and clicking **Done**. Another, and more common, method to open a site is to choose the **Language Club Web site** project from the drop-down menu in the **Files** panel.

(Page 195) **You Try It** **Activity 7B Organize the Site's File Structure** Students learn how to organize the pages they created in You Try It Activity 7A. Use the Solution Files noted in this chapter's Planning Guide.

(Page 196)
You Try It **Activity 7C Insert Page Headers** Students add a page header to each page in the site. This helps them understand how the similar elements in each page header gives consistency to the site, while the differences allow the user to know which individual Web page he or she is visiting. Use the Student Data Files and Solution Files noted in this chapter's Planning Guide.

(Page 197) ✓ **Reading Check** A page header identifies the site, the section the visitor is using, and possibly the site's primary navigation.

CHAPTER 7

ASSESS

(Page 197) Section 7.1 Assessment Answers

Reading Summary
Use the Reading Summary to help students review and reinforce the important points of the section.

What Did You Learn?

1. Students' definitions should be in their own words, but based on the information found in the section and in the book's glossary.

2. Consistency provides viewers with a sense of familiarity, comfort, and ease-of-use. Viewers are more likely to remain at your site if cues are easily available and the "look and feel" of a page is consistent. Repetition helps users find the buttons and links they need to navigate through the site quickly.

3. A Web site's repeating elements include the consistent use and placement of page banners, navigation buttons, and text-based links, which helps users navigate through the site.

Critical Thinking

4. Answers will vary, but should include points such as that the navigation, headings, and the site logo are all in the same location with a template, making it easier for users to navigate the site and find information faster. Students may specify that templates help the development of the site because developers can fill in the holes of a predesigned layout. In addition, updating a site is easier because developers only have to modify one template file to affect the look of the entire site.

   Students should also mention that templates can hurt development of the site because they may not be appropriate for unique sections of a site. In addition, templates can also make a site look too generic and may make the home page and subpages appear the same which takes away from the home page's importance.

5. Answers will vary. Examples may include meal times, school schedules, sports practice, bus schedules, etc.

Apply It!

Compare and Contrast Graphics The graphic that identifies the entire site (the logo graphic) appears on every page, providing the same visual cues, including color cues, on each page. The page's graphic (the title graphic) uses the same font (providing consistency), but a different font size and a different color. The smaller font size gives the reader the clue that the page is a child page of the home page. The page's graphic is more specific than the site's graphic, in that it describes the individual page. The elements work together. The page's graphic picks up a color from the site's graphic image.

CHAPTER 7

CLOSE

Reviewing Principles of Design Have students come up with a rubric for evaluating a Web page using the five presentation design principles discussed in this section. They should judge the following factors on a scale of one to four:

- How effectively white space is used
- How effectively related items are grouped
- Whether text/images are aligned consistently
- How easy it is to navigate using repeated design elements
- How consistent design elements are from page to page

CHAPTER 7

SECTION 7.2 CHOOSING COLORS
(Pages 198–201)

FOCUS

Understanding the Importance of Colors Colors are often associated with certain objects, activities, and feelings. To help students see this, ask the following: What color(s) do they associate with cheeriness? With solemnity? With patriotism? How might these associations affect their decision about which colors to use in a pre-school Web site? In a site for a funeral home? In a site for a political candidate? See if they can come up with additional examples of how color can be important in Web design.

(Page 198)

Focus on Reading

Read To Find Out
Use the Read to Find Out feature to focus student reading. Hold a quick starter discussion to find out what your students already know.

 Key Terms Online
Key term definitions and activities are available online at **WebDesignDW.glencoe.com**.

Reading Strategy Answer
Students should identify the four color scheme guidelines found under the heading *Color Scheme Guidelines* on page 198. Students' diagrams should look similar to this example:

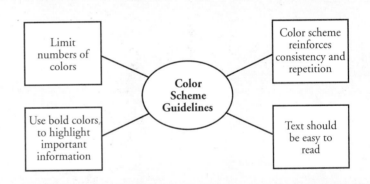

TEACH

Compare and Contrast Color Schemes As a class, visit several Web sites and lead a discussion about the color scheme of each site. Which site does the class think has the most effective scheme? Why? Make sure students consider the number of colors, the subject matter and purpose of the site, whether the colors distract the viewer or focus the viewer's attention appropriately, whether the colors make elements easy to read, and so on.

CHAPTER 7

Answers to Section 7.2 Captions and Activities

(Page 198) **Reading Focus** Colors that are appropriate for a site, a limited amount of colors, a text color that is easy to read, and using colors to reinforce consistency and repetition are the factors to consider when choosing a color scheme for a Web site.

(Page 198) **Activity 7.2** To give students additional experience with the use of color in Web pages, have them visit **WebDesignDW.glencoe.com**.

(Page 198) **Figure 7.7** Colors should contrast so the Web site content is easy to read.

(Page 198) ✓ **Reading Check** It is important to choose a color scheme that supports a Web site's theme because the site must look consistent, otherwise viewers may be confused or uncomfortable.

(Page 199) **Reading Focus** Web-safe colors are reliable on Web pages, which make sites more user-friendly.

(Page 199) **Activity 7D Add Content and Color to the Home Page** Students insert a header and a photo into the Language Club Web site's home page. They then use Web-safe colors to add colored text to the home page. Use the Student Data Files and Solution Files noted in this chapter's Planning Guide.

(Page 201) ✓ **Reading Check** Web designers originally decided to use Web-safe colors to provide reliable color within their pages on both Mac and PC computers.

ASSESS

(Page 201) ### Section 7.2 Assessment Answers

Reading Summary

Use the Reading Summary to help students review and reinforce the important points of the section.

What Did You Learn?

1. Students' definitions should be in their own words, but based on the information found in the section and in the book's glossary.

2. Students' answers will be in their own words but should include clicking within the editable region to be recolored, clicking on the Bg drop-down arrow in the Properties inspector and selecting a color, and saving the file.

3. Answers from students will vary but should include the following: choosing a color scheme reinforces consistency and repetition, using bold colors highlights important information, limiting the number of colors in a site creates a more unified look and feel, and avoiding excess use of color and use of color on color because it can make it difficult for a user to read and understand content.

Critical Thinking

4. Answers will vary, but should include thoughtful explanations for color choices.
5. Answers will vary, but should include thoughtful explanations for color choices.

Apply It!

Explore Background Colors Students change the background color of the Language Club home page and analyze the results. Students will likely note that the text becomes difficult to read with certain color choices. They may also note that the look of the site changes significantly when different background colors are used, and should be specific about these changes. For instance, a red background may not look as appropriate or professional for a home page about the ocean.

CLOSE

Using Color Scheme Guidelines Have students create a color scheme for a Web site about a summer camp that offers activities/classes in their favorite sport or hobby. The scheme should specify which Web-safe colors they would use. Have them do a sketch of the site's home page, indicating the elements on the page, and their color and placement. Let the class decide which sketch uses the most effective color scheme.

CHAPTER 7

SECTION 7.3 FONTS AND TYPOGRAPHY
(Pages 202–209)

FOCUS

Identifying Text Properties Students are probably familiar with many of the concepts in this section. To find out the extent of their knowledge, visit several Web sites with the class. Have them identify different font types, sizes, styles, and alignments. See if they have any thoughts about how these properties of text affect their response to the site. If students are familiar with HTML formatting, you may also want to note that some of the formatting terminology used by Dreamweaver does not always match that used in HTML. For example, and H1 heading in HTML often uses a 24 point font size. An H1 heading in Dreamweaver uses the font size of 6 which is equivalent to a 24 point font size.

(Page 202)

Focus on Reading

Read to Find Out
Use the Read to Find Out feature to focus student reading. Hold a quick starter discussion to find out what your students already know.

 **Key Terms Online**
Key term definitions and activities are available online at **WebDesignDW.glencoe.com**.

Reading Strategy Answer
Students can find information about serif and sans serif fonts under the heading *Readability* on page 206. Students' diagrams should look similar to this example:

Serif
- Extra curve or line at ends of some letters
- Easier to read on paper

- Affect readability
- Categories of fonts

Sans Serif
- No extra adornment on letters
- Easier to read on the screen

TEACH

Evaluating Font Type and Style Most students have used a variety of font types and styles, because it is fun and allows for creativity. However, these advantages must be balanced with readability and consistency in a Web site. To illustrate this, key a paragraph from Section 7.3 several times, applying a different font to each copy. How do students feel this affects the readability of the pages? What if these pages were all part of the same site? How might the lack of consistency affect a viewer?

CHAPTER 7

Answers to Section 7.3 Captions and Activities

(Page 202) **Reading Focus** When a Web page is properly formatted, visitors will find it easy to read and understand.

(Page 202) **Figure 7.11** Students' font lists will vary. You can review the fonts offered on classroom computers.

(Page 203) **Figure 7.12** Different sizes help the reader understand the structure of the content, such as, what is a title, what information is most important, and other aspects.

(Page 203) **Figure 7.13** Underlines are used for hyperlinks, not to emphasize text. Users may click on underlined text that is not a hyperlink and get frustrated.

(Page 204) **Figure 7.14** Most text on the Web is left-aligned.

(Page 204) **Figure 7.15** Different colors can be used to emphasize parts of the text on the page.

(Page 205) **Figure 7.16** The use of pre-defined styles is a quick and effective way to format text and to maintain consistency.

(Page 205) ✓ **Reading Check** The underline style isn't featured on the Dreamweaver Properties menu to discourage Web designers from using it for emphasis, because underlining is more commonly associated with hyperlinks.

(Page 206) **Reading Focus** Text that is consistent and readable makes a site user-friendly.

(Page 206) **Figure 7.17** A serif font has an extra line or curve at the end of some letters.

(Page 206) **Figure 7.18** Students should note that the example on the right contains a greater contrast between the background color and the text color and is therefore easier to read.

(Page 207) **Table 7.3** If a site is not readable, a visitor will move on.

(Page 207) **Figure 7.19** Based on the size of the text, the title is the most important element on the page.

(Page 208) **Table 7.4** Courier, Times, Courier New, and Times New Roman are serif fonts.

(Page 208) ✓ **Reading Check** A designer must consider readability, consistency, and appearance when deciding how to format text on a Web page.

(Page 208) **You Try It** **Activity 7E Format Text** Students complete the Language Club's home page by formatting text and alignment. Use the Solution Files noted in this chapter's Planning Guide.

(Page 209) ✓ **Reading Check** Use the Font drop-down menu to choose the font size.

CHAPTER 7

ASSESS

(Page 209) Section 7.3 Assessment Answers

Reading Summary

Use the Reading Summary to help students review and reinforce the important points of the section.

What Did You Learn?

1. Students' definitions should be in their own words, but based on the information found in the section and in the book's glossary.
2. Font is displayed differently by the Mac and Windows operating systems. The resolution settings on a monitor may affect size, whether set by the manufacturer or the user.
3. The three most common ways for specifying a font size are to enter a numerical value in the Size box of the Properties inspector, select a size from the Size drop-down menu on the Properties inspector, or choose a size from the menu bar by selecting Text>Size or Text>Size Change.

Critical Thinking

4. Students' answers will vary depending on the Web site they choose. They should demonstrate a good knowledge of the information included in the chapter, including the layout of the text for easy navigation, whether the text is serif or sans serif, and the different sizes of the text to indicate levels of importance.
5. Students' analyses should reflect an understanding of the section material. They should realize that the Web designer's personal preferences for certain colors (or fonts, and so on) should not take precedence over the needs of the site.

Apply It!

Evaluate Fonts Students experiment with different fonts for a photo caption. Their evaluations should note the way each choice affects the look of the page. For example, one font choice may compete with the text on the page, while another may look too small in relation to the rest of the page's content.

CLOSE

Applying Formatting Guidelines Have students work in pairs. Each student should copy a page of text (about 200 words) using a word processor. On this page, students should use many font types, sizes, styles, alignments, and colors. Then have the students correct each other's pages. They should align text consistently, limit the number of fonts, use formatting to emphasize text properly, and use styles and colors sparingly.

CHAPTER 7

(Page 210)

Ethics & Technology

RESPECTING INTELLECTUAL PROPERTY

Answers to Tech Check

1. Students' answers will vary, but should demonstrate a basic understanding of the nature of intellectual property, the rights associated with it, and the protections offered under copyright and trademark laws.

2. Before this activity, students should find real-world examples of copyright or trademark law violations and the consequences thereof. Encourage students to focus on various kinds of examples. Some may be more interested in the controversy surrounding the sharing of music files online, while others may focus on software piracy, movie piracy, trademark violations, or plagiarism. Ask students to focus on the actual and potential penalties in such cases. Also, ask students to determine what steps the violator could have taken to avoid getting into trouble.

CHAPTER 7 Answers to Chapter Review

The Chapter Review covers a wide range of student knowledge. Due to time constraints, students may not be able to complete every activity in the Chapter Review. Select the activities that are appropriate for your class needs and resources.

(Page 212) After You Read

Using Creative Study Tools Note that the classmate's study tool may or may not be as useful to the student as the one he or she devised. The point is not that only the student can create a good study tool for himself or herself, but that the tool must have meaning to the student in order to work. Although students will frequently come up with the most useful tool themselves, swapping tools or working together to create them can sometimes produce very effective results, and you may wish to encourage this.

(Page 212) Reviewing Key Terms

1. Repeating elements throughout a Web site may include:
   - Site logo placed on each page, linked to the home page
   - Banner, page title, or headline graphic, placed at top of each page
   - Navigation placement, whether graphical or text-linked
   - Color scheme
   - Text formatting

2. Consistency is a similarity among the parts of a whole. Repetition is the duplication of specific elements on all (or most) of a site's pages.

3. A page header, also known as a page banner, is typically a graphic that appears at the top of a page. The header is used to identify the site, the section of the site you are currently in, and, possibly, the site's primary navigation.

4. There were 216 Web-safe colors available and used in the past.

5. Typography is important on the Web because it can influence how clearly you communicate with your audience.

6. A pixel is a picture element and is also the most common unit of measurement on the Web for specifying font sizes.

7. Arial, Times New Roman, and Courier are three standard fonts.

8. Times Roman, Times New Roman, and Georgia are examples of serif fonts.

(Page 212) Understanding Main Ideas

9. Each page of the Language Club Web site includes the consistent use and placement of the logo, navigation, page titles, color scheme, and background image.

10. Use Web-safe colors to ensure consistent viewing, limit number of colors to three or four, and choose colors that appropriately convey your site's message.

11. Standard fonts are those that are found on most computer systems. A Web browser will substitute a different font from the one the designer has chosen if the browser's system does not have that font installed.

12. Five ways text can be formatted are: type, size, style, alignment, and color.

13. A serif font has an extra curve or line on the ends of certain letters and numbers. A sans serif font does not have end strokes. Serif fonts are considered most legible for printed text, while sans serif fonts are best on a computer screen.

Answers to Chapter Review — CHAPTER 7

14. Answers will vary, but can include article titles, which can be serif or sans serif font as, at a larger size, either are easily readable, and the contrast of font color and background, which should be sharp for easy readability.

15. Four types of alignment are left align, center align, right align and justified. The most common alignment is the left align.

(Page 212) ## Critical Thinking

16. Students' answers will vary and are speculative due to the ever-changing nature of the Web and how people use information. Students' reasoning should be based on real-world research if possible.

17. Students' analysis should include at least two ways the hardware and software used by the visitor affects the designer's choices. Examples may consider designer's use of fonts, text color and size, overall color scheme, and use of graphics or media.

18. Answers will vary based on the student's sense of design. Possible answers might include:

    a. A site about a children's theater would be created for a younger audience so a kidlike, playful, but readable typeface would be used for the logo, headings, and navigation. Using such a typeface would give the Web site a fun, more youthful appearance.

    b. A Web site about mountain climbing in the Swiss Alps might use a distinctive sans-serif typeface for headings and body text would also use sans-serif for legibility. For contrast, a serif typeface could be used for primary navigation to make it stand out from the other text.

19. Students' answers will vary but will compare and contrast the Web design principles of presentation design, consistency, and repetition with a television and a mobile phone.

20. Answers may vary. Formatting features for titles may include bold, a larger font size, and centering. Formatting features for important text may include bold or italic and perhaps a different font or color. Note that underlining should not be included in the list, since this is used on Web pages to indicate hyperlinks.

21. Answers may vary. A site might use many colors or unusual fonts if it:

    ◆ Is a site about rainbows, art supplies (such as paints), or something else multi-hued.
    ◆ Is a site for a printing shop which offers many font types and styles.
    ◆ Is a children's site that is colorful with small blocks of eye-catching information.
    ◆ Associates a certain color with a certain product/topic, and uses that color on the page about that product/topic.
    ◆ Is a game site with various themes.

    A site might use limited colors and traditional fonts if:

    ◆ Its expected audience is traditional or conservative.
    ◆ It contains scholarly information.
    ◆ It has a large amount of text.
    ◆ It is a site created for people with visual impairments.
    ◆ Its budget is limited.

CHAPTER 7 Answers to Chapter Review

(Page 213) **Command Center**

22. Ctrl + Shift + W = Close all open files in a site
23. Ctrl + N = Open New from Template dialog box
24. Ctrl + Alt + / = Open Insert Image dialog box

Standardized Test Practice

The correct answer is C. Advise students to read and review the definitions of repetition and consistency before they answer the question. A full comprehension of these terms is necessary to answer the question correctly.

Have students use the book's Web site **WebDesignDW.glencoe.com**.

- **Study with PowerTeach** Encourage your students to use the Chapter 7 PowerTeach Outline to review the chapter before they have a test.
- **Online Self Check** These quick five-question assessments may be used as an in-class activity, a homework assignment, or test review.

(Page 214) **Making Connections**

Science—Demonstrate Color Differences Students demonstrate the effect of color wavelength in identifying colors that come forward and colors that recede. Encourage students to try other combinations to see the effect.

(Page 214) **Standards at Work**

NETS-S 3 Analyze Text Styles and Color Students create a Web page to view the effect of different colors and font sizes. Encourage students to print this page and use it for reference as they build other Web sites.

(Page 215) **Teamwork Skills**

Create Web Content Students plan Web Design Tips and Resources page for your school's online handbook. Students write the content for the home page, which includes a paragraph and a bulleted list, and for the Graphics Resources page, which will contain links to graphics resources and descriptions of these resources. (Two good graphics resource links are Google and Yahoo, which both have images tabs.) Have students write brief content summaries of the other pages.

Answers to Chapter Review — CHAPTER 7

(Page 215) **Challenge Yourself**

Students create a color scheme for a store specializing in holiday decorations. They locate a graphic that they feel best represents the products and images of the store. Students then use Dreamweaver to refine the colors in the graphic (using Web-safe colors) to update the provided template with their new color scheme.

(Page 216)
1. **Format Text in Tables** Students add information about the Language Club's officers to the About Us page on the Language Club Web site.

2. **Add a Contact Us Page** Students add additional contact information to the Language Club's Contact Us page. Formatting for subheadings should match that described in the Skills Studio project. Information for teacher's name, school address, and school's phone number will vary but should be presented in an attractive, readable manner. Formatting for text underneath subheadings and for the table should match that described in the Skills Studio project. Check for spelling, formatting and grammatical errors.

Web Design Projects

(Page 217)
1. **Add Text to a Web Page** For this activity, students demonstrate their ability to create a new Web page called fundraiser.html from the Language_Main.dwt template. Students will store this new Web file in the pages subfolder. Students will insert the hdr_fundraiser.gif graphic (from the Student Data Files) into the page's header editable region. Students will copy, paste, or key in the content they created in You Try It Activity 6A (on page 165 of the student textbook). They will also format the text to be consistent with the rest of the Web site. Students will modify the Events page to include text from the Events.doc file included in the Student Data Files. They will also format this text to be consistent with the rest of the site. Last, students will select the word Fundraiser in the first paragraph and create a hyperlink that links to the fundraiser.html page.

2. **Refine Your Personal Web Site** Students refine the personal Web site they began in Chapter 6. They select and apply fonts for different text elements and create a color scheme for the entire site, including the background color. Students design a banner for their home page and a smaller banner for other pages. They also add a photograph and caption to the home page. The photograph becomes a hotspot to link to the personal interests page. Students do not need to add content to the personal interests page in this activity, although it would work as an extension activity.

UNIT 2

(Page 218) **BUILDING 21ST CENTURY SKILLS**

Project 1 Communicaton Skills: Write for a Web Audience

To quick start this project, bring in brochures, advertisements, or books that students can use for their Web page.

Have students print up a copy of their page. They should then have at least three other students in the class review the Web page and evaluate it in comparison to the original printed document. You can use the following rubric for student evaluations or have students come up with a rubric of their own.

Criteria	Excellent (3)	Satisfactory (2)	Poor (1)
Web page delivers the same information as printed material			
The subject and purpose are clear			
Web page targets the same audience as printed material			
Information is easy to understand			
Web page has an attractive appearance			
Page layout has sufficient white space and is not cluttered			
Text is easy to read			
Graphics relate to the text			
Links logically connect information			
Web page is successful adaptation of printed material			
Suggestions for improvement:			

Students should not see other students' evaluations. Afterwards, have students re-do their Web pages, using their classmates' reviews as a guide.

Project 2 Teamwork: Create a Web Site About Your Community

Students can form groups of four or less. Before beginning this project, you might want to have students brainstorm different people, places, or issues that are important to your town. Write their ideas on the board, and then have the class narrow down the list to ten topics. Remind students that they must present information in an ethical manner, citing sources and presenting issues fairly.

Teams should brainstorm ideas, assign roles to members, and discuss any problems or questions with you. Depending on their resources outside the classroom, students may continue this project outside of school. If they do, have them determine how they will communicate and review each other's work, for example, by e-mails, instant messaging, fax, phone, or meeting in person.

The final Web page should be presented to the class. Each group should explain the following:

◆ Why they chose their particular topic
◆ The purpose of their Web page
◆ The target audience of their Web page
◆ The role of each member of the group
◆ Any problems they had and how the problems were resolved

After each presentation, class members should give a brief review of the Web page. They should explain which elements work for them, which do not, and why.

(Page 219) ## BUILDING YOUR PORTFOLIO

The Portfolio projects are ongoing activities that build upon the material in the unit. By the end of the course, the students should have work samples that show every stage of their knowledge development. Explain to students how to save their samples as hard copies, online copies, or personal disks.

Create a Food Festival Web Page

Have students design their Web pages as if they were linked to a home page and other pages on their school's Web site.

This project will require students to do some research such as interviewing a teacher, other school staff, or staff from a local area restaurant that represents a particular type of food or culture. Help them plan how they will find the information and graphics they need for the Web page. Students should write out a list of suitable questions that they can ask the people they interview.

When reviewing the Web pages, students may create a class rubric based on the Web Page Checklist in their textbooks (page 219). If they like, they can add additional elements to the rubric. Reviews can be done as oral presentations to the whole class, or students can be given time to view each other's pages individually. Suggestions for improving the Web page may be given orally during a presentation, or students may write out suggestions to include with their rubrics.

You may choose to explain to students how to take and print screen shots for their portfolios. Also, suggest the process they should use to create an electronic copy of the finished product.

Unit 2 Designing Web Sites

Notes

Unit 3

Enhancing a Web Site

(Page 220)

Have students go to **WebDesignDW.glencoe.com**. Then have them click on **Unit Activities > Unit 3 Evaluating Web Sites**. Students can learn how to evaluate Web sites to make sure the information is accurate and reliable.

Students can find helpful Web site Evaluation Guides online. They can then use the guidelines to evaluate various Web sites, including the Evaluation Guide site itself. Have students practice evaluating more sites by clicking on the Web Design Resource links and Go Online Activity links provided on this book's Web site. Let students suggest their favorite sites and, with your approval, evaluate those as well. Take a class poll to see which sites were identified as highly reliable, somewhat reliable, or not very reliable.

Complete answers to each Unit Activity are available on the book Web site in the password-protected Teacher Center portion of the site.

(Page 221)

Think About It

In this activity students evaluate design elements, in particular those elements that are intended to catch a user's attention. To quick start your students on this project, bring in some examples of books and magazines that you think will help them recognize both good and poor design.

- Show students your examples and ask them to identify the layouts they like and which they do not. Have them explain the reasons for their preferences.
- Ask the students which elements work on the printed page but might not work as well on a Web page. Then have them explain why.

This activity can be completed as either a class discussion or as a topic for individual student papers. If you assign this activity as homework, ask students to use one of the examples you brought in or have students show you copies of the book or magazine pages they are evaluating.

As students complete the unit and add multimedia and interactive elements to their Web sites, encourage them to think about how these elements contribute to the overall design of the Web page. Students are often drawn to elements that flash or move. Encourage them to think about how these elements support the content and design of a page before they add them to their site.

CHAPTER 8 Planning Guide

Student Edition	Activities and Exercises
Chapter 8 Using Web Graphics (pages 222–249)	Quick Write Activity, page 222 Before You Read, page 223
Section 8.1 Web Graphic Types and File Formats (pages 224–227)	📁 Reading Strategy, page 224
Section 8.2 Obtaining and Modifying Graphics (pages 228–235)	📁 Reading Strategy, page 228 ⓘ Go Online Activity 8.1: Locate Graphics, page 228 𝒹 ⊙ You Try It Activity 8A: Insert an Inline Graphic, page 230 𝒹 You Try It Activity 8B: Crop, Resize, and Resample a Graphic, page 233 You Try It Activity 8C: Modify a Graphic, page 234
Emerging Technology Envisioning the Internet's Future (page 236)	Tech Check, page 236
Section 8.3 Image Maps and Web Albums (pages 237–242)	📁 Reading Strategy, page 237 𝒹 ⊙ You Try It Activity 8D: Create an Image Map with Hotspots, page 238 ⓘ Go Online Activity 8.2: Explore Image Editing Programs, page 239 𝒹 ⊙ You Try It Activity 8E: Create a Web Photo Album Using Fireworks, page 240
Chapter 8 Review (pages 243–249)	Making Connections: Math—Compare Download Times ⓘ Standards at Work: Copyrights and Permissions for Use (NETS-S 2) 𝒹 Teamwork Skills: Create Images and a Web Site Challenge Yourself: Compare Graphic File Types You Try It Skills Studio: 𝒹 —Add Graphics to a Web Page 𝒹 —Use Hotspots Web Design Projects: ⓘ 𝒹 —Create a Virtual Field Trip Web Site —Create an Art Styles Web Site Additional Activities You May Wish to Use: ⊙ ⓘ —PowerTeach Outlines Chapter 8 —Student Workbook Chapter 8

Planning Guide CHAPTER 8

Assessments

Section 8.1 Assessment, page 227

Section 8.2 Assessment, page 235

Section 8.3 Assessment, page 242

Chapter 8 Review and Assessment, page 243
You may also use any of the Chapter Review Activities and Projects as Assessments.
Additional Assessments You May Wish to Use:
—Self-Check Assessments Chapter 8
—*ExamView* Testbank Chapter 8

Estimated Time to Complete Chapter

18 week course = 5 days
36 week course = 10 days

To help customize lesson plans, use the Pacing Guide on pages 26–30 and the Standards Charts on pages 248–249.

Key to Recommended Materials

Icons represent elements that may require additional resources.

📁 Focus on Reading

ⓘ Internet access required

♩ Software: Dreamweaver

 Teacher Resource CD (contains Student Data Files, Solution Files, Reproducible Graphic Organizers, and Study with PowerTeach Outlines)

Data and Solution Files for Chapter 8

DataFiles
- BikeHike
- bike.jpg
- image_map.gif
- Photos

SolutionFiles
- SF_YTI_8ABC
- SF_YTI_8DE

Inclusion Strategies

For **Differentiated Instruction Strategies** refer to the **Inclusion in the Computer Technology Classroom** booklet.

Unit 3 Enhancing a Web Site

CHAPTER 8 — NETS Correlation For Students

ISTE NETS Foundation Standards

1. Basic operations and concepts
2. Social, ethical, and human issues
3. Technology productivity tools
4. Technology communications tools
5. Technology research tools
6. Technology problem-solving and decision-making tools

Performance Indicators	Textbook Correlation
1. Identify capabilities and limitations of contemporary and emerging technology resources and assess the potential of these systems and services to address personal, lifelong learning, and workplace needs. (NETS 2)	**SE:** Critical Thinking (227, 235, 242, 244, 245), Tech Check (236), Making Connections (246), Challenge Yourself (247)
2. Make informed choices among technology systems, resources, and services. (NETS 1, 2)	**SE:** You Try It (230, 233, 234, 238, 240), Critical Thinking (27, 235, 242, 244, 245), Apply It! (227, 235, 242), Making Connections (246), Teamwork Skills (247)
3. Analyze advantages and disadvantages of widespread use and reliance on technology in the workplace and in society as a whole. (NETS 2)	**SE:** Tech Check (236)
4. Demonstrate and advocate for legal and ethical behaviors among peers, family, and community regarding the use of technology and information. (NETS 2)	**SE:** Quick Tip (229), Standards at Work (246)
5. Use technology tools and resources for managing and communicating personal/professional information (e.g. finances, schedules, addresses, purchases, correspondence). (NETS 3, 4)	
6. Evaluate technology-based options, including distance and distributed education, for lifelong learning. (NETS 5)	**SE:** Go Online (228, 239), Tech Check (236)
7. Routinely and efficiently use online information resources to meet needs for collaboration, research, publications, communications, and productivity. (NETS 4, 5, 6)	**SE:** Tech Check (236), Go Online (228, 239), Standards at Work (246), Web Design Projects (249)
8. Select and apply technology tools for research, information analysis, problem-solving, and decision-making in content learning. (NETS 4, 5)	**SE:** Go Online (228, 239), Tech Check (236), Apply It! (235), Making Connections (246), Teamwork Skills (247), Challenge Yourself (247), Web Design Projects (249)
9. Investigate and apply expert systems, intelligent agents, and simulations in real-world situations. (NETS 3, 5, 6)	**SE:** You Try It (230, 233, 234, 238, 240), Apply It! (235), Web Design Projects (249)
10. Collaborate with peers, experts, and others to contribute to content-related knowledge base by using technology to compile, synthesize, produce, and disseminate information, models, and other creative works. (NETS 4, 5, 6)	**SE:** Teamwork Skills (247)

SCANS Correlation — CHAPTER 8

Foundation Skills

Basic Skills	
Reading	**SE:** Before You Read (223), Focus on Reading (224, 228, 237), Reading Strategies (224, 228, 237), After You Read (244)
Writing	**SE:** Quick Write Activity (222), Section Assessments (227, 235, 242), Chapter Review (244–249)
Mathematics	**SE:** Apply It! (227), Critical Thinking (245), Making Connections (246), Challenge Yourself (247)
Listening and Speaking	**SE:** Teamwork Skills (247)

Thinking Skills	
Creative Thinking	**SE:** Think About It (221), Quick Write Activity (222), Teamwork Skills (247), Web Design Projects (249)
Critical Thinking	**SE:** Think About It (221), Critical Thinking (227, 235, 242, 244, 245), Tech Check (236), Making Connections (246), Challenge Yourself (247)
Problem Solving	**SE:** Standards at Work (246), Web Design Projects (249)

Workplace Competencies

Resources Manage time, money, materials, facilities, human resources	**SE:** Command Center (245)
Interpersonal Work on teams, teach others	**SE:** After You Read (244), Teamwork Skills (247)
Information Acquire, evaluate, organize, maintain, interpret, communicate and use computers to process information	**SE:** You Try It (230, 233, 234, 238, 240), Critical Thinking (227, 235, 242, 244, 245), Apply It! (227, 235, 242), Tech Check (218, 230), Go Online (228, 239), Command Center (245), Making Connections (246), Standards at Work (246), Teamwork Skills (247), Challenge Yourself (247), Skills Studio (248), Web Design Projects (249)
Systems Understand, monitor, correct, improve, design systems	**SE:** You Try It (230, 233, 234, 238, 240), Skills Studio (248), Web Design Projects (249)
Technology Select, apply, maintain, and troubleshoot technology.	**SE:** You Try It (230, 233, 234, 238, 240), Apply It! (227, 235, 242, 244, 245), Go Online (228, 239), Making Connections (246), Teamwork Skills (247), Challenge Yourself (247), Skills Studio (248), Web Design Projects (249)

CHAPTER 8

Using Web Graphics

(Page 222) **Objectives**

Section 8.1: Web Graphic Types and File Formats
- Identify types of graphics
- Identify and compare graphic formats
- Describe compression schemes

Section 8.2: Obtaining and Modifying Graphics
- Identify image sources
- Use graphics ethically
- Insert and inline graphic
- Crop, resize, and resample a graphic
- Modify a graphic

Section 8.3: Image Maps and Web Albums
- Create an image map with hotspots
- Create a Web photo album
- Create a thumbnail

LEARNING LINK

Chapters 6 and 7 dealt with different aspects of how to sustain a viewer's interest in a Web site. Chapter 8 continues to explore this by showing students how to use graphics to create an interesting Web site that captures a viewer's attention.

(Page 222) **Why It Matters**

Find some emotion-evoking images in magazines. Describe the situation that the image is depicting, and lead a brief discussion about it. Then show the image to the students, and see if their reaction changes or intensifies.

(Page 222) **Quick Write Activity**

As an alternative activity, you could ask the students to think of a situation in their school that they have strong feelings about. Then ask them to make a list of images that might call attention to the topic.

(Page 223) **Before You Read**

Prior Knowledge You can help your students connect to a subject by showing how much they already know about it. Have students form small groups to go over each point in the "I Will Learn To..." objectives. They should make a list of what everyone in the group already knows about the subjects. Then they should make a list of questions about what they want to find out. Have them write their responses on the board.

CHAPTER 8

SECTION 8.1 WEB GRAPHIC TYPES AND FILE FORMATS
(Pages 224–227)

FOCUS

Analyzing Download Time Students have probably had the experience of waiting for images on a Web page to download. Lead a brief discussion about how long they might be willing to wait for an image to download before surfing to another site or another page on the site. Does it depend on what they expect the image to be? The expected quality of the image? Other factors? Discuss how this might be relevant when they are choosing graphics for a Web site. After finishing this section, ask how download time might affect which file formats they select for the graphic(s) they use.

(Page 224)

Focus on Reading

Read to Find Out
Use the Read to Find Out feature to focus student reading. Hold a quick starter discussion to find out what your students already know.

 Key Terms Online
Key term definitions and activities are available online at **WebDesignDW.glencoe.com**.

Reading Strategy Answer
Students can find information about GIF and JPEG file formats under the heading *Graphic File Formats* on page 225. Students' Venn diagrams should look similar to this example:

- **GIF Files** save only a maximum of 256 colors, are small files that download quickly, can be made transparent
- are based on pixels, most browsers will display images saved in either type of file
- **JPEG Files** can support millions of colors, better for photographs, are larger files that download more slowly

TEACH

Drawing Conclusions About File Quality If you have access to an image-editing program such as Macromedia Fireworks or Adobe Photoshop, you can show students how to adjust JPEG file quality. You can use an image from the Student Data Files images folder for Chapter 8.

To adjust JPEG file quality in Fireworks MX 2004, open a JPEG image using Open from the Start menu or by choosing **File>Open**. Choose **File>Export Preview** to adjust JPEG quality settings. To display two view windows for displaying the original and the optimized version, click the **2 preview windows** button at the bottom right of the dialog box. Remove the checkmark from the Preview box of either view window

Unit 3 Enhancing a Web Site 251

CHAPTER 8

to display the original. To see four view windows, click the **4 preview windows** button at the bottom right. Again, be sure to remove the checkmark from at least one of the Preview options in the four windows to display the original image alongside optimized image previews.

To adjust JPEG file quality in Photoshop, open a JPEG image using **File>Open**. Choose **File>Save** for Web to display the Save for Web dialog box. Choose either 2-Up or 4-Up from the tabs at the top of the dialog box. This will provide several view windows. One will display the file as it originally looks. Use the other windows to show the effects of adjusting the quality of the JPEG file. To modify JPEG settings, select JPG from the drop-down menu to the right of the dialog box. Adjust the quality setting and compare the file size against the quality of the image in the view window.

If you only have access to Dreamweaver, you can bring in a selection of photos and graphics into a Web page that have different file sizes and show students how file size and quality are related to download time.

Answers to Section 8.1 Captions and Activities

(Page 224) **Reading Focus** The two basic types of graphics are raster graphics and vector graphics.

(Page 224) ✓ **Reading Check** A raster graphic is made up of pixels. A vector graphic is composed of lines defined by mathematical equations.

(Page 225) **Reading Focus** A GIF file downloads quickly, is good for line drawings and simple graphics, supports a maximum of 256 colors, and can be used to create transparent images and animation effects. A JPEG file supports millions of colors, is good for saving photographs, and has a slower download time.

(Page 225) **Table 8.1** The GIF and PNG formats download quickly.

(Page 225) ✓ **Reading Check** The JPEG format is better for saving photographs.

(Page 226) **Reading Focus** Web designers compress image files so they download more quickly in a user's browser.

(Page 226) ✓ **Reading Check** Kbps stands for kilobytes per second.

(Page 227) **Figure 8.2** Use GIF for line drawings such as cartoons, simple graphics, and text objects. Also use GIF for drawings with transparency or animation.

ASSESS

(Page 227) ## Section 8.1 Assessment Answers

Reading Summary

Use the Reading Summary to help students review and reinforce the important points of the section.

CHAPTER 8

What Did You Learn?

1. Students' definitions should be in their own words, but based on the information found in the section and in the book's glossary.
2. Raster graphics are made up of pixels that, when viewed together, form a seamless image. Vector graphics are used for simple shapes using mathematical equations. Both types of graphics are used on the Web. You may want to note that a scanned photograph is an example of a raster graphic.

Critical Thinking

3. A long download time will frustrate many users, who will surf to another site.
4. Students' answers will vary, but should include a version of the following. When choosing graphic file formats for a new art gallery site, you will need to keep the following question in mind: do the graphics need to be clear and full of color (directly representing the original artwork), or is a quick download using less color and quality acceptable?

Apply It!

Convert File Formats Students use an image such as flower.jpg to compare the quality and the size of a JPEG file and a GIF file. They will find that the GIF is smaller than the JPEG file, but is of lesser quality.

CLOSE

Using Graphic File Formats Provide the students with a variety of graphics, and have them indicate which file format they would save them in. Ask them to explain their choices. (Their choices should take into consideration the size of the file that would be needed, its download time, the image quality they think is necessary, and so on.)

CHAPTER 8

SECTION 8.2 OBTAINING AND MODIFYING GRAPHICS
(Pages 228–235)

FOCUS

Using Graphics Many students have downloaded graphics. Ask them to describe what they used graphics for, what kinds of graphics they have used, and where they found them. Did students think about the ethical issues involved in graphic use beforehand? What do they think these issues might be?

(Page 228)

Focus on Reading

Read to Find Out
Use the Read to Find Out feature to focus student reading. Hold a quick starter discussion to find out what your students already know.

 Key Terms Online
Key term definitions and activities are available online at **WebDesignDW.glencoe.com**.

Reading Strategy Answer
Students should identify five ways to obtain or create graphics using information that can be found throughout the section. The students' Web diagrams should look similar to this example:

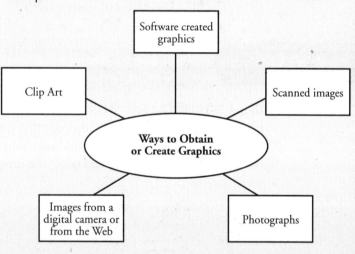

TEACH

Understanding Graphics Use As suggested in the student text by the "royalty free" example, the ethical use of graphics can be less than straightforward. Visit several Web sites that provide graphics with the class, and have them read the Terms of Use agreements. You might use a site like American Greetings (**www.americangreetings.com/legal.pd#top**) and Newsweek (**www.msnbc.com/modules/newsweek/info/nwinfo_reprints.asp**) Lead a discussion to see if they students have an accurate understanding of the ways in which they could use the graphics on these sites ethically.

254 Teacher Resource Manual *Introduction to Web Design Using Dreamweaver*

CHAPTER 8

Answers to Section 8.2 Captions and Activities

(Page 228) **Reading Focus** The two main ways of acquiring graphics are using premade graphics or creating original graphics.

(Page 228) **Activity 8.1** To provide students with additional help in locating graphics for Web pages, have them visit **WebDesignDW.glencoe.com**.

(Page 229) **Figure 8.3** A scanner converts a photo into a digital format.

(Page 229) ✓ **Reading Check** To use graphics ethically, a user must read a Web site's instructions for using a graphic, and/or obtain specific permission for that graphic.

(Page 230) **You Try It** **Activity 8A Insert an Inline Graphic** Students insert an inline graphic into the Bike and Hike Web site. Use the Student Data Files and Solution Files noted in this chapter's Planning Guide.

(Page 230) ✓ **Reading Check** `<IMG src>` is used to insert graphic files into a Web page.

(Page 231) **Reading Focus** Fireworks can be used to modify images in Dreamweaver.

(Page 231) **Figure 8.5** Filters might be useful when you want to create specific effects, such as making the image look like an oil painting.

(Page 232) **Figure 8.6** The size of an image can be changed by cropping, resizing, or resampling its dimensions.

(Page 233) **You Try It** **Activity 8B Crop, Resize, and Resample a Graphic** Students crop, resize, and resample an image in the Bike and Hike Web site. Use the Solution Files noted in this chapter's Planning Guide.

(Page 234) **You Try It** **Activity 8C Modify a Graphic** Students modify an image in the Bike and Hike Web site. Use the Solution Files noted in this chapter's Planning Guide.

(Page 235) ✓ **Reading Check** The four buttons in the Properties inspector you can use to edit images are Crop, Resample, Brightness and Contrast, and Sharpen.

ASSESS

(Page 235) **Section 8.2 Assessment Answers**

Reading Summary

Use the Reading Summary to help students review and reinforce the important points of the section.

What Did You Learn?

1. Students' definitions should be in their own words, but based on the information found in the section and in the book's glossary.

Unit 3 Enhancing a Web Site **255**

2. To resize an image in Dreamweaver, select the image, and drag the sizing handles to the desired size. Hold the Shift key down while performing this action to keep the image's aspect ratio constant and in proportion.

3. Resampling involves adding or removing pixels from a resized image in an effort to restore its quality. If the image size is decreased, resampling also decreases the file's size so that it downloads more quickly.

Critical Thinking

4. Cropping a photo involves the removal of some of the photo, while resizing keeps the photo intact. Cropping is useful when some portion of the photo is distracting or not needed for its intended use; resizing is useful when the entire photo is appropriate for use, but it is the wrong size for its intended space.

5. Answers will vary. A student might use a digital camera to take a photograph of the cast, scan the title graphic from the printed script using a scanner, use a Clip Art graphic of theater curtains, and use an image editing program to pull all of those images together to create a flyer to advertise the theater.

Apply It!

Create a Logo Students create a logo for a small business. Encourage students to be creative, use different tools to create different logos, and compare the results.

> **Teaching Tip**
>
> **NOTE:** Students in a lab with Studio MX will also have access to Fireworks and Freehand for creating logos. If applicable, you can suggest using these tools.

CLOSE

Locating Graphics In groups, students research at least two software applications with graphics. One should be commercial software. Ask them to compare and contrast the features of the programs, including the quantity and quality of the images. Based on their findings, when is it worthwhile to buy a commercial image package?

(Page 236)

EMERGING Technology

ENVISIONING THE INTERNET'S FUTURE

Answers to Tech Check

1. Answers will vary, but should show an understanding of the chosen technology or protocol and the W3C's role in its development. Students can find information about the technologies discussed in this feature at the W3C Web site. Students should also use other online or print resources and demonstrate effective search strategies and information-gathering skills.

2. Anyone can join the W3C. If students join, they will be encouraged to participate in some way. Even though they could not develop technologies or create protocols, they may be able to help with their testing.

CHAPTER 8

SECTION 8.3 IMAGE MAPS AND WEB ALBUMS
(Pages 237–242)

FOCUS

Understanding Image Maps and Web Albums Web designers use photo albums to help users navigate a section of a site in which many photographs or graphics need to be displayed. Ask students to name some examples of sites in which the photo album might be used.

(Page 237)

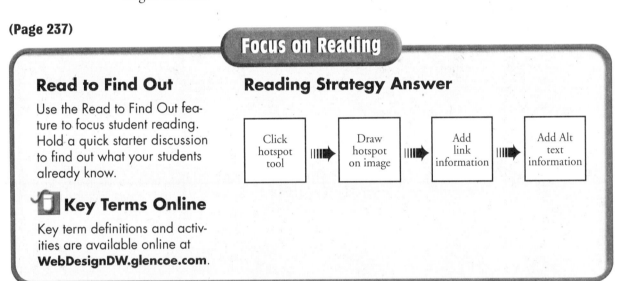

Read to Find Out
Use the Read to Find Out feature to focus student reading. Hold a quick starter discussion to find out what your students already know.

Key Terms Online
Key term definitions and activities are available online at **WebDesignDW.glencoe.com**.

TEACH

Creating Hotspots Have students explore the three hotspot tools using one image such as a world map. Ask students what type of hotspot is easiest to create for this type of image. Should any one type of hotspot be used over the others? Why or why not? A world map has irregular boundaries for countries. Ask students to identify the most appropriate type of hotspot in this situation. In Code view, have students examine the HTML code generated by the three types of image map hotspots.

Unit 3 Enhancing a Web Site **257**

CHAPTER 8

Answers to Section 8.3 Captions and Activities

(Page 237) **Reading Focus** An image map is a graphic that contains hotspots.

(Page 237) **Table 8.2** You need hotspots that are different shapes because there are different types of hotspot boundaries on graphics.

(Page 238) **You Try It** **Activity 8D Create an Image Map with Hotspots** Students use Dreamweaver to create an image map with hotspots in the Bike and Hike Web site. Use the Student Data Files and Solution Files noted in this chapter's Planning Guide.

Teaching Tip

Remind students about fair use guidelines regarding obtaining graphics and posting them on student created Web sites. Three specific questions to ask for a student created Web site are: 1) Is the graphic in the public domain or do you have permission to use the graphic from the publisher?; 2) Is the graphic going to be used on a temporary student project, or on a portfolio created site for college or employment purposes?; and 3) If the graphic is acceptable to use have you documented its source?

(Page 239)  **Activity 8.2** Image editing programs and their features change at a rapid pace. Up-to-date information on this topic can be found at **WebDesignDW.glencoe.com**.

(Page 239) ✓ **Reading Check** Clicking a hotspot takes a user to related pages or other areas on the current page.

(Page 240) **You Try It** **Activity 8E Create a Web Photo Album Using Fireworks** Students use the Fireworks or similar application to create a Web photo album on the Bike and Hike Web site. Use the Student Data Files and Solution Files noted in this chapter's Planning Guide. For an additional step-by-step activity that teaches students how to create a Web photo gallery using Adobe Photoshop, visit the online learning center at **www.WebDesignDW.glencoe.com**.

(Page 242) ✓ **Reading Check** A thumbnail is a small image that links to a larger version of the same image.

ASSESS

(Page 242) ### Section 8.3 Assessment Answers

Reading Summary

Use the Reading Summary to help students review and reinforce the important points of the section.

What Did You Learn?

1. Students' definitions should be in their own words, but based on the information found in the section and in the book's glossary.

2. A hotspot and a thumbnail are similar in that both are links from one graphic to another. They are different in that a thumbnail is typically a smaller representation of a larger photograph or image. A hotspot is a small area on a larger photograph or graphic that links to other pages. A graphic using image map hotspots can have multiple links within it whereas a thumbnail only links to one file or image.

3. To complete a Web photo album in Dreamweaver you need Fireworks or a similar application.

Critical Thinking

4. Student answers will vary. An example of a reason a Web designer might decide to use an image map as opposed to a navigation button or a text link is because adding a new navigation button to a page changes the design of the Web site's navigation menu. Using an image map is a way to add a link without changing that feel. Another reason is that the image map can enhance the connection between the image used as a link and the next page being linked.

5. Two situations in which thumbnails would be useful on a Web page are when many photographs are to be displayed, a page of thumbnails will download faster than a page of large size files, and when the site is being created with users in mind who have dial-up connections so the pages will load quickly when they contain thumbnails.

Apply It!

Create a Web Photo Album Encourage students to use their own digital photos of family members or friends for this assessment activity. If those are unavailable, provide suitable substitutes for use. Using Fireworks or a similar application and Dreamweaver, have students create a Web Photo Album using the steps outlined in Activity 8E (page 240 of the student textbook). Students should create a page with introductory text, thumbnails, and instructions for how to navigate through the photo album. Ensure the thumbnails link to the appropriate larger images and pages. The pages with the larger images should contain at least one interesting fact about the person pictured. See the book's Web site for an additional activity that teaches students how to create a Web photo gallery using Adobe Photoshop.

CLOSE

Creating an Album Directory Using knowledge of image maps and Web photo albums, have students create an image to be used as a directory for the photo album. Students will use hotspots on the image to help visitors navigate through the photo album. An example of this would be a collage of animals that helps visitors navigate through a "trip to the zoo" photo album.

CHAPTER 8 Answers to Chapter Review

The Chapter Review covers a wide range of student knowledge. Due to time constraints, students may not be able to complete every activity in the Chapter Review. Select the activities that are appropriate for your class needs and resources.

(Page 244) ## After You Read

Add to Your Knowledge To review the chapter, go over each item in your students' lists of what they already know and what they want to find out. See if the chapter confirmed what they originally knew. If not, ask students for the correct information. See if they can give you answers to the questions they wanted to answer. If some topics are not covered in the book, be prepared to supply answers, or use this as an extra-credit challenge assignment.

(Page 244) ## Reviewing Key Terms

1. A raster graphic can be used on the Web and a vector graphic cannot. A raster graphic is made up of pixels mapped to create an image. A vector graphic is achieved by graphical calculations, not by individual pixels.
2. PAINT is NOT a graphic file type.
3. The abbreviation "dpi" stands for dots per inch.
4. Scanners and digital cameras are two input devices you can use to create images for your Web site.
5. Image maps contain hotspots that you click to go to related topics.
6. To resize an image in Dreamweaver, select the image, and drag the sizing handles to the desired size. Hold the Shift key down while doing this to keep the image's aspect ratio constant and in proportion.

(Page 244) ## Understanding Main Ideas

7. The file extension (.jpg, .gif, .bmp, and so on) at the end of a graphic file's name will reveal its format.
8. You can obtain images from those already loaded on your hard drive, from a Clip Art Web site, from graphical software programs, by creating your own, or by using friends' art.
9. Raster graphics: Adobe Photoshop, Macromedia Fireworks
   Vector graphics: Adobe Illustrator, Macromedia Freehand
10. If you do not maintain a picture's aspect ratio, the image may become distorted.
11. Resizing an image differs from resampling it in that resizing an image changes the size of the image, but the file size stays the same. When an image is resampled, the number of pixels in the image changes, so the file size will be smaller or larger.
12. Image maps can save space text links may otherwise take up on a Web page. For example, instead of creating a page with links to all 50 states, you could simply create a map of the United States and include hotspots for each state.
13. Both change the image's look. Resizing just changes the dimensions of the image, whereas cropping deletes portions out of the image so the image is not just a smaller or larger version of the original.

Answers to Chapter Review — CHAPTER 8

14. GIF, JPG, and PNG are similar in that they are all graphic type file formats. They are different in that GIF is better for line drawings and simple graphics, JPG is better for photographs, and PNG is better for quick downloads and maintaining more colors than the GIF format.

(Page 244) ## Critical Thinking

15. Answers will vary, but students who have read this chapter material have been told that it is illegal to use other people's work without their permission. Students may choose to remind or teach the friend about the ethical use of others' work.

16. If bandwidth size is not an issue, you would use JPEG to compress files, and you would be able to maintain a high quality of the photographs.

17. You have to convert the JPEG files to GIF files, as animations are made of GIF files and JPG does not support multiple images within its file format.

18. The image is not linked correctly or is missing from the images/picture folder. A student would need to verify the graphic's location or that it exists or that its file name is correct and save the page again.

19. You would scan the image in at 72 dpi (for Web use), insert into a Web page and upload both the page and the image. If the image is a photograph, it will almost always be in JPEG format.

20. Most graphics, other than photographs, would be saved in the GIF format because the quality is high while the file size is low. If, however, some of the graphics use multi-colored blends—also known as gradients—you would most likely save those as JPEG files since the JPEG format supports more color information than the GIF file's 256 = color limit.

21. The higher an image's resolution and quality, the larger its file size and the longer its download time. However, long download times may cause users to surf to another site. Therefore, a Web designer has to choose images that are of sufficient quality to serve the site's purpose but will not take unduly long to download.

(Page 245) ## Command Center

22. **Ctrl + F2** = Opens Insert toolbar
23. **Ctrl + Z** = Undo
24. **F2** = Opens Dreamweaver Help Topics

Standardized Test Practice

The answer is D. Tell students that they should read the Graphic File Formats table carefully. Remind them that they will have to interpret the data in the table in order to answer the question. Then they can use the process of elimination when choosing the true statement.

CHAPTER 8 Answers to Chapter Review

Have students use the book's Web site **WebDesignDW.glencoe.com**.

- **Study with PowerTeach** Encourage your students to use the Chapter 8 PowerTeach Outlines to review the chapter before they have a test.
- **Online Self Check** These quick five-question assessments may be used as an in-class activity, a homework assignment, or test review.

(Page 246) Making Connections

Math—Compare Download Times Students create a line graph that shows the size of graphic files on one axis and the download time on the other. The elements of the line graph should be clearly and properly labeled. The students should conclude that as the file size declines, so does the quality and download time. Students create a pyramid table to report their findings for slowest to the fastest downloading file.

(Page 246) Standards at Work

NETS-S 2 Copyrights and Permissions for Use Students find sites that contain Clip Art or other visual images. They review the site's usage terms and licensing agreements and then summarize how the site's images could be used for the four purposes listed. Students also describe how they would obtain permission to use graphics for any of those purposes. Sites that students may want to visit include **www.corbis.com**, **www.clipart.com**, and **www.gettyimages.com**.

(Page 247) Teamwork Skills

Create Images and a Web Site Teams plan and create a three-page Web site using shared borders and a theme. The site will include various types of images that have been manipulated using Dreamweaver tools in the Properties inspector. The team selects the subject for the site. Students should use a rubric to evaluate each others' sites. A sample rubric is supplied in Appendix D of the student textbook, or rubrics can be located online.

(Page 247) Challenge Yourself

Compare Graphic File Types Students create a simple line drawing in Microsoft Paint or another paint program. They save this file in each of the formats available in the paint program and record the size of the file. Finally, they create a table that compares the file types and file sizes. They may add other descriptive information to the table such as a column to describe the quality of the image when saved in each format. Students should write a paragraph noting quality differences and explaining that the larger the file, the longer the download time.

Answers to Chapter Review — CHAPTER 8

You Try It Skills Studio

(Page 248)

1. **Add Graphics to a Web Page** Students add various types of graphics to the page they create from any sources available to them. They edit the images as needed and provide permission or licensing information for images from outside sources.

2. **Use Hotspots** Students should examine the logo's shape to determine which of the three hotspot tools is best suited for the task. For example, an irregularly shaped logo would use the Polygon Hotspot Tool while a logo that is circular in shape would use the Oval Hotspot Tool.

   > **Teaching Tip**
   > As students work through the second activity of the You Try It Skills Studio, remind them that not every graphic is a good candidate for a hotspot. Hotspots should exist to link to pages with important information for visitors.

   When complete, students will create a link from the logo to another page in the site where visitors can learn more about how to volunteer for the event described. Be sure students provide alternate text within the hotspot.

   Evaluate students' use of the hotspot tools on the remaining graphics and ensure they link to other pages properly and include alternate text information.

Web Design Projects

(Page 249)

1. **Create a Virtual Field Trip Web Site** Students create a virtual field trip Web site. The site contains a home page and six pages connected to the home page, one for each field trip planned. Students create a theme and text styles and use a title graphic and navigation bar to create a consistent look and feel. Students create an image map on the home page with an image (hotspot) linking to each of the six pages in the site. Encourage students to carefully review the site in a browser and make changes and refinements as needed.

2. **Create an Art Styles Web Site** Students create an art styles Web site. The site will contain a home page and four pages connected to the home page, one for each of four different styles of art. Students find representative images for one of these styles, and obtain permission for their use as needed. They create the home page and a page for each style, and apply a suitable theme, customizing as needed. They add navigation from the home page to each of the styles pages. Then they build the style page they selected, inserting the images they found and manipulating them as necessary. They should provide alternative text for each image and view the site in a browser.

CHAPTER 9 Planning Guide

Student Edition	Activities and Exercises
Chapter 9 Adding Multimedia to a Web Site (pages 250–275)	Quick Write Activity, page 250 Before You Read, page 251
Section 9.1 Multimedia and Web Design (pages 252–256)	Reading Strategy, page 252 Go Online Activity 9.1: Evaluate Multimedia Web Sites, page 254
Careers & Technology What Makes a Leader? (page 257)	Tech Check, page 257
Section 9.2 Adding Audio and Video to a Site (pages 258–264)	Reading Strategy, page 258 You Try It Activity 9A: Insert Background Sounds, page 260 Go Online Activity 9.2: Locate Clips Online, page 261 You Try It Activity 9B: Insert Video Clip, page 262
Section 9.3 Adding Animation to a Site (pages 265–268)	Reading Strategy, page 265 You Try It Activity 9C: Insert an Animation, page 266
Chapter 9 Review (pages 269–275)	Making Connections: Language Arts—Summarize a Book or Story Standards at Work: Use Technology Tools (NETS-S 1) Teamwork Skills: Create a Presidential Web Page Challenge Yourself: Compare and Contrast Plug-ins You Try It Skills Studio: —Add Sound to a Web Page —Use Animation on a Web Page Web Design Projects: —Create a Web Design Class History —Add Multimedia to the Virtual Field Trips Web Site Additional Activities You May Wish to Use: —PowerTeach Outlines Chapter 9 —Student Workbook Chapter 9

264 Teacher Resource Manual *Introduction to Web Design Using Dreamweaver*

Planning Guide — CHAPTER 9

Assessments

ⓘ Section 9.1 Assessment, page 256

ⓘ Section 9.2 Assessment, page 264

ⓘ Section 9.3 Assessment, page 268

Chapter 9 Review and Assessment, page 269
You may also use any of the Chapter Review Activities and Projects as Assessments.
Additional Assessments You May Wish to Use:
ⓘ —Self-Check Assessments Chapter 9
—*ExamView* Testbank Chapter 9

Estimated Time to Complete Chapter

18 week course = 2–3 days
36 week course = 10 days

To help customize lesson plans, use the Pacing Guide on pages 26–30 and the Standards Charts on pages 266–267.

Key to Recommended Materials

Icons represent elements that may require additional resources.

📁 Focus on Reading

ⓘ Internet access required

𝄞 Software: Dreamweaver

⊙ Teacher Resource CD (contains Student Data Files, Solution Files, Reproducible Graphic Organizers, and Study with PowerTeach Outlines)

Data and Solution Files for Chapter 9

DataFiles
- sound.swf
- bike.swf
- title_animate.gif
- registration.doc

SolutionFiles
- SF_YTI_9AB
- SF_YTI_9CD

Inclusion Strategies

For **Differentiated Instruction Strategies** refer to the **Inclusion in the Computer Technology Classroom** booklet.

CHAPTER 9 NETS Correlation For Students

ISTE NETS Foundation Standards

1. Basic operations and concepts
2. Social, ethical, and human issues
3. Technology productivity tools
4. Technology communications tools
5. Technology research tools
6. Technology problem-solving and decision-making tools

Performance Indicators	Textbook Correlation
1. Identify capabilities and limitations of contemporary and emerging technology resources and assess the potential of these systems and services to address personal, lifelong learning, and workplace needs. (NETS 2)	**SE:** Critical Thinking (256, 264, 268, 270,), Apply It! (264, 268), Challenge Yourself (273)
2. Make informed choices among technology systems, resources, and services. (NETS 1, 2)	**SE:** Critical Thinking (256, 264, 268, 270, 271), Apply It! (256, 264, 268), You Try It (260, 262, 266, 267), Making Connections (272), Standards at Work (272), Teamwork Skills (273), Skills Studio (274), Web Design Projects (275)
3. Analyze advantages and disadvantages of widespread use and reliance on technology in the workplace and in society as a whole. (NETS 2)	**SE:** Critical Thinking (271)
4. Demonstrate and advocate for legal and ethical behaviors among peers, family, and community regarding the use of technology and information. (NETS 2)	**SE:** Apply It! (256), Critical Thinking (264), Teamwork Skills (273), Web Design Projects (275)
5. Use technology tools and resources for managing and communicating personal/professional information (e.g. finances, schedules, addresses, purchases, correspondence). (NETS 3, 4)	**SE:** Making Connections (272), Standards at Work (272), Web Design Projects (275)
6. Evaluate technology-based options, including distance and distributed education, for lifelong learning. (NETS 5)	**SE:** Go Online (254, 261)
7. Routinely and efficiently use online information resources to meet needs for collaboration, research, publications, communications, and productivity. (NETS 4, 5, 6)	**SE:** Go Online (254, 261), Apply It! (256, 264, 268), Teamwork Skills (273), Challenge Yourself (273), Skills Studio (274), Web Design Projects (275)
8. Select and apply technology tools for research, information analysis, problem-solving, and decision-making in content learning. (NETS 4, 5)	**SE:** Go Online (254, 261), Standards at Work (272), Teamwork Skills (273), Skills Studio (274), Web Design Projects (275)
9. Investigate and apply expert systems, intelligent agents, and simulations in real-world situations. (NETS 3, 5, 6)	**SE:** You Try It (260, 262, 266, 267), Web Design Projects (275)
10. Collaborate with peers, experts, and others to contribute to content-related knowledge base by using technology to compile, synthesize, produce, and disseminate information, models, and other creative works. (NETS 4, 5, 6)	**SE:** Teamwork Skills (273)

SCANS Correlation — CHAPTER 9

Foundation Skills

Basic Skills

Reading	**SE:** Before You Read (251), Focus on Reading (252, 258, 265), Reading Strategies (252, 258, 265), After You Read (270), Making Connections (272)
Writing	**SE:** Quick Write Activity (250), Section Assessments (256, 264, 268), Tech Check (257), Chapter Review (270–275)
Mathematics	**SE:** What Did You Learn? (264), Web Design Projects (275)
Listening and Speaking	**SE:** Before You Read (251), Tech Check (257), After You Read (270), Making Connections (272), Teamwork Skills (273), Web Design Projects (275)

Thinking Skills

Creative Thinking	**SE:** Quick Write Activity (250), Making Connections (272), Standards at Work (272), Teamwork Skills (273), Web Design Projects (275)
Critical Thinking	**SE:** Critical Thinking (256, 264, 268, 270, 271), Tech Check (257), Challenge Yourself (273)
Problem Solving	**SE:** Apply It! (256), Teamwork Skills (273), Web Design Projects (275)

Workplace Competencies

Resources Manage time, money, materials, facilities, human resources	**SE:** Tech Check (257), Command Center (271), Standards at Work (272)
Interpersonal Work on teams, teach others	**SE:** Before You Read (251), Tech Check (257), After You Read (270), Teamwork Skills (273), Web Design Projects (275)
Information Acquire, evaluate, organize, maintain, interpret, communicate and use computers to process information	**SE:** Go Online (254, 261), Critical Thinking (256, 264, 268, 270, 271), Apply It! (256, 264, 268), You Try It (260, 262, 266, 267), Command Center (271), Making Connections (272), Standards at Work (272), Teamwork Skills (273), Challenge Yourself (273), Skills Studio (274), Web Design Projects (275)
Systems Understand, monitor, correct, improve, design systems	**SE:** Teamwork Skills (273), Skills Studio (274), Web Design Projects (275)
Technology Select, apply, maintain, and troubleshoot technology	**SE:** Go Online (254, 261), Apply It! (256, 264, 268), You Try It (260, 262, 266 267), Making Connections (272), Standards at Work (272), Teamwork Skills (273), Skills Studio (274), Web Design Projects (275)

CHAPTER 9

Adding Multimedia to a Web Site

CAUTION: In this chapter, students are asked to locate and download audio, video, and animation files. Review your school's policies on downloading files from the Web. If students will not have that capability, supply appropriate files and let students know where to find them. Students should be supervised whenever they use the Internet.

This book does not discuss the specific ways to use technology tools such as scanners and digital cameras. Review the operating procedures for any technology tools that you have available in the classroom, and make sure that students understand how to use this equipment responsibly. Also, consider posting operating instructions in a convenient location for easy reference.

(Page 250)

Objectives

Section 9.1: Multimedia and Web Design
- Identify multimedia design guidelines
- Identify sources of multimedia files
- Explain the ethical use of multimedia files
- Describe multimedia authoring tools
- Evaluate multimedia Web sites

Section 9.2: Adding Audio and Video to a Site
- Identify audio file formats
- Identify video file formats
- Insert audio files into a Web page
- Insert video files into a Web page
- Describe the equipment needed to create audio and video

Section 9.3: Adding Animation to a Site
- Identify animation file formats
- Insert animation into a Web page

> **LEARNING LINK**
>
> Chapter 8 explained how students can use graphics to create an interesting Web site that captures a viewer's attention. Use Chapter 9 to show students that the effective use of various media in their Web sites can generate further viewer interest, and to explain the guidelines for using multimedia.

(Page 250)

Why It Matters

Lead a class discussion about why it is often the case that people would rather see a movie than read the book that the movie is based on. For example, the audio and video (and sometimes animation) in a movie might make the subject matter more interesting or accessible to some people. Ask the students if they think multimedia elements also make it easier to learn particular topics in school. What types of educational topics are easier to grasp when multimedia is involved and why? For example, does seeing a re-creation of a historical event make it easier to understand why this event occurred and what it was like? What significance might this have for Web development and design?

(Page 250) ## Quick Write Activity

Play a short portion of an educational video for the students, and then have them make a list of any key points they can remember about it. For example, if it is about President Kennedy's assassination, the students' list might include:

- He was assassinated in Dallas in 1963.
- The assassination occurred during his third year in office.
- There are questions about whether the assassin acted alone or with others.

Then, read a description about a similar incident (e.g., the assassination of Lincoln or the attempted assassination of Ronald Reagan). Again, have the students make a list of any key points they recall. Do they remember more about the video? Ask them what relevance this might have to the use of multimedia in Web sites.

(Page 251) ## Before You Read

Prepare with a Partner Students become more involved in learning when they are active participants. Working with a partner lets students share their knowledge. This can give them a larger picture of a subject even before they start reading a chapter. In order to make sure students have meaningful conversations about the chapter, you need to prepare them first. Give them a specific task that they need to accomplish (e.g., read the objectives and come up with two or three questions about each). Finally, set ground rules, such as making sure they listen to their partner without interrupting.

CHAPTER 9

SECTION 9.1 MULTIMEDIA AND WEB DESIGN
(Pages 252–256)

FOCUS

Identifying Uses of Multimedia To generate enthusiasm about the concepts in this section, ask students to name some of their favorite interests. You will get a variety of responses, but they will likely include music, certain television shows, and activities that use high-tech equipment. Point out that these interests often make use of multimedia. Ask students which technologies use audio? Video? Animation? All three? Ask students how multimedia can stimulate their interest in a Web site.

(Page 252)

Focus on Reading

Read to Find Out
Use the Read to Find Out feature to focus student reading. Hold a quick starter discussion to find out what your students already know.

 Key Terms Online
Key term definitions and activities are available online at **WebDesignDW.glencoe.com**.

Reading Strategy Answer
Students identify six multimedia design guidelines noted in the section *Multimedia Design Guidelines* on pages 252–253. Students' diagrams should like this example:

- Use short audio clips when the site first loads or a button is clicked to listen to a clip
- Video should enhance a site, not convey its purpose
- Visitors should be allowed to specify the type of connection
- Supply a lower resolution presentation for users with slower connections
- Animations should draw the visitor's attention but not be distracting
- Always consider file size when creating multimedia files

(Multimedia Design Guidelines)

TEACH

Compare and Contrast Multimedia Visit several sites with the students that use video, audio, and animation. (You might suggest sites discussed in this chapter, as well as **Nick.com**, **CNN.com**, and **www.looneytunes.warnerbros.com**.) After identifying where and how these elements are used, explain why they do or do not follow the guidelines in this section. If possible, use some sites that take too long to download or do not work without specific software. Also discuss who the target audience might be and whether the multimedia enhances the sites' purpose. Emphasize that multimedia elements work best when they support the purpose and goal of a Web site.

CHAPTER 9

Answers to Section 9.1 Captions and Activities

(Page 252) **Reading Focus** It is important to consider file size when adding multimedia features to a Web site because larger files take longer to load, and visitors may get discouraged if they wait too long.

> **Teaching Tip**
> Wireless computers will also take longer to load. Remind students to consider the type of connection their audience will have when adding multimedia features to a site.

(Page 253) **Figure 9.1** Streaming technology can reduce a visitor's wait time, which makes a site more user-friendly.

(Page 253) ✓ **Reading Check** Streaming media works because a Web server breaks a transmission into pieces, and the user's computer starts playing the first piece, storing all the other pieces as they arrive and playing them in order.

(Page 254) **Reading Focus** The ethical use of multimedia files includes getting permission to use a file, follow the Web site's rules for using a file, and giving credit to the file's author if his or her work is published on a Web site.

(Page 254) **Figure 9.2** Dogpile lets a user search for image files, multimedia files, and Web pages.

(Page 254) **GO Online** **Activity 9.1** To give students additional experience with evaluating Web sites, have them visit the Online Learning Center at **WebDesignDW.glencoe.com**.

(Page 254) ✓ **Reading Check** Usage rules are a Web site's rules for using files, such as graphics or music, on other Web sites or for personal use.

(Page 255) **Reading Focus** Macromedia® Director®

(Page 255) ✓ **Reading Check** A multimedia authoring tool helps designers integrate media components, such as audio, video, animation, and images into a seamless whole.

(Page 255) **Reading Focus** Answers will vary, but students may note any of the guidelines listed in Figure 9.3 on page 255 of the student textbook.

(Page 255) **Figure 9.3** Too many multimedia elements on a Web page can make the page look cluttered and be confusing or distracting for visitors.

(Page 256) **Figure 9.4** The site might use audio cues to let visitors know when they have clicked on an item and when an action is taking place.

(Page 256) ✓ **Reading Check** Answers will vary, but students may note any of the following:

- Audio can be used to provide cues when a button is clicked.
- Audio can be used for narration in a Web site.
- Video can be used to demonstrate a concept that would otherwise be difficult to effectively get across with text, audio, or animation.
- Animation can be used to enhance and support content on a Web site.
- Animation can be used to demonstrate a concept that would otherwise be impossible or difficult with video, audio, or regular text.

CHAPTER 9

ASSESS

(Page 256) Section 9.1 Assessment Answers

Reading Summary

Use the Reading Summary to help students review and reinforce the important points of the section.

What Did You Learn?

1. Students' definitions should be in their own words, but based on the information found in the section and in the book's glossary.

2. Answers will vary. Guidelines include the following: audio files should only play for a short time when the site is first loaded or when the visitor clicks on a button to listen to an audio clip; video should be planned to enhance a site, not as a primary means of conveying its purpose; visitors should be allowed to specify the type of connection; you should supply a lower resolution presentation for those with slower connections; animations should be used to draw the visitor's attention but not be distracting; and always consider file size when creating multimedia files.

3. A well-designed multimedia Web site includes the following features: the audio, video, and/or animation adds to the page's goals; the page is not overly cluttered; there are no distracting components; the user has the option of skipping lengthy audio or video clips; and the sound and video components work properly and add to the enjoyment of the site.

Critical Thinking

4. Students' answers will vary. The friend's Web site needs some work to be an enjoyable and useful site. The distracting animation will have to be removed or "toned down." The video clip will have to be modified to load faster or a note should accompany the link warning of slow loading time.

5. Students' answers will vary. Some suggestions may be short audio clips of famous radio speeches, popular music of the time, sound effects of airplanes. Appropriate use of audio on any site includes the option to listen to audio or not, and careful choices as to what to include, for how long, and how much bandwidth it will demand from the user's computer.

Apply It!

Define Ethical Use Students summarize how files from Clip Art and image sites can be used ethically on Web sites. Students should note the difference on many sites between educational or personal use and commercial uses of the media. You can print out some examples of usage pages or suggest the URLs from the Teach activity at the beginning of this section.

CHAPTER 9

CLOSE

Applying Multimedia Design Guidelines In past chapter activities, students have thought about various aspects of a personal Web site. Now ask them to plan how they might use audio, video, or animation in such a site. Have them come up with at least five specific ideas. (For instance, if they are in a band, they might want to use audio and video of their music. They should also specify the page and length of the clip. Then let them work with another student, and receive feedback about whether their ideas would help meet the site's goals and purpose.

An alternative activity would be to have students research three multimedia software packages that are available for use on Macintosh or PCs. Ask them to compare and contrast the features of these programs in a table. Let them share this information with the rest of the class. They can do research online or from print sources.

(Page 257)

Careers & Technology

WHAT MAKES A LEADER?

Answers to Tech Check

1. Students may use the information in this feature to identify leadership skills. They can also apply the leadership goals and principles of the Business Professionals of America or the Future Business Leaders of America. Each student should choose a person who is his or her idea of a leader. It can be a friend, teacher, coach, business leader, politician, military leader, etc. Students should list the leadership qualities that their chosen person displays. Based on this list, students will evaluate their own strongest and weakest leadership skills, explain why the skill is valuable, and outline a plan for improving.

2. Divide the class into small groups. Each group should decide which aspects of leadership they will research. Examples might include leadership in business, sports, academics, volunteer organizations, religious groups, youth groups, or families. Students can perform research online, in a library, or in personal interviews. The groups will then plan a presentation of their research, with each student leading the presentation of his or her research.

CHAPTER 9

SECTION 9.2 ADDING AUDIO AND VIDEO TO A SITE
(Pages 258–264)

FOCUS

Describing Audio and Video Files Some students may have established e-zines, blogs, or personal Web sites that incorporate audio or video files. If anyone in the class has had such an experience, have the student(s) describe it. Ask if they created the files or inserted pre-existing ones. If they created them, let them explain how. Ask if their files require plug-ins, and if so which one(s). Ask what the response has been to the addition of these components to the site.

(Page 258)

Focus on Reading

Read to Find Out
Use the Read to Find Out feature to focus student reading. Hold a quick starter discussion to find out what your students already know.

 **Key Terms Online**
Key term definitions and activities are available online at **WebDesignDW.glencoe.com**.

Reading Strategy Answer
Students should identify two ways to incorporate audio into a Web site. This information can be found under the heading *Creating and Adding Audio Files* on page 260. The students' charts should look similar to this example:

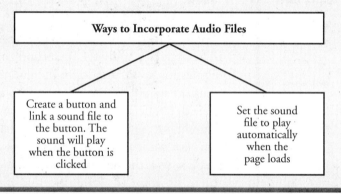

TEACH

Creating Audio Files If your school's computer system has the necessary requirements, show the students how to record audio and save it in a file. Insert the file into a Web page so that it plays automatically when the page loads. Set the file to repeat forever. Test the file, and see how soon students become annoyed by the repeating sound file. This reinforces the point that the number of loops should be limited.

CHAPTER 9

Answers to Section 9.2 Captions and Activities

(Page 258) **Reading Focus** The sampling rate of an audio file is important because the higher the sampling rate, the better the audio clip's sound quality.

(Page 258) **Table 9.1** A Midi file (.mid) would be the file created for a digital piano.

(Page 259) **Table 9.2** Recommended formats for low-speed connections are RAM RealVideo, and MPEG.

(Page 259) ✓ **Reading Check** A plug-in is an application that works with the Web browser to play a particular file format.

(Page 260) **Reading Focus** To create a sound file, a user needs a sound card, speakers, microphone, audio application, and audio editing software.

(Page 260) **Activity 9A Insert Background Sounds** Students insert an audio file into a Web page, and set the file to play twice. Students preview the page to be certain the file plays correctly. Use the Student Data Files and the Solution Files provided in this chapter's Planning Guide.

(Page 260) ✓ **Reading Check** Two ways to incorporate sound into Web pages are by linking an audio file to a button that a user clicks to play the sound, and setting the sound to play automatically when the page loads.

(Page 261) **Reading Focus** Video recorders are used to create video files.

(Page 261) **GO Online** **Activity 9.2** To give students additional experience with finding audio, video, and animation clips online, have them visit **WebDesignDW.glencoe.com**.

(Page 261) **Figure 9.6** Students' answers will vary. Video could be used to show a scene from a school play or students creating a project.

(Page 262) **Activity 9B Insert a Video Clip** Students insert a video clip that uses the Flash plug-in into the Bike and Hike's Video page. Then they preview the page and test the video. Use the Student Data Files and Solution Files noted in this chapter's Planning Guide (see Teaching Tip).

(Page 264) ✓ **Reading Check** Significant download time, different file format requirements for compression, and a Web browser's ability to understand the file's format and its codec can make it difficult to include video on a Web page.

> **Teaching Tip**
> Instructions to insert a different audio and video file format have been provided on the Online Learning Center. Students may need to test different file formats in You Try It activities 9A and 9B to see which format works best with their computer system and the systems of their target audience. Remind students to preview the page in several browsers to determine that the file plays correctly.

CHAPTER 9

ASSESS

(Page 264) Section 9.2 Assessment Answers

Reading Summary

Use the Reading Summary to help students review and reinforce the important points of the section.

What Did You Learn?

1. Students' definitions should be in their own words, but based on the information found in the section and in the book's glossary.

2. Video file formats include AVI (Audio Visual Interleaved); MPEG (Moving Picture Experts Group); QuickTime; RAM RealVideo; and WMV (Windows Media Video). Audio file formats include Wave; Midi; RealAudio; AIFF; AU, SND; and MPEG Audio-Layer 3.

3. A video's FPS (Frames Per Second) should be about 15 FPS to run acceptably over the Internet. A higher FPS closer to 30 FPS will mean a larger file size, and therefore a longer download time. A lower FPS closer to 1 FPS will be a smaller file size and download faster; however, the video will appear jerky.

Critical Thinking

4. Students might want to use video to show the school and its students or historical clips of the school. Audio might be used to record interviews with current and former students and teachers. Audio and video should be used moderately, taking into account the bandwidth each format demands. Ethical use means getting permission to use files obtained off the Web or that belong to someone else.

5. A microphone records sound, while a video recorder records images. A video recorder often has a microphone that captures sound simultaneously with the video. Both a microphone and a video recorder can be used to create multimedia for a Web site.

Apply It!

Evaluate Multimedia Components Students' answers will vary but their evaluation should be based on the questions on page 255 of the student textbook. Popular movie sites include the following: **www.hollywood.com/movies**, **www.apple.com/trailers**, and **www.foxmovies.com**. NOTE: You should preview sites first to make sure the material is suitable for students and that videos will download to classroom computers.

CHAPTER 9

CLOSE

List the Steps in Creating and Inserting Audio and Video Files To both reinforce the concepts in this section and to have an outline of the key points for later review, ask the students to make two lists: one that indicates the steps in creating and inserting audio files in Dreamweaver, and one that indicates the steps in creating and inserting video files in Dreamweaver (steps may vary depending on the version of Dreamweaver being used). The first list, for creating and inserting a background sound in Dreamweaver, might look like this:

- Record audio and save it in a file.
- If desired, use audio editing software to modify the file.
- Open the Web page in Dreamweaver, right-click anywhere, click **Page Properties**.
- In the **Page Properties** dialog box, under Background sound, click in the **Location** text box.
- Enter the file location and open the file.
- Under Loop, select the desired number of times the file should repeat, click **OK**.
- Preview the page in several different browsers and on both Windows and Macintosh computers to make certain the file works correctly.

CHAPTER 9

SECTION 9.3 ADDING ANIMATION TO A SITE
(Pages 265–268)

FOCUS

Identifying Types of Animation Ask your students what kinds of animation they have seen on Web sites they have visited. They may be surprised to find out that something as simple as a blinking ad can be considered animation. Some Web animation, however, can be very complex. What kinds of animation have your students seen on Web sites? Which of these best advanced the purpose of the site, and why?

(Page 265)

Focus on Reading

Read to Find Out
Use the Read to Find Out feature to focus student reading. Hold a quick starter discussion to find out what your students already know.

 Key Terms Online
Key term definitions and activities are available online at **WebDesignDW.glencoe.com**.

Reading Strategy Answer
Students can find information under the headings *Animation Files* and *Incorporating Animation Files into a Site* on pages 265 and 266. Students' diagrams should look similar to this example:

GIF
simpler animation files; images can be animated using a number of graphic applications and Dreamweaver

types of animations; provide the appearance of motion in graphics or text

Flash
more sophisticated; need Flash plug-in; created with Macromedia's Flash software or a similar program; faster download time

TEACH

Analyzing the Use of Animation Files Visit several Web sites with the class and identify different kinds of animation, whether they are Flash or GIF animations, and what kinds of applications were needed to create them. Ask the students which they find interesting, and which they feel enhance the effectiveness of the site. Do the two things always go hand in hand? Make sure they consider the use of interactive buttons when discussing which animations enhance site effectiveness.

CHAPTER 9

Answers to Section 9.3 Captions and Activities

(Page 265) **Reading Focus** GIF animation files are the simplest type of animation file, while Flash animation is more sophisticated and interactive.

(Page 265) **Table 9.3** GIF files contain instructions that tell the browser the order in which images should load, the position where each image should appear, and how long each image should appear on the screen.

Teaching Tip

Chapter 8 compared the different graphic file formats. Remind students that the GIF file format only supports a maximum of 256 colors, which means the format does not work well for photographs. (Refer students to Table 8.1 on page 225 of the textbook to review the formats.)

(Page 265) ✓ **Reading Check** Flash animation is more sophisticated and interactive than GIF animation.

(Page 266) **Reading Focus** A GIF animation is inserted into a Web page in the same way as a static (nonanimated) GIF. (See page 266 of the student textbook).

(Page 266) **You Try It** **Activity 9C Insert an Animation** Students learn how to insert an animated GIF into a Web page. Use the Student Data Files and Solution Files noted in this chapter's Planning Guide (see Teaching Tip).

(Page 266) ✓ **Reading Check** Students should use their own words, but should note the following: 1) Start Dreamweaver; 2) Open the Web page containing the animated .GIF file; 3) Select the .GIF image; 4) Resize the image using the handles that appear in the selection box around the image. Hold down the Shift key to constrain proportions and aspect ratio as you resize. (Students' answers might also say to select the image and adjust the values in the Width and Height box located in the Properties inspector.)

(Page 267) **Reading Focus** A Flash button changes when the user points to or clicks on it, which can make a site more interactive and user-friendly.

(Page 267) **You Try It** **Activity 9D Create and Insert a Flash Button** Students create and insert a Flash button into the Bike and Hike Web site, and preview it in a browser. Use the Student Data Files and Solution Files noted in this chapter's Planning Guide.

(Page 268) ✓ **Reading Check** The button animates when the insertion point is placed over it.

ASSESS

(Page 268) **Section 9.3 Assessment Answers**

Reading Summary

Use the Reading Summary to help students review and reinforce the important points of the section.

Unit 3 Enhancing a Web Site 279

CHAPTER 9

What Did You Learn?

1. Students' definitions should be in their own words, but based on the information found in the section and in the book's glossary.
2. GIF animations can be created with Macromedia Fireworks, Adobe ImageReady, and Microsoft PhotoDraw. Flash animation can be created with Macromedia Flash or a similar application that supports this format.
3. Video captures live motion and breaks it down into separate pieces called frames. Animation takes separate images and puts them together so that the finished product looks continuous and creates the appearance of motion.

Critical Thinking

4. Flash is more sophisticated and downloads more quickly relative to size than GIF animation. But Flash requires special software that is more difficult to use.
5. Students' answers will vary. Any animation, if used properly, can add visual interest or provide information. For example, the radar animation in a weather forecast suggests the passage of time. A user can see more quickly the boundaries and location of a storm that is passing through their region than a written or oral description could present.

Apply It!

Evaluate Animation Students' answers should demonstrate good understanding of section material. Students will present three examples of animations, state each animation's purpose, and explain their initial attraction to the animation and how they could use each animation on a Web page. Students might mention animations such as ads that blink or change color or images that move. If students have trouble finding animation to evaluate, suggest that they use a search engine such as Google or Alta Vista to locate a soft drink company or a popular fast food restaurant.

CLOSE

Using Animation in Web Sites Have the students work in pairs or small groups, and plan what kinds of animations they might use in a Web site for:

- A day care center for children between the ages of two and six
- A rock group (or other musical group) of their own choosing
- A school program that is teaching students how to handle peer pressure

Have the students explain to the class why they would use the kinds of animations they selected, and let the rest of the class provide feedback about their choices.

Answers to Chapter Review — CHAPTER 9

The Chapter Review covers a wide range of student knowledge. Due to time constraints, students may not be able to complete every activity in the Chapter Review. Select the activities that are appropriate for your class needs and resources.

(Page 270) ## After You Read

Compare Notes with Your Partner By now, student teams should be more comfortable and have more notes that they can use to respond to each other. After students have shared their ideas with each other, follow up with a class discussion. See if the teams can answer each others' unanswered questions.

(Page 270) ## Reviewing Key Terms

1. The media forms that can be combined to produce multimedia are audio, video, and animation.
2. Animation is a technique used to create a sense of motion in graphics or text.
3. A codec compresses and decompresses the data when media is being streamed.
4. Sentence should be rewritten as *Using streaming media can help reduce a file's download time.*
5. A plug-in is a separate application that is needed to properly display a certain type or types of media in a browser.
6. A video capture card is a special circuit board that can translate video from an analog video recorder into digital format.
7. *A GIF animation is made up of individual GIF files combined into a single file.*

(Page 270) ## Understanding Main Ideas

8. When downloading files from the Web, check any available license agreement or usage rules for specific information about how the files can be used. Ask permission for use if necessary.
9. Multimedia authoring tools let you integrate multimedia components such as video, audio, and animation into a Web page. Macromedia Director is a multimedia authoring tool.
10. Some tools used to create audio and video files are microphones, audio applications, and analog or digital video recorders.
11. A digital video recorder creates video that can be used directly by a computer and video editing software. Video created with an analog video recorder must be converted to a digital format before it can be viewed on a computer.
12. To play audio, your computer needs a sound card (or sound capabilities integrated into the motherboard) and speakers. If you are going to create your own audio files, you also need a microphone and an audio application that lets you record audio and save it in a file.
13. To insert a sound file into a Web page, you can create a button and link a sound file to the button. Or, you can specify that the sound file be automatically played when a page is loaded.

CHAPTER 9 Answers to Chapter Review

14. Animation is a common feature on the Web because it is relatively easy to use. It provides a fairly simple way to bring Web pages to life and thereby stimulate interest in the site. In addition, features such as rollover buttons provide users with visual cues as to what is happening, making the site easier to use.

15. An animated GIF is a series of static GIFs, while a static GIF only contains a single image.

16. 1) Read and follow any rules stated on the Web site about how to use the files legally; 2) Give credit to a file's author if you use someone else's work on your Web site.

17. Answers will vary, but may include any of the following:

    ◆ Problem: Large file downloads slowly; Solution: Stream media

    ◆ Problem: Large file downloads slowly; Solution: provide link to file

    ◆ Problem: Audio file is distracting; Solution: Set file to loop only once

    ◆ Problem: Video file uses format that audience may not have; Solution: Link file to page instead of inserting into page

(Page 270) Critical Thinking

18. Students' answers will vary. Animations can be appealing or distracting. Advertisements are often animated to draw the viewer's eyes to it and elicit a "must click this" response.

19. Students' tables may look similar to the one below:

Hardware/Software Needed	Why Needed
Video recorder	To make video of summer vacation.
Video capture card	If video is analog, video capture card translates video into digital format.
Digital video camera	Includes cables needed to connect the video recorder to computer so video can be transferred to hard disk.
Video editing software	To make changes to the video once it is on the computer.

20. Flash would be the best application to create the animation because it generates much smaller file sizes for complicated images. Student examples will vary, but can include suggestions of a crowded workout room with people using different equipment, or an instructional video of the proper way to hold and lift weights.

Answers to Chapter Review — CHAPTER 9

21. Students should consider each type of multimedia discussed in this chapter when making their analysis of the strategy "If in doubt, leave it out." They might discuss problems like clutter or slow download times. You may want students to identify effective and ineffective uses of multimedia on others' Web sites. Students' charts may look similar to the one below:

Multimedia Problem	Proposed Solution
Video on the site starts playing immediately.	Show a preview image of the video and provide instructions for how to play the video or explain to users that they can click a video icon link to view the video in a player they have installed on their computer.
Flash animation "splash screen" precedes entry to Web site.	Provide a "SKIP INTRO" link to allow visitors to get to the site quickly. This is also useful for visitors who access the Web on dial-up connections.
Music plays continuously in the background of a Web site.	Provide an option to stop the music, or turn down the volume. Another option would be to give users a choice of whether they want audio or not.

22. Students create a list of sources of free audio, video, and animation files. Good sources of audio and animation files include **www.microsoft.com**, **www.barrysclipart.com**, and **www.animations.com**. Sources of free video are more difficult to locate. Students can try using a search engine such as Alta Vista to locate free video clips.

(Page 271)

Command Center

23. **Ctrl + Alt + F** = Opens Source File dialog box to insert Flash files
24. **Ctrl + C** = Copy item
25. **Ctrl + V** = Paste item

Standardized Test Practice

The correct answer is C. As students review the possible answers, suggest that they re-read the paragraph about multimedia and streaming video carefully, and compare each statement. When they find a statement that is false, they can cross it out, thereby eliminating it from the choices and concentrate on the remaining statements until only one is left.

Unit 3   Enhancing a Web Site   283

CHAPTER 9 Answers to Chapter Review

Have students use the book's Web site **WebDesignDW.glencoe.com**.

- **Study with PowerTeach** Encourage your students to use the Chapter 9 PowerTeach Outline to review the chapter before they have a test.
- **Online Self Check** These quick five-question assessments may be used as an in-class activity, a homework assignment, or test review.

(Page 272) ## Making Connections

Language Arts—Summarize a Book or Story Students write and record a summary of a book they have recently read. They create a site recommending the book to others. The audio file should be included on the site, as well as the book's title, the list of characters, and appropriate graphic or visual elements.

(Page 272) ## Standards at Work

NETS-S 1 Use Technology Tools Students plan a site for an upcoming event at school, such as a sports event, a play, a dance, etc. Students create a three-column chart to list the Web site's pages, the multimedia elements to be included on each page, and the technology tools that are available in your class to create the multimedia element. They create the multimedia elements and save them in a folder.

(Page 273) ## Teamwork Skills

Create a Presidential Web Page Students can find links to presidential libraries at www.archives.gov/presidential_libraries/index.html. Teams plan and create a Web page about a recent American president. They use resources found at the presidential library and any other resources to add multimedia components to the site. The page should contain a photo of the president and a well-known statement from the president. Teams add audio and video resources to enhance the page or add hyperlinks to the site to direct visitors to these resources. Students should review usage guidelines before downloading and using materials from another site.

(Page 273) ## Challenge Yourself

Compare and Contrast Plug-ins Students create a Venn diagram summarizing their research on two popular plug-ins: Windows Media Player and QuickTime Player. The diagram should indicate the similarities and differences between the two resources.

Answers to Chapter Review — CHAPTER 9

You Try It — Skills Studio

(Page 274)

1. **Add Sound to a Web Page** Students add sound or sound effects to the community event page they created in Chapter 8 on page 248. Students choose how and what to add to their site. Options include creating sound effects, downloading appropriate effects from the Web, or creating a voice recording about the event. Students decide if the sound file should loop and how many times. Students preview the site in a browser to test the audio file.

2. **Use Animation on a Web Page** Students locate an animation file online. Students are to review all usage agreements and to ask your permission before downloading any files. Students create a Web page, add the animation, and preview it. Students add a sentence or two to the Web page describing the animation's movement. Encourage students to display the animation and text in an attractive manner.

> **Teaching Tip**
>
> Many sources of free audio, video, and animation files ask visitors to register or provide information about themselves. Remind students that they should never give out personal information over the Internet. When they do that, they may unknowingly be letting others track their online activities.

Web Design Projects

(Page 275)

1. **Create a Web Design Class History** Students create a two-page Web site that presents an oral history of the class. Students use the multimedia tools available to them to create the multimedia elements for this site. The project suggests that students interview you or other students to create audio or video files. The project also suggests that if time is available, students add a third page titled "Projects I Have Completed." This page contains descriptions of projects completed and links to those projects. Students should preview their site in a browser.

2. **Add Multimedia to the Virtual Field Trips Web Site** Students continue to build the Virtual Field Trips Web site from Chapter 8. In this activity, they add the content for one of the field trips. The content should be relatively brief and should include lists or short paragraphs to make it easy to read. Students create or obtain one multimedia component and add it to the Web site. Encourage students to be creative in deciding what to add, and to consider the site's purpose and audience in making their decision (for example, students can include music from the period, sound effects, clips of speeches or video clips from the period, etc.). Students should test the site in a browser to see that the multimedia element works correctly.

CHAPTER 10 Planning Guide

Student Edition	Activities and Exercises
Chapter 10 Adding Interactivity to a Web Site (pages 276–305)	Quick Write Activity, page 276 Before You Read, page 277
Section 10.1 Scripting and Markup Languages (pages 278–281)	Reading Strategy, page 278 Go Online Activity 10.1: Compare Scripting Languages, page 278
Real World Technology Accessibility on the Web (page 282)	Tech Check, page 282
Section 10.2 Adding Dynamic Effects (pages 283–291)	Reading Strategy, page 283 You Try It Activity 10A: Insert a Banner Ad, page 284 You Try It Activity 10B: Add Update Information, page 285 You Try It Activity 10C: Remove a Page From a Template, page 286 You Try It Activity 10D: Insert Show-Hide Layers Behavior, page 288
Section 10.3 Adding a Form to a Web Site (pages 292–298)	Reading Strategy, page 292 Go Online Activity 10.2: Create Well-Designed Forms, page 292 You Try It Activity 10E: Create a Form with Fields, page 293 You Try It Activity 10F: Add a Jump Menu to a Web Page, page 297
Chapter 10 Review (pages 299–305)	Making Connections: Social Studies—Analyze Your Environment Standards at Work: Plan Interactivity (NETS-S 6) Teamwork Skills: Add Interactive Elements to a Web Site Challenge Yourself: Research JavaScripts You Try It Skills Studio: —Create a Drama Club Web Site —Add an Order Form to a Web Site Web Design Projects: —Create a Sandwich Takeout Site —Create a Form to Collect Survey Data Additional Activities You May Wish to Use: —PowerTeach Outlines Chapter 10 —Student Workbook Chapter 10

Planning Guide — CHAPTER 10

Assessments

Section 10.1 Assessment, page 281

Section 10.2 Assessment, page 291

Section 10.3 Assessment, page 298

Chapter 10 Review and Assessment, page 299
—Building 21st Century Skills
—Building Your Portfolio
You may also use any of the Chapter Review Activities and Projects as Assessments.
Additional Assessments You May Wish to Use:
—Self-Check Assessments Chapter 10
—*ExamView* Testbank Chapter 10

Estimated Time to Complete Chapter

18 week course = 4–6 days
36 week course = 10 days

To help customize lesson plans, use the Pacing Guide on pages 26–30 and the Standards Charts on pages 288–289.

Key to Recommended Materials

Icons represent elements that may require additional resources.

- Focus on Reading
- Internet access required
- Software: Dreamweaver
- Teacher Resource CD (contains Student Data Files, Solution Files, Reproducible Graphic Organizers, and Study with PowerTeach Outlines)

Data and Solution Files for Chapter 10

DataFiles
- banner01.gif
- banner02.gif
- button_funds.gif
- button_resale.gif
- quotes.html

SolutionFiles
- SF_YTI_ABCD
- SF_YTI_EF
- SF_Bike_Hike

Inclusion Strategies

For **Differentiated Instruction Strategies** refer to the **Inclusion in the Computer Technology Classroom** booklet.

Unit 3 Enhancing a Web Site 287

CHAPTER 10 NETS Correlation For Students

ISTE NETS Foundation Standards

1. Basic operations and concepts
2. Social, ethical, and human issues
3. Technology productivity tools
4. Technology communications tools
5. Technology research tools
6. Technology problem-solving and decision-making tools

Performance Indicators	Textbook Correlation
1. Identify capabilities and limitations of contemporary and emerging technology resources and assess the potential of these systems and services to address personal, lifelong learning, and workplace needs. (NETS 2)	**SE:** Critical Thinking (281, 291, 298, 300, 301), Apply It! (281, 291, 298), Tech Check (282)
2. Make informed choices among technology systems, resources, and services. (NETS 1, 2)	**SE:** Critical Thinking (281, 291, 298, 300, 301), Tech Check (282), You Try It (284, 285, 286, 288, 293, 297), Apply It! (291, 298), Standards at Work (302), Teamwork Skills (303), Skills Studio (304), Web Design Projects (305), Building 21st Century Skills (306), Building Your Portfolio (307)
3. Analyze advantages and disadvantages of widespread use and reliance on technology in the workplace and in society as a whole. (NETS 2)	**SE:** Tech Check (282)
4. Demonstrate and advocate for legal and ethical behaviors among peers, family, and community regarding the use of technology and information. (NETS 2)	**SE:** Tech Check (282)
5. Use technology tools and resources for managing and communicating personal/professional information (e.g. finances, schedules, addresses, purchases, correspondence). (NETS 3, 4)	**SE:** Skills Studio (304), Web Design Projects (305), Building 21st Century Skills (306)
6. Evaluate technology-based options, including distance and distributed education, for lifelong learning. (NETS 5)	**SE:** Go Online (278, 292), Tech Check (282), Building Your Portfolio (307)
7. Routinely and efficiently use online information resources to meet needs for collaboration, research, publications, communications, and productivity. (NETS 4, 5, 6)	**SE:** Go Online (278, 292), Apply It! (291), Tech Check (282), Challenge Yourself (303), Building Your Portfolio (307)
8. Select and apply technology tools for research, information analysis, problem-solving, and decision-making in content learning. (NETS 4, 5)	**SE:** Go Online (278, 292), Apply It! (291, 298), Tech Check (282), Web Design Projects (305), Building 21st Century Skills (306), Building Your Portfolio (307)
9. Investigate and apply expert systems, intelligent agents, and simulations in real-world situations. (NETS 3, 5, 6)	**SE:** You Try It (293, 297), Standards at Work (302), Skills Studio (304), Web Design Projects (305), Building 21st Century Skills (306), Building Your Portfolio (307)
10. Collaborate with peers, experts, and others to contribute to content-related knowledge base by using technology to compile, synthesize, produce, and disseminate information, models, and other creative works. (NETS 4, 5, 6)	**SE:** Teamwork Skills (303), Building Your Portfolio (307)

SCANS Correlation — CHAPTER 10

Foundation Skills

Basic Skills

Reading	**SE:** Before You Read (277), Focus on Reading (278, 283, 291), Reading Strategies (278, 283, 291), After You Read (300)
Writing	**SE:** Quick Write Activity (276), Section Assessments (300–305), Building 21st Century Skills (306), Building Your Portfolio (307)
Mathematics	**SE:** Standardized Test Practice (301)
Listening and Speaking	**SE:** Teamwork Skills (303)

Thinking Skills

Creative Thinking	**SE:** Quick Write Activity (276), Standard at Work (302), Teamwork Skills (303), Web Design Projects (305), Building 21st Century Skills (306), Building Your Portfolio (307)
Critical Thinking	**SE:** Critical Thinking (281, 291, 298, 300, 301), Tech Check (282), Challenge Yourself (303)
Problem Solving	**SE:** Standards at Work (302), Skills Studio (304), Web Design Projects (305)

Workplace Competencies

Resources Manage time, money, materials, facilities, human resources	**SE:** Command Center (301), Building 21st Century Skills (306)
Interpersonal Work on teams, teach others	**SE:** After You Read (300), Teamwork Skills (303), Building Your Portfolio (307)
Information Acquire, evaluate, organize, maintain, interpret, communicate and use computers to process information	**SE:** Go Online (278, 292), Apply It! (281, 291, 298), You Try It (284, 285, 286, 288, 293, 297), Critical Thinking (281, 291, 298), Command Center (301), Making Connections (302), Standards at Work (302), Teamwork Skills (303), Challenge Yourself (303), Skills Studio (304), Web Design Projects (305), Building 21st Century Skills (306), Building Your Portfolio (307)
Systems Understand, monitor, correct, improve, design systems	**SE:** You Try It (284, 285, 286, 288, 293, 297), Teamwork Skills (303), Challenge Yourself (303), Web Design Projects (305)
Technology Select, apply, maintain, and troubleshoot technology.	**SE:** Go Online (278, 292), You Try It (284, 285, 286, 288, 293, 297), Apply It! (291), Standards at Work (302), Teamwork Skills (303), Challenge Yourself (303), Skills Studio (304), Web Design Projects (305), Building 21st Century Skills (306), Building Your Portfolio (307)

CHAPTER 10

Adding Interactivity to a Web Site

(Page 276) ## Objectives

Section 10.1: Scripting and Markup Languages
- Define scripting
- Summarize interactivity design guidelines
- Identify scripting languages
- Compare common scripting languages
- Identify markup languages

Section 10.2: Adding Dynamic Effects
- Apply DHTML effects
- Create a banner ad
- Add update information
- Remove a page from a template
- Insert layers

Section 10.3: Adding a Form to a Web Site
- Create a form
- Identify different field types
- Place fields and labels into forms
- Add a jump menu

LEARNING LINK

Chapter 9 showed students that the use of various media in their Web sites can generate significant viewer interest. Use Chapter 10 to show how interactivity, in addition to helping viewers navigate a site, can also be used to make their Web sites much more interesting to their audience.

(Page 276) ## Why It Matters

Discuss experiences students have had that showed them the importance of interactivity. For instance, they may not care for museums, but may have found "hands on" museums interesting. Or, they may have been at a party where they did not know anyone, and may compare that negatively with one where they interacted a lot.

(Page 276) ## Quick Write Activity

As an alternate activity, you might want to discuss with students what a Web site on dogs that uses no interactive elements except for navigation might be like. Then have them think of some way of making the site more interesting, by including an interactive element. Have them write a paragraph about the interactive element.

(Page 277) ## Before You Read

Managing Time Emphasize to students that reading faster does not necessarily mean that they are reading better. Students need to come up with reading strategies that work well for them. If they are slow readers or have short chunks of time, they should concentrate on reading one section of a chapter thoroughly. If they rush through a whole chapter, they may not remember a word. Visual learners might want to allow more time to look at figures and captions to reinforce the concepts in the text.

CHAPTER 10

SECTION 10.1 SCRIPTING AND MARKUP LANGUAGES
(Pages 278–281)

FOCUS

Analyzing Interactive Elements Have students work in teams and see which team can come up with the longest list of interactive elements they have used on Web sites. Then have a class discussion about the effect of these elements, including why interactivity does not inherently make a site more useful or interesting. Sometimes too much interactivity is annoying, like when you have to go through a lot of steps to get information you want.

(Page 278)

Focus on Reading

Read to Find Out
Use the Read to Find Out feature to focus student reading. Hold a quick starter discussion to find out what your students already know.

 **Key Terms Online**
Key term definitions and activities are available online at **WebDesignDW.glencoe.com**.

Reading Strategy Answer
Students will find information for this activity under the heading *Scripting Languages* on page 279. Students' tables should look similar to this example:

Types of Scripting	Use
JavaScript	Makes a page dynamic and interactive
Java applets	Makes a small, cross-platform Java application that is designed to be executed within another application
Common Gateway Interface (CGI)	Makes it possible to search online databases and to fill out, submit, and process forms over the Internet
Dynamic HTML (DHTML)	Uses HTML, CSS, and JavaScript to create interactive Web sites

TEACH

Explaining the Advantages and Disadvantages of Dreamweaver Explain to the class which interactive elements Dreamweaver allows you to insert, and which elements Dreamweaver would not be able to add to a Web page, requiring a Web designer to learn one or more scripting languages.

Unit 3 Enhancing a Web Site

CHAPTER 10

Answers to Section 10.1 Captions and Activities

(Page 278) **Reading Focus** A script is a short program that can be inserted into a Web page's HTML code in order to make the page dynamic.

(Page 278) **GO Online** **Activity 10.1** For additional information about scripting languages and their different purposes, have students visit **WebDesignDW.glencoe.com**.

(Page 278) ✓ **Reading Check** A Web page is dynamic when it contains information that changes regularly and allows interactivity.

(Page 279) **Reading Focus** The Common Gateway Interface is used to search online databases and to fill out, submit, and process forms over the Internet.

(Page 279) **Figure 10.1** Players can use the computer's keyboard to make the onscreen figure shoot a basketball.

(Page 279) ✓ **Reading Check** Rollover buttons, banner displays, clocks, forms, and games are types of interactivity that can be created using scripting languages.

(Page 280) **Reading Focus** HTML is a markup language that defines the appearance of data. XML is a markup language that defines the meaning, and not the appearance, of Web elements.

(Page 280) **Figure 10.2** XML defines the meaning of Web elements, while HTML defines the appearance of data.

(Page 280) ✓ **Reading Check** XHTML stands for Extensible Hypertext Markup Language.

(Page 281) **Reading Focus** Interactivity enhances a Web site by providing a more dynamic and enjoyable experience for the users.

(Page 281) **Figure 10.3** Too many interactive elements on a Web site can make the site cluttered and confusing.

(Page 281) ✓ **Reading Check** Students' answers may vary. Two guidelines related to interactivity are to keep the page simple and to use interactivity only when it enhances the site.

ASSESS

(Page 281) ### Section 10.1 Assessment Answers

Reading Summary

Use the Reading Summary to help students review and reinforce the important points of the section.

What Did You Learn?

1. Students' definitions should be in their own words, but they should be based on the information found in this section and in the book's glossary.

2. XML code resembles HTML in that it uses open and close tags enclosed in angle brackets (< >). HTML describes how to display a page, while XML defines the data and how it is organized.

Critical Thinking

3. CGI allows browsers to interact with other applications such as databases. This allows a user to send and receive information to and from an application through a server. This development allows form information to be processed and used, which greatly increases the interactivity of a Web site.

4. Interactive pages make Web pages dynamic because they can change. Other information sources are static and do not change once they are published. Interactivity also allows communication between the visitor and the information source.

Apply It!

Identify Scripting Students view the source code of a Web site in a browser to identify examples of scripting. Encourage students to view the graphics on the site first. Then, ask students to guess the type of scripting used to create the site before they view the source code and explain what function the scripting performs on the site. JavaScript will likely be found more often than other scripts. Java applets may be identified, but the student may not be able to detect how the applet functions. Good code often contains descriptive statements that allow the viewer to understand the basic use of the script. Common scripts include hit counters, clocks, login information, and so on.

> **Troubleshooting**
>
> If your school does not allow students to view source code, ask students to use a search engine such as Google or Alta Vista to locate and view the source code of free Javascripts, Java applets, or free CGI bins.

CLOSE

Applying Interactivity Guidelines Choose a topic for a Web site, such as a particular sport or hobby. Let the students work in small groups to come up with a dozen or more interactive elements they might want to add to such a site. Then have them use the interactivity design guidelines on page 281 of the student textbook to determine which of these elements they would actually use. Ask students what scripting languages they would be likely to need to add these interactive elements.

CHAPTER 10

(Page 282)

Real World Technology

ACCESSIBILITY ON THE WEB

Answers to Tech Check

1. Students should choose only one type of application for this activity. Have them use the Help menu in that application to find out about the accessibility tools. They should list at least five accessibility options. After students have explained the options, have them try them out or demonstrate them to the rest of the class. Charts may look like the partial example below.

Microsoft Windows 2000 Accessibility Tools	Disability that is addressed	Tool Function	How to Activate
Magnifier	Low vision	displays a magnified portion of the screen	**Start menu> Programs> Accessories> Accessibility> Magnifier**
Narrator	Low vision	text-to-speech utility that reads what is displayed on the screen	**Start menu> Programs> Accessories> Accessibility> Narrator**

2. Students can go to the W3C Web site at **www.w3.org** to find out more information about the Web Accessibility Initiative (WAI) and its Accessibility Guidelines. To learn more about Section 508, they can visit **www.section508.gov**. Microsoft also has information about accessibility on its own Web site at **http://www.microsoft.com/enable**. Checklists can be developed as an individual, group, or class project to evaluate a Web page they have designed and make changes to make it more accessible (students can convert their checklists into a rubric if desired.) Some (but not all) of the features students should use in their list include:
   ◆ Provides text-based options for all graphic content, including navigation.
   ◆ Provides text-based options for audio content.
   ◆ Text-only display is clear and easy to use as graphics-based page.
   ◆ Text stands out clearly from background.

CHAPTER 10

SECTION 10.2 ADDING DYNAMIC EFFECTS
(Pages 283–291)

FOCUS

Describing Dynamic Effects Since students will have had experience with rollover buttons, banner ads, and so on, let them describe these experiences. Did they find these effects useful, interesting, or annoying? Have them explain why. Since a portal site's goal is to make money by placing banner ads on its home page, should it remove them if the ads annoy viewers? This consideration illustrates the constant need to keep the Web site's purpose and goals in mind.

(Page 283)

Focus on Reading

Read To Find Out
Use the Read to Find Out feature to focus student reading. Hold a quick starter discussion to find out what your students already know.

 Key Terms Online
Key term definitions and activities are available online at **WebDesignDW.glencoe.com**.

Reading Strategy Answer
Students can find answers for this activity throughout the section. The students' diagrams should look similar to this example:

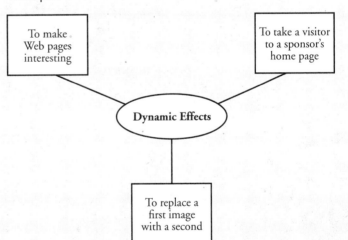

TEACH

Comparing Dreamweaver with Scripting Languages If you are familiar with a scripting language, show the students how to add a dynamic effect by writing a script or obtaining a script online for that effect. Let them compare this experience with adding that effect using Dreamweaver. The students will observe that the latter process is quicker and easier.

Unit 3 Enhancing a Web Site   **295**

CHAPTER 10

Answers to Section 10.2 Captions and Activities

(Page 283) **Reading Focus** A banner ad is an advertisement that takes visitors to the sponsor's home page when clicked.

(Page 284) **You Try It** **Activity 10A Insert a Banner Ad** Students insert a banner ad into a Web page, so that when visitors position their mouse over the ad, it changes from one image to another. Use the Student Data Files and Solution Files noted in this chapter's Planning Guide.

(Page 284) ✓ **Reading Check** A banner ad is an advertisement that, when clicked, takes the visitor to the sponsor's home page.

> **Teaching Tip**
>
> In You Try It Activity 10A, students learn how to insert a simple banner ad that links to the external Web site that it advertises. While this activity is oriented toward teaching students the basics, you may want to remind students that banner ads tend to be dynamic (for example, they rotate) to better catch the viewer's attention. You may also want to note that most banner ads are placed at the top, right, or bottom of a page—where the viewer is most likely to see and click the ad.

(Page 285) **Reading Focus** News sites usually display update information so that users know that the site's content is current and up-to-date.

(Page 285) **You Try It** **Activity 10B Add Update Information** Students learn how to add update information. Use the Solution Files noted in this chapter's Planning Guide.

(Page 285) ✓ **Reading Check** To insert update information in Dreamweaver, choose **Insert>Date**. In the **Insert Date** dialog box, select a date format option and click **OK**. (Students may note that the file should be saved or that the **Update automatically on save** check box should be checked.)

(Page 286) **Reading Focus** The Behaviors panel can be used to create custom effects.

(Page 286) **You Try It** **Activity 10C Remove a Page From a Template** Students learn to remove a page from a template in order to insert unique information. Use the Solution Files provided in this chapter's Planning Guide.

(Page 288) **You Try It** **Activity 10D Insert Show-Hide Layers Behavior** Students add Show-Hide layers to the Bike and Hike Web site. Use the Student Data Files and Solution Files provided in this chapter's Planning Guide.

(Page 291) ✓ **Reading Check** Adding too many layers could be distracting or confusing.

ASSESS

(Page 291) **Section 10.2 Assessment Answers**

Reading Summary

Use the Reading Summary to help students review and reinforce the important points of the section.

296 Teacher Resource Manual *Introduction to Web Design Using Dreamweaver*

What Did You Learn?

1. Students' definitions should be in their own words, but based on the information found in the section and in the book's glossary.

2. To use the behaviors panel to apply effects, click on the desired object and select the appropriate action for the object in the panel. Students' answers will be in their own words but should reflect the basic Steps in You Try It activity 10D.

3. Answers may include the following: banner ads that are hyperlinked to bring a visitor to the sponsor's home page, rollover buttons that change their appearance in response to a user's action, and layers such as forms that allow users to add their information and/or comments to a Web page.

Critical Thinking

4. Students' answers will vary. Students will note that banner ads often include motion to attract the visitor's attention and they link the visitor directly to the sponsor's home page. It is therefore likely that more people will visit your site if you use a banner ad than if you use a static ad.

5. If a Web site has not updated information for a long time, the information can be out-of-date and therefore inaccurate. You may want to note the caveat that some sites automatically change a page's date, regardless of whether or not any information on the page was recently updated. While update information can help students identify pages that have not been updated in a while, they should not solely rely on this information when evaluating the accuracy of a page's content.

Apply It!

Apply Dynamic Effects Students use the Behaviors panel to apply various effects to text on a Web page. They identify how different effects change text and evaluate when these effects would be appropriate and how they might be used. Remind students that overusing effects may be annoying or distracting.

Evaluating Dynamic Effects In previous Close activities, the students have planned various aspects of a personal Web site. Now have them consider how they might effectively add dynamic effects to such a site. They should take into account each of the effects discussed in this section. Would a banner ad be appropriate? (Probably not, unless they happen to have a sponsor to visit.) Rollover effects? (Possibly, to make navigation easier.) Update information? (Yes, it shows their information is up-to-date.)

CHAPTER 10

SECTION 10.3 ADDING A FORM TO A WEB SITE
(Pages 292–298)

FOCUS

Analyzing Form Design Ask students to describe experiences they have had, preferably online, filling out forms. Specifically, what kinds of problems have they run into? (Students may have been confused about what information to enter or felt forced to provide information they believed was too personal, etc.) Use their answers to identify important concerns of this section (e.g., the advantages of clear labels, avoiding asking for more than basic information, etc.)

(Page 292)

Focus on Reading

Read to Find Out
Use the Read to Find Out feature to focus student reading. Hold a quick starter discussion to find out what your students already know.

 **Key Terms Online**
Key term definitions and activities are available online at **WebDesignDW.glencoe.com**.

Reading Strategy Answer
Students can find information for this activity under the heading *Form Fields* on page 292. Students' tables should look similar to this example:

Field Type	Description
Text Box	for entering a line of text
Text Area	for entering many lines of text
Check Box	for selecting one of two options
Option Button	for selecting one or more options from a list
Drop-Down Box	for selecting from a list of choices

TEACH

Cause and Effect: Identifying Confusing Labels Design a form, either online or on paper, that uses confusing labels. Make copies of the form and have the students fill them out. Compare the answers that students gave in response to the labels. Afterwards, lead a class discussion about which elements of the form worked well (if any), which did not, and why.

For example, a job application might be confusing if you had to choose from the following labels under Past Experience:

- Retail
- Restaurant
- Telemarketing
- Customer Service

298 Teacher Resource Manual *Introduction to Web Design Using Dreamweaver*

CHAPTER 10

Answers to Section 10.3 Captions and Activities

(Page 292) **Reading Focus** Most forms include a field and label button.

(Page 292) **GO Online** **Activity 10.2** For additional examples of forms and information about designing forms, have students visit **WebDesignDW.glencoe.com**.

(Page 292) **Reading Focus** A text box lets users enter a relatively small amount of text, such as a name or address, into a form. A text area lets users enter larger amounts of text, such as comments and suggestions.

(Page 293) **Table 10.1** A radio button can be used when a user only needs to select one option on a form, such as True/False or Yes/No.

(Page 293) **You Try It** **Activity 10E Create a Form with Fields** Students create a form that lets users send contact information. Use the Solution Files included in this chapter's Planning Guide.

(Page 296) ✓ **Reading Check** A well-designed form includes labels, text fields, a drop-down list, and limited option fields such as check boxes and radio buttons.

(Page 297) **Reading Focus** Adding a jump menu makes a form more dynamic because it allows users to access hyperlinks from a single drop-down menu.

(Page 297) **You Try It** **Activity 10F Add a Jump Menu to a Web Page** Students learn to add a jump menu to their Bike and Hike Web site. Use the Solution Files noted in this chapter's Planning Guide.

(Page 298) ✓ **Reading Check** Radio buttons, check boxes, list/menus and Submit/Reset buttons are all examples of limited option fields.

✎ **Teaching Tip**

If students are having trouble clicking in the cell below the E-mail Address: label in Step 9 of You Try It activity 10E, have them press **Tab** to move to the next cell.

⚠ **Troubleshooting**

Some students may not be able to reset the form in Step 18 of You Try It activity 10E. This may be because there is an error in the Reset button code. If students' forms do not reset when they click the Reset button, have them view the Reset button code. It should be written as follows:

`<input type="reset" name="Submit2" Value="Reset">`

If you select the Reset button in Design view, the Properties inspector should show the Button name as "Submit 2", the Label as "Reset", and the Action option set to "Reset form".

CHAPTER 10

ASSESS

(Page 298) Section 10.3 Assessment Answers

Reading Summary

Use the Reading Summary to help students review and reinforce the important points of the section.

What Did You Learn?

1. Students' definitions should be in their own words, but based on the information found in the section and in the book's glossary.

2. Visitors will be more likely to give you correct information when you clearly label all the fields in a form.

3. Check boxes allow users to select only one of two options. Radio buttons allow users to select one option from multiple options. Both allow users to select from predefined choices and are ways in which you can get information from a Web site's visitors.

Critical Thinking

4. Students should recognize that a drop-down list (the type of list provided in a drop-down box) would not be a good option for listing visitors' last names. Since a drop-down list could not include all possible last names, visitors would not know how to respond.

5. Answers will vary. Fields would include first name, last name, middle initial, street address, city, state, ZIP, student number, class choices, etc. Students should identify appropriate field types for each field. For instance, a text box would be appropriate for student names. Classes might be listed in a drop-down list.

Apply It!

Identify Form Fields Students' answers will vary depending on the form selected. Students should appropriately identify the type of field required. For example, text area would not be appropriate for name or age, since the length of the fields can be determined. A text area would be appropriate, however, for a field that asks someone to tell about awards they have earned or honors they have received.

CLOSE

Using Field Types Have the students (individually or in groups) plan a form for receiving online discount coupons for an office supply store. The coupons are for specific products sold in the store (e.g. software, pens, notebooks, etc). Students should draw a sketch of the form, using each of the fields discussed in this section. Have students exchange forms and give each other feedback. Students can use the guidelines in this section to create a rubric for their evaluations.

Answers to Chapter Review — CHAPTER 10

The Chapter Review covers a wide range of student knowledge. Due to time constraints, students may not be able to complete every activity in the Chapter Review. Select the activities that are appropriate for your class needs and resources.

(Page 300) After You Read

Reading Without Distractions Ask students which elements in this chapter they thought were most useful and helped their comprehension. For example, did it help to first check the section assessment questions and then look for answers as they read the section? Did it help to look at illustrations? With that in mind, how would students incorporate these elements into their reading? Would they review them as they read or before they read? How does this affect the speed of their reading?

(Page 300) Reviewing Key Terms

1. Students should properly identify three interactive Web sites they have visited. Common examples include e-commerce sites, game sites, movie sites, and so on. Students should also identify interactive elements on each Web site.
2. Scripting is often used to add interactivity and functionality to Web pages on a Web site.
3. Three scripting languages are JavaScript, Java applets, and CGI.
4. Three markup languages are HTML, XML, and XHTML.
5. CGI stands for Common Gateway Interface.
6. Sentence should read: A *hit counter* keeps track of the number of visitors to the site.
7. A form allows visitors to supply specific kinds of information to the business or person who developed the Web site.
8. Labels describe the form fields. For example, the label "First Name" indicates that the field should contain a person's first name.

(Page 300) Understanding Main Ideas

9. Interactivity should be used after careful planning. Usage guidelines include using interactivity only when it enhances the site, making the interactivity simple and not distracting, making certain that users understand the response expected of them, checking interactive components in all the browsers that your users are likely to use, and providing alternative text for those who cannot use the interactive components.
10. JavaScript can be used to create rollover buttons, banner displays, and games.
11. HTML code creates a static Web page that does not allow interactivity. DHTML is an extension of HTML allowing interactive elements such as banner ads and rollover buttons.
12. Answers may include news and sports site that contain current information. Visitors may want to know if the latest news or sports scores have been posted to the site.
13. Forms allow users to submit information to a Web site.

CHAPTER 10 Answers to Chapter Review

14. Answers will vary. Advantages include allowing users to stack information on a page and making a Web page easier to update. One disadvantage might be that if there are too many layers being used it will cause a page to download very slowly.

15. Students will likely note the following:
    - Text Field: Allows user to enter a line of text.
    - Text Area: Allows user to enter many lines of text.
    - Radio Button: Allows user to select only one option from multiple ones.
    - Check Box: Allows user to select one or more options from a list.
    - List/Menu: Allows user to select from a list of choices.
    - Submit/Reset: Allows user to submit a form and to erase the form's content.

(Page 300) ## Critical Thinking

16. A clearly written label tells the user exactly what information to enter into a field. The only way to get reliable information from users is to have them provide information in a systematic and orderly way. Labels help achieve that goal.

17. Students may note that CGI is used to connect the browser to the database that stores your list of preferences. Students may also list JavaScript as a way to check the validity of data, such as whether data has been entered into all required fields.

18. Students will likely note that the use of interactive Web sites will increase over the next decade. As applications become more powerful and as hardware and communications technologies improve, authors, publishers, and educators will likely find dynamic ways to use interactivity to help students learn.

19. Banner ads make the sponsor's Web site only a click away. Visitors are more likely to visit a site by clicking than by typing the URL. One disadvantage to the Web site is that the visitor may not return to the original site.

20. Advantages include forcing the visitor to enter the correct type of information and making it easier for the visitor to respond. One disadvantage might be that you may not learn important information because the form does not contain a field for the specific type of information the visitor could provide.

21. Web pages that only contain HTML code are not dynamic because HTML is not a dynamic language. Scripts must be inserted into an HTML page to make it dynamic. Answers will vary, but may include that scripting languages enabled visitors to interact with Web pages instead of just viewing those pages. For example, visitors can enter information into a page, and have something happen (visitors receive an answer to a question, or purchase a product and have it sent to them).

22. Any action plan to incorporate interactive elements should be acceptable, as long as the student follows the guidelines on page 281 of the student textbook. An example of an interactive element and function appears below:

Interactive Element	Function
Navigation options that change color when the mouse is positioned over them.	The change of color indicates to the user that an action is occurring and that clicking the button will take you to another Web page.

Answers to Chapter Review — CHAPTER 10

(Page 301)

Command Center

23. When in a table, press **Tab** = Move to next cell
24. **Shift + F4** = Open Behaviors panel
25. **F2** = Open Layers panel to view layers

Standardized Test Practice

The correct answer is B. Help students review the correct way to read the Popularity of Scripting Languages bar graph including estimating unique percentages, so that they can identify the correct answer.

Have students use the book's Web site **WebDesignDW.glencoe.com**.

- **Study with PowerTeach** Encourage your students to use the Chapter 10 PowerTeach Outline to review the chapter before they have a test.
- **Online Self Check** These quick five-question assessments may be used as an in-class activity, a homework assignment, or test review.

(Page 302) ## Making Connections

Social Studies—Analyze Your Environment Encourage students to list all the things that grab their attention during the course of one 24-hour period. Students analyze what elements were attention grabbers. Some ideas include color, motion, loud noises, silence, and so on.

Answers will vary, but students' tables may look similar to the one below:

Attention Getting Item	Web Site Equivalent	Evaluation
Billboard with bold, fluorescent colors.	A banner ad with similar colors.	Including a banner ad with bold colors would be attention getting and more appealing than having the banner flash with those colors.

(Page 302) ## Standards at Work

NETS-S 6 Plan Interactivity Students need to come up with specific recommendations for interactive elements that are suitable for a clothing store's Web site. This might include banner ads, advertising that links to store coupons, forms that allow visitors to be informed of future sales by e-mail, etc. Students then create the banner ad in Dreamweaver to advertise the upcoming sale.

CHAPTER 10 Answers to Chapter Review

(Page 303) ## Teamwork Skills

Add Interactive Elements to a Web Site Teams add two forms of interactivity to the presidential Web site created in Chapter 9. It would be best to use the same teams as you used in Chapter 9. After creating the interactivity using Dreamweaver, students test the site in two browsers and describe any differences between the browsers. Students also add three page transitions to the site and test each in a browser. Students retain the page transition that is most effective.

(Page 303) ## Challenge Yourself

Research JavaScripts Students find and print two JavaScripts for clocks. Scripts can be found at: **http://javascript.internet.com/, http://www.bodo.com/javacool.htm**, and **http://www.w3schools.com/js/js_examples.asp** (make sure that students review the site's Terms of Use before downloading scripts). Students compare the two source codes and note similarities and differences. Students evaluate the advantages and disadvantages in using others' JavaScripts.

(Page 304)
1. **Create a Drama Club Web Site** Students create a drama club Web site to announce an upcoming play or musical. Encourage students to select a theme that is in keeping with the play they will be advertising. If your school does not have a play, drama, or musical scheduled, students can use the text noted in the student textbook instead. The site includes a banner ad that reads "Buy Your Tickets Now." Other elements to appear on the site are update information and a short applause sound that plays upon loading the page, but does not play continuously. If students cannot locate an applause sound, they can use any other appropriate sound on their site.

2. **Add an Order Form to a Web Site** Students add an order form to the drama club site they created in You Try It Skills Studio 1. The form includes fields for first name, last name, e-mail address, date of performance, and cost of ticket. The completed page should be viewed in a browser and any corrections or adjustments should be made.

Answers to Chapter Review — CHAPTER 10

Web Design Projects

(Page 305)

1. **Create a Sandwich Takeout Site** Students create a one-page Web site for a sandwich restaurant. The restaurant takes orders online and delivers the orders to customers.

   - The restaurant's telephone number should appear in a banner ad, and the students should also create an order form.
   - Students decide on the menu. Some students will want to create a complex menu; encourage them to keep their choices simple so that the form is easy to create.
   - At a minimum, the order form must include the customer's name, address, telephone number, and e-mail address. The delivery address should also be included, even if it is the same as the customer's address. The order form must lay out the menu in such a way that people can tell easily what they have ordered and are unlikely to make mistakes.
   - Since students do not publish the site and it is not connected to a database, note that the Submit button will not work.

2. **Create a Form to Collect Survey Data** Students create a form to gather survey data about reading preferences of young people. Students should decide what labels they need in the form by first making a list of questions that would help them gather the information they need. Remind students that they should only ask for useful information. This is a good opportunity to discuss when forms might need personal information like names and addresses, and when personal information is not necessary or appropriate.

UNIT 3

(Page 306) BUILDING 21ST CENTURY SKILLS

Project 1 Civic Responsibility: Create a Web Site for Voters

Students plan and create a three-page Web site, using a hierarchical structure, to encourage people 18 or older to vote. The basic information for each page is listed in the project.

Students plan the pages, develop the content, obtain or create a graphic to include on each page, and identify links, especially for the voter registration information. Students add a JavaScript (quotes.html) that is provided on the CD. Use the Student Data File noted in the Chapter 10 Planning Guide.

Students design a custom theme in Dreamweaver that uses a patriotic motif. They add the text, graphics, and JavaScript. They will want to edit the JavaScript so that the colors work with the custom theme. Discourage students from making major changes to the JavaScript unless they have experience with this scripting language.

Students check the quality of their work before finalizing the project. If time is available, you may want to add the peer review process to this project.

Project 2 Use Technology Tools: Create a Web Photo Album

Students create an image gallery by creating a table on a Dreamweaver page and inserting the images. Review with students all the technology tools available to them at school. Discuss other technology tools and allow students to use other tools that may be available to them. Have students give you a list of the technology tools they used. As you evaluate the image galleries, consider the variety of tools used, as well as the variety of the images included.

Students should crop, resize, adjust brightness/contrast, sharpen, and resample the images as needed. Evaluate the cropping choices and the resizing techniques. For example, crops generally should not cut off the tops of peoples' heads and the resizing generally should maintain the aspect ratio. If images are stretched or skewed, students should provide a specific explanation of why they made that choice.

Students create a form that can be used to gather names and e-mail addresses from the site's visitors. The forms should not gather unneeded information. This form may be included at the bottom of the image gallery page or may be a separate page.

If any images are copyrighted, students should cite the sources. They should check the Terms of Use page if the image is from a Web site. When they have completed their Web site, students check the quality of their work, testing the page in a browser before finalizing it.

(Page 307) # BUILDING YOUR PORTFOLIO

The Portfolio projects are ongoing activities that build upon the material in the unit. By the end of the course, the students should have work samples that show every stage of their knowledge development. Explain to students how to save their samples as hard copies, online copies, or on a personal disk.

Create an Educational Web Site

Students create a Web site about the seven continents targeted to elementary-age children. The site includes a home page and a page for each continent.

Students research and create the content for the site. They gather or create multimedia elements for the site, following copyright guidelines where necessary. Review with students the tools that the school has available for creating audio, video, and animation files. If possible, students should include an example of each type on their site. You may want students to work together to create the multimedia components, even though each student will create his or her own Web site. This technique works especially well if you have some students who are familiar with the multimedia creation tools and others who are not. By pairing them, the experienced students can teach the other students.

Students use a Dreamweaver premade page design or create a template that fits with their target audience and their site's goals. Students add the content and multimedia elements to the site. They use a quote about Earth as a banner element. Quotes can be found online or in books of quotes. Quotes of only a few words work best. Encourage students to include the name of the person quoted in a smaller font at the end of the quote.

Students evaluate their page using the Web page checklist provided in the student textbook. Based on their evaluations, they should make any needed corrections before peer review. The peer reviewers should use the same checklist to evaluate the page.

Students create screen shots for their portfolios. They should also make an electronic copy of the finished product. The instructions also suggest publishing the site to the school or class Web site. If this is possible, Chapter 14 discusses the steps needed to publish a Web site. At this point, it would be best to walk students through the steps they should follow to publish the site.

Notes

UNIT 4

The Web Site Development Process

(Page 308)

Visit Glencoe Online

Have students go to **WebDesignDW.glencoe.com**. Then have them click on **Unit Activities > Unit 4 Copyright and Fair Use.** Students can learn how to recognize the importance of understanding copyright policies, and they can learn what information you can and cannot use legally.

Students can complete this four-question activity to familiarize themselves with the concepts of copyright and fair use by browsing a "free Clip Art" Web site. Point out that understanding copyright policies is very important when collecting information or files from the Web—incorrectly using data or documents can have serious legal consequences. Students can also use this information to help them protect their own creative works from copyright infringement.

Complete answers to each Unit Activity are available on the book Web site in the password-protected Teacher Center portion of the site.

(Page 309)

Think About It

In Units 1 through 3, students learned how to create basic Web sites. In Unit 4, they will continue to develop their skills while learning about how Web development project teams function. Have students identify interpersonal and communication skills they have used while working with other students on team projects. (They may identify the need to clearly state what task each person on the team is responsible for completing; the need to resolve conflicts between team members in order to keep the project moving forward; and the need to work as a group to identify solutions to problems.) Then have students discuss how these skills might be the same as or different from the soft skills needed to complete a Web development project.

CHAPTER 11 Planning Guide

Student Edition	Activities and Projects
Chapter 11 Project Planning (pages 310–333)	Quick Write Activity, page 310 Before You Read, page 311
Section 11.1 The Project Life Cycle (pages 312–319)	Reading Strategy, page 312 Go Online Activity 11.1: Explore Web Programming, page 313 You Try It Activity 11A: Identify Team Responsibilities, page 317 You Try It Activity 11B: Enable Source Control, page 318
Ethics & Technology Ethics in the Workgroup (page 320)	Tech Check, page 320
Section 11.2 Determining Project Scope (pages 321–326)	Reading Strategy, page 321 Go Online Activity 11.2: Explore E-Commerce, page 321 You Try It Activity 11C: Identify Tasks and Milestones, page 325
Chapter 11 Review (pages 327–333)	Making Connections: Math—Conduct a Salary Survey Standards at Work: List Confidential Items (NETS-S 2) Teamwork Skills: Identify Project Team Strengths Challenge Yourself: Compare Storefront Solutions You Try It Skills Studio: —Evaluate Web Sites —Compare Evaluations Web Design Projects: —Identify Client Goals —Create a Schedule Additional Activities You May Wish to Use: —PowerTeach Outlines Chapter 11 —Student Workbook Chapter 11

310 Teacher Resource Manual *Introduction to Web Design Using Dreamweaver*

Planning Guide — CHAPTER 11

Assessments

ⓘ Section 11.1 Assessment, page 319

Section 11.2 Assessment, page 326

Chapter 11 Review and Assessment, page 327
You may also use any of the Chapter Review Activities and Projects as Assessments.
Additional Assessments You May Wish to Use:
ⓘ —Self-Check Assessments Chapter 11
—*ExamView* Testbank Chapter 11

Estimated Time to Complete Chapter

18 week course = 2–3 days
36 week course = 7–8 days

To help customize lesson plans, use the Pacing Guide on pages 26–30 and the Standards Charts on pages 312–313.

Key to Recommended Materials

Icons represent elements that may require additional resources.

📁 Focus on Reading

ⓘ Internet access required

𝒅 Software: Dreamweaver

⊙ Teacher Resource CD (contains Student Data Files, Solution Files, Reproducible Graphic Organizers, and Study withPowerTeach Outlines)

Data and Solution Files for Chapter 11

DataFiles
◆ proposal.doc

There are no Solution Files for this activity.

Inclusion Strategies

For **Differentiated Instruction Strategies** refer to the **Inclusion in the Computer Technology Classroom** booklet.

Unit 4 The Web Site Development Process

CHAPTER 11 NETS Correlation For Students

ISTE NETS Foundation Standards

1. Basic operations and concepts
2. Social, ethical, and human issues
3. Technology productivity tools
4. Technology communications tools
5. Technology research tools
6. Technology problem-solving and decision-making tools

Performance Indicators	Textbook Correlation
1. Identify capabilities and limitations of contemporary and emerging technology resources and assess the potential of these systems and services to address personal, lifelong learning, and workplace needs. (NETS 2)	**SE:** Apply It! (319), Go Online (321), Critical Thinking (326), Challenge Yourself (331)
2. Make informed choices among technology systems, resources, and services. (NETS 1, 2)	**SE:** You Try It (325), Critical Thinking (319, 328, 329), Challenge Yourself (331), Skills Studio (332), Web Design Projects (333)
3. Analyze advantages and disadvantages of widespread use and reliance on technology in the workplace and in society as a whole. (NETS 2)	**SE:** Go Online (321), Critical Thinking (326)
4. Demonstrate and advocate for legal and ethical behaviors among peers, family, and community regarding the use of technology and information. (NETS 2)	**SE:** Standards at Work (330)
5. Use technology tools and resources for managing and communicating personal/professional information (e.g. finances, schedules, addresses, purchases, correspondence). (NETS 3, 4)	**SE:** You Try It (317, 325), Web Design Projects (333)
6. Evaluate technology-based options, including distance and distributed education, for lifelong learning. (NETS 5)	**SE:** Go Online (313, 321)
7. Routinely and efficiently use online information resources to meet needs for collaboration, research, publications, communications, and productivity. (NETS 4, 5, 6)	**SE:** Go Online (313, 321), Apply It! (319, 326), Making Connections (330), Challenge Yourself (331), Skills Studio (332)
8. Select and apply technology tools for research, information analysis, problem-solving, and decision-making in content learning. (NETS 4, 5)	**SE:** Go Online (313, 321), You Try It (325), Making Connections (330), Challenge Yourself (331), Skills Studio (332)
9. Investigate and apply expert systems, intelligent agents, and simulations in real-world situations. (NETS 3, 5, 6)	**SE:** You Try It (325), Challenge Yourself (331), Skills Studio (332), Web Design Projects (333)
10. Collaborate with peers, experts, and others to contribute to content-related knowledge base by using technology to compile, synthesize, produce, and disseminate information, models, and other creative works. (NETS 4, 5, 6)	**SE:** Tech Check (320), Skills Studio (332)

SCANS Correlation — CHAPTER 11

Foundation Skills

Basic Skills

Reading Skills	**SE:** Before You Read (311), Focus on Reading (312, 321), Reading Strategies (312, 321), After You Read (328)
Writing	**SE:** Quick Write Activity (310), Section Assessments (319, 326), Chapter Review (327–333)
Mathematics	**SE:** Making Connections (330), Challenge Yourself (331)
Listening and Speaking	**SE:** Tech Check, (320) Skills Studio (332)

Thinking Skills

Creative Thinking	**SE:** Think About It (309), Quick Write Activity (310)
Critical Thinking	**SE:** Critical Thinking (319, 326, 328, 329), Tech Check (320), Standards at Work (330), Teamwork Skills (331), Challenge Yourself (331), Web Design Projects (333)
Problem Solving	**SE:** Tech Check (320), You Try It (325), Skills Studio (332), Web Design Projects (333)

Workplace Competencies

Resources Manage time, money, materials, facilities, human resources	**SE:** You Try It (317, 325), Critical Thinking (319, 326, 328, 329), Command Center (329), Web Design Projects (333)
Interpersonal Work on teams, teach others	**SE:** Think About It (309), Quick Write Activity (310), You Try It (317, 325), Critical Thinking (319), Tech Check (320), Teamwork Skills (331), Skills Studio (332)
Information Acquire, evaluate, organize, maintain, interpret, communicate and use computers to process information	**SE:** Go Online (313, 321), Apply It! (319, 326), You Try It (325) Critical Thinking (328, 329), Command Center (329), Making Connections (330), Standards at Work (330), Challenge Yourself (331), Skills Studio (332), Web Design Projects (333)
Systems Understand, monitor, correct, improve, design systems	**SE:** Skills Studio (332), Web Design Projects (333)
Technology Select, apply, maintain, and troubleshoot technology.	**SE:** Go Online (313, 321), Challenge Yourself (331), Skills Studio (332)

CHAPTER 11

Project Planning

(Page 310) ## Objectives

Section 11.1 The Project Life Cycle
- Identify the stages of the Web site development life cycle
- Identify the responsibilities of project team members
- Use a checklist to evaluate progress
- Explain the use of source control

Section 11.2 Determining Project Scope
- Explain project scope
- Define e-commerce
- Identify types of e-commerce
- Summarize guidelines for developing e-commerce Web sites

LEARNING LINK

Past units of this book showed students how to design and create various aspects of a Web site. Use Chapter 11 to explain how project teams often divide these various tasks among a number of team members to produce an effective Web site.

(Page 310) ## Why It Matters

Ask students to identify examples of products, events, or people that have impressed them. Their answers may range from a recording artist to a car model to historic events such as a person walking on the moon. For each example, ask the class if they can think of who else might have contributed to the positive result. (For example, a recording artist would have a producer, manager, sound engineers, backup singers, musicians, personal assistants, etc.) Use the students' responses to reinforce the concept that successful projects often involve teamwork, and that teamwork has a tremendous impact on the finished product.

(Page 310) ## Quick Write Activity

Have the students write about an experience that was difficult for them because they were working alone. In a paragraph or two, ask them to explain how having team members would have helped both them and the project. Students must be more specific than just saying it would have been easier and the project would have been better.

(Page 311) ## Before You Read

Use Notes Explain to students that it is normal to have questions when they read. Having questions means that the reader is checking his or her understanding of the material. Good readers realize that their understanding can be impeded by a difficult word or concept. When people are involved in the material they are reading, they try to fill in the missing knowledge as a way of getting the most out of the text.

CHAPTER 11

SECTION 11.1 THE PROJECT LIFE CYCLE
(Pages 312–319)

FOCUS

Identifying Web Development Tasks Based on previous reading and their experience in creating Web sites, have students identify some of the different tasks performed by a project team. Write all appropriate responses on the board. After finishing this section, come back to this list and see if the students identified all the tasks required to create a Web site. If not, have them identify which ones are missing from their initial list.

(Page 312)

Focus on Reading

Read to Find Out
Use the Read to Find Out feature to focus student reading. Hold a quick starter discussion to find out what your students already know.

 **Key Terms Online**
Key term definitions and activities are available online at **WebDesignDW.glencoe.com**.

Reading Strategy Answer
Students can find information about team members' responsibilities under the heading *Forming a Project Team* on page 314. Students' tables should look similar to this example:

Team Member	Responsibility
Client Liaison Representative	maintains contact with client
Project Manager	oversees the work of all team members
Web Author	writes the content for the Web site
Web Designer	provides the visual direction for the Web site
Web Developer	programs the Web site using tools such as Dreamweaver
Webmaster	maintains the completed Web site

TEACH

Understanding Teamwork Issues One of the less enjoyable parts of working in a team is dealing with members who do not have a good work ethic and do not perform their tasks well or even at all, making other group members pick up the slack or suffer the consequences. Lead a discussion about this, and ask students if they have encountered such a situation, and what they did about it. Use their responses to explain how they could handle the problem effectively. Some solutions might be: identifying each member's task to the teacher in advance of a problem developing, having a teacher meet with the team periodically to discuss each person's progress, or having regular peer evaluations, anonymous or not.

CHAPTER 11

Answers to Section 11.1 Captions and Activities

(Page 312) **Reading Focus** The basic stages of the Web development life cycle are Analysis and Planning, Design and Development, Testing, Implementation, and Evaluation and Maintenance.

(Page 312) **Figure 11.1** A circle illustrates the process because most Web sites are being continually improved and refined.

(Page 312) ☑ **Reading Check** Answers will vary, but students should recognize that the amount of time assigned to each stage of the life cycle varies by project, and stages may overlap. A designer may begin designing the site's navigation scheme before the entire site's content has been determined.

(Page 313) **Reading Focus** Answers will vary, but students should recognize the importance for each Web site development team member to understand the project's life cycle and know how his or her role fits into the model.

(Page 313) **Go Online** **Activity 11.1** For more information about the resources available to Web developers, have students visit **WebDesignDW.glencoe.com** and check out the links at that site.

(Page 313) **Table 11.1** The responsibilities of certain team members mean that they must participate in the entire life cycle of the project. For example, the client liaison representative maintains contact with the client throughout the entire life cycle of the Web site.

(Page 313) ☑ **Reading Check** The Web development project team members that take part in all stages of a project are the client liaison representative and the project manager.

(Page 314) **Reading Focus** The team members that are essential to the Web development process are the client liaison representative, project manager, Web author, Web designer, Web developer, and Webmaster.

(Page 314) **Figure 11.2** Answers will vary, but may include select images, develop content, determine basic design, and determine navigation.

(Page 315) **Figure 11.3** Answers will vary. Many students will note that project managers participate in all stages of the Web site life cycle; others may suggest that they enjoy problem solving or working with other people to accomplish a goal.

(Page 315) **Figure 11.4** Web authors and Web designers must work together so that the content and the visual elements complement each other. Visual elements need to be relevant to and enhance the site's text. Sites with lots of content and many pages may require different navigation design than sites with small blocks of content and few pages.

> **Teaching Tip**
> Have students justify or explain why they prefer one project management task over another. Ask them to write a paragraph about why they prefer this task and have them share it with the class. Afterwards, ask the students if they still prefer the same task. Have them explain why.

CHAPTER 11

(Page 316) **Figure 11.5** Answers will vary, but students should recognize that the Web developer's goal is to enable visitors to successfully load the Web site in their browser, to navigate within the site, and to navigate to external links.

(Page 316) ✓ **Reading Check** Some students will note that Web developers use software applications, such as Dreamweaver, and authoring languages, such as HTML, to develop or program the Web site; others may suggest that Web developers focus on the interactivity of the site, determining how visitors will move between pages. The Web designer provides visual direction for the site, selects a color palette, gives shape and definition to each page, and provides a consistent look to the site.

(Page 316) **Reading Focus** A Web site development checklist can help to evaluate a Web site's progress and identify the team members responsible for performing specific tasks during the site's development. Students may also note that a checklist enables team members to use consistent criteria when evaluating the interaction, information, and presentation design of a site.

(Page 317) **You Try It** **Activity 11A Identify Team Responsibilities** Students can use Table 11.1 on page 313 to help identify which team members are active at which stage of the MyDiskDesigns.biz project's life cycle. The tasks performed by various team members are described throughout the section. Together, these resources will help students identify who is responsible for which task on the checklist and at which stage of the project cycle this task should be performed (for example, the Web author would be responsible for determining the accuracy of a site's content; the Web author would check the content during the Design and Development stage of the project's life cycle).

> **Teaching Tip**
> It may be a good learning experience to have the class complete You Try It activity 11A in teams, with each team member assigned to a specific job. Having students work in teams at this time may make them more aware of their responsibilities when they create a Web site as a group.

(Page 318) **You Try It** **Activity 11B Enable Source Control** Students open the Language Club Web site and learn how to enable Dreamweaver's Check In/Check Out feature, also referred to as source control, for the Language Club Web site. To reinforce the skills learned in this activity, have students enable the Check In/Check Out feature in Chapter 15 after they have put their MyDiskDesigns.biz site on an FTP server (page 430 of the student textbook).

> **Troubleshooting**
> The e-mail address in Figure 11.7 of You Try It activity 11B is for reference only. If students do not have their own e-mail address, you may want to assign dummy e-mail addresses or provide them with one of your own so they can complete the activity.

(Page 319) ✓ **Reading Check** Source control ensures that only one person at a time can edit a particular file, thus avoiding one person overwriting another's changes.

Unit 4 The Web Site Development Process **317**

CHAPTER 11

ASSESS

(Page 319) Section 11.1 Assessment Answers

Reading Summary

Use the Reading Summary to help students review and reinforce the important points of the section.

What Did You Learn?

1. Students' definitions should be in their own words, but based on the information found in the section and in the book's glossary.

2. Project managers oversee the work of all members of the project team. They assign specific tasks to team members and they track the progress of each team member. Project managers focus on delivering the desired Web site on time and on budget.

3. Team members use checklists to evaluate the effectiveness of a site's interaction, information, and presentation design. They can also use the checklists to make good decisions about their portion of the assigned tasks.

Critical Thinking

4. Answers will vary, but students should recognize that the project manager needs the team to work together. The project manager could help the team review the client's goals to see if any of them are better served by one design over the other. If both designs meet the client's goals, both could be presented to the client to seek his or her reaction.

5. Web site design and development are complex tasks, involving many people. Thorough testing before implementation ensures that when the site goes live it works the way the team intended.

Apply It!

Research Team Jobs Students research the educational requirements and experience needed to perform one of the team roles. Students may find alternate names for some of the roles. For example, Web authors may be called content developers, Web writers, or technical writers. Suggested sites for searches include America's Job Bank (**www.ajb.org**), America's Career InfoNet (**www.acinet.org/acinet**), and Career Explorer (**careerexplorer.net**).

CHAPTER 11

CLOSE

Understanding Team Member Responsibilities
Have students pair up. One will take the role of a client liaison representative for a Web design project team. The other is the client: a car dealership. Have the liaison make a list of questions to ask the client. The client should then come up with possible answers. Students should also create a set of milestones for the development of the site, and dates for the completion of these milestones. Let teams present their work to the class and have the class decide which team has the most realistic goals.

> **Teaching Tip**
> Although students will find out more about milestones in the next section, it will be interesting for them to make estimates here and compare it to the guidelines in Section 11.2.

(Page 320)

Ethics & Technology

ETHICS IN THE WORKGROUP

Answers to Tech Check

1. Students' answers will vary, but should reflect an appreciation for diversity of skills and backgrounds in the workplace. They might discuss the challenges and rewards of working with people from different educational backgrounds, different cultural perspectives, and different fields. Answers should reflect an understanding of why conflicts can emerge in a diverse workgroup, and reasonable methods for resolving conflicts, such as negotiation and compromise. This could make a good class discussion or an opinion essay.

2. Students' responses can be in the form of a written report or an oral presentation. Before the activity, it might be helpful to review some conflict resolution techniques. This might include basic rules of parliamentary procedure, such as recognizing a leader, speaking in turn, voting, taking notes, and so on. The group should create a list or diagram showing the elements of their Web page. While doing so, students should demonstrate effective teamwork, including how to negotiate and work cooperatively with other students. Afterwards, group members should explain the techniques they used to complete the project successfully as a team.

CHAPTER 11

SECTION 11.2 DETERMINING THE PROJECT SCOPE
(Pages 321–326)

FOCUS

Drawing Conclusions About Site Development Many students will have purchased products online, or at least seen them offered. Ask them to describe a favorite site that offers products for sale. What features does it offer the viewer? List as many answers as possible on the board. Ask the students what this means for the Web designer and the project team. (Having various features means the site needs certain pages and certain interactive elements, all of which will take a certain amount of money and time to develop.)

Focus on Reading

Read to Find Out
Use the Read to Find Out feature to focus student reading. Hold a quick starter discussion to find out what your students already know.

 **Key Terms Online**
Key term definitions and activities are available online at **WebDesignDW.glencoe.com**.

Reading Strategy Answer
Students can find information for this activity under the headings *Designing an E-commerce Web Site* on page 323. The students' diagrams should look similar to this example:

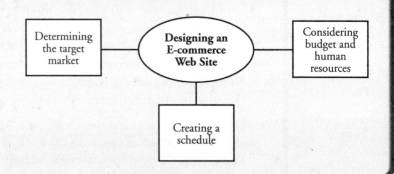

TEACH

Evaluating a Site's Scope To demonstrate that an unlimited budget does not necessarily determine a site's scope, have the class suggest ideas for a site for a clothing manufacturer, assuming an unlimited budget. Then have the class narrow down the list by considering the target market and its likely uses of the site. (For instance, a visitor might be uninterested in the company's mission statement, but would like photos of celebrities wearing the clothes.) You may wish to create a schedule that allows little time before the site goes live. Show the students how this could have an impact on decisions about what to include on the site.

CHAPTER 11

Answers to Section 11.2 Captions and Activities

(Page 321)  **Activity 11.2** For additional information about the significance of e-commerce, have students visit WebDesignDW.glencoe.com and check out the links at that site.

(Page 321) **Reading Focus** During the analysis and planning stage it is important to identify a site's purpose, goals, and audience.

(Page 321) ✓ **Reading Check** A project's scope is the set of features and content that can be provided given the amount of time and resources available.

(Page 322) **Reading Focus** Answers will vary. Advantages of running an e-commerce site include customers can shop from home, 24 hours a day, seven days a week, and businesses can sell merchandise that is not available in the customer's local community.

(Page 322) **Figure 11.9** Answers may include the following: online businesses must decide how to market their products, they must provide a secure site, and they must provide a way for customers to feel comfortable buying online, such as establishing policies for returns and exchanges.

(Page 322) **Table 11.3** Answers will vary. Many students will note the conveniences of being able to compare prices and shop from home at any time as most helpful.

(Page 323) **Figure 11.10** Business-to-business (B2B) and business-to-consumer (B2C).

(Page 323) ✓ **Reading Check** A business-to-business e-commerce site sells goods and services to other businesses. A business-to-consumer site sells goods and services to individual consumers.

(Page 323) **Reading Focus** When designing an e-commerce Web site, you must market, or target, your Web site to the group of potential customers for the product or services that you are selling.

(Page 323) **Figure 11.11** Students may note that the graphics, colors, type, and text used are designed for different age groups.

(Page 324) **Figure 11.12** Testing needs to occur throughout the design and development process so that any changes can be implemented into the site's design in order to make it more effective.

(Page 325)  **Activity 11C Identify Tasks and Milestones** Students list the tasks and milestones for the MyDiskDesigns.biz Web site development project. They should use table 11.4 to help them determine time frames. Use the Student Data file noted in this chapter's Planning Guide.

(Page 326) ✓ **Reading Check** Businesses with limited resources can use a less costly solution, such as an instant storefront, to set up an online presence. An instant storefront helps businesses create their own e-commerce Web sites in a few hours. Some instant storefronts help businesses market their sites; others help businesses through the maze of privacy and security issues that can be difficult for small businesses to handle on their own.

CHAPTER 11

ASSESS

(Page 326) **Section 11.2 Assessment Answers**

Reading Summary

Use the Reading Summary to help students review and reinforce the important points of the section.

What Did You Learn?

1. Students' definitions should be in their own words, but they should be based on the information found in this section and in the book's glossary.

2. In-house solutions use the company's employees to develop and maintain the e-commerce site. Instant storefronts are businesses that help other businesses quickly and efficiently develop an e-commerce site. The storefront provides the human and programming resources to launch and maintain the site.

Critical Thinking

3. Answers may include that some types of goods and services may be primarily available online, replacing traditional stores. However, for other types of goods, online sales will exist alongside traditional sales. For example, people will still want to try on clothes, whereas CDs can easily be sampled and ordered online.

4. The available budget will set limits on the complexity of the e-commerce site. Some features may have to be postponed until later, such as online payments. The budget will help the business prioritize which features are most important.

Apply It!

Compare E-commerce Sites Students compare two e-commerce sites that sell similar products. Their comparisons should focus on such things as features available and ease of use. Students may also compare policies for refunds, returns, and exchanges. Two sites you might suggest are two online booksellers: Barnes and Noble (**www.barnesandnoble.com**) and Amazon.com (**www.amazon.com**).

CLOSE

Applying Web Site Development Guidelines Have students think of a small business they might establish. (It can be a personal service, such as giving skateboarding lessons, or involve the sale of items they make, such as jewelry.) Have them determine their target market, create a schedule, and determine a budget for a Web site for their business. (Budget should be based on the potential sales the site might generate and any income they may be earning that they can spend on the site.) Have them present their work to the class, and receive feedback.

Answers to Chapter Review — CHAPTER 11

The Chapter Review covers a wide range of student knowledge. Due to time constraints, students may not be able to complete every activity in the Chapter Review. Select the activities that are appropriate for your class needs and resources.

(Page 328)

After You Read

Revisit Your Notes After students have gone back over their own notes, have them share some of their questions with the class, particularly ones for which they could not find answers in the chapter. See if anyone else had the same questions. If a number of students have the same question, discuss why they found the particular material difficult. See if anyone in the class has answers and how they found them. Ask students how they might find the answers to any of the questions that are still unresolved and encourage them to follow through.

(Page 328)

Reviewing Key Terms

1. Answers could include client liaison representative, project manager, Web author, Web designer, Web developer, and Webmaster.

2. Clients may include companies that want a corporate presence, organizations that need to stay in touch with members, or retail stores that want to develop an e-commerce site.

3. The client liaison representative works to understand the client's needs and goals. This person helps all team members understand the client's point of view. The project manager works with all team members to deliver what the client wants.

4. A milestone is a specific step in the Web building process that includes a date for completion. Creating milestones will help in setting the parameters for a project.

5. Source control limits the amount of people working on the same page at a certain time. It only allows one team member to access a page at a time.

6. E-commerce is the electronic buying and selling of goods and services.

7. Business-to-Business
Business-to-Consumer

8. Instant storefronts

(Page 328)

Understanding Main Ideas

9. Project managers help all team members work together toward a common goal—meeting the client's goals. Web developers use various tools to program the Web site.

10. The Web designer selects the color palette, gives shape and definition to each page, provides a consistent look to the site, creates the graphics, and creates or obtains photographs, maps, and other visual elements.

11. Checklists help all team members to know the tasks to be accomplished. When teams meet, they can measure individual and team progress against the checklist.

12. The project's scope is determined by balancing the list of desired items for the Web site with the time, money, and other resources available.

13. B2B sites focus their selling efforts on other businesses, while B2C sites focus their selling efforts on individual consumers.

CHAPTER 11 Answers to Chapter Review

14. Businesses must market their e-commerce sites in order to service their target market or group of potential customers. This creates a site that revolves around a common interest making it easier to sell your product.

15. The stages of Web site development are Analysis and Planning, Design and Development, Testing, Implementation, and Evaluation and Maintenance.

16. Answers may vary. Three types of e-commerce transactions include customers ordering products online, businesses providing online technical support for a fee, and online events to which people subscribe and pay a fee.

(Page 328) ## Critical Thinking

17. Businesses use age, income, educational background, interests, and activities as ways to identify market segments.

18. Students' answers will vary. The project manager will likely make this decision based on several factors including the amount of experience each person has with the animation program, the list of tasks yet to be performed by each person, and how the animation will be used in the site. For example, if the Web designer knows the animation program well and the animation affects the interaction design created by the designer, the Web designer will likely be assigned the task.

19. Students will likely note that the goals of the site (such as shipping within 48 hours of the order) will need to be balanced with the cost and resources needed to build and maintain the site.

20. It is important to test your Web site throughout the design and development stage, testing stage, implementation stage, and evaluation and maintenance stage. Testing throughout the development process and even throughout the site's life cycle helps deliver a better product to the client.

21. The student will need to list milestones that they think they will encounter in this project. Opposite to the milestones they will need to list the deliverables. A guide for this table can be found on page 314 of the student textbook.

(Page 329) ## Command Center

22. **Ctrl + Z =** Undo
23. **Ctrl + Shift + Z =** Redo
24. **Ctrl + A =** Select all

Standardized Test Practice

The correct answer is B. As students review the paragraph about project team members and then review the answer statements, remind them to read each one carefully and use the process of elimination to find the correct answer.

Answers to Chapter Review — CHAPTER 11

e-Review

Have students use the book's Web site **WebDesignDW.glencoe.com**.

- **Study with PowerTeach** Encourage your students to use the Chapter 11 PowerTeach Outline to review the chapter before they have a test.
- **Online Self Check** These quick five-question assessments may be used as an in-class activity, a homework assignment, or test review.

(Page 330) ## Making Connections

Math—Conduct a Salary Survey Students research salary ranges for various types of jobs related to Web site design and development, and construct a bar chart based on their findings. The chart should have a title and the axes should be appropriately labeled. Students can look for Web development salaries on Web sites like: Payscale (**www.payscale.com/salary-survey**) and the Lewis and Clark College salary survey (**www.lclark.edu/ karic/salarystudy/index.html**). Students should be consistent with their data: all salaries should be from the same region and be shown either as annual or hourly wages, but not both.

(Page 330) ## Standards at Work

NETS-S 2 List Confidential Items Students create a list of items that they would need to know about a toy store to design an e-commerce site for the store. Information would include such things as its products, product pricing, how orders are placed and fulfilled, company history, target markets, and so on. Beside each item on the list, students check the ones that should not be discussed outside the project team in order to maintain confidentiality. Students should find that most items should be checked. Discuss with students the importance of honoring confidentiality agreements. Students may find a few items that could be mentioned without breaking confidentiality. For example, they may be able to mention that they are working on a Web site in a certain industry.

CHAPTER 11 Answers to Chapter Review

(Page 331) **Teamwork Skills**

Identify Project Team Strengths Answers may vary. Suggested answers are as follows:

PROJECT TEAM STRENGTHS	
Intelligence	**Project Team Member**
• Works well with spoken and written language	Client liaison representative, project manager, Web author
• Works well with numbers and understands the relationship between objects	Project manager, Web designer, Web developer, Webmaster
• Understands how something drawn on paper will look when created	Web designer, Web developer
• Coordinates the body effectively (for example, dancers and athletes)	Does not necessarily apply to any team members
• Works well with music	Web designer, Web developer if adding audio to the site
• Deals well with the behavior, emotions, and motivations of other people	Client liaison representative, project manager, Webmaster
• Deals well with one's own emotions and motivations	All team members
• Works well with one's physical surroundings	Web designer, Web developer

(Page 331) **Challenge Yourself**

Compare Storefront Solutions Students test two demos from instant storefronts and make a chart comparing features of the two storefronts. Students recommend one of the sites to a friend who wants to use the storefront to market video games, and explain why. Storefront Web sites with demos include **www.thriftestore.com**, **www.merchantspace.com**, and **www.coolcart.com**.

Answers to Chapter Review — CHAPTER 11

You Try It — Skills Studio

(Page 332)

1. **Evaluate Web Sites** Students work with a partner to rate three different sites, including an e-commerce site, an entertainment site, and a college or university site. The partners use the checklist provided in Figure 11.6 (page 317 of the student textbook) to rate the sites. The Web sites that students choose should be approved by you, or you can assign Web sites suggested in this TRM or any of the Go Online activities.

2. **Compare Evaluations** Two sets of partners should work together to compare their evaluations from You Try It Skills Studio 1. Each set of partners completes an evaluation of the other set's Web sites. The two sets of partners meet and note the similarities and differences in the evaluations. Students discuss reasons for any differences noted and summarize what they have learned. Often students find that they become comfortable with a certain navigation scheme or a certain presentation design. When they find other sites with similar features, they give them a higher rating. Students should also observe that different backgrounds of individuals can lead to different evaluations of the same site.

Web Design Projects

(Page 333)

1. **Identify Client Goals** Students recommend the pages for a corporate presence site. Recommendations may include a home page with a clear identity for Outdoor Excursions, a page of special interest related to camping and camping gear, a Contact Us page with store hours, a Meet the Staff page with information about a different employee each month (focus on camping experience of each employee), a Links page to campgrounds in a 100-mile radius of the store, a Recommendations page with comments from satisfied customers, and so on.

   Follow-up questions for developing content may include:

   a. questions related to company history (how long in business, location of store, brands of products sold, and so on)

   b. questions related to how people typically learn about the store

   c. questions related to the types of camping experiences each staff member has had

2. **Create a Schedule** Students' schedules for the Web site development of Candles by Carol should show an end date three months from now. Based on the schedule shown in Table 11.4, students should allot two to three weeks for analysis and planning, four to five weeks for design and development, two to three weeks for testing, and one week for implementation. Evaluation and maintenance should be ongoing after publication.

CHAPTER 12 Planning Guide

Student Edition	Activities and Projects
Chapter 12 Developing a Web Site (pages 334–363)	Quick Write Activity, p. 334 Before You Read, p. 335
Section 12.1 Examining an E-Commerce Web Site (pages 336–341)	Reading Strategy, p. 336 YTI Activity 12A: Explore the MyDiskDesigns.biz Web Site, p. 337 YTI Activity 12B: Create an Internal Style Sheet, p. 338 YTI Activity 12C: Attach an External Style Sheet, p. 339 YTI Activity 12D: Edit an External Style Sheet, p. 340
Section 12.2 Using Feedback Forms (pages 342–346)	Reading Strategy, p. 342 YTI Activity 12E: Add a Feedback Form, p. 343 YTI Activity 12F: Add Radio Buttons, p. 344 YTI Activity 12G: Add Check Boxes, p. 345
Emerging Technology Security on the Web (page 347)	Tech Check, p. 347
Section 12.3 Web Site Privacy and Security (pages 348–352)	Reading Strategy, p. 347 Go Online Activity 12.1: Explore Web Site Privacy, p. 349 YTI Activity 12H: Add a Privacy Policy, p. 349 Go Online Activity 12.2: Investigate Web Site Security, p. 351
Section 12.4 Web Site Accesibility (pages 353–356)	Reading Strategy, p. 353 YTI Activity 12I: Run an Accessibility Report, p. 355
Chapter 12 Review (pages 357–363)	Making Connections: Social Studies—Debate an Issue Standards at Work: Evaluate Home Pages (NETS-S 2) Teamwork Skills: Plan a Web Site Challenge Yourself: Research Web Site Security You Try It Skills Studio: —Create an Order Form —Add a Privacy Policy Web Design Projects: —Create a Feedback Form —Plan a Web Site with Feedback Additional Activities You May Wish to Use: —PowerTeach Outlines Chapter 12 Student Workbook Chapter 12

Planning Guide — CHAPTER 12

Assessments

(i) Section 12.1 Assessment, p. 341

Section 12.2 Assessment, p. 346

Section 12.3 Assessment, p. 352

Section 12.4 Assessment, p. 356

Chapter 12 Review and Assessment, p. 357
You may also use any of the Chapter Review Activities and Projects as Assessments.
Additional Assessments You May Wish to Use:
(i) —Self-Check Assessments Chapter 12
—*ExamView* Testbank Chapter 12

Estimated Time to Complete Chapter

18 week course = **4–6 days**
36 week course = **7–8 days**

To help customize lesson plans, use the Pacing Guide on pages 26–30 and the Standards Charts on pages 330–331.

Key to Recommended Materials

Icons represent elements that may require additional resources.

📁 Focus on Reading

(i) Internet access required

♂ Software: Dreamweaver

⊙ Teacher Resource CD (contains Student Data Files, Solution Files, Reproducible Graphic Organizers, and Study with PowerTeach Outlines)

Data and Solution Files for Chapter 12

DataFiles
- MyDiskDesigns
- mydiskdesigns.css
- hdr_privacy.gif
- privacy.doc

SolutionFiles
- SF_YTI_12B
- SF_YTI_12CD
- SF_YTI_12EFG
- SF_YTI_H

Inclusion Strategies

For **Differentiated Instruction Strategies** refer to the **Inclusion in the Computer Technology Classroom** booklet.

Unit 4 The Web Site Development Process

CHAPTER 12 NETS Correlation For Students

ISTE NETS Foundation Standards

1. Basic operations and concepts
2. Social, ethical, and human issues
3. Technology productivity tools
4. Technology communications tools
5. Technology research tools
6. Technology problem-solving and decision-making tools

Performance Indicators	Textbook Correlation
1. Identify capabilities and limitations of contemporary and emerging technology resources and assess the potential of these systems and services to address personal, lifelong learning, and workplace needs. (NETS 2)	**SE:** Critical Thinking (346, 352, 356), Apply It! (353), Making Connections (360), Standards at Work (360), Challenge Yourself (361)
2. Make informed choices among technology systems, resources, and services. (NETS 1, 2)	**SE:** Critical Thinking (346, 352, 356), Apply It! (353), Standards at Work (360), Teamwork Skills (361), Challenge Yourself (361)
3. Analyze advantages and disadvantages of widespread use and reliance on technology in the workplace and in society as a whole. (NETS 2)	**SE:** Go Online (349, 351), Critical Thinking (352)
4. Demonstrate and advocate for legal and ethical behaviors among peers, family, and community regarding the use of technology and information. (NETS 2)	**SE:** Go Online (349, 351), You Try It (349), Critical Thinking (352), Challenge Yourself (361), Skills Studio (362)
5. Use technology tools and resources for managing and communicating personal/professional information (e.g. finances, schedules, addresses, purchases, correspondence). (NETS 3, 4)	**SE:** You Try It (343), Apply It! (346, 353), Skills Studio (362)
6. Evaluate technology-based options, including distance and distributed education, for lifelong learning. (NETS 5)	**SE:** Go Online (349, 351)
7. Routinely and efficiently use online information resources to meet needs for collaboration, research, publications, communications, and productivity. (NETS 4, 5, 6)	**SE:** Go Online (349, 351), Apply It! (352), Tech Check (347), Standards at Work (360)), Teamwork Skills (361)
8. Select and apply technology tools for research, information analysis, problem-solving, and decision-making in content learning. (NETS 4, 5)	**SE:** You Try It (337, 349), Apply It! (346, 352), Tech Check (347), Teamwork Skills (361), Challenge Yourself (361), Skills Studio (362), Web Design Projects (363)
9. Investigate and apply expert systems, intelligent agents, and simulations in real-world situations. (NETS 3, 5, 6)	**SE:** You Try It (337, 343, 344, 345), Challenge Yourself (361), Skills Studio (362), Web Design Projects (363)
10. Collaborate with peers, experts, and others to contribute to content-related knowledge base by using technology to compile, synthesize, produce, and disseminate information, models, and other creative works. (NETS 4, 5, 6)	**SE:** Making Connections (360)

SCANS Correlation — CHAPTER 12

Foundation Skills

Basic Skills

Reading	**SE:** Before You Read (335), Focus on Reading (336, 342, 348, 353), Reading Strategies 336, 342, 348, 353), After You Read (358)
Writing	**SE:** Quick Write Activity (334), Section Assessments (341, 346, 352, 356), Tech Check (347), Chapter Review (358-363), Standards at Work (360)
Mathematics	
Listening and Speaking	**SE:** Making Connections (360), Teamwork Skills (361)

Thinking Skills

Creative Thinking	**SE:** Quick Write Activity (334)
Critical Thinking	**SE:** Critical Thinking (341, 346, 352, 356, 358, 359), Tech Check (347), Making Connections (360), Teamwork Skills (361), Challenge Yourself (361), Web Design Projects (363)
Problem Solving	**SE:** Critical Thinking (358, 359)

Workplace Competencies

Resources Manage time, money, materials, facilities, human resources	**SE:** You Try It (343), Apply It! (346), Critical Thinking (358, 359), Command Center (359), Web Design Projects (363)
Interpersonal Work on teams, teach others	**SE:** Quick Write Activity (334), Making Connections (360), Teamwork Skills (361)
Information Acquire, evaluate, organize, maintain, interpret, communicate and use computers to process information	**SE:** Go Online (349, 351), You Try It (337, 338, 339, 343, 344, 345, 349, 355), Critical Thinking (346, 358, 359), Apply It! (343, 352), Tech Check (347), Command Center (359), Making Connections (360), Standards at Work (360), Teamwork Skills (361), Challenge Yourself (361), Skills Studio (362), Web Design Projects (363)
Systems Understand, monitor, correct, improve, design systems	**SE:** You Try It (337, 344, 345), Apply It! (343), Skills Studio (362), Web Design Projects (363)
Technology Select, apply, maintain, and troubleshoot technology.	**SE:** Go Online (349, 351), You Try It (337, 338, 339, 343, 344, 345, 349, 355), Apply It! (343, 352), Skills Studio (362), Web Design Projects (363)

CHAPTER 12

Developing a Web Site

(Page 334) ## Objectives

Section 12.1: Examining an E-Commerce Web Site
- Discuss the functions of a Web site
- Compare and contrast style sheets
- Apply cascading style sheets (CSS) to a Web site

Section 12.2: Using Feedback Forms
- Create a feedback form
- Compare and contrast radio buttons and check boxes

Section 12.3: Web Site Privacy and Security
- Explain the use of privacy policies
- Compare and contrast Web site privacy and security
- Discuss security measures used by e-commerce sites

Section 12.4: Web Site Accessibility
- Identify and describe accessibility issues
- Identify strategies for maximizing site accessibility
- Validate accessibility

LEARNING LINK

Chapter 11 explained how project team members work together to create an effective Web site. Such sites may be owned by businesses that want to conduct e-commerce. Use Chapter 12 to show students some of the features that e-commerce sites might incorporate.

(Page 334) ## Why It Matters

Lead a brief discussion about what the main foundations of a business Web site should be. What other kinds of organizations might have similar needs? (For example, charities and political organizations need to explain their goals clearly and to provide accurate information to visitors. They might also need to gather information about individuals, and might want to be able to process transactions.)

(Page 334) ## Quick Write Activity

Tell students to think of a personal project or interest that might add an e-commerce element to their personal Web site. For example, they may be part of a band and want to sell t-shirts or create a mailing list to notify fans of upcoming concerts. Have them write down the kinds of features they would want to add to their Web site to accomplish these goals.

(Page 335) ## Before You Read

Check Your Understanding By now, students should be familiar with the graphic organizers used in the Reading Strategies at the beginning of each section. Explain to students that they can use those types of charts and tables to take their own notes. They should choose one or two of the organizers that they think work best. Different sections might need different types of diagrams. For each section, they should use an organizer to summarize and connect the key points as they read.

CHAPTER 12

SECTION 12.1 EXAMINING AN E-COMMERCE WEB SITE
(Pages 336–341)

FOCUS

Identifying E-Commerce Site Features Discuss e-commerce sites with the class, and ask them to identify features that are common to the sites they have visited. List these common features on the board. Ask students to draw conclusions about why certain features are common to many e-commerce sites. What benefits do they provide to the consumer? To the site owner?

(Page 336)

Focus on Reading

Read to Find Out
Use the Read to Find Out feature to focus student reading. Hold a quick starter discussion to find out what your students already know.

Key Terms Online
Key term definitions and activities are available online at **WebDesignDW.glencoe.com**.

Reading Strategy Answer
Students can find information for this activity under the heading *Cascading Style Sheets* on page 338. Students' diagrams should look similar to this example:

Internal Style Sheet
Style sheet is embedded into every page. Gives control over specific elements on one page.

Both internal and external style sheets contain information that styles HTML elements.

External Style Sheet
There is only one style sheet for the Web site. Maintenance and changes to the look of the site are easier with one file.

TEACH

Using and Editing Cascading Style Sheets Have students use Dreamweaver to open the Language Club Web site in Design view. Then, have them open the CSS styles panel, select the style sheet, and click the trashcan icon to remove the link. Lead a discussion about what happens.

CHAPTER 12

Answers to Section 12.1 Captions and Activities

(Page 336) **Reading Focus** Businesses use Web sites to introduce visitors to the business, provide an overview of the business's products or services, provide the opportunity to buy goods or services over the Internet, answer questions about the business, and provide contact information to visitors.

(Page 337) **You Try It** **Activity 12A Explore the MyDiskDesigns.biz Web Site** Students visit the MyDiskDesigns.biz site and analyze the content of each page, identify its purpose, and describe how it contributes to the site. Use the Student Data Files noted in this chapter's Planning Guide.

> **Teaching Tip**
> Students will use the MyDiskDesigns.biz site in Chapters 12 through 15. Since the site will be modified frequently, students should be reminded to always save their work.

(Page 337) ✓ **Reading Check** A FAQ page provides users with answers to frequently asked questions about a business and its services or products.

(Page 338) **Reading Focus** CSS can be used to format a Web site because it helps make the presentation elements of a Web site consistent.

(Page 338) **You Try It** **Activity 12B Create an Internal Style Sheet** Students create a simple Web page that uses an internal style sheet. Use the Solution File noted in this chapter's Planning Guide.

(Page 339) **You Try It** **Activity 12C Attach an External Style Sheet** Students open the MyDiskDesigns.biz Web site and attach an external style sheet to each page within the site. Use the Student Data File and Solution Files noted in this chapter's Planning Guide.

(Page 340) **You Try It** **Activity 12D Edit an External Style Sheet** Students modify the external style sheet they attached in exercise 12C. Use the Solution Files noted in this chapter's Planning Guide.

(Page 341) ✓ **Reading Check** Internal and external style sheets are the two main types of style sheets that can be applied to a Web site.

ASSESS

(Page 341) ### Section 12.1 Assessment Answers

Reading Summary

Use the Reading Summary to help students review and reinforce the important points of the section.

CHAPTER 12

What Did You Learn?

1. Students' definitions should be in their own words, but based on the information found in the section and in the book's glossary.

2. Each page helps to promote the company and its products in a different way:
   - **Home Page** Provides visitors with an introduction to the products offered on the Web site.
   - **Products Page** Provides details and an overview of products available.
   - **FAQ Page** Provides answers to frequently asked questions visitors may have about the products.
   - **News Page** Provides visitors with news about the company and their products.
   - **Contact Page** Provides visitors with a way of contacting MyDiskDesigns.biz.

3. An internal style sheet embeds CSS information within an individual Web page's header HTML code. An external style sheet is a separate file that contains CSS information. This file is not embedded in a single Web page but instead can be linked to multiple Web pages.

Critical Thinking

4. CSS allows the user to make items consistent by separating presentation information from content information.

5. Students' answers will vary. Students may note that using an external style sheet makes maintenance and updating the design of a site easier. Information on the style sheet can be found on page 339 of the student textbook.

Apply It!

Edit CSS Reference Activity 12D on page 340 of the student textbook for steps on how to open the MyDiskDesigns.biz Web site and modify its style sheet.

CLOSE

Reviewing E-commerce Functionality To ensure that students understand that business Web sites have different degrees of e-commerce functionality, have them create a list that indicates how a business site might progress from an online presence to a fully functional e-commerce site. An example of a partial list might be the following:

- Show business's products and give descriptions
- Provide a Contact Us page to answer questions
- Allow online ordering; processing orders by phone
- Allow online ordering and electronic processing of orders (e.g., credit card orders)

Unit 4 The Web Site Development Process 335

CHAPTER 12

SECTION 12.2 USING FEEDBACK FORMS
(Pages 342–346)

FOCUS

Using Feedback Forms Many students will have already been to Web sites in which a feedback form is used. Have students look at the school Web site and determine which sections of the site could benefit from having a feedback form to gain information from parents. List their ideas on the board and see if they can make predictions about how to effectively use a feedback form on the Web sites that they've created using this textbook.

(Page 342)

Focus on Reading

Read to Find Out
Use the Read to Find Out feature to focus student reading. Hold a quick starter discussion to find out what your students already know.

 Key Terms Online
Key term definitions and activities are available online at **WebDesignDW.glencoe.com**.

Reading Strategy Answer
Students can find information about radio buttons and check boxes under the headings *Radio Buttons* and *Check Boxes* on pages 344 and 345. Students' Venn diagrams should look similar to the one below:

Radio Buttons Allow users to select one choice from a list | Allow visitors to select from a list | **Check Boxes** Allow visitors to select preset choices and allow site owner to gather information

TEACH

Comparing and Contrasting Feedback Forms Since the client is the one paying the project team to develop its site, it is likely that the team members will have the client's goals in mind when they develop feedback forms. Impress upon the students that it is equally important to have the visitor's needs in mind. Lead a discussion as to why this is so. Which sites might most need a feedback form? (Sites where customers are making purchases might want customers to provide feedback about their purchasing experience or product concerns, etc.) Visit several business Web sites that have feedback forms, and compare them with the class. Which do students feel is most effective, and why? You might look at the different types of "Contact Us" pages at Lands End (**www.landsend.com**) and Dell (**www.dell.com**).

CHAPTER 12

Answers to Section 12.2 Captions and Activities

(Page 342) **Reading Focus** A feedback form can enhance an e-commerce site by giving customers a way to voice opinions, comments, and suggestions.

(Page 343) **You Try It** **Activity 12E Add a Feedback Form** Students add a feedback form to the Contact Us page of the MyDiskDesigns.biz site. Use the Solution Files noted in this chapter's Planning Guide.

(Page 343) ✓ **Reading Check** A company might add a feedback form to its Web site in order to make the site more dynamic, and to have an opportunity to get feedback from its customers.

(Page 344) **Reading Focus** Preset choices make it easy for visitors to provide feedback because they make it easy for visitors to select an answer.

(Page 344) **You Try It** **Activity 12F Add Radio Buttons** Students learn how to add a feedback question that uses radio buttons for preset choices. Use the Solution Files noted in this chapter's Planning Guide.

(Page 345) **You Try It** **Activity 12G Add Check Boxes** Students learn how to add a feedback question that uses check boxes as preset choices. Use the Solution Files noted in this chapter's Planning Guide.

(Page 346) ✓ **Reading Check** Two types of Web site feedback response mechanisms are radio buttons and check boxes.

ASSESS

(Page 346) ## Section 12.2 Assessment Answers

Reading Summary

Use the Reading Summary to help students review and reinforce the important points of the section.

What Did You Learn?

1. Students' definitions should be in their own words, but based on the information found in the section and in the book's glossary.

2. A feedback form provides customers with a way to voice opinions, comments, and suggestions.

3. A radio button gives visitors a chance to select only one choice from a list. A check box allows visitors to select multiple items from a list.

Critical Thinking

4. Answers will vary, but should indicate that a business would want to provide the level of service that it can dependably handle until it is sure it is getting sufficient customer response to make it worth investing more in the site.

CHAPTER 12

5. Answers will vary. If the business wants visitors to choose from a specific list of hobbies, check boxes would be a good option. If the business wants visitors to list any hobby or hobbies, a text area would work. (Note: Radio buttons and pull-down menus would not be good choices, since they force visitors to make only one choice and people tend to have more than one hobby.)

Apply It!

Develop a Form Students add questions to the MyDiskDesigns.biz feedback form. Make sure that the student's choice regarding the type of response (text box, text area, radio button, check box, and so on) matches the question asked. Other questions that might be asked include: How did you hear about us? (check box) Would you be likely to visit this site again? (radio button) Why or why not? (text box or text area)

CLOSE

Using Tools That Help Gather Information To ensure that students understand that if the purpose of a Web site is to communicate information or a message, then knowing who the user is, and what information is needed is important, ask them how they think a feedback form can help provide a process for communication between the designer and the user. Then have them determine the best type of form component to perform this task. Then have them explain to the class why they made their choice.

(Page 347)

EMERGING Technology

SECURITY ON THE WEB

Answers to Tech Check

1. Students should use the Internet or available print resources to find information about Web security measures. A search engine or well-known security site (such as McAfee, Norton, or Panda) are good places to start. Suggest that students create a table with columns for the system name, its purpose, strengths, and flaws.

2. Students' responses can be in the form of a written report or an oral presentation. Students can work individually or as a team to research on the Internet or available print resources. A search engine or major news Web site (such as CNN.com) are good places to conduct a search for current or archived news reports. Students' reports should outline the type of organization hit, the method of attack, the security in place at the time, the consequences of the attack, and any measures the organization took to improve or increase its security.

CHAPTER 12

SECTION 12.3 WEB SITE PRIVACY AND SECURITY
(Pages 348–352)

FOCUS

Understanding Privacy and Security Concerns Lead a brief discussion of students' experiences with privacy and security on the Web. Are students concerned about privacy and security when they use the Internet? Why or why not? Have they or their friends had any site or individual try to find out information they did not want to share? (Students might have had such experiences in chat rooms or sites with shared files, like music swapping sites.) What did they do? What did they feel the site should have done to prevent this? Use any concerns or negative experiences to show why e-commerce sites must consider these issues.

(Page 348)

Focus on Reading

Read to Find Out
Use the Read to Find Out feature to focus student reading. Hold a quick starter discussion to find out what your students already know.

 Key Terms Online
Key term definitions and activities are available online at **WebDesignDW.glencoe.com**.

Reading Strategy Answer
Students can find information about this activity throughout the section. The students' tables should look similar to this example:

Protecting Privacy	Ensuring Security
legal forms of protection, e.g., COPPA	data encryption
read the Web site's privacy policy	digital certificates

TEACH

Explaining the Importance of Privacy and Security Since many students do not worry about credit ratings, they may not understand the importance of privacy and security issues. Read with students the privacy policy pages at sites such as Dell (**www.Dell.com**) and Citibank (**www.citibank.com/us/index.htm**). Ask students why visitors to these sites might want to consider these policies. Is there anything students would add to or delete from these policies? Explain to the students the various ways in which unauthorized use of personal information can create problems for them. (For example, fraudulent use of their credit card could lead to bad credit, which could result in an inability to purchase a car or buy a house in the future.)

CHAPTER 12

Answers to Section 12.3 Captions and Activities

(Page 348) **Reading Focus** E-commerce sites gather customer data through cookies.

(Page 349)  **Activity 12.1** For more information about Web site privacy, have students visit **WebDesignDW.glencoe.com**.

(Page 349) **Activity 12H Add a Privacy Policy** Students add a privacy policy to the MyDiskDesigns.biz Web site. They format the text to make it consistent with the font and sizes on the home page. Use the Student Data File and Solution File noted in this chapter's Planning Guide.

> ⚠ **Troubleshooting**
>
> In Step 6 of You Try It activity 12H, if students are working in the Macintosh version of Dreamweaver, have them open the privacy.doc file and copy the text. Students should then return to the privacy.html page in Dreamweaver and paste the text under the page header.

(Page 350) ✓ **Reading Check** Web sites post privacy policies to outline the information the site is collecting and to explain how the organization will use that information.

(Page 351) **Reading Focus** Privacy is an important issue for e-commerce Web sites because the businesses need to prevent intruders from stealing or altering sensitive company or customer information contained on their servers.

(Page 351)  **Activity 12.2** Additional information about data encryption can be found at **WebDesignDW.glencoe.com**.

(Page 351) **Figure 12.18** Data encryption provides security to an e-commerce site by encoding data about the order and payment as it is sent over the Internet, so that only the intended receiver with the proper decryption algorithm is allowed to process the order and payment.

(Page 352) **Figure 12.19** Secure Server Certification Authority issued the digital certificate.

(Page 352) ✓ **Reading Check** A commonly used data encryption method among Web publishers is Secure Socket Layer (SSL).

ASSESS

(Page 352) ### Section 12.3 Assessment Answers

Reading Summary

Use the Reading Summary to help students review and reinforce the important points of the section.

What Did You Learn?

1. Students' definitions should be in their own words, but based on the information found in the section and in the book's glossary.

2. Privacy relates to what information can be ethically and legally collected about visitors to a Web site. Security relates to protecting the data that is stored on Web servers and transmitted over the Web.

3. Privacy policies let the customers of an e-commerce site know how the information it collects will be used. Customers are more likely to make online purchases when they know that the information they supply will be used ethically and will be transmitted securely.

Critical Thinking

4. Students should recognize that the Internet can be used by anyone, including people seeking to exploit underage users. Such legislation seeks to protect these young users, making the Internet a safer place for everyone. It also protects legal businesses from selling to young people who cannot pay for the goods and services.

5. Answers should acknowledge that such forgeries would disrupt e-commerce because people would have less confidence in the identity of businesses. They would not, for example, want to give credit card information over the Internet if that information were going to be misused.

Apply It!

Research Digital Certificates Students research the requirements that businesses must meet to get a digital certificate. Possible sites for research are VeriSign (**www.verisign.com**), thawte (**www.thawte.com**), and TRUSTe (**www.truste.com**).

CLOSE

Using Privacy Policies Have the students work in teams and agree on a business they might one day create. Ask them to list what kinds of information they would gather on a Web site for their business. Then have them write a privacy policy that explains this to the viewer, and any options the viewer might have. Have each team explain to the class why they made their privacy policy choices, and receive feedback.

Questions the students might consider include:

- If they use cookies, do they tell the viewer?
- Can the site be used if cookies have been disabled by the viewer?
- Is there any other way the viewer can control what information the site collects?
- Will they share their information with other businesses as a source of income?
- If so, are there any limitations on this, or on the kinds of collected information they will share?
- Can the viewer agree to some types of sharing and not others?

CHAPTER 12

SECTION 12.4 WEB SITE ACCESSIBILITY
(Pages 353–356)

FOCUS

Identifying Web Site Accessibility Open a Web site with vivid colors and sound, perhaps a children's Web site or a site with video. Have some students close their eyes, and some cover their ears. Ask them to discuss how they could enjoy the site if they could not see or hear. What ideas do they have?

(Page 353)

Focus on Reading

Read to Find Out
Use the Read to Find Out feature to focus student reading. Hold a quick starter discussion to find out what your students already know.

Key Terms Online
Key term definitions and activities are available online at **WebDesignDW.glencoe.com**.

Reading Strategy Answer
Students can find the Web page elements under the heading *Making a Site Accessible* on page 354 of the student textbook. Encourage students to provide specific examples for each Web page element. For example, what type of multimedia elements should always include alternative text?

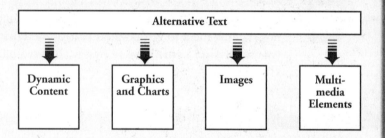

TEACH

Understanding Accessibility in Web Design Some Web site users need accessible Web sites. They may not be able to navigate the menu, see the colors, or even see the monitor. To help students understand more about this accommodating those with different needs, show students the accessibility section of the Web browser. Designers need to keep in mind the purpose of the site, and the users who will visit the site.

CHAPTER 12

Answers to Section 12.4 Captions and Activities

(Page 353) **Reading Focus** Accessibility is important to Web design because it allows individuals with different needs to access and receive online information more efficiently.

(Page 354) **Table 12.3** Alternative text describes a site's audio elements for people who have difficulty hearing. It also enables those browsing the Web with images turned off or browsing with assistive devices to see a description of the image.

> **Teaching Tip**
> If students have trouble locating the answer to this question (Table 12.3), suggest that they check the book's glossary for the term's definition or the Chapter's Reading Review on page 357 of the student textbook. Remind them that the answer should be in their own words.

(Page 354) **Reading Check** Accessibility standards ensure that Web sites are accessible to all visitors, including those with disabilities.

(Page 355) **Reading Focus** Dreamweaver provides a built-in validation tool to check the accessibility of a Web site or document.

(Page 355) **You Try It** **Activity 12I Run an Accessibility Report** Students learn how to run an accessibility report for the MyDiskDesigns.biz site.

(Page 356) **Reading Check** An accessibility report is a list of accessibility errors in a Web page or document, and the identification of what part of Section 508 of the U.S. Rehabilitation Act the error violates.

ASSESS

(Page 356) ### Section 12.4 Assessment Answers

Reading Summary

Use the Reading Summary to help students review and reinforce the important points of the section.

What Did You Learn?

1. Students' definitions should be in their own words, but based on the information found in the section and in the book's glossary.

2. Accessibility enables individuals with different needs to access and receive online information more efficiently. A site should present information in as many ways as possible.

3. Using alternative text in place of or in addition to a site's multimedia elements allows the site to be more accessible to differently abled individuals.

CHAPTER 12

Critical Thinking

4. Section 508 of the U.S. Rehabilitation Act requires Federal agency Web sites to be accessible to all visitors, including those with disabilities. This allows no restrictions to be put on the Web site so the information can be utilized by everyone.

5. 1) Provide alternative text and content for information contained in scripts, plug-ins, and applets.

   2) Include alternative text or the `alt` attribute for every image element in the Web site.

   3) Provide alternative text for all animations, videos, and audio items, along with descriptions of video content and transcriptions of presentations.

Apply It!

Add Alternative Text Students open the Hardware Devices Web site, select each individual image, and modify the alternative text by clicking in the Alt text field in the Properties inspector.

CLOSE

Validating Accessibility Have students select their favorite Web sites. Then have them use an accessibility checker to verify the site's accessibility. Have the students discuss the results and share recommendations for the site to make the site accessible.

Answers to Chapter Review — CHAPTER 12

The Chapter Review covers a wide range of student knowledge. Due to time constraints, students may not be able to complete every activity in the Chapter Review. Select the activities that are appropriate for your class needs and resources.

(Page 358) ## After You Read

Use Diagrams to Help Understanding Students should practice diagramming the information in each section, but they should also understand how the different sections relate to each other. Have them create a diagram that connects the titles or main topics of all the sections of the chapter.

(Page 358) ## Reviewing Key Terms

1. CSS allows the designer to separate presentation information from content information.
2. Feedback forms allow visitors to e-commerce sites to voice their opinions and give the business ideas.
3. *Check lists* allow visitors to select as many choices from a list as they desire. Or radio buttons allow visitors to select *one choice from a predetermined list of choices.*
4. The small data file is called a cookie.
5. A digital certificate tells a visitor that the business's credentials have been verified.
6. E-commerce sites can benefit from Web accessibility by creating a user-friendly environment for all potential clients or customers.

(Page 358) ## Understanding Main Ideas

7. Using an external style sheet makes it quick and easy to make a change to an entire Web site. Any changes made to an external style sheet are reflected in every Web page to which the CSS file is linked.
8. Information includes a statement of what information is collected about visitors, how the organization will use that information, how visitors can control the amount of information gathered, and how visitors can review and correct errors in the information collected.
9. Cookies can gather data about visitors without their knowledge. If security measures are not in place, this information could be used improperly.
10. Customers must have confidence that the information they provide, especially personal information, is not being used improperly.
11. Data encryption alters the appearance of data as it is being transmitted. This ensures that only the proper recipient who can decode the information has access to it.

CHAPTER 12 Answers to Chapter Review

12. 1) Provide alternative text and content for information contained in scripts, plug-ins, and applets.

    2) Include alternative text or the alt attribute for every image element in the Web site.

    3) Provide alternative text for all animations, videos, and audio items, along with descriptions of video content and transcriptions of presentations.

    4) Use colors that provide a high contrast between a site's content and background.

    5) Use link text that is descriptive and makes sense when read out of context.

13. Digital certificate information is shown about that particular site, including:
    - Authorized names
    - The certificate serial number
    - Expiration dates
    - A copy of the certificate holder's public key
    - The digital signature of the certificate-issuing authority

14. A text area allows a visitor to type specific comments to the company. A text box allows the visitor to type specific text that is asked for, like your name or e-mail address.

(Page 358) ## Critical Thinking

15. Students' answers will vary. Suggestions may include pages with contact information, answers to common questions, press releases about the company, information about the company's products and services, and so on.

16. Answers will vary, but students should recognize that privacy and security issues will likely grow in importance as the amount of business conducted on the Web increases and more personal information is stored on databases.

17. Recommended form features are as follows: a text box for visitor's name; a text box for visitor's e-mail address; radio buttons for visitor's age range; check boxes for products used; check boxes for products about which more information is desired; and a text area for suggestions for product improvements.

18. Web site privacy creates a safe environment for users and gives the consumer confidence that they will not be taken advantage of.

19. Students' answers will vary. Students will use the privacy policy from You Try It activity 12H on page 349 of the student textbook as a guideline in determining what elements to keep and what to change and create a table for their answers.

Answers to Chapter Review — CHAPTER 12

(Page 359)

Command Center

21. Ctrl + D = Duplicates file
22. Shift + F1 = Displays Reference panel
23. Shift + F11 = Displays CSS Styles panel

Standardized Test Practice

The correct answer is C. As students review the possible answers, suggest that they re-examine the bar chart carefully, and compare each statement. When they find a statement about a particular country that is false, they can eliminate the choice and focus on the remaining statements.

Have students use the book's Web site **WebDesignDW.glencoe.com**.

- **Study with PowerTeach** Encourage your students to use the Chapter 12 PowerTeach Outline to review the chapter before they have a test.
- **Online Self Check** These quick five-question assessments may be used as an in-class activity, a homework assignment, or test review.

(Page 360)

Making Connections

Social Studies—Debate an Issue Students research the globalization of business and the role the Internet has in globalization. Students use this research to debate whether the Internet has made it possible for international companies to improve the lives of people in developing countries. Students might search the Internet or print sources to find out about the international activities of American companies such as Walmart, Ford, Nike, and IBM. Some Web sites they might find useful are "What is the WTO (World Trade Organization)" at **www.wto.org**, the International Forum on Globalization (**www.ifg.org**), and the World Bank Group (**www.worldbank.org**).

Students' flow charts may look like the one below:

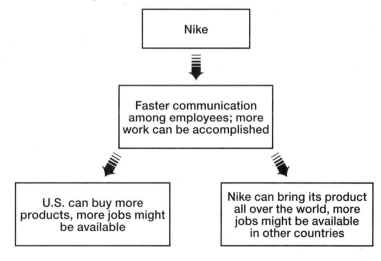

CHAPTER 12 Answers to Chapter Review

(Page 360) ## Standards at Work

NETS-S 5 Evaluate Home Pages Students evaluate the home pages of three e-commerce companies in the same industry. Students' evaluations focus on ease of navigating to product and service information, ease of locating ways to contact the company, the prominence of special offers from the company, and the attractiveness of the home page. Students create a chart based on the information to compare the three companies. You can suggest the following e-commerce sites:

- Clothing—Lands' End, Tony Hawk, Niketown
- Entertainment— Amazon.com, Internet Chess Club, Apple iTunes
- Computer Equipment—Gateway, Dell, CNET.com
- Travel—Travelocity, American Airlines, Expedia

(Page 361) ## Teamwork Skills

Plan a Web Site The team divides into two groups to plan a Web site update. One group plans the revision of the site's navigation structure and the other decides what features to add to the site. Both groups should research sites that sell CDs for ideas. Suggested sites include **www.buy.com**, **www.amazon.com**, **www.cdnow.com** (actually takes you into the Amazon site to CDs), **www.barnesandnoble.com**, and **cdconnection.com**. Based on their research, the entire team works together to storyboard the revised site.

(Page 361) ## Challenge Yourself

Research Web Site Security Students, with the teacher's permission, download a demonstration version of a digital certificate for evaluation. Students recommend a digital certificate company based on their research and their experience with the download. Possible sites for research are **www.Verisign.com** (offers an SSL trial ID), **www.thawte.com** (offers a free test SSL certificate), and **www.ecommercepki.com**.

Students' tables may look similar to the one below:

Digital Certificate	Features	Requirements	Costs
Verisign.com	Secure Site Pro: True 128-Bit SSL Certificates	1 of over 20 types of Web server software	$995/year
Thawte.com	Premium Server Gated Cryptography SSL certificates with full authentication, and capable of 256-bit encryption with automatic 128-bit step-up encryption (using IE 4.x or Netscape 4.06 and later)	1 of over 50 types of Web server software	$449/year
Ecommercepki.com	WISe-Server Certificate	Could not find	$190/year

Answers to Chapter Review — CHAPTER 12

You Try It — Skills Studio

(Page 362)

1. **Create an Order Form** Students select a theme for a site that sells mouse pads. They create an order form similar to the one shown in the text. Students should us the correct form feature for each field.

2. **Add a Privacy Policy** Students review privacy policies at e-commerce sites on the Web to identify the key elements of the policies. Students then adapt the MyDiskDesigns.biz privacy policy to reflect what they have learned in their review and to customize it to work for a company that sells mouse pads. Students add a link on the order form to the privacy policy page.

Web Design Projects

(Page 363)

1. **Create a Feedback Form** Students build a feedback form to gather information to be used in planning upcoming trips. The feedback form should gather basic contact information such as name, address, telephone number, and e-mail address. Students could use a simple check box list of the domestic and international trips and have visitors check all trips in which they are interested. A more complex feedback form would list each trip and then have visitors rate their likelihood of participating in such a trip. Ratings could be very likely, likely, not likely, and definitely not. This more complex form would provide more useful feedback when Outdoor Excursions plans and promotes these trips. The feedback form could also include a text area for visitors to add their suggestions for camping trips.

2. **Plan a Web Site with Feedback** Students create a two-page Web site for the Speckled Band. The home page should present the information from the band's flyer in an attractive way. Students should select an appropriate theme. The second page is a feedback form that gathers contact information from visitors and asks visitors to rate each of the band's 10 services for level of interest. Each statement is followed by a radio button list for the rating. Remind students that once they have one of theses statements set up with the radio button ratings, they can copy and paste it nine times. Then they can edit these for each of the remaining statements.

CHAPTER 13 Planning Guide

Student Edition	Activities and Projects
Chapter 13 Adding Web Site Functionality (pages 364–391)	Quick Write Activity, page 364 Before You Read, page 365
Section 13.1 Tracking Visitors and Collecting Information (pages 366–369)	☐ Reading Strategy, page 366 ⓘ Go Online Activity 13.1: Explore Tracking Software, page 367
Careers & Technology Starting an E-business (page 370)	Tech Check, page 370
Section 13.2 Making Information Easy to Find (pages 371–374)	☐ Reading Strategy, page 371 ⓘ Go Online Activity 13.2: Identify Search Features, page 372 𝒅 You Try It Activity 13A: Add Named Anchors, page 373
Section 13.3 Building a Sense of Community (pages 375–379)	☐ Reading Strategy, page 375 𝒅 You Try It Activity 13B: Create a Guest Book, page 377
Section 13.4 Frames (pages 380–384)	☐ Reading Strategy, page 380 𝒅 ⦿ You Try It Activity 13C: Use Frames on a Site, page 382
Chapter 13 Review (pages 385–391)	Making Connections: Language Arts—Design a Table of Contents ⓘ Standards at Work: Evaluate Guest Books (NETS-S 1) 𝒅 Teamwork Skills: Design a Database Interface ⓘ Challenge Yourself: Research Tracking Software You Try It Skills Studio: 𝒅 —Add a Guest Book 𝒅 —Create a Frames-Based Page Web Design Projects: 𝒅 —Create Named Anchors for a Resume 𝒅 —Create an Investing for Teens Web Site Additional Activities You May Wish to Use: ⦿ ⓘ —PowerTeach Outlines Chapter 13 —Student Workbook Chapter 13

Planning Guide — CHAPTER 13

Assessments

ⓘ Section 13.1 Assessment, page 369

ⓘ Section 13.2 Assessment, page 374

Section 13.3 Assessment, page 379

Section 13.4 Assessment, page 384

Chapter 1 Review and Assessment, page 385
You may also use any of the Chapter Review Activities and Projects as Assessments.
Additional Assessments You May Wish to Use:
ⓘ —Self-Check Assessments Chapter 13
—*ExamView* Testbank Chapter 13

Estimated Time to Complete Chapter

18 week course = 4–6 days
36 week course = 10 days

To help customize lesson plans, use the Pacing Guide on pages 26–30 and the Standards Charts on pages 352–353.

Key to Recommended Materials

Icons represent elements that may require additional resources.

📁 Focus on Reading

ⓘ Internet access required

𝒅 Software: Dreamweaver

⊙ Teacher Resource CD (contains Student Data Files, Solution Files, Reproducible Graphic Organizers, and Study with PowerTeach Outlines)

Data and Solution Files for Chapter 13

DataFiles
- hdr_guestbook.gif
- logo_mydiskdesigns.gif
- frames_privacy.doc

SolutionFiles
- SF_YTI_13A
- SF_YTI_13B
- SF_YTI_13C
- SF_MyDiskDesigns

Inclusion Strategies

For **Differentiated Instruction Strategies** refer to the **Inclusion in the Computer Technology Classroom** booklet.

Unit 4   The Web Site Development Process

CHAPTER 13 NETS Correlation For Students

ISTE NETS Foundation Standards

1. Basic operations and concepts
2. Social, ethical, and human issues
3. Technology productivity tools
4. Technology communications tools
5. Technology research tools
6. Technology problem-solving and decision-making tools

Performance Indicators	Textbook Correlation
1. Identify capabilities and limitations of contemporary and emerging technology resources and assess the potential of these systems and services to address personal, lifelong learning, and workplace needs. (NETS 2)	SE: Critical Thinking (369, 374, 379, 384, 386, 387), Apply It! (369, 374, 384), Tech Check (370), Challenge Yourself (389)
2. Make informed choices among technology systems, resources, and services. (NETS 1, 2)	SE: Critical Thinking (369, 374, 379, 384, 386, 387), Apply It! (369, 374, 379, 384), Tech Check (370), Challenge Yourself (389)
3. Analyze advantages and disadvantages of widespread use and reliance on technology in the workplace and in society as a whole. (NETS 2)	SE: Plan Ahead (381)
4. Demonstrate and advocate for legal and ethical behaviors among peers, family, and community regarding the use of technology and information. (NETS 2)	SE: Critical Thinking (369)
5. Use technology tools and resources for managing and communicating personal/professional information (e.g. finances, schedules, addresses, purchases, correspondence). (NETS 3, 4)	SE: You Try It (373, 377, 382), Making Connections (388), Skills Studio (390), Web Design Projects (391)
6. Evaluate technology-based options, including distance and distributed education, for lifelong learning. (NETS 5)	SE: Go Online (367, 372), Web Design Projects (391)
7. Routinely and efficiently use online information resources to meet needs for collaboration, research, publications, communications, and productivity. (NETS 4, 5, 6)	SE: Go Online (367, 372), Apply It! (369, 374), Critical Thinking (374), You Try It (377, 382), Standards at Work (388), Teamwork Skills (389), Challenge Yourself (389), Web Design Projects (391)
8. Select and apply technology tools for research, information analysis, problem-solving, and decision-making in content learning. (NETS 4, 5)	SE: Apply It! (369, 374), Critical Thinking (374), Teamwork Skills (389), Challenge Yourself (389), Web Design Projects (391)
9. Investigate and apply expert systems, intelligent agents, and simulations in real-world situations. (NETS 3, 5, 6)	SE: You Try It (373, 377, 382)
10. Collaborate with peers, experts, and others to contribute to content-related knowledge base by using technology to compile, synthesize, produce, and disseminate information, models, and other creative works. (NETS 4, 5, 6)	SE: Tech Check (370), Teamwork Skills (389)

SCANS Correlation — CHAPTER 13

Foundation Skills

Basic Skills

Reading	SE: Before You Read (365), Focus on Reading (366, 371, 375, 380), Reading Strategies (366, 371, 375, 380), After You Read (386), Standardized Test Practice (387)
Writing	SE: Quick Write Activity (364), Section Assessments (369, 374, 379, 384), Tech Check (370), Chapter Review (386-391), Challenge Yourself (389)
Mathematics	SE: Critical Thinking (386), Web Design Projects (391)
Listening and Speaking	SE: Tech Check (370), Teamwork Skills (389)

Thinking Skills

Creative Thinking	SE: Quick Write Activity (364), Standards at Work (388), Web Design Projects (391)
Critical Thinking	SE: Critical Thinking (369, 374, 379, 384, 386, 387), Tech Check (370), Making Connections (388), Teamwork Skills (389), Challenge Yourself (389), Web Design Projects (391)
Problem Solving	SE: Apply It! (379), Critical Thinking (386, 387), Teamwork Skills (389), Web Design Projects (391)

Workplace Competencies

Resources Manage time, money, materials, facilities, human resources	SE: You Try It (377, 382), Command Center (387), Skills Studio (390), Web Design Projects (391)
Interpersonal Work on teams, teach others	SE: Tech Check (370), Critical Thinking (386, 387), Teamwork Skills (389)
Information Acquire, evaluate, organize, maintain, interpret, communicate and use computers to process information	SE: You Try It (377), Apply It! (369), Command Center (387), Making Connections (388), Challenge Yourself (389)
Systems Understand, monitor, correct, improve, design systems	SE: You Try It (373, 377, 382), Teamwork Skills (389), Skills Studio (390), Web Design Projects (391)
Technology Select, apply, maintain, and troubleshoot technology.	SE: You Try It (373, 377, 382), Go Online (367, 372), Teamwork Skills (389), Challenge Yourself (389), Skills Studio (390), Web Design Projects (391)

CHAPTER 13

Adding Web Site Functionality

(Page 364) ## Objectives

Section 13.1: Tracking Visitors and Collecting Information
- Identify the limitations of hit counters
- Monitor Web site traffic
- Describe the information gathered by tracking systems
- Identify database interface pages

Section 13.2: Making Information Easy to Find
- Identify Web site search features
- Add named anchors to a Web page

Section 13.3: Building a Sense of Community
- Identify tools used to share news
- Identify tools used to collect visitor information
- Create a guest book

Section 13.4: Frames
- Explain how frames work
- Identify guidelines for frames pages
- Create a frames-based page
- Use frames on a site

> **LEARNING LINK**
>
> Chapter 12 discussed some of the features that e-commerce sites might incorporate. Use Chapter 13 to introduce students to additional features that Web sites can incorporate to increase their usefulness to both visitors and site owners.

(Page 364) ## Why It Matters

Briefly discuss some of the useful features on students' favorite Web sites. One example is the search feature. What if this feature were not available? How would visitors find the information they were looking for? Would the site be one of their favorites if information were not easily accessible? What are the design implications?

(Page 364) ## Quick Write Activity

With students, go through the features in this textbook that make it user friendly. They might notice the Table of Contents, the index, the glossary, and the different fonts and colors used for different parts and elements. Discuss what features on a Web site these features can be compared to.

(Page 365) ## Before You Read

Organize Information It is easier for students to remember information if they group it in ways that make sense. For example, rather than trying to remember everything about computer hardware, a student might break it down into smaller groups such as input devices, output devices, storage, and so on. Recommend that students take notes on index cards.

CHAPTER 13

SECTION 13.1 TRACKING VISITORS AND COLLECTING INFORMATION
(Pages 366–369)

FOCUS

Identifying Information for Site Owners Web designers need to think like site owners if they are to produce effective Web sites. To begin developing this skill, ask students to imagine they have created a Web site for a business they are starting. Have them generate a list of the information they would like to know about the site's effectiveness. List their ideas on the board. As you proceed through the chapter, have students identify the tools that are available to provide each kind of information. Write these tools next to the appropriate list item.

NOTE: You may want to let students know that some Web components will only work once the site is published to a remote Web server. Therefore, students should not become discouraged if some component elements do not work.

(Page 366)

Focus on Reading

Read to Find Out
Use the Read to Find Out feature to focus student reading. Hold a quick starter discussion to find out what your students already know.

 Key Terms Online
Key term definitions and activities are available online at **WebDesignDW.glencoe.com**.

Reading Strategy Answer
Students can find the information for this activity under the headings *Hit Counters, Page Views, and Unique Visits* and *Tracking Software* on pages 366 and 367. Students' tables should look similar to this example:

Information Provided by Hit Counters	Information Provided by Tracking Software
Number of times visitors accessed Web page (i.e., number of times browsers request a file from the Web server)	What country visitors are from
	How visitors navigated to your site
	What browser visitors used
	Which pages are most popular

TEACH

Comparing Information Tracking Students have a tendency to think that privacy issues and a site owner's quest for information are always at odds. However, not all information that a site owner might want raises privacy issues. Lead a discussion about the different kinds of information collected on the Internet and the methods used to collect this information. Which methods tend to create conflicts, and which ones are less controversial? (For example, hit counters do not reveal the identity of the user. Information collected in guest book log files can.)

Unit 4 The Web Site Development Process 355

CHAPTER 13

Answers to Section 13.1 Captions and Activities

(Page 366) **Reading Focus** Web developers use dynamic components, such as hit counters, pages views, and unique visitors, to keep track of Web site traffic.

(Page 367) **Table 13.1** Page views and hit counters are more accurate ways to track visitors than a hit counter because hit counters do not measure the length of a visit, whether a visitor goes to other site pages, and whether a visitor has previously accessed the site.

(Page 367) **Activity 13.1** For additional information about tracking software, have students visit **WebDesignDW.glencoe.com**.

(Page 367) ✓ **Reading Check** Tracking software records what country visitors are from, how they navigated to your site, and what browser they used.

(Page 368) **Reading Focus** In this section, students focus on how they can use a database to collect information. Many companies use a database to send information about a product or service to users or to collect the information from users.

(Page 368) **Figure 13.1** The information a database sends to users or receives from users is organized by fields and records. A field is one piece of information, such as a first name or last name. A record is a group of related fields that contains the information gathered about a particular person or item, such as a product's item number, type, quantity, and price.

(Page 369) **Figure 13.2** The E-Catalog page interacts with a database that stores and updates information about new products on the **Glencoe.com** Web site.

(Page 369) ✓ **Reading Check** A database sends information to users. Users submit information to the database.

ASSESS

(Page 369) ### Section 13.1 Assessment Answers

Reading Summary

Use the Reading Summary to help students review and reinforce the important points of the section.

What Did You Learn?

1. Students' definitions should be in their own words, but based on the information found in the section and in the book's glossary.

2. Tracking systems provide a significant amount of information about a site's visitors. They help individuals and companies decide where and how to advertise their sites, and identify the most popular pages at a site.

3. A static page contains fixed information. A dynamic page contains information that is capable of change. On a static page, information is embedded in the HTML code that makes up the page. Dynamic pages are shells that contain changing information.

Critical Thinking

4. Tracking systems provide information about what country visitors are from, how they navigated to your site, and what browser they used. This information can help an owner to decide where to place a banner ad. For example, if tracking information suggests the site's visitors navigate there from a certain search engine, then the owner might want to place a banner ad on other search engines where the site needs more promotion.

5. Answers will vary. Since restricting access to the results page helps to keep personal customer information secure, it would be best to set up the results page for your order forms as private to protect your visitors' privacy.

Apply It!

Students create a list categorizing the information tracking software will gather. Possible sites for students to research include: DeepMetrix (**www.deepmetrix.com**), Site Stats (**www.sitestats.com**), and Enterprise Marketing Solutions (**www.goemsi.com**).

CLOSE

Reviewing Tracking Methods To ensure that students understand the concepts in this section, you may want to discuss the following:

- Why might a site use a hidden hit counter? (If the site is not yet popular, a small number of hits might give a negative impression of it to a viewer. By using a hidden hit counter, the owner can check for hits without risking this.)
- Should every page of a Web site have a hit counter? (If the hit counters are not hidden, then it might be annoying to see one on every page. If the hit counters are hidden, there would seem to be no reason not to have them on each page.)
- What are the advantages of using tracking software? (It can provide much more information than a hit counter, such as how long a visitor stays on the site, whether she or he visits other site pages, and so on.)

Restate the fact that hit counters have certain limitations. For example, refreshing a page may count as a hit, even though a new visitor is not accessing the page. Students should consider these limitations when evaluating the information that is provided by hit counters.

CHAPTER 13

(Page 370)

Careers & Technology

STARTING AN E-BUSINESS

Answers to Tech Check

1. Lead the class in creating a checklist for evaluating commercial Web sites as marketing tools. Have students first create a checklist individually, then compile all their findings into a single evaluation tool. When evaluating a site, students should consider its effectiveness in presenting basic information about the company, as well as specific information about products or services. They should look at elements such as visual appeal, interactive tools, navigation, media elements, ease of use, special promotions, etc. Students should also consider whether the site gives them positive feelings and makes them want to do business with the company. Afterwards, students can make suggestions for improving poor sites. Students should be supervised when using the Internet.

   Example of a partial checklist:

	1 Poor Marketing Tool	2 Fair Marketing Tool	3 Good Marketing Tool	4 Excellent Marketing Tool
Visual Appeal	Difficult to find information, too cluttered or sparse, poor graphics or layout	Can find information, but graphics or layout is unappealing.	Information is easy to find. Layout and graphics are effective, but unimaginative	Graphics and layout are eye-catching. Information is clearly laid out.
Information	Insufficient information or information is not clearly presented.	Information may be available, but requires a lot of clicking or scrolling.	Information is sufficient and clear, but does not use media elements effectively.	Uses media elements to present information in a clear and interesting manner.
Interactive Tools (e.g. product photos and prices, reservation forms, online purchasing, etc.)	No tools. Provides basic information only.	Allows some interaction, such as close-up photos and prices.	Allows users to complete a transaction, such as making a reservation or purchasing a product. Requires some patience.	Allows users to complete a transaction easily, quickly, and efficiently.

2. Each student's plan should be tailored to the specific type of business he or she chooses. Make sure that students understand that the business should be service-oriented, rather than one that sells products. Students can look at commercial Web sites offering similar services for ideas. Students should list the specific types of information the site would provide, the type of customers they hope to attract, and the methods they would use to attract prospective clients. Ask students to write a brief message that they would use on the site. Students should also describe the design and graphics they would use to

CHAPTER 13

SECTION 13.2 MAKING INFORMATION EASY TO FIND
(Pages 371–374)

FOCUS

Finding Information Most students will have used some or all of the methods for finding information that are discussed in this section. Have them describe these experiences. Which methods have they used most often? Why? Are they more comfortable using particular methods, or does the method they use depend on the kind of information they are looking for? Does the usefulness of a method depend at all on the type or size of the Web site being searched? See if students can draw any conclusions about when and why they would use each of these Web site features.

(Page 371)

Focus on Reading

Read to Find Out
Use the Read to Find Out feature to focus student reading. Hold a quick starter discussion to find out what your students already know.

 Key Terms Online
Key term definitions and activities are available online at **WebDesignDW.glencoe.com**.

Reading Strategy Answer
Students should find the information they need to complete this activity throughout the section. Students' diagrams should look similar to this example:

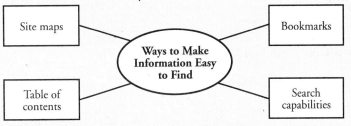

Note: Students may also note that FAQ pages make information easy to find.

TEACH

Evaluating Methods for Finding Information Lead a discussion about the limitations of each information-finding method discussed in this section. (For example, site maps will only list categories of information. A category may be named so that it is difficult to know if it contains the information the user wants. Or there may be too few categories to be very useful.) List these limitations on the board for each method discussed in this section. Encourage the students to see the implications of these limitations for the Web designer. (He or she must figure out how many categories are needed to be thorough, but not overwhelming. The Web designer must also be good at organizing information and must anticipate categories used to find information.)

CHAPTER 13

Answers to Section 13.2 Captions and Activities

(Page 371) **Reading Focus** Tools such as site maps, tables of contents, named anchors, and search capabilities make information easier for visitors to locate on a site.

(Page 372) **Figure 13.3** The online table of contents is similar to a printed book's table of contents, making it convenient and comfortable for readers.

(Page 372) **GO Online** **Activity 13.2** For additional information about search features, have students visit **WebDesignDW.glencoe.com**.

(Page 372) ✓ **Reading Check** A site map organizes a Web site's contents into logical categories, making it easy for visitors to target their search by identifying the categories that may contain the information they need. A table of contents functions the same way as a table of contents in a book. It allows users to see the contents and organization of the site in one glance.

(Page 373) **Reading Focus** Named anchors are used to transport a visitor to a specific place in another document or to a specific pace within a document. An intrapage (within the same page) named anchor is useful when you have long pages that are divided into logical sections. When clicked, the intrapage named anchor will transport visitors to the marked section.

(Page 373) **You Try It** **Activity 13A Add Named Anchors** Students learn how to add named anchors to the MyDiskDesigns.biz Frequently Asked Questions page. Use the Solution File noted in this chapter's Planning Guide.

(Page 374) ✓ **Reading Check** A named anchor is a hyperlink to a specific place in another document or to a specific place within a document.

ASSESS

(Page 347) **Section 13.2 Assessment Answers**

Reading Summary

Use the Reading Summary to help students review and reinforce the important points of the section.

What Did You Learn?

1. Students' definitions should be in their own words, but they should be based on the information found in this section and in the book's glossary.

2. Site maps and tables of contents help visitors navigate to the specific information they are seeking, which is especially important when the site is large and contains a great deal of information.

CHAPTER 13

3. FAQ pages answer common questions that visitors are likely to have about the site. This helps visitors find the information they seek and reduces the number of queries a site is likely to receive.

Critical Thinking

4. Students should recognize that information about products, how to place orders, how to make payments, shipping costs, and how to process returns are critical types of information for an e-commerce site. Other answers are acceptable, but students should provide their reasoning.

5. Answers should provide specific sites that students have searched. Answers may identify that searches located specific information on a site quickly. Other students may note that it is important to carefully select the key words or phrases to search for. Some searches can be frustrating if the search criteria are not specific.

Apply It!

Identify Search Features Students search a local newspaper Web site or an e-zine to identify the features included in the site. Students should describe how the feature is used. This activity may lead to a class discussion of the preferred ways of searching a site. No one way is right or wrong, but some choices are better based on the type of information being sought. For example, if you want to find sports information at a newspaper site, its site map or table of contents will likely be the quickest way to access the sports news. However, if you are seeking information about a specific person in the news, it may be better to use the site's search capabilities.

CLOSE

Using Tools That Help Locate Information Have students work in teams. Tell them they are the Web designers for a new Web site for the Library of _____ (in filling in this blank, the students should agree on a topic of interest to the team. For instance, it can be the Library of Skateboarding, or the Library of Alternative Music, and so on). Ask them to develop one or more of the following for their site:

◆ a site map

◆ a table of contents

◆ a frequently asked questions page

After they have sketched out the page, you may want them to create it. If they are creating a FAQ page, tell them to insert named anchors that will allow visitors to immediately go to the answer when they click a question and then return to the questions when they have finished reading the answer.

Unit 4   The Web Site Development Process   **361**

CHAPTER 13

SECTION 13.3 BUILDING A SENSE OF COMMUNITY
(Pages 375–379)

FOCUS

Communicating with Web Site Visitors Including features that are useful and interesting will motivate visitors to return to a Web site. These types of demographically targeted features also make it easier to share news and information with users and helps build a sense of community. To reinforce the importance of building a sense of community, lead a discussion about the kinds of tools students use regularly to communicate with family and friends and why they think they are effective. Alternately, ask students to think of communication tools that a business might use to share news and information with its customers. If students can't come up with any answers, visit some e-commerce sites with the class that use newsletters, blogs, bulletin boards, or a guest book. Are there features that might help make visitors feel that they are part of a community? What features, if any, will help to motivate visitors to return to the sites?

(Page 375)

Read to Find Out
Use the Read to Find Out feature to focus student reading. Hold a quick starter discussion to find out what your students already know.

Key Terms Online
Key term definitions and activities are available online at 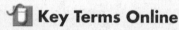WebDesignDW.glencoe.com.

Focus on Reading

Reading Strategy Answer
Students can find the information for this activity throughout the section. Students' diagrams should look similar to this example:

Share Information	Receive Information
Newsletters	Bulletin Boards
Blog	Guest Books
Syndicated Content	

TEACH

Comparing Communication Tools Encourage the students to think of Web-specific communication tools that would be useful for charitable concerns and other non-commerce organizations. (For example, an environmental Web site might use a blog or a newsletter to encourage visitors to e-mail politicians about an environmental issue. It might then use a bulletin board or guestbook to allow visitors to post information about events of interest to them.) You may want to visit a site like your local newspaper with the class, and see what communication tools it uses, and discuss whether those tools enhance the feeling of community in your area.

362 Teacher Resource Manual *Introduction to Web Design Using Dreamweaver*

Answers to Section 13.3 Captions and Activities

(Page 375) **Reading Focus** Tools such as newsletters, Web blogs, and syndicated content allow Web sites to share information with visitors.

(Page 376) **Figure 13.6** The acronym RSS stands for Really Simple Syndication. RSS can also stand for Rich Site Summary or RDF (Resource Description Framework) Site Summary.

(Page 376) ✓ **Reading Check** A blog, short for Web log, is a public journal in which one or more individuals share their thoughts on a variety of subjects.

(Page 377) **Reading Focus** Tools such as bulletin boards and guest books allow Web sites to gather information from a Web site's visitors.

(Page 377)

You Try It **Activity 13B Create a Guestbook** Students learn how to add a guest book page to the MyDiskDesigns.biz Web site. For Step 1, after renaming the guestbook.html file, remind students to change the page title in the Title box.

(Page 379) ✓ **Reading Check** A feedback form communicates information to the site's owners. A guest book communicates information to a site's owners and to anyone else who visits the site; it is a public record.

ASSESS

(Page 379) **Section 13.3 Assessment Answers**

Reading Summary
Use the Reading Summary to help students review and reinforce the important points of the section.

What Did You Learn?

1. Students' definitions should be in their own words, but based on the information found in the section and in the book's glossary.

2. Students' answers should reflect the steps outlined in You Try It activity 13B Create a Guest Book (page 377).

3. Many Web sites distribute monthly or quarterly newsletters to share news, information, and ideas about a particular topic; others use newsletters to stay in touch with users and to motivate users to visit the site again.

Critical Thinking

4. Answers will vary. Answers should provide specific examples of the types of syndicated content that students would include on the site. Students may identify RSS news feeds, headlines, blog entries, company news, and event listings.

5. Answers will vary. An example would be Adobe Forums (**http://www.adobeforums.com/**) which provides support for Adobe products such as Photoshop, Illustrator, and GoLive. This bulletin board is used is to post questions about a product or provide answers to others who have posted questions.

Apply It!

Write a Proposal Students create a proposal identifying the three communications tools to include in the site. Students should describe how each feature is used. Possible tools for students to include: newsletters, blogs, syndicated content, bulletin boards, and guest books. This activity may lead to a discussion of the preferred method of communicating with visitors. No one tool is right or wrong, but some choices are better based on the type of news and information that is included on the school district's site.

CLOSE

Comparing Communication Tools The need of Web sites to communicate with visitors is easy to see. To ensure that students understand the concepts in this section and how they relate to creating a Web site that keeps users coming back to a site, have them compare and contrast the functions of each tool discussed in this chapter section. Have them use a Venn diagram to illustrate their answers.

CHAPTER 13

SECTION 13.4 FRAMES
(Pages 380–384)

FOCUS

Evaluating Frames-Based Sites Once you have discussed the key terms, ask students for examples of sites they are familiar with that use frames. (If they cannot remember any, you may want to visit some with the class.) Ask them what advantages, if any, such sites offer the user. What advantages, if any, do they offer the site owner? Do they think every site is a good candidate for being a frames-based site? Why or why not?

(Page 380)

Focus on Reading

Read to Find Out
Use the Read to Find Out feature to focus student reading. Hold a quick starter discussion to find out what your students already know.

Key Terms Online
Key term definitions and activities are available online at **WebDesignDW.glencoe.com**.

Reading Strategy Answer
Students can find the information for this activity throughout the section. Students' diagrams should look similar to this example:

Frames – Can make information easier to access and navigate. Using frames on a site, however, can make it difficult for visitors to bookmark specific pages. Search engines can have trouble indexing content in frames.

Both framed and non-framed sites are easy to access and navigate.

No Frames – Pages display more quickly and, without frames, it is easier for visitors to understand the site's structure. Pages are easy to bookmark and search engines can easily index the content.

TEACH

Understanding the Need for Accessibility Frames can make a site more difficult to navigate for those with accessibility issues. Although these issues were discussed in Chapter 12, students often have a hard time appreciating the problems of people with disabilities. Lead a discussion that lets students describe the experiences of people they know who face challenges in performing everyday tasks. You may want to have students try to use the Internet while wearing scarves over their eyes that allow only limited vision, or ask them to tape their fingers together to simulate the lack of dexterity that can go along with arthritis. What implications does accessibility have for Web designers?

CHAPTER 13

Answers to Section 13.4 Captions and Activities

(Page 380) **Reading Focus** A frames-based page usually consists of three separate files.

(Page 381) **Figure 13.11** Four files are needed to create a Web page with three frames.

(Page 381) ☑ **Reading Check** A frameset is the shell, or container page, that defines how the separate frames files will display on the Web page. The frameset includes information about the size, setting, and placement of each frame on the Web page.

(Page 382) **Reading Focus** In this section, students focus on how to create a frames-based page using Dreamweaver. Dreamweaver provides predefined frameset templates for creating frames-based pages in Dreamweaver's Start page.

(Page 382) **You Try It** **Activity 13C Use Frames on a Site** Students convert the MyDiskDesigns.biz site into a frames-based site with top and bottom frames. Suggest that students define the My Frames Site in Dreamweaver as part of Step 1. Use the Student Data File and Solution File noted in this chapter's Planning Guide. Also point out the accessibility tip in the Quick Tip! on page 382.

> **Teaching Tip**
>
> In Step 12 of You Try It activity 13C, if students are working in the Macintosh version of Dreamweaver, have them open the frames_privacy.doc file and copy the text. Students should then return to the index.html page in Dreamweaver and paste the text into the bottom frame.

(Page 384) ☑ **Reading Check** Three files are contained in a Web site with two frames.

ASSESS

(Page 384) ### Section 13.4 Assessment Answers

Reading Summary

Use the Reading Summary to help students review and reinforce the important points of the section.

What Did You Learn?

1. Students' definitions should be in their own words, but based on the information found in the section and in the book's glossary.

2. A frameset contains information about the size and placement of each frame on the Web page.

3. Three problems with using frames are as follows: dividing the page into too many frames can confuse visitors; some older browsers do not support frames; frames create accessibility issues (for example, screen readers have difficulty making sense of pages with frames).

Critical Thinking

4. Frames organize the content of Web pages. Frames actually divide the page into separate frames, each containing its own Web page. They are similar in that they both are easy to navigate and contain accessible information.

5. The number of frames sites has been decreasing and will likely continue to decrease. (One reason for the decrease is that some individuals have difficulty accessing sites that use frames.) Other, newer techniques such as shared borders will likely replace frames-based techniques.

Apply It!

Evaluate Frames Students' analyses will vary. This book could be set up as a frames site with the table of contents being used to navigate to each chapter. However, students need to consider the length of the document. If the book is posted to one page, then visitors will have to scroll a long way to reach Chapter 12. Students should support their analysis with reasons.

CLOSE

Using Frames in Web Sites Have the students work in teams. Ask each team to sketch an idea for a new frames site advertising a business in the community. (Students can make up a business if they prefer.) The sketch should indicate where the frames would be and how they would interact. As they plan the site, students will need to identify the target audience of the site and the site's basic goals.

CHAPTER 13 Answers to Chapter Review

The Chapter Review covers a wide range of student knowledge. Due to time constraints, students may not be able to complete every activity in the Chapter Review. Select the activities that are appropriate for your class needs and resources.

(Page 386) ## After You Read

Organize to Remember Review the chapter by helping students organize the information they learned in recognizable groups. Write a main heading or topic word on the board. Have students suggest related topics that they read about in the chapter. Write these around the main topic. Under each subtopic, write down examples that students remember from the chapter. For example, if tracking was your main topic, you might have subtopics such as hit counters, tracking software, and guest books. Under a subtopic like hit counters, students might suggest public and hidden.

(Page 386) ## Reviewing Key Terms

1. A record is *a group of related fields that contain the information about a particular person or item*. Or a *field* is one piece of information, such as a last name or telephone number.
2. Search capabilities allow a visitor to search the site by key words or phrases.
3. A named anchor is a hyperlink to another document or to a specific place within the same document.
4. A blog, or Web log, is a public journal in which one or more individuals share their thoughts on a variety of subjects.
5. A newsletter is used to send information to users, while a bulletin board is used to receive/exchange information from users.
6. guest book
7. The name of the shell page that includes the information about the size and shape of each frame on the page is the frameset.

(Page 386) ## Understanding Main Ideas

8. Hit counters do not measure how long a visitor stays on the site, whether he or she visits other site pages, or if this visitor has previously accessed the site.
9. Tracking systems provide a significant amount of information about a site's visitors and help companies decide where and how to advertise their sites, and identify the most popular pages at a site.
10. Databases are organized by fields and records.
11. A database interface page connects to and interacts with a database.
12. Search capabilities help visitors locate information on large sites.
13. Intrapage named anchors move visitors directly to information that may otherwise require scrolling to find.
14. A guest book communicates information to a site's owners and to anyone else who visits the site; it is a public record, whereas a feedback form communicates information only to the company.

Answers to Chapter Review — CHAPTER 13

15. Answers may vary. Static pages contain fixed information that only changes if the HTML code is revised. Dynamic pages change based on information that comes from an external source such as a database. Blogs are an example of dynamic content because the site owner writes information for the blog via a blogging interface and this information is stored in a database that appears on the blog Web page. An example of static content would be a privacy policy on a Web site or the About Us page.

16. Newsletters are typically delivered via e-mail to a subscriber's inbox. Blogs are usually displayed on a Web site that visitors can access. RSS is delivered via RSS feeds. People can subscribe to the feed and have it delivered in their browser or through an RSS feed application.

(Page 386) ## Critical Thinking

17. Students' answers will vary. A site map would be a good way to allow visitors to access the writings by person and genre. A Web search form that allows visitors to search by person or genre would also be helpful.

18. Students should recognize that four frames will not work well. People will view the site with various size monitors. There is no way to assign equal sizes to each frame without restricting the size of the page. If you assign a size to each frame, some people will see lots of empty space on the screen.

19. A blog would provide regular communication from the yearbook staff to the student body, and would require frequent information updates; a newsletter would provide an extension of the yearbook on an ongoing basis, and could reflect the same style and information as what would be in the yearbook; a bulletin board would provide the yearbook staff with a means for obtaining student body input on topics and content to be included in the yearbook

20. Students' answers will vary based on their design concepts for the library site. As an example, they might use the left frame to help users navigate through the frames and Web site, and the right frame to contain the main content that users access through the left frame navigation.

(Page 387) ## Command Center

21. **Ctrl + Alt + A** = Named anchor
23. **F2** = Layers
24. **Shift + F2** = Frames

Standardized Test Practice

The correct answer is A. As students review the statements, encourage them to go back to the reading *Connecting Web Sites to Databases* to determine whether an answer statement is true or false.

CHAPTER 13 Answers to Chapter Review

e-Review

Have students use the book's Web site **WebDesignDW.glencoe.com**.

◆ **Study with PowerTeach** Encourage your students to use the Chapter 13 PowerTeach Outline to review the chapter before they have a test.

◆ **Online Self Check** These quick five-question assessments may be used as an in-class activity, a homework assignment, or test review.

(Page 388) ## Making Connections

Language Arts—Design a Table of Contents Students should understand that this activity is a good way of understanding how to organize a table of contents or a site map for a Web site. They will create a table of contents by organizing their class notes by class and then adding appropriate subcategories. Subcategories might include class dates, chapters in the textbook, or curriculum standards. Students will use a fishbone diagram as a model for each class and should identify whether it would be beneficial to distribute the notes by blog or newsletter and explain why. Students' diagrams will vary, but may look similar to the partial example below:

Class: Biology 10

—Why It's Important: Week of September 1-7

—Lab Guidelines: Week of September 8-14

—Microorganisms: Week of September 15-21

(Page 388) ## Standards at Work

NETS-S 1 Evaluate Guest Books Students locate and evaluate a site that includes a guest book by creating a chart that lists the strengths and weaknesses of the site. Students identify the greatest strength of the site and suggest a specific improvement to the site. Students use this information to make an entry in the guest book. Students also visit the site after posting the entry to see how it appears. Students should share their entry with a classmate and discuss the similarities and differences between the two guest books. **NOTE:** Some guest books contain material that is inappropriate for students. Either assign pre-screened sites or make sure students are closely supervised during this activity.

Teaching Tip
Students may need to close and reopen their browser to see their guest book entry.

Some suggested sites where students can view guest books are: Beaufort Online (**www.beaufortonline.com/guestbook**), Nantucket Online (**http://nantucketonline.com/cgi-bin/guestbook/guestbook.cgi**), and http://guestbooks.pathfinder.gr/sign/lancelot68.

Answers to Chapter Review — CHAPTER 13

(Page 389) ## Teamwork Skills

Design a Database Interface Students should review sites that include book reviews and used book sales such as **www.amazon.com** and **barnesandnoble.com**. Based on their analysis, they design a review form that could be used by the school's book review site. Then students use a table to identify the database fields needed to manage the book buying and trading. Each database field must be assigned a field name (remind students that field names should be short and contain no spaces). Students' diagrams will vary, but may look similar to the partial example below:

Form Information Needed	Field Name	Form Element
Book Title	ISBN	Text Field
Harry Potter and the Half-Blood Prince (Book 6)	0439784549	Used to enter ISBN number.

Finally, students use Dreamweaver to create the buying and trading form.

(Page 389) ## Challenge Yourself

Research Tracking Software Students create a chart that compares three tracking software applications and write a report that explains the types of Web sites that could effectively use tracking software. Possible sites students can use for their research are **www.deepmetrix.com**, **www.sitestats.com** (note: This site first offers a free trial; however, students can navigate to the site's home page and discover the information they need without signing up for the free trial), and **www.goemsi.com**.

(Page 390)

1. **Add Guest Book** Students use the site they created in Chapter 12. They select a name, create a home page, and add a simple logo to the home page. The home page is added and the order form becomes a sub page to it. The home page content describes the custom mouse pads. Students should use good Web authoring skills to create this content. Students add a hit counter to the home page. Students then add a second child page to the home page that contains a guest book. Students preview their work in a browser.

2. **Create a Frames-Based Page** Students change a page from the MyDiskDesigns.biz Web site into a frames-based page. Students use a Dreamweaver frameset template to create a new Fixed Top frames-based Web page. Students name the frameset file and save all the site's files to a new root folder. Students then open the frameset page in Design view and use the Frames panel to control height and formatting options for each frame within the page. Once completed, students can then add content to the individual frame pages. To make the framed pages easier to see, suggest changing the background color on each page.

CHAPTER 13 Answers to Chapter Review

Web Design Projects

(Page 391)

1. **Create Named Anchors for a Résumé** Students create a résumé in Dreamweaver, using their own personal information. They add named anchors to allow visitors to quickly move to each section of the résumé. Remind students that a résumé must display a student's best work and should have no errors. Students should test their site in a browser, making sure that all named anchors work properly and that there are no spelling or formatting errors.

2. **Create an Investing for Teens Web Site** Students create a four-page Web site that includes a hit counter on the home page and named anchors on the glossary page. The other pages are a membership form page and an informational page. Students should research information for the site, especially the informational and glossary pages. The informational page should include links to investing sites aimed at teens.

Notes

CHAPTER 14 Planning Guide

Student Edition	Activities and Projects
Chapter 14 Publishing a Web Site (pages 392–421)	Quick Write Activity, p. 392 Before You Read, p. 393
Section 14.1 Web Servers (pages 394–397)	▢ Reading Strategy, p. 394 ⓘ Go Online Activity 14.1: Explore Web Hosts, p. 396 d YTI Activity 14A: Calculate Web Site Size and Bandwidth, p. 396
Section 14.2 The Publishing Process (pages 398–403)	▢ Reading Strategy, p. 398 ⓘ Go Online Activity 14.2: Explore File Transfers, p. 401 d YTI Activity 14B: Publish a Web Site Using FTP, p. 401
Real World Technology How We Use the Web (page 404)	Tech Check, p. 404
Section 14.3 Results and Site Reports in Dreamweaver (pages 405–409)	▢ Reading Strategy, p. 405 d YTI Activity 14C: Validate a Web Site, p. 406 d YTI Activity 14D: Check for Broken Links, p. 407 d YTI Activity 14E: Perform a Target Browser Check, p. 408
Section 14.4 Promoting a Web Site (pages 410–414)	▢ Reading Strategy, p. 410 ⓘ YTI Activity 14F: Register a Site with a Search Engine, p. 411 d YTI Activity 14E: Add Meta Tags to a Web Site, p. 412
Chapter 14 Review (pages 415–421)	Making Connections: Language Arts— Conduct a Debate d Standards at Work: Create a Web Page with Meta Tags (NETS-S 3) Teamwork Skills: Publicize a Web Site ⓘ Challenge Yourself: Recommend a "Pay-per-click-Service" YTI Skills Studio: d —Calculate Web Site Size d ⓘ —Add Meta Tags and Publish a Site Web Design Projects: d —Organize Web Site Structure d —Publish a Site Additional Activities You May Wish to Use: ⊙ ⓘ —PowerTeach Outlines Chapter 14 —Student Workbook Chapter 14

Planning Guide CHAPTER 14

Assessments

Section 14.1 Assessment, page 397

Section 14.2 Assessment, page 403

Section 14.3 Assessment, page 409

Section 14.4 Assessment, page 414

Chapter 14 Review and Assessment, page 415
You may also use any of the Chapter Review Activities and Projects as Assessments.
Additional Assessments You May Wish to Use:
(i) —Self-Check Assessments Chapter 14
—*ExamView* Testbank Chapter 14

Estimated Time to Complete Chapter

18 week course = 2–3 days
36 week course = 7–8 days

To help customize lesson plans, use the Pacing Guide on pages 26–30 and the Standards Charts on pages 376–377.

Key to Recommended Materials

Icons represent elements that may require additional resources.

☐ Focus on Reading

(i) Internet access required

♪ Software: Dreamweaver

⊙ Teacher Resource CD (contains Student Data Files, Solution Files, Reproducible Graphic Organizers, and Study with PowerTeach Outlines)

Data and Solution Files for Chapter 14

There are no Data Files for this chapter.
There are no Solution Files for this chapter.

Inclusion Strategies

For **Differentiated Instruction Strategies** refer to the **Inclusion in the Computer Technology Classroom** booklet.

Unit 4   The Web Site Development Process   375

CHAPTER 14 NETS Correlation For Students

ISTE NETS Foundation Standards

1. Basic operations and concepts
2. Social, ethical, and human issues
3. Technology productivity tools
4. Technology communications tools
5. Technology research tools
6. Technology problem-solving and decision-making tools

Performance Indicators	Textbook Correlation
1. Identify capabilities and limitations of contemporary and emerging technology resources and assess the potential of these systems and services to address personal, lifelong learning, and workplace needs. (NETS 2)	SE: Critical Thinking (397, 403, 409, 414, 416, 417), Apply It! (397), Tech Check (404), Challenge Yourself (419)
2. Make informed choices among technology systems, resources, and services. (NETS 1, 2)	SE: You Try It (396, 411, 412), Critical Thinking (397, 403, 414), Apply It! (403, 414), Tech Check (404), Teamwork Skills (419), Challenge Yourself (419), Skills Studio (420), Web Design Projects (421)
3. Analyze advantages and disadvantages of widespread use and reliance on technology in the workplace and in society as a whole. (NETS 2)	SE: Tech Check (404), Making Connections (418)
4. Demonstrate and advocate for legal and ethical behaviors among peers, family, and community regarding the use of technology and information. (NETS 2)	SE: Making Connections (418)
5. Use technology tools and resources for managing and communicating personal/professional information (e.g. finances, schedules, addresses, purchases, correspondence). (NETS 3, 4)	SE: Apply It! (397)
6. Evaluate technology-based options, including distance and distributed education, for lifelong learning. (NETS 5)	SE: Go Online (396, 401)
7. Routinely and efficiently use online information resources to meet needs for collaboration, research, publications, communications, and productivity. (NETS 4, 5, 6)	SE: Go Online (396, 401), Apply It! (397), Tech Check (404), You Try It (401), Making Connections (418), Challenge Yourself (419), Skills Studio (420)
8. Select and apply technology tools for research, information analysis, problem-solving, and decision-making in content learning. (NETS 4, 5)	SE: Go Online (396, 401), You Try It (396, 411, 412), Apply It! (397), Tech Check (404), Making Connections (418), Standards at Work (418), Challenge Yourself (419), Skills Studio (420), Web Design Projects (421)
9. Investigate and apply expert systems, intelligent agents, and simulations in real-world situations. (NETS 3, 5, 6)	SE: Apply It! (403, 414), Skills Studio (420), Web Design Projects (421)
10. Collaborate with peers, experts, and others to contribute to content-related knowledge base by using technology to compile, synthesize, produce, and disseminate information, models, and other creative works. (NETS 4, 5, 6)	SE: Making Connections (418), Teamwork Skills (419)

SCANS Correlation — CHAPTER 14

Foundation Skills

Basic Skills

Reading	**SE:** Before You Read (393), Focus on Reading (394, 398, 405, 410), Reading Strategies (394, 398, 405, 410), After You Read (416)
Writing	**SE:** Quick Write Activity (392), Section Assessments (397, 403, 409, 414), Chapter Review (416-421)
Mathematics	**SE:** You Try It (396), Challenge Yourself (419), Skills Studio (420)
Listening and Speaking	**SE:** Making Connections (418), Teamwork Skills (419)

Thinking Skills

Creative Thinking	**SE:** Quick Write Activity (392), Teamwork Skills (419), Web Design Projects (421)
Critical Thinking	**SE:** Critical Thinking (397, 403, 409, 414, 416, 417), Tech Check (404), Making Connections (418), Standards at Work (418), Teamwork Skills (419), Challenge Yourself (419), Web Design Projects (421)
Problem Solving	**SE:** Apply It! (403, 414), Challenge Yourself (419)

Workplace Competencies

Resources Manage time, money, materials, facilities, human resources	**SE:** You Try It (396), Apply It! (397), Command Center (417)
Interpersonal Work on teams, teach others	**SE:** Teamwork Skills (419)
Information Acquire, evaluate, organize, maintain, interpret, communicate and use computers to process information	**SE:** Go Online (396, 401), You Try It (396, 401, 406, 407, 408, 411, 412), Critical Thinking (397, 403, 409, 414, 416, 417), Apply It! (397), Tech Check (404), Command Center (417), Making Connections (418), Standards at Work (418), Teamwork Skills (419), Challenge Yourself (419), Skills Studio (420), Web Design Projects (421)
Systems Understand, monitor, correct, improve, design systems	**SE:** You Try It (401, 411, 412), Skills Studio (420), Web Design Projects (421)
Technology Select, apply, maintain, and troubleshoot technology.	**SE:** Go Online (396, 401), You Try It (396, 401, 406, 407, 408, 411, 412), Apply It! (397), Tech Check (404), Standards at Work (418), Skills Studio (420), Web Design Projects (421)

CHAPTER 14

Publishing a Web Site

(Page 392) ## Objectives

Section 14.1: Web Servers
- Identify the technical needs of a Web server
- Evaluate Web hosts
- Compare and contrast internal and external Web hosting

Section 14.2: The Publishing Process
- Select a Web site name
- Register a domain name
- Maintain a site's directory structure
- Publish and test a Web site

Section 14.3: Results and Site Reports in Dreamweaver
- Validate a Web site against W3C standards
- Check for broken links
- Check your Web site against target browsers

Section 14.4: Promoting a Web Site
- Identify techniques for publicizing Web sites
- Insert meta tags
- Evaluate the use of cookies for targeted marketing

LEARNING LINK

In Chapter 13, students learned how to add features such as search capabilities, hit counters, and guest books to an e-commerce site. They also learned about frame pages, and how to monitor Web site traffic. Chapter 14 takes students through the steps for successfully publishing a site to a remote Web server.

(Page 392) ## Why It Matters

It is important for students to remember that most Web sites are created for an audience. A writer may find it personally satisfying to write a novel. However, if that writer wants to develop an audience, then he must make that novel accessible to the public. Publishing the novel and selling it in a bookstore or elsewhere allows the public to obtain and read the writer's work. The same is true with publishing a Web site.

(Page 392) ## Quick Write Activity

It used to be that word-of-mouth was an extremely important way to increase sales of a product, because there were fewer ways of reaching target audiences before television and the Internet. Students may think that word-of-mouth is not as important today. Have them write a paragraph about why this may or may not be true.

(Page 393) ## Before You Read

Take Good Notes Formal outlines can be intimidating and confusing for students. They worry about whether they should use numbers or letters, not to mention Roman numerals, to differentiate the outline's different levels. A simplified version of an outline can help students learn to distinguish between main ideas and supporting details without worrying about formatting correctly. They can quickly and easily use levels 1, 2, and 3 to determine the importance of the content they read as they take notes.

CHAPTER 14

SECTION 14.1 WEB SERVERS
(Pages 394–398)

FOCUS

Identifying Web Servers and How They Function Lead a brief discussion to see what students may already know about publishing Web sites. Ask them to identify Web servers and Web hosts they have heard of. See if they can distinguish between the two. See if they understand how Web servers function so as to allow a site to be used on the Internet. Ask students what they think they still need to know about these topics. After finishing this section, make sure the students have filled in the holes in their knowledge.

(Page 394)

Focus on Reading

Read to Find Out
Use the Read to Find Out feature to focus student reading. Hold a quick starter discussion to find out what your students already know.

 Key Terms Online
Key term definitions and activities are available online at **WebDesignDW.glencoe.com**.

Reading Strategy Answer
Students can find the information they need for this activity under the heading *Internal Versus External Hosting* on page 397. Students' tables should look similar to this example:

Internal
- Companies provide their own Web server
- Allows greater control of site
- Lets companies determine content and functionality of site

(Overlap)
- Use servers
- Are ways companies' sites gain access on the Internet

External
- Companies pay someone else to host their site
- Can be more cost effective
- Allows access to up-to-date hardware and equipment

TEACH

Defining Appropriate Content Chapter 14 discusses publishing a Web site. Because of the potential legal ramifications of students publishing Web sites under the school's name or auspices, it is critical that the students understand their responsibility to avoid any content that is controversial. Lead a discussion about what might be appropriate and inappropriate content. Make sure the students also know that they must always check with you before publishing a Web site.

Teaching Tip
This chapter contains exercises that direct students to publish Web sites on an FTP server. Although your students may not be able to perform these exercises due to limited or unavailable capability, you may find the remaining sections of the chapter to be useful, as they contain valuable Webmaster information that is excellent "real world" material.

CHAPTER 14

Answers to Section 14.1 Captions and Activities

(Page 394) **Reading Focus** Answers will vary, but students should indicate that selecting an appropriate server involves evaluating a Web server's CPU power, hard drive speed and capacity, communications channel bandwidth, scalability, and reliability.

(Page 394) **Figure 14.1** A server's hardware largely determines its efficiency. The factors involved are CPU power, hard drive speed and capacity, communications channel bandwidth, scalability, and reliability.

(Page 395) ✓ **Reading Check** Scalability refers to a Web server's ability to meet response time and to handle increasing Web traffic.

(Page 395) **Reading Focus** Instead of purchasing their own Web servers, many companies pay Web hosts to store their Web site files for them. Web hosts provide Web server space to customers for a fee so that they can post their Web site on the server.

(Page 395) **Figure 14.2** A Web host provides server space to customers for a fee, so that they can post their Web site on the server.

(Page 396) **Go Online** **Activity 14.1** For additional information about the services provided by various Web hosts, have students visit **WebDesignDW.glencoe.com**.

(Page 396) **You Try It** **Activity 14A Calculate Web Site Size and Bandwidth** Students check the size and calculate the transfer bandwidth of the MyDiskDesigns.biz site, to determine the amount of space and the minimum amount of bandwidth a Web host should have to effectively administer this site.

(Page 397) **Figure 14.4** Three advantages of external hosting are as follows: more cost effective than Web server; can provide more up-to-date computer hardware and communications equipment; provide benefits such as Internet and backup services.

(Page 397) ✓ **Reading Check** The three ways bandwidth is measured are as follows: Kilobytes per second(Kbps); Megabytes per second (Mbps); or Gigabytes per second (Gbps).

> **Teaching Tip**
> When students are working in Dreamweaver, point out the load time in the bottom right corner of the screen. Explain to students that, as a rule of thumb, their Web site load time should not be larger than 60 seconds if they want their Web sites to be user-friendly for visitors with a slow connection speed.

ASSESS

(Page 397) **Section 14.1 Assessment Answers**

Reading Summary

Use the Reading Summary to help students review and reinforce the important points of the section.

What Did You Learn?

1. Students' definitions should be in their own words, but based on the information found in the section and in the book's glossary.

2. Individuals should consider cost, performance, reliability, tech support, and storage space and bandwidth.

Critical Thinking

3. With internal Web hosting, a company uploads its Web site to its own Web server. The company retains all the control over the site and how it functions on the server. External Web hosting involves transferring the Web site files to the Web server of another company that typically hosts many other Web sites. By sharing the costs of the server with other companies, the cost is often less than what it would be if the site were internally hosted.

4. A Web server bought by an individual is likely not to be as powerful (less CPU power, smaller hard drive) as a Web server purchased by a large company.

Apply It!

Evaluate Web-Hosting Services Students create a chart to compare the setup costs, monthly fees, performance, and reliability of two local Web hosting companies. Students will likely need to make some judgments based on the information about the performance and reliability of the two services. Students may need to infer that companies with RAID or other highly reliable types of backup systems will be more reliable than a service that uses offline backups. Or they may be able to find testimonials from customers.

CLOSE

Reviewing Factors Affecting Server Choice Have students write a paragraph describing a situation in which a company might buy its own server. Then have them write a second paragraph describing a situation in which a company might want to use a Web host's server. In the first paragraph, students may note one or more of the following: the company's site may be complex and contain applications that access large databases; the company's site may need constant updating of information and features; the company has the funds to make such a purchase. In the second paragraph, the students may note one or more of the following: the company's funds are limited; the company may need frequent tech support; the Web host's server may be better than one it could afford. Let students know that external hosting sometimes provides perks such as access to special Web components such as hit counters, CGI scripts, e-mail forwarding, and so on. If these are important to a company, then it might want to use external hosting.

CHAPTER 14

SECTION 14.2 THE PUBLISHING PROCESS
(Pages 398–403)

FOCUS

Evaluating Web Site Names Most Internet users have at times experienced difficulties in locating a Web site, due to an ineffective Web site name. To reinforce the importance of having an effective Web site name, ask students to describe such experiences. Alternatively, ask students what they think the URLs are for the Web sites for Dickies clothing (**www.dickies.com**), the Miami Beach Chamber of Commerce (**www.miamibeachchamber.com**), the American Broadcasting Company (**abc.go.com**) and other business sites. See if their guesses about the Web site names are accurate. Let them draw conclusions about naming Web sites, and about what this means for Web developers and their clients. You may also want to note that, in general, people never really own a domain name. Instead, people usually lease the right to use a domain name. The term of this lease varies.

(Page 398)

Focus on Reading

Read to Find Out
Use the Read to Find Out feature to focus student reading. Hold a quick starter discussion to find out what your students already know.

 **Key Terms Online**
Key term definitions and activities are available online at **WebDesignDW.glencoe.com**.

Reading Strategy Answer
Students can find the three guidelines for this activity under the heading *Selecting a Name* on page 398 of the student textbook. Students' diagrams should look similar to this example:

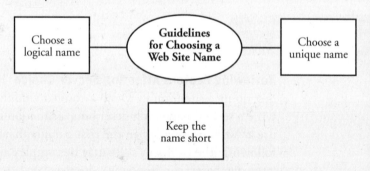

TEACH

Dreamweaver Server Extensions Invite a Webmaster or other representative from a Web hosting company to discuss the Web site publishing process. Also, have the person discuss the types of hosting services and technical support available from the Web hosting company. Encourage students to ask questions about Web hosting and the Web publishing process.

CHAPTER 14

Answers to Section 14.2 Captions and Activities

(Page 398) **Reading Focus** Web site names should be as unique, logical, and short as possible. Students' answers may indicate that the Web site name is often the same as the Web site's URL.

(Page 399) **Figure 14.5** Every domain name must be unique so that a Web browser connected to the Internet can locate the correct site.

(Page 399) **Reading Focus** A site is ready to be published when its directory structure is well organized to speed download times and when it has a consistent style for naming files and referencing those files so that errors do not occur.

(Page 400) **Figure 14.6** Case sensitive means that the system distinguishes between a file name that uses uppercase and lowercase letters and one that uses only lowercase letters.

(Page 400) **Figure 14.7** Good organization will improve download times.

(Page 401) **Reading Check** It's difficult to manage many files if they all reside in the same directory. Users will experience slow download times if the server has to scan hundreds of files every time they click a site's hyperlink.

(Page 401) **Reading Focus** You can transfer Web files to a server using HTTP (Hypertext Transfer Protocol) or FTP (Files Transfer Protocol).

(Page 401) **GO Online** **Activity 14.2** Additional information about transferring files to a server is available at **WebDesignDW.glencoe.com**.

(Page 401) **You Try It** **Activity 14B Publish a Web Site Using FTP** Students learn how to use the Dreamweaver FTP client to publish a Web site. You will need to supply them with the remote Web site location, FTP client address, user name, and password.

CAUTION: Students should not publish a site to an FTP server without your permission.

(Page 402) **Reading Check** HTTP is a two-way protocol because it can download, or transfer, data from a file server to a client (user) machine, and it can also be used to upload, or transfer, data from a client's computer system to a server as well.

Teaching Tip

If students are using Dreamweaver to create their Web site, file organization is part of their designed system. Have students go online to various news related Web sites and examine the page file names. Do they make sense? Is it important for news sites to maintain logical file names or does the site's navigational structure make this unnecessary? Remember to remind students that all of the Web site's folders must be named exactly the same on the server as on the local computer.

Troubleshooting

Remind students to avoid using spaces in file and folder names. Point out that many older servers do not have the ability to read file names that contain spaces. Emphasize the importance of limiting the number of characters in a file or folder name, but suggest that, if necessary, students should use the underscore (_) character in a file or folder name instead of a space.

CHAPTER 14

(Page 403) • **Reading Focus** It is important to test a Web site on a variety of platforms to ensure that the site functions properly.

(Page 403) **Reading Check** Cross-platform testing is the process of testing sites on a variety of computer hardware and software configurations.

ASSESS

(Page 403) ### Section 14.2 Assessment Answers

Reading Summary

Use the Reading Summary to help students review and reinforce the important points of the section.

What Did You Learn?

1. Students' definitions should be in their own words, but based on the information found in the section and in the book's glossary.
2. When developing a large Web site, a logical directory structure helps developers keep files organized. It also improves download time when a user visits the site.
3. HTTP is the Internet protocol used to access Web pages via a browser. FTP is the protocol used to transfer files between a client computer and a Web server.

Critical Thinking

4. Domain names are registered so that no one else can use the name.
5. Answers should note that both site names and page names should be logical and be kept as short as possible. Site names need to attract visitors to the site and set the site apart from similar sites. These considerations are not as important for page names. Also, page names must be unique within the site, but they do not need to be registered or researched to make certain that no one else is using the name.

 ### Apply It!

Create a Directory Structure Answers may vary to a certain extent. However, the directory structure should include folders for genre (Pop/Rock, Classical, Country, and so on). Some students may recommend including folders for artists; however, this is likely to create too many folders since many artists will have only one or two CDs. A good extension activity would be to supply a list of CDs and have students list the artist/CD title within the correct folder. This will help students determine if further categorization is needed.

CHAPTER 14

CLOSE

Comparing the Transfer of Files to a Server with HTTP and FTP To make sure the students have grasped the similarities and differences between transferring Web files to a Web server using HTTP and FTP, have them create a chart comparing the two methods. Students' charts will vary but may look similar to this:

HTTP	FTP
Main protocol used to download files over the Internet	Not used to download files over the Internet
A method of transferring or uploading files to a server	A method of transferring or uploading files to a server
Does not use an FTP server	You need to know the name of the FTP server that will receive your files
	You need a valid user name and password

(Page 404)

Real World Technology

HOW WE USE THE WEB

Answers to Tech Check

1. Answers will vary, but one example would be Bank of America (**www.bankofamerica.com**). Personal services are more numerous and easier to locate on the site than business services, and include online banking, education loans, and Teen Visa cards. Business services include payroll and direct deposit services, and business loans.

2. Students' answers will vary, but should focus on one specific field and how it is expanding its emerging technology. Students should make predictions about the different directions the field may take, and any of the social, economic, or political consequences.

CHAPTER 14

SECTION 14.3 RESULTS AND SITE REPORTS IN DREAMWEAVER
(Pages 405–409)

FOCUS

Validating a Web Site In small groups, have students take different pages of a previously created Web site, such as the Language Club Web site, and validate them online using the W3C's validation service at **http://validator.w3.org/**. Do all of the pages validate correctly? If not, what errors are being produced and what steps can students take to correct them to successfully validate their pages? Have them revalidate the pages once corrections are made.

(Page 405)

Focus on Reading

Read to Find Out
Use the Read to Find Out feature to focus student reading. Hold a quick starter discussion to find out what your students already know.

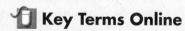
Key Terms Online
Key term definitions and activities are available online at **WebDesignDW.glencoe.com**.

Reading Strategy Answer
Students can find the information for this activity throughout this section. Students' diagrams should look similar to this example:

Report	Function
Accessibility	Checks the Web page or site to ensure it meets accessibility standards.
Missing Alt Text	Generates a report indicating whether any images or graphics do not have alternate text.
Untitled Documents	Checks a Web page or site for Web pages that do not have any text within the TITLE tags of a page.

TEACH

Performing a Target Browser Check In Dreamweaver, have students open a previously created Web site. Using the Results panel, have students select the Target Browser Check tab. Do any errors appear? If so, have students correct them. Next, have students change the browser versions and perform a Target Browser Check. For instance, lower Internet Explorer (or similar Web browser) from version 6.0 to 3.0. (If students are using a different Web browser, lower the version of that Web browser.) To access the settings, choose the green arrow in the upper-left corner of the Results panel.

CHAPTER 14

Answers to Section 14.3 Captions and Activities

(Page 405) **Reading Focus** Dreamweaver provides Workflow reports to track a Web site's files, and HTML reports to spot code errors such as missing or alternate text or empty tags.

(Page 405) **Figure 14.10** The two main types of reports available in the Reports dialog box are: Workflow and HTML Reports.

(Page 405) ✓ **Reading Check** A Web design program, such as Dreamweaver.

(Page 406) **Reading Focus** Dreamweaver's Results panel provides a variety of reports that validate a site's code, check for broken hyperlinks, and confirm that a site will display correctly in a variety of Web browsers.

(Page 406) **You Try It** **Activity 14C Validate a Web Site** Students learn how to validate the MyDiskDesigns.biz Web site against the HTML 4.0 standards.

> ⚠ **Troubleshooting**
>
> In You Try It activity 14C, students may be inclined to move ahead without your permission. Encourage them to wait for your instruction or provide them with this instruction before starting the activity.

(Page 407) **You Try It** **Activity 14D Check for Broken Links** Students learn how to check for the MyDiskDesigns.biz Web site for broken links.

(Page 408) **You Try It** **Activity 14E Perform a Target Browser Check** Students learn how to check the MyDiskDesigns.biz Web site against common browsers.

(Page 409) ✓ **Reading Check** A Link Checker report identifies broken links and orphaned files. The report also identifies the number of links in the site, the number of HTML files checked, and the number of orphaned links. It also displays how many of those links are OK, Broken, or External.

ASSESS

(Page 409) **Section 14.3 Assessment Answers**

Reading Summary

Use the Reading Summary to help students review and reinforce the important points of the section.

1. Students' definitions should be in their own words, but based on the information found in the section and in the book's glossary.

2. Reports are useful tools that help you spot errors or make maintenance easier. Web developers use reports and validations to be sure their Web sites are ready to run smoothly before being published.

CHAPTER 14

Critical Thinking

3. A target browser check will allow the user to specify which type and version of browser they will want to check the site against.

4. A link checker report identifies broken links in your site or within a particular file. A target browser will allow the user to specify which type and version of browser they will want to check the site against.

Apply It!

Check Links Answers will vary, but students should indicate that an orphaned file is a file that does not link to other files in the site. To locate orphaned files in a Web site with Dreamweaver, students run the Link Checker report under the Results panel.

CLOSE

Using Reports and Validating a Web Site In Dreamweaver, have students open a previously created Web site. Use the Site Reports option in the Results panel to check the Web site for any errors. Once students correct the errors, have them run the Site Reports again.

CHAPTER 14

SECTION 14.4 PROMOTING A WEB SITE
(Pages 410–414)

FOCUS

Analyzing Publicizing Methods Most students have already been consumers for many years. Lead an activity in which students list the various methods that businesses have used to make them aware of certain products, and then discuss whether these methods were effective (led to a sale). You may wish to start this as a general discussion, and then focus on methods encountered online.

(Page 410)

Focus on Reading

Read to Find Out
Use the Read to Find Out feature to focus student reading. Hold a quick starter discussion to find out what your students already know.

 **Key Terms Online**
Key term definitions and activities are available online at **WebDesignDW.glencoe.com**.

Reading Strategy Answer
Students can find the information for this activity under the heading *Publicizing Web Pages* on page 410. Students' tables should look similar to this example:

Publicizing Method	Pros	Cons
E-mail advertising	Cost effective; easy to connect to site through hyperlink	May be filtered by ISP
Print advertising	Can reach people who do not use e-mail	Relatively expensive; cannot use hyperlinks
Link trading	Cost effective	Would not make sense to add a link on a competitor's site
Registering with search tools	Exposes site to millions of Internet users	Site may be buried in a large list of related hits; there may be a delay in becoming part of database
Using meta tags	Easy to implement and increases likelihood of a search engine hit	May not include the keyword the searcher uses

TEACH

Comparing Meta Tags Visit several Web sites with students that sell products or services of the same type. Hotel sites like **www.hilton.com** and **www.ramada.com** are good examples. View each site's source code and look at its meta tags. Then use a search engine to locate these same businesses. How do the businesses display on the search tool's hit list? Is there a relationship between where the site displays in the list and the type of meta tags it used in its source code? Have the students draw conclusions about what this means for advertising a Web site.

Unit 4 The Web Site Development Process **389**

CHAPTER 14

Answers to Section 14.4 Captions and Activities

(Page 410) **Reading Focus** E-mail, print media, and link trading are often used to publicize a Web site.

(Page 411) *You Try It* **Activity 14F Register a Site with a Search Engine** Students learn how to register a Web site with a search engine.

(Page 412) *You Try It* **Activity 14G Add Meta Tags to a Web Site** Students add meta tags to the MyDiskDesigns.biz Web site. Before starting this activity, you may want to come up with a list of keywords that students can use for this site.

(Page 413) ✓ **Reading Check** The description meta tag describes the Web site's purpose.

(Page 413) **Reading Focus** In order to expand their user base, some Web site publishers: offer periodic sales and promotions; give away prizes; or offer recognition.

(Page 413) **Figure 14.19** Answers will vary. Answers should note that visitors could visit a local computer store to get the same computer, but limited time offers and other online promotions that may expire, such as gift certificates, referral bonuses, discounts, and free shipping may sway many of these customers to purchase online.

(Page 413) ✓ **Reading Check** Promotions that Web sites often use to increase Web traffic include: gift certificates, referral bonuses, discounts, and free shipping.

(Page 414) **Reading Focus** Many Web sites use a cookie, or small file stored on the user's computer, to gather information about their target audience.

(Page 414) ✓ **Reading Check** A cookie is a small file stored on the user's computer that contains specific information about the user, including information regarding: what sites the user has visited; the products the user has purchased; how much time and money the user has spent online; the user's credit card or checking account information.

ASSESS

(Page 414) ### Section 14.4 Assessment Answers

Reading Summary

Use the Reading Summary to help students review and reinforce the important points of the section.

What Did You Learn?

1. Students' definitions should be in their own words, but based on the information found in the section and in the book's glossary.

2. Publicizing methods include e-mail advertising, print advertising, link trading, registering with search engines, and embedding meta tags in HTML code.

3. A cookie is a small file stored on the user's computer that contains information about the user, such as what sites the user has visited, what products he or she has purchased, and so on.

Critical Thinking

4. Web sites, especially e-commerce sites, depend on repeat visitors for a steady stream of income from the site. Repeat visitors require less advertising than is necessary to attract first-time visitors.

5. Answers should note that e-mail and print ads are both used to promote Web sites. E-mail is less expensive than print ads and makes it easier for people to connect to the site. E-mail messages can, however, be filtered out as spam by ISPs. Print ads require more work for consumers, since they must remember the information until they actually log onto their computers and then enter the Web site address into the browser.

Apply It!

Promote a Web Site Proposals will vary. Students should state that the objective is to sell extreme sports gear (i.e. skateboarding, snowboarding, mountain biking, rock climbing, etc.) to a broad market. Specific proposals to promote the site may include any of the methods mentioned in the section. Students may also recommend publicity methods not included in the text, such as sponsoring an extreme sports event at which banners, billboards, hats, t-shirts, and so on contain the company's Web site address. Since this is an e-commerce site, students will want to consider various promotions to encourage repeat customers.

CLOSE

Using Meta Tags and Applying Publicizing Methods Have students work in teams of two or three. Tell them they are starting a small business that offers courses in how to write for television comedies. Have each team come up with appropriate description and keywords meta tags to increase the effectiveness of how the site will display on a search tool's hit list. Have them decide how else the business will publicize the Web site, given that it is new and has a limited budget. Have the teams explain their meta tag and publicizing decisions to the class.

CHAPTER 14 Answers to Chapter Review

The Chapter Review covers a wide range of student knowledge. Due to time constraints, students may not be able to complete every activity in the Chapter Review. Select the activities that are appropriate for your class needs and resources.

(Page 416) **After You Read**

Create an Outline The outline for the first section of this chapter would look like this:

1. Web Servers
    2. The Technical Needs of a Web Server
    2. Web Hosts
        3. Choosing a Web Host
        3. Internal Versus External Hosting

(Page 416) **Reviewing Key Terms**

1. A Web server is a powerful computer that maintains a constant connection to the Internet and on which Web site files reside.

2. Internal Web hosting means the company uploads its Web site to its own Web server, while external Web hosting involves transferring the Web site files to the Web server of another company that typically hosts many other Web sites.

3. When you download files you transfer them from a *server* to a *client computer system*. Or when you *upload* files, you transfer them from a client computer system to a server.

4. InterNIC is a Web site that provides information about the Web name registration process. It is hosted by the Internet Corporation for Assigned Names and Numbers (ICANN) that assigns Web site names and IP addresses.

5. HTTP

6. Cross-platform testing helps ensure that your Web site will work as expected on many different computer configurations.

7. Checked Out By, Design Notes, Recently Modified

8. Spam refers to massive unsolicited e-mailing to advertise a company, product, or service.

(Page 416) **Understanding Main Ideas**

9. Until the files are on a Web server, which maintains a constant Internet connection, other people's browsers will not be able to locate the site.

10. Web server efficiency is affected by CPU power, hard drive speed and capacity, communications channel bandwidth, scalability, and reliability.

11. A site's directory structure should be well organized to speed download times and to maintain a clear organization of the site's files.

Answers to Chapter Review — CHAPTER 14

12. Some servers see a file that has uppercase and lowercase letters as a different file from one that is all lowercase. As a result, students should use a consistent style when naming files and referencing those files so that errors do not occur.

13. Publicizing methods include e-mail advertising, print advertising, registering with search engines, link trading, and using meta tags.

14. E-mail advertising is inexpensive and provides an easy way for people to connect to the site. Disadvantages include the fact that some people see this advertising as spam and some ISPs block these e-mail messages.

15. Three ways to increase Web site traffic are offering periodic sales and promotions, giving away prizes, and offering recognition to visitors.

(Page 416) ## Critical Thinking

16. You register a domain name on the InterNIC Web site, after checking to see that the domain name is not currently registered by someone else.

17. 1) Cost

    2) Performance

    3) Reliability

    4) Tech Support

    5) Storage Space and Bandwidth

    Descriptions can be found on page 396 of the student textbook.

18. Factors that a company should use to select a Web host include cost, performance (bandwidth), reliability, availability of technical support, and storage space on the server. Cost and tech support are likely to be very important to a small company. Technical support is important to small businesses that do not employ technical people to maintain the site, perform upgrades, or fix problems that may arise.

19. Scalability refers to a Web server's ability to handle increasing traffic, meaning that there is sufficient capacity for additional files to be added to sites. Reliability refers to the ongoing availability of Web sites. Sites should be available to visitors 24 hours a day, seven days a week. This is especially important for e-commerce sites that depend on the site being available to generate income.

20. The log of publishing events provides clear evidence of when files were transferred from the client to the Web server. It can also help with file updates by revealing which files have been updated and whether the files were uploaded to the correct place on the server.

21. Students' answers will vary, but students should indicate how they will market the Web site and use a pyramid chart to explain whether they would use cookies, spam, or link trading as a first choice and why.

22. Answers will vary. Students should explain why they think their Web site is getting fewer hits and discuss how they intend to increase traffic to their Web site. Students may suggest some of the following techniques: e-mail advertising, print advertising, link trading, registering with a search engine, embedding meta tags in HTML code. Students may also note any of the following: offering sales and promotions, giving away prizes, and offering recognition.

CHAPTER 14 Answers to Chapter Review

(Page 417) Command Center

23. F7 = Open the results panel
24. Ctrl + F8 = Open Check Links Sitewide report
25. Ctrl + ' = Change view

Standardized Test Practice

The correct answer is B. As students review the possible answers and re-read the internal and external hosting advantages, remind them to use the process of elimination to find the correct answer.

Have students use the book's Web site **WebDesignDW.glencoe.com**.

◆ **Study with PowerTeach** Encourage your students to use the Chapter 14 PowerTeach Outline to review the chapter before they have a test.

◆ **Online Self Check** These quick five-question assessments may be used as an in-class activity, a homework assignment, or test review.

(Page 418) Making Connections

Language Arts—Conduct a Debate Students research and prepare for a debate on the use of cookies. Assign students randomly to one of the teams. Then tell the team which side of the debate they will take. Encourage students to use facts, rather than opinions, to state their case. Also, focus your assessment of this activity on the clarity of the points that are made, the research to back up the position, and the ability to defend the position.

Student's main idea charts will vary, but may include some the following:

Cookies	Against Cookies
Can be used to help customize search engine results	Can be used to track visitors through a Web site without them knowing
Can be used to customize the features or look of a Web site	Could transmit personal information such as what a visitor looks at and how long they stay on a particular page.
Can be used to store shopping lists of items a user has selected while browsing a virtual shopping mall.	
Can be used to ensure a visitor to a site enters an online contest only once.	

394 Teacher Resource Manual *Introduction to Web Design Using Dreamweaver*

Answers to Chapter Review — CHAPTER 14

(Page 418) ## Standards at Work

NETS-S 3 Create a Web Page with Meta Tags Students create a Web page that lists four services or businesses in your community targeted at families with young children. The page should include a one-sentence description of each service or business and provide links to these services. Meta tags should be added to the HTML code. Meta tags may vary but should include the name of the community, important words such as children's services, preschools, health care, and so on that relate to the information supplied on the page.

(Page 419) ## Teamwork Skills

Publicize a Web Site Students plan a name and a Web site domain name for a business that offers courses in English as a second language. Students also write an advertising plan for this site. Factors about potential customers that students should consider in choosing the name and creating the advertising plan include: limited English skills, different ethnic backgrounds, varying educational backgrounds, and so on. They might consider using meta tags in different languages and advertising on search engines that cater to non-English speakers.

Student's answers will vary, but may look similar to the example below:

Method	Reason	Results
Web page banner ads	They would be seen by those browsing the Internet.	May not effectively reach target audience unless the ads are placed on sites new immigrants may visit.
Create flyers	Could be placed in locations that immigrants go to such as government offices.	May not be noticed.
Billboards	They are large and easy to see.	Can be placed in areas that immigrants travel to, live, or frequent. High visibility may mean good results.

(Page 419) ## Challenge Yourself

Recommend a "Pay-per-click Service" Students research the "pay-per-click" services of at least three search engines and create a chart that compares pricing structures. Students then write a paragraph recommending one of the services and stating the reasons for the choice. Students' decisions should be based on the needs of a local bed and breakfast that is launching a Web site.

CHAPTER 14 Answers to Chapter Review

(Page 420)
1. **Calculate Web Site Size** Students calculate the size of each file in the Language Club Web site. They estimate the number of visitors to the site in a month based on 15 percent of students in the school, plus 50 additional visitors per month. Based on this information, students calculate the approximate transfer bandwidth for the site.

2. **Add Meta Tags and Publish a Site** Students select a site they have created, add relevant meta tags, and publish the site. Student's answers will vary, but may look similar to the example below:

Description	Keywords
Annual International Food Festival	Food
	International
	Festival
	Annual

(Page 421)
1. **Organize Web Site Structure** Students use Dreamweaver to create the Tools for Home and Business Web site. The focus of this project is on creating a logical directory structure for the site, using a consistent naming structure for files and folders. All file and folder names should use lowercase letters and should be logical. Students insert placeholder text for graphics.

> **Teaching Tip**
> Students' may provide only one description entry for their Tools for Home and Business Web site.

2. **Publish a Site** Students publish the Tools for Home and Business site. You will need to direct students as to how to publish the site. If possible, have students publish the site to a Web server using Dreamweaver's FTP client. If no server is available, they can publish the site to their hard drive or a network drive. Students then update the site by adding a graphic and publishing only the changed page. If possible, make different hardware configurations available so that students can test the site in various browsers and with various hardware configurations.

Notes

CHAPTER 15 Planning Guide

Student Edition	Activities and Projects
Chapter 15 Maintaining a Web Site (pages 422–443)	Quick Write Activity, page 422 Before You Read, page 423
Section 15.1 Web Server Maintenance (pages 424–427)	Reading Strategy, page 424 Go Online Activity 15.1: Explore Web Server Maintenance, page 424 You Try It Activity 15A: Research Webmaster Jobs, page 427
Ethics & Technology Privacy Issues and the Internet (page 428)	Tech Check, page 428
Section 15.2 Updating Information (pages 429–432)	Reading Strategy, page 429 You Try It Activity 15B: Download and Upload Files from a Remote Server, page 430
Section 15.3 Keeping a Web Site Secure (pages 433–436)	Reading Strategy, page 433 You Try It Activity 15C: Create a Login Screen, page 434 Go Online Activity 15.2: Explore Global Access Controls, page 435
Chapter 15 Review (pages 437–443)	Making Connections: Create an Oral Presentation Standards at Work: Create Technical Documentation (NETS-S 4) Teamwork Skills: Update a Web Site Challenge Yourself: Identify Security Procedures You Try It Skills Studio: —Update a Web Site —Create a Job Description Web Design Projects: —Document a Procedure —Plan and Develop a Web Site Additional Activities You May Wish to Use: —PowerTeach Outlines Chapter 15 —Student Workbook Chapter 15

Planning Guide CHAPTER 15

Assessments

Section 15.1 Assessment, page 427

Section 15.2 Assessment, page 432

Section 15.3 Assessment, page 436

Chapter 15 Review and Assessment, page 437
Building 21st Century Skills
Building Your Portfolio
You may also use any of the Chapter Review Activities and Projects as Assessments.
Additional Assessments You May Wish to Use:
ⓘ —Self-Check Assessments Chapter 15
—*ExamView* Testbank Chapter 15

Estimated Time to Complete Chapter

18 week course = 4–6 days
36 week course = 7–8 days

To help customize lesson plans, use the Pacing Guide on pages 26–30 and the Standards Charts on pages 400–401.

Key to Recommended Materials

Icons represent elements that may require additional resources.

📄 Focus on Reading

ⓘ Internet access required

d Software: Dreamweaver

◉ Teacher Resource CD (contains Student Data Files, Solution Files, Reproducible Graphic Organizers, and Study with PowerTeach Outlines)

Data and Solution Files for Chapter 15

There are no Data Files for this chapter.
SolutionFiles
◆ SF_YTI_15C

Inclusion Strategies

For **Differentiated Instruction Strategies** refer to the **Inclusion in the Computer Technology Classroom** booklet.

Unit 4 The Web Site Development Process   399

CHAPTER 15 NETS Correlation For Students

ISTE NETS Foundation Standards

1. Basic operations and concepts
2. Social, ethical, and human issues
3. Technology productivity tools
4. Technology communications tools
5. Technology research tools
6. Technology problem-solving and decision-making tools

Performance Indicators	Textbook Correlation
1. Identify capabilities and limitations of contemporary and emerging technology resources and assess the potential of these systems and services to address personal, lifelong learning, and workplace needs. (NETS 2)	**SE:** Critical Thinking (427, 432, 436, 438, 439), Apply It! (427, 436), Tech Check (428), Making Connections (440), Challenge Yourself (441), Web Design Projects (443)
2. Make informed choices among technology systems, resources, and services. (NETS 1, 2)	**SE:** Critical Thinking (427, 432, 436, 438, 439), Apply It! (427, 432, 436), Making Connections (440), Teamwork Skills (441), Web Design Projects (443), Building 21st Century Skills (444), Building Your Portfolio (445)
3. Analyze advantages and disadvantages of widespread use and reliance on technology in the workplace and in society as a whole. (NETS 2)	**SE:** Tech Check (428), What Did You Learn? (436), Challenge Yourself (441)
4. Demonstrate and advocate for legal and ethical behaviors among peers, family, and community regarding the use of technology and information. (NETS 2)	**SE:** Tech Check (428), Go Online (435), Section Assessment (436), Challenge Yourself (441), Web Design Projects (443)
5. Use technology tools and resources for managing and communicating personal/professional information (e.g. finances, schedules, addresses, purchases, correspondence). (NETS 3, 4)	**SE:** Standards at Work (440), Building Your Portfolio (445)
6. Evaluate technology-based options, including distance and distributed education, for lifelong learning. (NETS 5)	**SE:** Go Online (424, 435), You Try It (427)
7. Routinely and efficiently use online information resources to meet needs for collaboration, research, publications, communications, and productivity. (NETS 4, 5, 6)	**SE:** Go Online (424, 435), You Try It (427), Apply It! (427, 432, 436), Tech Check (428), Teamwork Skills (441)
8. Select and apply technology tools for research, information analysis, problem-solving, and decision-making in content learning. (NETS 4, 5)	**SE:** You Try It (427, 430, 434), Apply It! (427, 436), Tech Check (428), Standards at Work (440), Teamwork Skills (441), Skills Studio (442), Web Design Projects (443), Building 21st Century Skills (444)
9. Investigate and apply expert systems, intelligent agents, and simulations in real-world situations. (NETS 3, 5, 6)	**SE:** You Try It (427, 430, 434), Apply It! (436), Web Design Projects (443)
10. Collaborate with peers, experts, and others to contribute to content-related knowledge base by using technology to compile, synthesize, produce, and disseminate information, models, and other creative works. (NETS 4, 5, 6)	**SE:** Tech Check (428), Teamwork Skills (441), Challenge Yourself (441), Building Your Portfolio (445)

SCANS Correlation — CHAPTER 15

Foundation Skills

Basic Skills

Reading	**SE:** Before You Read (423), Focus on Reading (424, 429, 433), Reading Strategies (424, 429, 433), After You Read (438), Standardized Test Practice (439)
Writing	**SE:** Quick Write Activity (422), Section Assessments (427, 430, 434), Tech Check (428), Chapter Review (438-443), Challenge Yourself (441), Building 21st Century Skills (444), Building Your Portfolio (445)
Mathematics	**SE:** Apply It! (427)
Listening and Speaking	**SE:** Tech Check (428), Making Connections (440), Teamwork Skills (441), Challenge Yourself (441)

Thinking Skills

Creative Thinking	**SE:** Quick Write Activity (422), Making Connections (440), Building 21st Century Skills (444)
Critical Thinking	**SE:** Critical Thinking (427, 432, 436, 438, 439), Tech Check (428), Standards at Work (440), Teamwork Skills (441), Challenge Yourself (441), Web Design Projects (443), Building 21st Century Skills (444), Building Your Portfolio (445)
Problem Solving	**SE:** Standards at Work (440), Web Design Projects (443), Building 21st Century Skills (444)

Workplace Competencies

Resources Manage time, money, materials, facilities, human resources	**SE:** You Try It (427), Command Center (439), Standards at Work (440), Web Design Projects (443)
Interpersonal Work on teams, teach others	**SE:** Teamwork Skills (441)
Information Acquire, evaluate, organize, maintain, interpret, communicate and use computers to process information	**SE:** Go Online (424, 435), You Try It (427, 430, 434), Critical Thinking (427, 432, 436, 438, 439), Apply It! (427, 432, 436), Tech Check (428), Command Center (439), Making Connections (440), Standards at Work (440), Teamwork Skills (441), Challenge Yourself (441), Skills Studio (442), Web Design Projects (443), Building 21st Century Skills (444), Building Your Portfolio (445)
Systems Understand, monitor, correct, improve, design systems	**SE:** You Try It (430, 434), Teamwork Skills (441), Building 21st Century Skills (444), Building Your Portfolio (445)
Technology Select, apply, maintain, and troubleshoot technology.	**SE:** Go Online (424, 435), Apply It! (427, 436), You Try It (430, 434), Teamwork Skills (441), Skills Studio (442), Web Design Projects (443), Building 21st Century Skills (444), Building Your Portfolio (445)

CHAPTER 15

Maintaining a Web Site

(Page 422) ## Objectives

Section 15.1: Web Server Maintenance
- Identify Webmastering Tasks
- Identify Web server maintenance techniques
- Describe the importance of backups

Section 15.2: Updating Information
- Identify guidelines for updating a site
- Explain the purpose of archiving a Web site
- Edit and update a Web page

Section 15.3: Keeping a Web Site Secure
- Identify Web site access controls
- Create a login screen

> **LEARNING LINK**
>
> Chapter 14 explained how to publish and promote a Web site. Use Chapter 15 to show that publishing and promoting a site are only the first steps towards the site's usefulness. Ongoing maintenance is crucial if the site is to be an effective one for its owner.

(Page 422) ## Why It Matters

Lead a brief discussion about some of the students' favorite Web sites. Do they offer products, information, promotions, or services that change frequently? (Sites offering CDs, information about television shows or celebrities, and so on, will be good topics of discussion.) Would students still like these sites if they were not routinely updated? Why or why not? What other maintenance might be required regularly on these sites?

> **Teaching Tip**
>
> This chapter contains exercises that direct students to edit a published Web site on an FTP server. Although your students may not be able to perform these exercises due to limited or unavailable capability, you may find the remaining sections of the chapter to be useful, as they contain valuable Webmaster information that is excellent "real world" material.

(Page 422) ## Quick Write Activity

Have the students write a paragraph about what the maintenance needs of a non-business Web site might be. (The site could be a personal Web site, a government educational Web site, a fan club Web site, and so on.) Then have them write a paragraph about the possible maintenance needs of a business Web site. What specific elements of each site might need updating or repair, and how often?

(Page 423) ## Before You Read

Two-Column Notes Two-column notes can be used in a variety of ways. They can be main idea/detail notes, as in this activity. They can also be used in other ways, depending on students' instructional needs. For example, if students need to solve a problem, they might write the problem in the left column and the solution in the right column. They can also use this technique to list opinions and supporting facts or conclusions and supporting facts.

CHAPTER 15

SECTION 15.1 WEB SERVER MAINTENANCE
(Pages 424–427)

FOCUS

Describing Web Server Problems and Their Effects Frequent users of the Internet will have had experience with Web server problems. To see what the students already know about these, ask them to describe some incidents. Have they experienced difficulties logging on or crashes? Do they know if it was a hardware failure? A software glitch? Too much traffic? What was their reaction? What implications does this have for Webmasters and Web hosting companies?

Teaching Tip

Remind students that this section is meant to provide a brief overview of Web server maintenance. Make certain they understand they should not attempt to service a Web server on their own. Such skills require a serious understanding of server architecture and configuration that cannot be attempted in an introductory Web design class.

(Page 424)

Focus on Reading

Read to Find Out
Use the Read to Find Out feature to focus student reading. Hold a quick starter discussion to find out what your students already know.

 Key Terms Online
Key term definitions and activities are available online at **WebDesignDW.glencoe.com**.

Reading Strategy Answer
Students will find the three tasks under the heading *Maintaining a Web Server* on page 424. Students' tables should look similar to this example:

Maintenance Task	Purpose of Task
Maintaining uploading and downloading capabilities	To maintain communication hardware and software
Maintain storage	To delete unused or outdated files and to upgrade storage capacity as needed
Backing up data	To protect a company's valuable data

TEACH

Explaining the Importance of Backing Up Data Regardless of what system or medium is used, it is extremely important for a Webmaster to make sure data are backed up. Explain to the students that backed up data need to be stored at a location other than the location where the server is located, because if there is damage to the server room and the server is damaged, chances are any other items in the room would be damaged as well. A good manager of these servers will have a plan for regular backups and for emergency recovery. It is critical that he or she restore order with little loss of time.

Unit 4 The Web Site Development Process **403**

CHAPTER 15

Answers to Section 15.1 Captions and Activities

(Page 424) **Reading Focus** A Webmaster monitors a server's hardware and software by making sure the servers can properly upload, download, store, and back up Web sites.

(Page 424) **Go Online Activity 15.1** For more information about Web server maintenance, have students visit **WebDesignDW.glencoe.com**.

(Page 425) **Figure 15.1** Commercial customers, especially e-commerce businesses, would most likely use high-speed data lines.

(Page 426) **Table 15.1** Answers may vary. Since cost is usually an issue with small businesses, they would probably choose hard drive mirroring, since it is inexpensive to replace the drives in the system.

(Page 426) ✓ **Reading Check** A Webmaster must regularly delete a site's unused or outdated files in order to free up storage space and prevent a server crash.

(Page 427) **Reading Focus** Some skills needed to become a Webmaster are an ability to work with server hardware and software, and programming and design skills in order to make minor updates to a site.

(Page 427) **You Try It Activity 15A Research Webmaster Jobs** Students locate information about the career of Webmaster, locate Webmaster jobs, and identify job skills required for these positions. An article that students might find helpful is "What is a Webmaster?" on the Web Developer's Personal Library site (**http://www.wdvl.com/Internet/Web/Jobs/webmaster.html**). Students should be supervised when they do research on the Internet.

(Page 427) ✓ **Reading Check** A Webmaster's primary role is to maintain a Web site.

ASSESS

(Page 427) ### Section 15.1 Assessment Answers

Reading Summary

Use the Reading Summary to help students review and reinforce the important points of the section.

What Did You Learn?

1. Students' definitions should be in their own words, but based on the information found in the section and in the book's glossary.

2. The important aspects of maintaining a Web server include maintaining uploading and downloading capabilities, maintaining storage, and backing up data.

3. Storage maintenance may include using hot-swappable drives, or hard drive mirroring. Students may also note that creating backups is an important part of protecting important data.

CHAPTER 15

Critical Thinking

4. Both types of backup protect data. A complete backup makes a copy of a specific set of data. An incremental backup only stores data that has changed since the last complete backup was done.

5. A skilled Webmaster is an important person in maintaining a Web site. The Webmaster ensures that the hardware and software work correctly, makes updates as needed, upgrades storage capacity as necessary, and ensures that backups are done as scheduled.

Apply It!

Choose a Data Backup Utility Students research backup utilities, determining the cost and features of each one. Based on their research, students recommend the one that they believe provides the best overall value. Recommended sites for student research include: **www.cellarstone.com/backtrakpro.htm**, **www.han-soft.com/habt.php**, and **www.cmfperception.com**.

CLOSE

Understanding the Job of Webmaster If possible, arrange for a Webmaster to speak to the class, and offer more detailed information about their job and specific examples of tasks and problems he or she routinely handles. Have the students prepare questions in advance that they can ask the Webmaster. If you have the capability, you can also conduct an online interview using instant messaging.

(Page 428)

Real World Technology

PRIVACY ISSUES AND THE INTERNET

Answers to Tech Check

1. Encourage each student or group to focus on one specific threat to employee/employer privacy that exists primarily online. This can include privacy issues such as unauthorized access to financial or health information, libel, personal usage, vulnerability to hackers, selling confidential information to marketers, etc. In their reports, students should describe the threat in detail, along with the potential consequences for computer users who ignore the problem. Students can present their findings in the form of a written report or a presentation.

2. Essays should demonstrate how the value of technology may change depending on how it is used. Even if students write from a personal viewpoint, they should back up their arguments with facts and examples. If necessary, have students do research to find out about recent privacy issues related to the Internet. One source for information is the World Wide Web Consortium's Platform for Privacy Preferences Project (**http://www.w3.org/P3P**). After students have completed their essay, you might conduct a class discussion or informal debate about this subject.

CHAPTER 15

SECTION 15.2 UPDATING INFORMATION
(Pages 429–432)

FOCUS

Analyzing the Need for Updates E-commerce sites often need updating because the available services, products, or prices change over time. Ask students to think of other reasons why these sites would need updating. (One possible answer is to keep up with what competitors are doing.) If the students cannot come up with any reasons, visit some sites that sell similar products. Are there features some sites have that others do not that make them more attractive?

Teaching Tip
Ask students why they think files are archived rather than deleted. They should understand the importance of archiving files, and be able to come up with a few examples of when an archived file might be essential to a process or situation.

(Page 429)

Focus on Reading

Read to Find Out
Use the Read to Find Out feature to focus student reading. Hold a quick starter discussion to find out what your students already know.

 Key Terms Online
Key term definitions and activities are available online at **WebDesignDW.glencoe.com**.

Reading Strategy Answer
Students can find the information for this activity under the heading *Managing and Archiving Web Files* on page 430. The students' diagrams should look similar to this example:

Direct Server
- File is updated directly on Web server where it resides
- Quick way to make changes for immediate viewing
- Viewers may see imcomplete changes

- Are ways to update Web page
- Can use a text editor to make changes

Local Client
- File is updated on a client workstation and revised page is uploaded to server
- Viewers will not see changes until complete

TEACH

Using Direct Server Updates Emphasize to your students the problems with updating a live site. Also remind them that if they need to do this, they must thoroughly test all changes. Once customers (or potential customers) lose confidence in a site or company, it is hard to re-claim that customer. Also, in the event that a direct server update is necessary, tell students to always rename the files they are going to replace instead of overwriting them, so they have them to fall back on if they need them.

CHAPTER 15

Answers to Section 15.2 Captions and Activities

(Page 429) **Reading Focus** The factors to be considered when updating a Web site are how changes will benefit visitors, content elements such as graphics, text, last-updated date, and recommended links, being consistent with the site's overall structure, and scheduling regular updates.

(Page 429) **Figure 15.3** Other types of sites that should be updated frequently include news sites, weather sites, and movie theater and other entertainment-related sites that provide schedules of events/showings, and so on.

(Page 429) ✓ **Reading Check** Sites that depend on current information, such as news, weather, and entertainment sites, require constant updating to remain useful.

(Page 430) **Reading Focus** File management helps to maintain Web sites by keeping files organized, updated, and archived.

(Page 430) **You Try It** **Activity 15B Download and Upload Files from a Remote Server** Students will use Dreamweaver's FTP capability or a standalone FTP program to download and upload files to a Web server. Uploading files to a Web server will make them accessible through a Web browser.

(Page 432) ✓ **Reading Check** A local client update is an update to a file stored on a regular computer such as a desktop or laptop. These files are not visible through a Web browser unless uploaded to a Web server.

ASSESS

(Page 432) ### Section 15.2 Assessment Answers

Reading Summary

Use the Reading Summary to help students review and reinforce the important points of the section.

What Did You Learn?

1. Students' definitions should be in their own words, but based on the information found in the section and in the book's glossary.

2. Old pages can serve as a good template for new pages and the graphics can be reused in the future. Archived pages can also be used if the current Web page is unexpectedly damaged or lost.

3. Technical documentation provides useful information about the Web site. It can be used by Webmasters or system administrators to perform some technical process. Or it can provide specific instructions to help Web site users or developers complete a process.

CHAPTER 15

Critical Thinking

4. Direct server updates involve updating the files directly on the Web server where it resides, making the files immediately available on the Internet. Local client updates involve changing a copy of the Web page on a client workstation, then uploading the revised page to the server. The changed page is not available on the Web until the Webmaster uploads the new file to the server. Both are effective ways to update Web sites.

5. A diagram of the process of downloading a file from an FTP site can be found on pages 430 and 431.

Apply It!

Plan Updates to a Site Students' plans should include adding disk cases to the Products page and including disk cases on the Order form. Students may also suggest adding a press release about the addition to the product line and/or adding a question to the FAQ page.

CLOSE

Reviewing How to Update Information To make sure the students have grasped the concepts in this section, have them work in teams of two. Each member of the team should open a Web site he or she has previously created that contains hyperlinks. Then the other member should break several of the hyperlinks by changing the links so they contain incorrect URLs. The first member should then use Dreamweaver's site reports to check the condition of the site, and should fix any broken hyperlinks. In addition, have students add new information to the site, or modify old information. With your permission, they can publish the site and view their changes through Dreamweaver's FTP capabilities or via a standalone FTP program.

SECTION 15.3 KEEPING A WEB SITE SECURE
(Pages 433–436)

FOCUS

Identifying Web Site Security Issues Lead a discussion about what kinds of information the students feel need to be kept from unauthorized access. What kinds of information do they think do not need protection? (Possible answers may be that names, addresses, phone numbers, credit card numbers, and social security numbers need to be kept secure, while types of products purchased and e-mail addresses may be of less concern.) If they become Webmasters, they will need to understand both the technology available and the ethical issues involved in Web site security.

(Page 433)

Focus on Reading

Read to Find Out
Use the Read to Find Out feature to focus student reading. Hold a quick starter discussion to find out what your students already know.

 Key Terms Online
Key term definitions and activities are available online at **WebDesignDW.glencoe.com**.

Reading Strategy Answer
Students can find the information for this activity under the heading *Controlling Access to a Site* on page 433. The students' diagrams should look similar to this example:

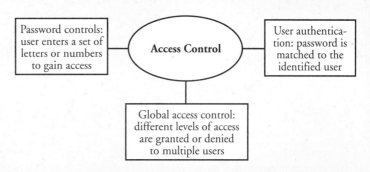

TEACH

Describing Global Access Controls If your school uses a system that employs global access controls, explain to the students how it works. To what do you have access? To what do others have access? If it is inappropriate to discuss your school's specific system, give students other examples of global access controls. For example, schools or universities may have a system that allows students to access an individual course's Web page, but does not allow them to make changes to it. The course instructor may be able to access the page and make changes to it (e.g., post homework assignments, provide links to relevant articles, and so on), but may not have access to other parts of the system.

CHAPTER 15

Answers to Section 15.3 Captions and Activities

(Page 433) **Reading Focus** Webmasters can control access to data on a site by restricting the sites' availability to a specific set of authorized users.

(Page 434) **You Try It** **Activity 15C Create a Login Screen** Students learn how to create a login screen using Dreamweaver. This screen will require users to enter a username and password to gain access to a site.

(Page 435) **Go Online** **Activity 15.2** You can have students learn more about global access control by having them visit **WebDesignDW.glencoe.com**.

(Page 435) **Figure 15.8** User Group 3 is probably the administrator group.

(Page 435) ✓ **Reading Check** A password is a set of letters or numbers that a user enters to gain access to a site.

(Page 435) **Reading Focus** A Webmaster must make choices about what is and is not appropriate material to include on Web sites.

(Page 436) ✓ **Reading Check** A Webmaster must decide whether an image that a user uploads is appropriate for the site.

ASSESS

(Page 436) ### Section 15.3 Assessment Answers

Reading Summary

Use the Reading Summary to help students review and reinforce the important points of the section.

What Did You Learn?

1. Students' definitions should be in their own words, but based on the information found in the section and in the book's glossary.

2. Security is intended to protect the confidentiality of users' personal data, such as names, addresses, phone numbers, and credit card information. Business can only be conducted on the Web when users have confidence that Web sites are secure.

3. Webmasters encounter ethical considerations when deciding if files can be uploaded to the Web server, including what is appropriate and inappropriate material.

Critical Thinking

4. Global access controls make system data available only to people who are authorized to access it. Various levels of access are given as appropriate. For example, Webmasters and system administrators have a high level of access to database information, while other users may be granted rights only to view the system data.

5. Access controls provide security to a Web site, similar to data encryption. Data encryption involves decoding and encoding data as it is transmitted over communication lines. Access controls limit access to information, such as database information, stored on the server.

Apply It!

Analyze Security Students identify means that various sites such as e-commerce, auction, or banking sites use to keep customer data secure. Suggested sites to visit include: **pages.ebay.com/securitycenter**, **www.amazon.com**, and **www.bankofamerica.com**. This information can usually be found on the Privacy Notice page of the site.

CLOSE

Evaluating Web Site Security Measures As is noted in this section, the exact nature of the responsibility to keep information secure is not perfectly clear. Have the class discuss the possibilities. Should Web sites be prohibited from collecting certain information? If so, what kinds should they be prohibited from collecting? Should sites be required to allow individuals to opt out of providing certain information? Would this be a sufficient measure? Why or why not? Should passwords and user IDs be considered legally sufficient measures for protecting information? (If students tend to consider only one side or the other, remind them that the interests of both the public and those who maintain Web sites must be considered.) After a preliminary discussion, you may want to have a class debate on this topic.

CHAPTER 15 Answers to Chapter Review

The Chapter Review covers a wide range of student knowledge. Due to time constraints, students may not be able to complete every activity in the Chapter Review. Select the activities that are appropriate for your class needs and resources.

(Page 438) ## After You Read

Study with Two-Column Notes Demonstrate to students how they can use two-column notes to review the chapter. Cover the notes in the right column with a sheet of paper. Then read a question or idea on the left. Have the class come up with as much information as they can about the topic. Uncover the notes on the right to see if they covered the same information. Then ask if they can add any new information or conclusions that go beyond just memorizing the material.

(Page 438) ## Reviewing Key Terms

1. Hot-swappable hard drives allow a Webmaster to replace a bad hard drive without powering down the server.
2. Hard drive mirroring means the same data is written to two or more drives at the same time so that if the primary drive fails, a secondary drive will automatically take over.
3. Webmasters use tapes, CD-ROMS, hard drives, or floppy disks to make backups.
4. A direct server update involves updating the file directory on the Web server where it resides. A local client update is done by downloading a Web page and modifying it on a client workstation.
5. Restricting the availability of a site to a specific set of authorized users is known as access control.
6. The process of saving old Web pages is called *archiving*.
7. The process is user authentication.

(Page 438) ## Understanding Main Ideas

8. Webmasters make sure that Web sites function properly, that sites are updated properly, and that all server hardware and software is functioning properly so the server can upload, download, store and back up Web site files. Students may have additional ideas based on their research in You Try It activity 15A (page 427).
9. Webmasters use hot-swappable hard drives and hard drive mirroring.
10. Guidelines include making changes that will benefit visitors, updating content elements frequently to maintain visitor interest, maintaining the site's overall structure and navigation with all updates, and creating a schedule for regular updates.
11. Web sites that need to be updated frequently might use an automated update process, because it allows multiple users to make updates to a site, and then posts all of the new content files in a single operation.
12. Documentation may be provided in online help files or in downloadable PDF files.
13. The most common form of access control is using passwords to verify that the user has the right to gain access to information at the site.

Answers to Chapter Review — CHAPTER 15

14. Web tracking systems can be used to generate information about which pages visitors are hitting, how often, and from where. Companies' marketing staffs use this information to plan their marketing efforts. Webmasters can use the information to manage Web site security.

15. When maintaining a site's hardware capabilities, a Webmaster must ensure the hardware is capable of handling traffic that visits a Web site, and ensure it has enough memory and processing capability to service visitors. For software capabilities, a Webmaster must ensure the software can handle file requests and other functions that are on a Web site, and ensure that the software is protected against viruses and hackers. For storage capabilities, a Webmaster must ensure enough storage space is available for the files needed to run a Web site.

16. **Step 1:** Think about how your changes will benefit your visitors.

    Step 2: Frequently update content elements such as the site's graphics, text, last-updated date, and recommended links.

    Step 3: Try to maintain the site's overall structure, navigation bars, logos, color schemes, and contact information.

    Step 4: Schedule regular updates.

(Page 438) ## Critical Thinking

17. Students' answers will vary. There are many reasons for an unexplained graphic, such as a misunderstanding with the Webmaster or even the site being hacked. The problem should be resolved by taking down the graphic, discovering the source of the problem, and putting controls in place to make sure it does not happen again.

18. Students answers will vary, but should include answers to all questions. For instance, the archive policy may include maintaining files for one year, and the backup policy may require creating a backup of files on the Web server once a week.

> **Teaching Tip**
> Consider asking the school district's Webmaster to talk to your class about his or her responsibilities. Or, ask permission for the students to e-mail him or her with their questions.

19. A local client update is the best practice for updating a Web site. Student answers will vary, but should include an applied understanding of the material in the chapter.

20. Answers may vary. Salespeople should be allowed to view and enter customer information, but should not be able to change product information. Product line managers should be able to view, enter, and change product information, but do not need specific customer information. Customers should be able to place orders and check on the status of an order. However, they should not be allowed access to other customer data or to alter product information. Warehouse personnel should be allowed to view product information and part of the customer order information, but should not be able to view credit card numbers. They also do not need to be able to change customer or product information. Top-level managers primarily need access to summary information, and should be able to query all portions of the database, but won't need to change database information.

CHAPTER 15 Answers to Chapter Review

(Page 439) **Command Center**

21. **Ctrl + F** = Find and Replace
22. **Ctrl + Shift + D** = Get selected files or folders from a remote site
23. **Ctrl + Shift + U** = Put selected files or folders to a remote site

Standardized Test Practice

The correct answer is C. As students review the paragraph about the automated update process and the possible answers, make sure they look for words like "must," and "only." These may help them eliminate possible answers such as A and B.

Have students use the book's Web site **WebDesignDW.glencoe.com**.

- **Study with PowerTeach** Encourage your students to use the Chapter 15 PowerTeach Outline to review the chapter before they have a test.
- **Online Self Check** These quick five-question assessments may be used as an in-class activity, a homework assignment, or test review.

(Page 440) **Making Connections**

Language Arts—Create an Oral Presentation Students research various storage devices and prepare an oral presentation for a company that sells all these solutions. The presentation should focus on the features, benefits, and cost of each. Students should have conducted enough research to be able to answer questions about the various storage devices included in the presentation. Students can find information about storage hardware at Hewlett-Packard (**www.hp.com**) and Iomega (**www.iomega.com**).

Students' tables may look similar to the one below:

Web Server Storage Devices		
Storage Options	Benefit	Cost
Shared Server	Lower cost to customer because they do not have to purchase an entire server for their Web site.	$6.95/month
Dedicated Server	Ability to control every aspect of the server including upgrades, maintenance, and storage capacity.	$175.00/month
Custom Server	Includes features of dedicated server but also allows for customers to have custom features not available through a dedicated server.	Price varies

(Page 440) **Standards at Work**

NETS-S 4 Create Technical Documentation Students create a set of procedures that outline how to update the Web site. These procedures should describe how to perform a local client update. Students can write out these procedures, and include other elements such as drawings or screen shots as needed to help clarify specific

Answers to Chapter Review — CHAPTER 15

steps in the procedure. Students should then use their set of procedures to update the product prices on the Products page of the MyDiskDesigns.biz site. The purpose of this action is to see if students can follow their own guidelines without becoming confused. If students become confused, have them revise their written procedures as needed. Alternatively, you can have students exchange procedures to see if they can follow each other's guidelines. Have students give each other feedback as to how they can make their guidelines clearer and easier to follow.

(Page 441) ## Teamwork Skills

Update a Web Site Students publish a site that they have created. Instruct students where they should publish the site. Students then identify and make at least three improvements to the site, making the changes as a local client update. Students publish the site again and view the published site in a browser. Students should verify that their changes appear. Students' diagrams may look like the one below:

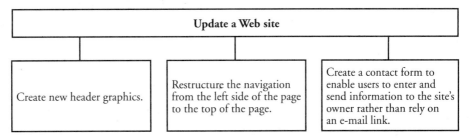

(Page 441) ## Challenge Yourself

Identify Security Procedures Students write a series of interview questions related to security procedures used to manage access to Web sites. Questions may include: What software do you use to help you manage security? Have you ever had a security breach? If so, what did you do to safeguard the information at the site? How important is security to the sites you manage? What kinds of access levels do different users have? Students then conduct an interview with a Webmaster from your school, school district, or a local business. They can do this in person, by phone, or by e-mail. Students write a two-page report based on what they have learned. Student diagrams may look similar to the one below:

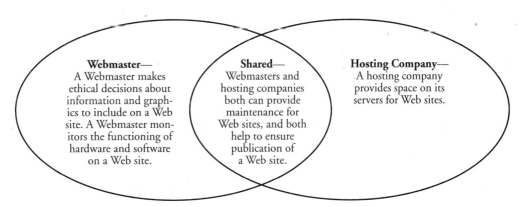

CHAPTER 15 Answers to Chapter Review

You Try It Skills Studio

(Page 442)

1. **Update a Web Site** Students update the MyDiskDesigns.biz Web site by adding a question and answer to the FAQ page. The question is provided, and students create their own response. They also add an appropriate named anchor. Students publish the revised site and test it in a browser.

2. **Create a Job Description** Students use the Internet to research realistic skills and salaries for Webmasters. A sample job description and salary table are listed below.

MyDiskDesigns.biz Webmaster This position is responsible for technical aspects of the MyDiskDesigns.biz Web site to include programming and documentation. This position also needs to be able to troubleshoot performance issues such as speed of access and site content. One to three years related experience required. Good communication skills (verbal and written) and good customer service skills (internal and external). Database knowledge is required. Adobe Photoshop or similar knowledge preferred. The ability to update Web pages using FTP, basic HTML and related tools; experience with a variety of languages; and HTML (hypertext markup language).

Years Experience	Salary Range
0–1 Years	$20,000—$23,000
2–5 Years	$25,000—$30,000
6+ Years	$30,000—$50,000

Web Design Projects

(Page 443)

1. **Document a Procedure** Students write a set of procedures that detail how and when backups are to be made. The procedures should include instructions for incremental backups, daily incremental backups, and a monthly complete backup, and a daily complete backup. Students are directed to schedule incremental backups for the early afternoon and complete backups to run overnight and be checked in the morning. Students' procedures should include this timing information.

2. **Plan and Develop a Web Site** Students will use the knowledge they acquired throughout the book to create a Web site for their business. Their work should include a basic plan of the Web site, with a mission statement, page sketches, and content overview. They should use Dreamweaver to create their sites, which should conform to the rules of consistency and repetition, include clear formatting, concise and correctly structured content, and may include graphics and multimedia elements such as feedback forms and/or guest books. Students should also take accessibility guidelines into account when creating their sites and include alternative text and other accessibility-related options.

UNIT 4

(Page 444) BUILDING 21ST CENTURY SKILLS

Project 1 Problem Solving:
Develop a Commercial Web Site

CAUTION: Students should not publish a site to an FTP server without your permission.

Students determine a site name and write a mission statement, site goals, and description of the target market for a Web site that will feature a line of high-quality computer furniture intended for home-office use. Students storyboard the site which will include a home page, product pages for each line, an FAQ page, an order form, and a privacy policy.

If possible, provide catalogs of home-office furniture for students to review as they are planning the site's order form. Students may also review online order forms from e-commerce sites that sell office furniture. Suggested sites are: **www.officefurniture.com**, **www.ofconcepts.com**, and **www.staples.com**.

Students create the site using Dreamweaver. They should add a logo using the site's name and include images as needed. The privacy policy may be adapted from ones that are available at the Web sites suggested above, or students can use the MyDiskDesigns.biz privacy policy as a model. Students add search capabilities to the site.

Students test the site in a browser. If possible, have students use the Dreamweaver FTP client to publish the site.

UNIT 4

(Page 445)

BUILDING YOUR PORTFOLIO

The Portfolio projects are ongoing activities that build upon the material in the unit. By the end of the course, the students should have work samples that show every stage of their knowledge development. Explain to students how to save their samples as hard copies, online copies, or personal disks.

Create an Online Portfolio

CAUTION: Students should not publish a site to an FTP server without your permission.

Students create a frames site to house an online portfolio of their work. Students should select their best six to eight pages to include in the portfolio. Even though the pages they created in HTML using a text editor may not seem like their best work, encourage students to include one of these pages as a way to demonstrate their familiarity with HTML.

Students design and create a site that may be viewed by potential employers. They will link the content pages appropriately to the link bar in the left frame, then add a hit counter in the left frame and a guest book. Make sure that students use contrasting colors when designing their portfolio site's pages, so that their content is easy to read.

Students evaluate their site. You may want to provide a customized Web site checklist or have them use examples from the textbook. Based on their evaluations, they should make any needed corrections before peer review. The peer reviewers provide feedback and also add an entry in the guest book.

Students create screen shots for their portfolios. They should also make an electronic copy of the finished product.

The instructions also suggest publishing the site to the school or class Web site. Have students complete this part of the project if you have a Web server available and they have permission to do so.

UNIT 5

Advanced HTML

(Page 446)

> **Visit Glencoe Online**
>
> Introduce students to the resources that are available online at **WebDesignDW.glencoe.com**. Have students select **Unit Activities > Unit 5 Cyber Manners and Netiquette.** Students can take a quiz to check their knowledge of safe and effective online communication. Have them review the Technology Handbook located at the front of their textbooks and then complete this four-question quiz. Point out that even though computers make it easy to communicate with one another, online communication can sometimes be risky. When you cannot see the other person to whom you are talking, you might misinterpret that person's meaning because you cannot see their facial expressions or gestures or hear their tone of voice. Encourage students to follow good netiquette guidelines at school, at home, and with friends. Provide ample opportunities in class to practice these skills through hands-on lessons or class discussions and oral quizzes.
>
> Complete answers to each Unit Activity are available on the book Web site in the password-protected Teacher Center portion of the site.

(Page 447)

Think About It

Student answers will vary. One way to approach this activity is to have students identify how methods of communication have changed over the past ten years. Ask them to list the types of technology developed during that period. Students can identify new technology, and technology that improved or expanded the use of existing technology. Then have students discuss why this new technology was developed, and why it became popular. (They should realize that new technology does not progress far unless it is adopted and endorsed by users.) Students can use their analysis of the past ten years as a foundation to predict what might happen in the next ten years.

CHAPTER 16 Planning Guide

Student Edition	Activities and Exercises
Chapter 16 HTML Tables and Frames (pages 448–473)	Quick Write Activity, page 448 Before You Read, page 449
Section 16.1 Creating Tables in HTML (pages 450–454)	Reading Strategy, page 450 Go Online Activity 16.1: Explore Table Attributes, page 452 You Try It Activity 16A: Create a Table Using HTML, page 453
Emerging Technology The Home and Workplace of the Future (page 455)	Tech Check, page 455
Section 16.2 Creating Frames in HTML (pages 456–461)	Reading Strategy, page 456 You Try It Activity 16B: Create a Frames-Based Web Page, page 459 Go Online Activity 16.2: Explore Frames, page 460
Section 16.3 Cascading Style Sheets (pages 462–466)	Reading Strategy, page 462 You Try It Activity 16C: Create an External Style Sheet Using HTML, page 464 You Try It Activity 16D: Use CSS to Position Page Elements, page 465
Chapter 16 Review (pages 467–473)	Making Connections: Social Studies—Create a Table Standards at Work: Explore Accessibility (NETS-S 5) Teamwork Skills: Create a Frames-Based Web Site Challenge Yourself: Create a Nested Table You Try It Skills Studio: —Create a Table —Create Frames Web Design Projects: —Create an Inventory Table —Create a Frames-Based Recipe Index Additional Activities You May Wish to Use: —PowerTeach Outlines Chapter 16 —Student Workbook Chapter 16

Planning Guide CHAPTER 16

Assessments

Section 16.1 Assessment, page 454

Section 16.2 Assessment, page 461

Section 16.3 Assessment, page 466

Chapter 16 Review and Assessment, page 467
You may also use any of the Chapter Review Activities and Projects as Assessments.
Additional Assessments You May Wish to Use:
- —Self-Check Assessments Chapter 16
- —*ExamView* Testbank Chapter 16

Estimated Time to Complete Chapter

18 week course = 3–5 days
36 week course = 10 days

To help customize lesson plans, use the Pacing Guide on pages 26–30 and the Standards Charts on pages 422–423.

Key to Recommended Materials

Icons represent elements that may require additional resources.

- Focus on Reading
- Internet access required
- Software: Dreamweaver
- Teacher Resource CD (contains Student Data Files, Solution Files, Reproducible Graphic Organizers, and Study with PowerTeach Outlines)

Data and Solution Files for Chapter 16

DataFiles
- stylesheet.html

SolutionFiles
- SF_YTI_16A
- SF_YTI_16B
- SF_YTI_16C
- SF_YTI_16D

Inclusion Strategies

For **Differentiated Instruction Strategies** refer to the **Inclusion in the Computer Technology Classroom** booklet.

Unit 5 Advanced HTML 421

CHAPTER 16 NETS Correlation For Students

ISTE NETS Foundation Standards

1. Basic operations and concepts
2. Social, ethical, and human issues
3. Technology productivity tools
4. Technology communications tools
5. Technology research tools
6. Technology problem-solving and decision-making tools

Performance Indicators	Textbook Correlation
1. Identify capabilities and limitations of contemporary and emerging technology resources and assess the potential of these systems and services to address personal, lifelong learning, and workplace needs. (NETS 2)	**SE:** Critical Thinking (454, 461, 466, 468, 469), Tech Check (455), Challenge Yourself (471)
2. Make informed choices among technology systems, resources, and services. (NETS 1, 2)	**SE:** Critical Thinking (454, 461, 466), Apply It! (454, 461), Making Connections (470), Standards at Work (470), Teamwork Skills (471), Challenge Yourself (471), Web Design Projects (473)
3. Analyze advantages and disadvantages of widespread use and reliance on technology in the workplace and in society as a whole. (NETS 2)	**SE:** Tech Check (455)
4. Demonstrate and advocate for legal and ethical behaviors among peers, family, and community regarding the use of technology and information. (NETS 2)	**SE:** Plan Ahead (459), Critical Thinking (469)
5. Use technology tools and resources for managing and communicating personal/professional information (e.g. finances, schedules, addresses, purchases, correspondence). (NETS 3, 4)	**SE:** Web Design Projects (473)
6. Evaluate technology-based options, including distance and distributed education, for lifelong learning. (NETS 5)	**SE:** Go Online (452, 460), Tech Check (455)
7. Routinely and efficiently use online information resources to meet needs for collaboration, research, publications, communications, and productivity. (NETS 4, 5, 6)	**SE:** Go Online (452, 460), Tech Check (455), Making Connections (470)
8. Select and apply technology tools for research, information analysis, problem-solving, and decision-making in content learning. (NETS 4, 5)	**SE:** Go Online (452, 460), Tech Check (455), Making Connections (470), Standards at Work (470)
9. Investigate and apply expert systems, intelligent agents, and simulations in real-world situations. (NETS 3, 5, 6)	**SE:** Making Connections (470), Skills Studio (472), Web Design Projects (473)
10. Collaborate with peers, experts, and others to contribute to content-related knowledge base by using technology to compile, synthesize, produce, and disseminate information, models, and other creative works. (NETS 4, 5, 6)	**SE:** Tech Check (455), Teamwork Skills (471)

SCANS Correlation — CHAPTER 16

Foundation Skills

Basic Skills

Reading	SE:	Before You Read (449), Focus on Reading (450, 456, 462), Reading Strategies (450, 456, 462), After You Read (468)
Writing	SE:	Think About It (447), Quick Write Activity (448), Section Assessments (454, 461, 466), Chapter Review (468-473)
Mathematics	SE:	Challenge Yourself (471)
Listening and Speaking	SE:	Tech Check (455), Teamwork Skills (471)

Thinking Skills

Creative Thinking	SE:	Think About It (447), Quick Write Activity (448), Making Connections (470), Web Design Projects (473)
Critical Thinking	SE:	Critical Thinking (454, 461, 466, 468, 469), Tech Check (455), Standards at Work (470), Teamwork Skills (471), Challenge Yourself (471), Web Design Projects (473)
Problem Solving	SE:	Standards at Work (470), Challenge Yourself (471)

Workplace Competencies

Resources Manage time, money, materials, facilities, human resources	SE:	Command Center (469)
Interpersonal Work on teams, teach others	SE:	Apply It! (461), Teamwork Skills (471)
Information Acquire, evaluate, organize, maintain, interpret, communicate and use computers to process information	SE:	Go Online (452, 460), You Try It (453, 459, 464, 465), Critical Thinking (454, 461, 466, 468, 469), Apply It! (454, 461, 466), Tech Check (455), Command Center (469), Making Connections (470), Standards at Work (470), Teamwork Skills (471), Challenge Yourself (471), Skills Studio (472), Web Design Projects (473)
Systems Understand, monitor, correct, improve, design systems	SE:	You Try It (453, 459, 464, 465), Tech Check (455), Skills Studio (472), Web Design Projects (473)
Technology Select, apply, maintain, and troubleshoot technology	SE:	Go Online (452, 460), You Try It (453, 459, 464, 465), Apply It! (454), Tech Check (455), Making Connections (470), Teamwork Skills (471), Challenge Yourself (471), Skills Studio (472), Web Design Projects (473)

CHAPTER 16

HTML Tables and Frames

(Page 448) **Objectives**

Section 16.1: Creating Tables in HTML
- Create a basic table using HTML
- Define borders
- Merge cells
- Align content in tables

Section 16.2: Creating Frames in HTML
- Create a frames-based Web page using HTML
- Create a link bar page
- Create a content page
- Create a container page
- Control Web page layout with frames
- Create links between frames

Section 16.3: Cascading Style Sheets
- Identify inline CSS
- Identify internal style sheet code
- Create an external style sheet
- Use CSS for page layout

> **LEARNING LINK**
>
> In Chapter 6, students learned how to use Dreamweaver to create tables. Use this chapter to show them how to build a table using HTML tags. Emphasize that sometimes manipulating the actual HTML code is the only way to achieve certain effects.

(Page 448) **Why It Matters**

Comprehension is easier when material is organized. Tables allow information to be presented in a way that viewers can understand without a great deal of effort or confusion. Ask the class to imagine a sports Web site that presents all information in prose form without using any tables to indicate statistics. Lead a brief discussion about other kinds of Web sites that might present information in tabular form.

(Page 448) **Quick Write Activity**

The Quick Write Activity in the Student Edition may be done on computer if students' notes are on a computer. An additional or alternate activity is to have the students visit a few of their favorite Web sites, and ask them to write a paragraph describing some tables these Web sites might use to organize the information they present. (For instance, on a music site, there could be a table listing the various albums of a performer and the price for each. An additional column could offer a brief review or rating.)

(Page 449) **Before You Read**

Study with a Partner Working with a partner makes learning interactive and social. This can motivate students. It helps them focus and become active participants in the study process. They also get exposure to others' ideas and immediate responses to questions or problems.

CHAPTER 16

SECTION 16.1 CREATING TABLES IN HTML
(Pages 450–454)

FOCUS

Reviewing HTML Basics Students learned about basic HTML tags and attributes in Chapter 4. Since Chapter 16 builds on this knowledge, it is a good idea to review HTML basics at this time.

(Page 450)

Focus on Reading

Read to Find Out
Use the Read to Find Out feature to focus student reading. Hold a quick starter discussion to find out what your students already know.

 Key Terms Online
Key term definitions and activities are available online at **WebDesignDW.glencoe.com**.

Reading Strategy Answer
Students can find information about tag sets under the heading *Defining a Basic Table* on page 450. Students' tables should look similar to this example:

HTML Table Tags	What Tag Set Defines
`<TABLE><\TABLE>`	Marks the beginning and end of the table area
`<TR><\TR>`	Marks the beginning and end of the table row
`<TD><\TD>`	Marks the beginning and end of the table column

TEACH

Using Table Attributes To show how tables can be used to modify page layout, enter the HTML source code in Figure 16.5, and show the students how to change the border width and color. View the changes in a browser, so students can see the results of the changes. Then show the students as you make changes to the cell spacing, cell padding, and the alignment of the table and of items in the cells. Have them view the changes in a browser.

CHAPTER 16

Answers to Section 16.1 Captions and Activities

(Page 450) **Reading Focus** Web designers define and modify a table using HTML coding.

(Page 450) **Figure 16.1** In a single table cell there is one row and one column.

(Page 450) ✓ **Reading Check** The <TR></TR> tag set marks the beginning and end of a table row.

(Page 451) **Reading Focus** Attributes are used to modify: borders, cells, and alignment.

(Page 451) **Figure 16.2** The number associated with the border attribute defines the width of the border.

(Page 451) **Figure 16.3** A cell padding of 5 means that the space between the cell border and the cell's content is 5 pixels.

(Page 452) **Figure 16.4** The header row contains the titles for each column in the table.

(Page 452) **GO Online** **Activity 16.1** Additional information about table attributes can be found at **WebDesignDW.glencoe.com**.

(Page 453) **Figure 16.5** It would align the table to the right side of the browser screen.

(Page 453) **You Try It** **Activity 16A Create a Table Using HTML** Students create a table with a border and a header column. They can use either a text editor such as Notepad or Dreamweaver to enter the HTML source code that is provided in the activity.

(Page 454) ✓ **Reading Check** A header row is a row in a table that contains titles for each column in the table. By merging columns, you create a header row.

ASSESS

(Page 454) ### Section 16.1 Assessment Answers

Reading Summary

Use the Reading Summary to help students review and reinforce the important points of the section.

What Did You Learn?

1. Students' definitions should be in their own words, but they should be based on the information found in this section and in the book's glossary.

2. Tables both define the layout space and can be used to position elements on the user's screen very precisely.

3. Table tags are: <TABLE></TABLE>, which mark the beginning and end of the table area; <TR></TR>, which mark the beginning and end of a table row; and

`<TD></TD>`, which mark the beginning and end of a table column. The attributes that define a table are the `border` attribute, the `bordercolor` attribute, the `cellspacing` attribute, the `cellpadding` attribute, and the `align` attribute.

Critical Thinking

4. The `align` attribute, when used with the table tag, changes the alignment of the entire table. When it is used with the column tag, it only affects the alignment of the contents of one particular table cell.

5. Header columns are used to provide row titles and should generally be used to help visitors understand the content of a table. For example, a table showing a student's daily schedule might use a header column to identify class time periods.

Apply It!

Merge Cells HTML code would be as follows:

```
<HTML>
<HEAD>
<TITLE>Simple Table</TITLE>
</HEAD>
<BODY>
<TABLE border="1" bordercolor="FF0000" cellspacing="0" cellpadding="5" align="center">
<TR>
<TD>
<TABLE border="1" bordercolor="FF0000" cellspacing="0" cellpadding="5" align="center">
<TR>
<TD rowspan="2" align="center">Table<BR>Header</TD>
<TD>Row 1 Column 1</TD>
<TD>Row 1 Column 2</TD>
</TR>
<TR>
<TD>Row 2 Column 1</TD>
<TD>Row 2 Column 2</TD>
</TR>
</TABLE>
</TD>
</TR>
</TABLE>
</BODY>
</HTML>
```

CLOSE

Analyzing Tables and Their Effectiveness Have students visit several Web sites that use tables and examine the source code for these tables. You can use the Chicago Cubs schedule and stats at **www.chicagocubs.mlb.com** (or find your local team on the Major League Baseball site at **www.mlb.com**). Discuss the following with students:

◆ What attributes does the table use?

◆ What are the resulting effects?

◆ Why is this table a useful way of organizing the information it contains?

◆ Would the table be more effective if the content or layout were changed in any way?

◆ Would the table be more effective if the attributes were changed in any way?

(Page 455)

EMERGING Technology

THE HOME AND WORKPLACE OF THE FUTURE

Answers to Tech Check

1. Students can show the results of their research in a written, oral, or Web-based report. Answers will vary, but should show an understanding of the chosen technology and present persuasive arguments supporting the students' views. Students should also demonstrate effective information-gathering skills, using either online or printed resources. When using the Internet, students should be supervised.

2. Answers will vary, but should demonstrate an understanding of essential ways in which technologies have become the underpinnings of various social or commercial activities. Encourage students to be objective when expressing their views, and to be prepared to support them. This activity can be used for a class discussion or informal debate.

CHAPTER 16

SECTION 16.2 CREATING FRAMES IN HTML
(Pages 456–461)

FOCUS

Identifying Uses of Frames Link bars are one obvious use of frames. Lead a brief discussion to see if students can identify any other uses, based on their experience surfing the Internet. If not, visit some Web sites with the class, and see if the students can find other uses of frames. (For example, the Web page shown in Figure 16.8 uses the frame on the left to list content highlighted in the site.) Alternatively, have the students imagine what other uses might be made of frames.

(Page 456)

Focus on Reading

Read to Find Out
Use the Read to Find Out feature to focus student reading. Hold a quick starter discussion to find out what your students already know.

Key Terms Online
Key term definitions and activities are available online at **WebDesignDW.glencoe.com**.

Reading Strategy Answer
Students can find information they need for this activity under the heading *Creating Frame Pages in HTML* on page on page 457. Students' diagrams should look similar to this example:

Content Pages Web pages with the site's content, should be site's main focus and fulfill site's purpose

Are pages in a frameset

Container Pages Describe the characteristics of the frames that contain the content pages

TEACH

Explaining Tags, Attributes, and Their Effects Use HTML to create a simple Web page with multiple (two or three) frames. Then go over parts of the code you have created with the class, indicating the different tags and attributes, and the different effects they will produce. Once you have provided at least one example of the various tags, attributes, and effects included in the code, see if students can identify other examples of these elements in parts of the code that you have not discussed. You may wish to intentionally include errors in some of the code, and see if students can spot them.

CHAPTER 16

Answers to Section 16.2 Captions and Activities

(Page 456) **Figure 16.8** Frames effectively divide a browser page into two or more rectangular regions that contain their own Web pages. These pages can operate completely independently or they can interact with each other.

(Page 457) **Reading Focus** A two-page Web site is composed of three separate HTML documents.

(Page 457) **Figure 16.9** The link bar, or document that defines the Web page.

(Page 457) **Figure 16.10** A bulleted list is created by this code.

(Page 458) **Figure 16.11** The code for the page starts with <HTML> and ends with </HTML>.

(Page 458) **Figure 16.12** Both identify the source of information, either an image or a Web page.

(Page 459) **You Try It** **Activity 16B Create a Frames-Based Web Page** Students enter HTML code to create a frame page with a horizontal layout. Explain to the students that, as an alternative to using a number to specify the height of a frame (or the width of a frame in a vertical layout), they can use a percentage (i.e., width = 30%).

> **Teaching Tip**
> Point out the Plan Ahead on page 459 to students and ask them why frames might be difficult for disabled Web users to navigate.

(Page 460) **Activity 16.2** For additional information about frames, have the students visit **WebDesignDW.glencoe.com**.

(Page 460) **Reading Check** The asterisk represents the remaining space on the screen.

(Page 460) **Reading Focus** The target attribute tells the browser to load the target Web page into a specified frame.

(Page 460) **Figure 16.14** The target attribute tells the browser to load the target Web page into a specified frame, rather than into the current frame.

(Page 461) **Figure 16.15** The name attribute specifies the frame into which the Web page will be loaded.

Page 461) **Reading Check** To keep the link bar from changing, include the target attribute in the link's anchor tag.

ASSESS

(Page 461) Section 16.2 Assessment Answers

Reading Summary

Use the Reading Summary to help students review and reinforce the important points of the section.

What Did You Learn?

1. Students' definitions should be in their own words, but based on the information found in the section and in the book's glossary.
2. The container page tells the Web browser where to position the page's frames, how big to make them, and what HTML files to display in them.
3. The `target` and `name` attributes are needed to tell the browser to load the Web page into the correct frame.

Critical Thinking

4. Answers may include that left-handed navigation is friendlier to visitors who are used to reading from left to right or that it allows the remainder of the horizontal space on the browser's window to display the main information of the site.
5. On a frame page, the link bar does not need to change because the links reference the main content pages; the links themselves do not change.

Apply It!

Explain Frame Placement Students' reasoning may include that people are more comfortable with left-handed navigation and that left-handed navigation is far more widely used than other placements. Site designers want visitors to be comfortable navigating the site. Placing the link bar on the left side could also avoid the problem that on small monitors the far right of the page may not display if the sizes of the frames are stated in pixels, leaving the navigation inaccessible on such monitors.

CLOSE

Applying Frame Tags and Attributes To make sure the students have grasped the concepts in this section, have them create the source code needed for a frame page with a vertical layout and three frames. (You may either let the students make up the title, file names, and file text that they will need, or you may give students this information.) Remind the students that they may find it easier, since there are to be three frames, to use percentages rather than numbers and asterisks to indicate column width. Have students exchange their finished work with another student, and have that student sketch what he or she thinks would appear in a browser if the code were entered.

CHAPTER 16

SECTION 16.3 CASCADING STYLE SHEETS
(Pages 462–466)

FOCUS

Reviewing the Benefits of Cascading Style Sheets In Chapter 12 students learned to apply cascading style sheets to Web sites. Have students discuss the purpose and benefits of designing Web sites using cascading style sheets. Remind them about the three types of CSS: inline, internal, and external.

(Page 462)

Focus on Reading

Read to Find Out

Use the Read to Find Out feature to focus student reading. Hold a quick starter discussion to find out what your students already know.

 Key Terms Online

Key term definitions and activities are available online at **WebDesignDW.glencoe.com**.

Reading Strategy Answer

Students can find the information they need for this activity throughout the section. Students' diagrams should look similar to this example:

Internal Specifies style attributes within the `<HEAD>` section of an HTML document. Controls position and appearance of elements on a page (i.e., the position of a paragraph or the color of a page). Style sheet is embedded into every page.

Both internal and external style sheets contain information that styles HTML elements.

External Referenced in an HTML document's `<HEAD>` section. Maintenance and changes to the look of the position and appearance of elements in the entire site can be controlled by editing only one style sheet (i.e., the background color of the Web site).

TEACH

Many Web browsers have the capability of displaying Web sites using CSS, or allowing CSS attributes to be removed. Removing the CSS attributes can help Web designers determine how the site might look using accessibility programs, how they might be viewed on handhelds or mobile phones, or on older browsers that do not support CSS technology.

CHAPTER 16

Answers to Section 16.3 Captions and Activities

(Page 462) **Reading Focus** The three ways to use or apply CSS to an HTML document are inline, internal style sheets, and external style sheets.

(Page 464) **You Try It** **Activity 16C Create an External Style Sheet Using HTML** Students enter HTML code to create an external style sheet. Use the Student Data files and Solution Files noted in this chapter's Planning Guide.

> **Teaching Tip**
>
> In You Try It Activity 16C Step 3, in the stylesheet.html file, have students select **View>Source** before positioning their insertion point after the </TITLE> tag.

(Page 464) ✓ **Reading Check** A selector is HTML coding that contains properties and corresponding values within curly braces that control the appearance of HTML elements.

(Page 465) **Reading Focus** Students learn how to use CSS to control the position and appearance of elements on a Web page. The <DIV></DIV> tag set is used to control blocks of information in paragraphs, images, or forms. The <SPAN></SPAN> tag is typically used in individual inline tags. The <DIV> and <SPAN> tags specify the right, left, top, and bottom position of an HTML element.

(Page 465) **You Try It** **Activity 16D Use CSS to Position Page Elements** Students enter HTML code to position page elements on a simple Web page.

(Page 466) ✓ **Reading Check** Absolute positioning uses numeric values to place elements precisely on a page, relative to the top and left of a browser window. Static positioning places elements on a page normally, just as if you had laid out the page with tables or <DIV> tags. Relative positioning also places elements on a page normally. However, you can adjust the position of an element relative to how it would normally appear on a page.

ASSESS

(Page 466) **Assessment Answers**

Reading Summary

Use the Reading Summary to help students review and reinforce the important points of the section.

What Did You Learn?

1. Students' definitions should be in their own words, but based on the information found in the section and in the book's glossary.

Unit 5 Advanced HTML 433

2. Internal style sheets specify style attributes within the <HEAD> section of an HTML document and do not separate content from presentation. External style sheets are separate text documents that only contain selectors along with their properties and values. They allow you to change the look of an entire Web site by editing only one style sheet.

3. A class selector is a special selector. A selector contains properties and corresponding values that control the appearance of HTML elements. The class selector is a selector that can be applied over and over in an HTML document. An example of a class selector is setting a background color.

Critical Thinking

4. Inline and internal style sheets are rarely used because they do not separate content from presentation information.

5. A Web designer would want to specify exactly where an element appears on a Web page so the page viewed matches the design intended by the designer. Without the specified placement, Web pages would look different on each computer, therefore the message intended may not be communicated.

Apply It!

Use CSS

Answers will vary. CSS can be used to change the background colors, text color, headlines, and more.

Teaching Tip

If students have difficulty determining what to define in their style sheets, suggest that they change the background color of the **MySkills.html** site, or change the text formatting of paragraphs on the site.

The use of cascading style sheets can help customize and edit a Web site more easily than if the designer had to edit each separate page for the same attribute. Using CSS will also ensure that if others are involved in editing the site, the attributes are not affected, and content managers can make changes without being involved in the coding affecting other areas of the site.

Answers to Chapter Review — CHAPTER 16

The Chapter Review covers a wide range of student knowledge. Due to time constraints, students may not be able to complete every activity in the Chapter Review. Select the activities that are appropriate for your class needs and resources.

(Page 468) After You Read

Study for Success It might help to team up weaker and stronger students so that the less successful student can learn from the study strategies of his or her partner. Working with a partner can also lead to further discussion that can help students gain a greater understanding and perspective about the topics they have read about.

(Page 468) Reviewing Key Terms

1. Cell spacing refers to the space between the outer border and the cell border. Cell padding refers to the space between the cell border and the cell's content.
2. Column titles are placed in a header row.
3. Row titles are placed in a header column.
4. container page
5. The navigation frame is at the left of the page in a vertical frame layout.
6. Inline CSS are integrated within tags in an HTML page.
7. Internal style sheets specify style attributes in an HTML document's `<HEAD>` section.

(Page 468) Understanding Main Ideas

8. A table border is created using the `border` attribute. This attribute uses a number to identify the pixel width of the border. The higher the number, the wider the border. You can specify the border color with the `bordercolor` attribute.
9. Alignment is controlled with the `align` attribute. When added to the `<TABLE>` tag it affects the alignment of the entire table. When used in the `<TR>` tag, it aligns the contents of all the cells in that row. When used in the `<TD>` tag, it aligns the contents of that particular table cell.
10. Common attributes include `border`, `bordercolor`, `align`, `cellspacing`, and `cellpadding`.
11. You control the width by using the `cols` attribute and specifying the number of pixels for each frame. The width of the second frame is usually defined with an asterisk (*), which indicates the remaining space on the page.
12. A selector contains properties and corresponding values within curly braces that control the appearance of HTML elements.

(Page 468) Critical Thinking

13. The HTML documents include the container page and the content pages.
14. The user is taken to the Web page in the main content frame that is indicated by the link bar item that was selected. Although the content frame changes, the

CHAPTER 16 Answers to Chapter Review

link bar remains the same. Attributes needed to make this action occur include creating a hyperlink and using a `target` attribute within the anchor tag to target which frame changes when clicking on the link.

15. Student answers will vary. Perhaps one of the best ways to convince the owner would be to show examples of live sites that use left-hand navigation. Another approach would be to prepare a sample of both left-hand and right-hand navigation and have the owner ask for input from employees, friends, and family about which approach is preferred. The size could also be displayed in a browser that cuts off the right side of the page.

16. One advantage in building a frames-based Web site is the ability of Web designers to create separate rectangular areas on the screen that operate independently or interact with each other. A disadvantage is the potential accessibility problems of frames. Issues to consider are what other design techniques are available, as well as the needs of the site and of the target market. For example, if the target market includes older adults, a frame-based site might confuse some users or might be difficult to navigate.

17. Students' answers will vary, but may be similar to the following:

    Web Site Changes:

    ◆ Use an external style sheet over inline CSS because you only need to make a change to one CSS file in order to change the appearance of the entire Web site. Using inline CSS requires you to go into each HTML file and make changes.

    ◆ Use `<DIV>` and `<SPAN>` tags as a replacement layout technique over tables. By doing this, the site will be easier to maintain, will load within a Web browser quicker, is more accessible to all kinds of users and devices, and relies on Web standards established by the World Wide Web Consortium.

(Page 469)

Command Center

18. **F1** = Open Notepad Help feature
19. **Ctrl + P** = Print a Notepad file
20. **Ctrl + D** = Open the Open dialog box in Notepad

> **Teaching Tip**
>
> Point out the shortcuts on page 469 to students and explain that they are universal. The shortcuts will work with any text editor.

Standardized Test Practice

The correct answer is B. As students review the possible answers, make sure they pay close attention to the wording in each statement. Suggest that students carefully evaluate each statement before eliminating any answers.

Have students use the book's Web site **WebDesignDW.glencoe.com**.

Answers to Chapter Review — CHAPTER 16

- ◆ **Study with PowerTeach** Encourage your students to use the Chapter 16 PowerTeach Outline to review the chapter before they have a test.
- ◆ **Online Self Check** These quick five-question assessments may be used as an in-class activity, a homework assignment, or test review.

(Page 470) ## Making Connections

Social Studies–Create a Table Students create a work of art based only on squares and rectangles. If possible, provide samples of Piet Mondrian's work to provide inspiration. You can find examples on the Web Museum (**www.ibiblio.org/wm/paint/auth/mondrian**) and the Art Archive (**www.artchive.com/artchive/M/mondrian**). Students should be able to explain the event or place that provided inspiration for their artwork. Remind students to use the hexadecimal color table in Appendix C to select a variety of colors for their artwork.

(Page 470) ## Standards at Work

NETS-S 5 Explore Accessibility Students research Section 508 of the Americans with Disabilities Act to find the provisions that Web pages must meet to ensure adequate accessibility. They select one of the provisions and show an HTML code sample that does not meet the guideline and one that does meet the guideline. Recommended sites to use for this research are **http://usability.gov/web_508**, **www.usdoj.gov/crt/508**, and **www.webaim.org/standards/508/checklist**. (The last one is good for students to get the information they need for this project.) Have students review Chapter 12 to learn more about this topic.

(Page 471) ## Teamwork Skills

Create a Frames-Based Web Site Students work to create a frames-based site that has two frames. The left frame lists the school's faculty. The right frame displays a picture and text about each faculty member. Students only need to create the content for one teacher. Students should already know how to complete this task in Dreamweaver, but here they should use HTML code.

> **Teaching Tip**
> In the Teamwork Skills activity, have students clear the content for the Web page about a faculty member before proceeding to Step 3. Students should obtain permission before going any further in this activity.

CHAPTER 16 Answers to Chapter Review

(Page 471) **Challenge Yourself**

Create a Nested Table Sample code needed to create the nested table is:

```
<HTML>
<HEAD>
<TITLE>Simple Table</TITLE>
</HEAD>
<BODY>
<TABLE border ="1" bordercolor="FF0000" cellspacing="0" cellpadding="5" align="center">
<TR>
<TD>
<TABLE border="1" bordercolor="FF0000" cellspacing="0" cellpadding="5" align="center">
<TR>
<TD rowspan="2" align="center">Table<BR>Header</TD>
</TR>
<TR>
<TD>Row 1 Column 1</TD>
<TD>Row 1 Column 2</TD>
</TR>
<TR>
<TD>Row 2 Column 1</TD>
<TD>Row 2 Column 2</TD>
</TR>
</TABLE>
</TD>
</TR>
</TABLE>
</BODY>
</HTML>
```

(Page 472) 1. **Create a Table** Students create a table based on research about the trees that grow in your community. Students can find information about trees at Urban Forest Ecosystems Institute (**www.ufei.calpoly.edu**). You may want to give students a specific number of trees to include in the table, such as five or seven trees. The table should include a header row that spans the entire table and a header row labeling each column. Make certain that students use a text editor, rather than Dreamweaver, to complete this activity.

Answers to Chapter Review — CHAPTER 16

2. **Create Frames** Students create a frames-based site that will include the trees table created in You Try It Skills Studio 1. The site will have a link bar frame on the left and the main content page on the right. The only page that students need to create is the Trees in Our Community page that will contain the table.

Web Design Projects

(Page 473)

1. **Create an Inventory Table** Students sketch a table that they could use to organize one of their collections, such as their CDs or DVDs. Encourage students to have at least three columns in their tables. Then they write the HTML code to create the table. They do not need to enter information for their entire collection, but they should enter several items to check how the table appears in a browser. After they are satisfied with the functioning of their table, they add a row with an additional item for the table. Encourage students to use the copy and paste feature in their text editor to make this a simpler task.

2. **Create a Frames-Based Recipe Index** Students create a frames-based site that lists one recipe. The link bar will be expanded as recipes are added to the site. The recipe page should contain a title, a table listing the ingredients, and an ordered list of the steps needed to complete the recipe.

CHAPTER 17 Planning Guide

Student Edition	Activities and Projects
Chapter 17 HTML, Scripting, and Interactivity (pages 474–495)	Quick Write Activity, page 474 Before You Read, page 475
Section 17.1 Adding Interactivity Using HTML (pages 476–481)	Reading Strategy, page 476 You Try It Activity 17A: Add an Audio File Using HTML, page 476 Go Online Activity 17.1: Explore HTML Resources, page 477 You Try It Activity 17B: Add Text Boxes Using HTML, page 477 You Try It Activity 17C: Add Radio Buttons and Check Boxes Using HTML, page 478 You Try It Activity 17D: Add a Pull-down Menu Using HTML, page 479 You Try It Activity 17E: Add a Text Area Using HTML, page 480 You Try It Activity 17F: Use CSS to Style a Form, page 480
Careers & Technology What Does a Webmaster Do? (page 482)	Tech Check, page 482
Section 17.2 Adding Interactivity Using Scripting (pages 483–486)	Reading Strategy, page 483 Go Online Activity 17.2: Explore Scripts, page 483 You Try It Activity 17G: Create a Rollover Button Using JavaScript, page 484
Chapter 17 Review (pages 487–495)	Making Connections: Social Studies—Create a Survey Form Standards at Work: Debug Scripts (NETS-S 3) Teamwork Skills: Convert a Printed Form into an Electronic Form Challenge Yourself: Create a Dictionary of Terms You Try It Skills Studio: —Create a Web Page with Audio in HTML —Create a Ticket Order Form Web Design Projects: —Create a Survey Form —Use JavaScript to Add a Submit Button Additional Activities You May Wish to Use: —PowerTeach Outlines Chapter 17 —Student Workbook Chapter 17

Planning Guide — CHAPTER 17

Assessments

Section 17.1 Assessment, page 481

Section 17.2 Assessment, page 486

Chapter 17 Review and Assessment, page 487
Building 21st Century Skills
Building Your Portfolio
You may also use any of the Chapter Review Activities and Projects as Assessments.
Additional Assessments You May Wish to Use:
—Self-Check Assessments Chapter 17
—*ExamView* Testbank Chapter 17

Estimated Time to Complete Chapter

18 week course = 2–3 days
36 week course = 7–8 days

To help customize lesson plans, use the Pacing Guide on pages 26–30 and the Standards Charts on pages 442–443.

Key to Recommended Materials

Icons represent elements that may require additional resources.

- Focus on Reading
- Internet access required
- Software: Dreamweaver
- Teacher Resource CD (contains Student Data Files, Solution Files, Reproducible Graphic Organizers, and Study with PowerTeach Outlines)

Data and Solution Files for Chapter 17

DataFiles	SolutionFiles
◆ birds.wav	◆ SF_YTI_17A
◆ button1.gif	◆ SF_YTI_17B
◆ button2.gif	◆ SF_YTI_17C
	◆ SF_YTI_17D
	◆ SF_YTI_17E
	◆ SF_YTI_17F
	◆ SF_YTI_17G

Inclusion Strategies

For **Differentiated Instruction Strategies** refer to the **Inclusion in the Computer Technology Classroom** booklet.

CHAPTER 17 NETS Correlation For Students

ISTE NETS Foundation Standards

1. Basic operations and concepts
2. Social, ethical, and human issues
3. Technology productivity tools
4. Technology communications tools
5. Technology research tools
6. Technology problem-solving and decision-making tools

Performance Indicators	Textbook Correlation
1. Identify capabilities and limitations of contemporary and emerging technology resources and assess the potential of these systems and services to address personal, lifelong learning, and workplace needs. (NETS 2)	**SE:** Critical Thinking (481, 486, 488, 489), Apply It! (481, 486)
2. Make informed choices among technology systems, resources, and services. (NETS 1, 2)	**SE:** Critical Thinking (481, 486, 488, 489), Apply It! (481, 486), Making Connections (490), Standards at Work (490), Teamwork Skills (491), Building 21st Century Skills (494), Building Your Portfolio (495)
3. Analyze advantages and disadvantages of widespread use and reliance on technology in the workplace and in society as a whole. (NETS 2)	**SE:** Quick Write Activity (474)
4. Demonstrate and advocate for legal and ethical behaviors among peers, family, and community regarding the use of technology and information. (NETS 2)	**SE:** Building 21st Century Skills (494)
5. Use technology tools and resources for managing and communicating personal/professional information (e.g. finances, schedules, addresses, purchases, correspondence). (NETS 3, 4)	**SE:** Tech Check (482), Skills Studio (492), Web Design Projects (493)
6. Evaluate technology-based options, including distance and distributed education, for lifelong learning. (NETS 5)	**SE:** Go Online (477, 483)
7. Routinely and efficiently use online information resources to meet needs for collaboration, research, publications, communications, and productivity. (NETS 4, 5, 6)	**SE:** Go Online (477, 483), Apply It! (481, 486), Tech Check (482), Standards at Work (490), Challenge Yourself (491)
8. Select and apply technology tools for research, information analysis, problem-solving, and decision-making in content learning. (NETS 4, 5)	**SE:** Go Online (477, 483), Apply It! (481, 486), Tech Check (482), Standards at Work (490), Challenge Yourself (491)
9. Investigate and apply expert systems, intelligent agents, and simulations in real-world situations. (NETS 3, 5, 6)	**SE:** You Try It (476, 477, 478, 479, 480, 484), Tech Check (482), Apply It! (486), Web Design Projects (493)
10. Collaborate with peers, experts, and others to contribute to content-related knowledge base by using technology to compile, synthesize, produce, and disseminate information, models, and other creative works. (NETS 4, 5, 6)	**SE:** Standards at Work (490), Teamwork Skills (491), Building Your Portfolio (495)

SCANS Correlation — CHAPTER 17

Foundation Skills

Basic Skills

Reading	**SE:** Before You Read (475), Focus on Reading (476, 483), Reading Strategy (476, 483), After You Read (488)
Writing	**SE:** Quick Write Activity (474), Section Assessments (481, 486), Tech Check (482), Chapter Review (488-493), Building 21st Century Skills (494), Building Your Portfolio (495)
Mathematics	
Listening and Speaking	**SE:** Standards at Work (490), Teamwork Skills (491)

Thinking Skills

Creative Thinking	**SE:** Quick Write Activity (474), Making Connections (490), Standards at Work (490), Teamwork Skills (491), Challenge Yourself (491), Web Design Projects (493), Building 21st Century Skills (494)
Critical Thinking	**SE:** Critical Thinking (481, 486, 488, 489), Tech Check (482), Making Connections (490), Standards at Work (490), Teamwork Skills (491), Web Design Projects (493), Building 21st Century Skills (494), Building Your Portfolio (495)
Problem Solving	**SE:** Standards at Work (490), Building 21st Century Skills (494)

Workplace Competencies

Resources Manage time, money, materials, facilities, human resources	**SE:** Tech Check (482)
Interpersonal Work on teams, teach others	**SE:** Standards at Work (490), Teamwork Skills (491)
Information Acquire, evaluate, organize, maintain, interpret, communicate and use computers to process information	**SE:** Go Online (477, 483), You Try It (476, 477, 478, 479, 480, 484), Critical Thinking (481, 486, 488, 489), Apply It! (481, 486), Tech Check (482), Command Center (489), Making Connections (490), Standards at Work (490), Teamwork Skills (491), Challenge Yourself (491), Skills Studio (492), Web Design Projects (493), Building 21st Century Skills (494), Building Your Portfolio (495)
Systems Understand, monitor, correct, improve, design systems	**SE:** Web Design Projects (493), Building 21st Century Skills (494)
Technology Select, apply, maintain, and troubleshoot technology.	**SE:** Go Online (477, 483), You Try It (476, 477, 478, 479, 480, 484), Apply It! (481, 486), Tech Check (482), Making Connections (490), Standards at Work (490), Teamwork Skills (491), Challenge Yourself (491), Skills Studio (492), Web Design Projects (493), Building 21st Century Skills (494), Building Your Portfolio (495)

CHAPTER 17

HTML, Scripting, and Interactivity

(Page 474) ### Objectives

Section 17.1: Adding Interactivity Using HTML
- Add an audio file using HTML
- Create a form using HTML
- Add text boxes using HTML
- Add radio buttons and check boxes using HTML
- Add a pull-down menu using HTML
- Add a text area using HTML
- Modify a text box using CSS

Section 17.2: Adding Interactivity Using Scripting
- Identify client-side scripting languages
- Create a rollover button using JavaScript
- Identify server-side scripting languages
- Debug code

LEARNING LINK

Chapter 16 showed students how to build a table using HTML code. Use Chapter 17 to explain how to use HTML to create forms and insert multimedia elements into a Web page, and also to show how scripting languages can add functionality to a Web site.

(Page 474) ### Why It Matters

See if the class can identify some features a Web designer might want or need that would not be available were HTML the only tool at his or her disposal. Lead a brief discussion about why other languages are used to expand the capabilities of HTML. Emphasize that technologies which provide additional functionality to Web sites increase a Web designer's options and allow for creativity.

(Page 474) ### Quick Write Activity

After finishing this section, you may wish to have the students write a paragraph or two comparing the experience of adding interactivity using Dreamweaver, HTML, and scripting languages.

(Page 475) ### Before You Read

How Can You Improve? Students can use many different strategies for studying, but with experience they should be able to find an approach that works best for them. Successful students know how a particular strategy works for them and might use different approaches for different circumstances. Students who do not perform as well are usually less aware of what they need to do to learn material. They often think that reading the chapter is enough. That is why they need to be exposed to a variety of study strategies.

CHAPTER 17

SECTION 17.1 ADDING INTERACTIVITY USING HTML
(Pages 476–481)

FOCUS

Exploring Alternative Methods to Dreamweaver Since students have already learned how to add audio files and form features using Dreamweaver, they may not feel there is much point in knowing an alternative way of completing these tasks. Ask them to think of and describe experiences in which having an alternative method or backup of some kind would be helpful to them. For example, if they store a friend's number on a cell phone, and then lost it, they could not contact the friend unless they had written the number down elsewhere. Or, if their car breaks down, they might have to take a bus or use some other mode of transportation. Emphasize that just as alternative ways of handling situations, such as recording information, can help alleviate the problems students describe, alternative methods can be used to address problems a Webmaster might encounter.

(Page 476)

Focus on Reading

Read to Find Out
Use the Read to Find Out feature to focus student reading. Hold a quick starter discussion to find out what your students already know.

 **Key Terms Online**
Key term definitions and activities are available online at **WebDesignDW.glencoe.com**.

Reading Strategy Answer
Students can find the four HTML tags under the heading Creating a Registration Form on page 477. Students' tables should look similar to this example:

HTML Tag	Function
`<INPUT></INPUT>`	Defines placement of text field on page
`<SELECT></SELECT>`	Defines pull-down menu
`<OPTION></OPTION>`	Defines options on pull-down menu
`<TEXTAREA></TEXTAREA>`	Defines text area

TEACH

Understanding Cause (HTML Code) and Effect (Web Page Features) The You Try It activities in this section ask students to enter provided HTML code to add certain features to a Web page. To make sure students understand how the code is producing the desired features, go through the HTML code in You Try It Activity 17B with the class. Ask the class what each line of code will cause to happen and correct any erroneous or incomplete answers. Then go on to the other activities, and have students explain how the provided code produces the desired effect. While this section covers certain HTML basics, you may want to note that some tasks such as adding animated GIFs to a page often require special software to complete.

CHAPTER 17

Answers to Section 17.1 Captions and Activities

(Page 476) **Reading Focus** With HTML coding, multimedia elements such as audio files and animation can be inserted into a Web site.

(Page 476)
You Try It **Activity 17A Add an Audio File Using HTML** Students learn how to use HTML code to insert an audio file into a Web page. The code is provided in the activity. Use the Student Data File and Solution File noted in this chapter's Planning Guide. While this activity teaches students how to insert an audio file using a text link, students may want to research other methods for adding audio using HTML.

> **Teaching Tip**
> In this section, students learn how to create form elements using HTML. Remind students that the form they create will not actually work, although students can test the Reset button. Note that Project 2 in the Web Design Projects (see page 493) teaches students how to use JavaScript to add functionality to a Submit button.

(Page 477)  **Activity 17.1** Students can gain additional experience with advanced HTML by visiting **WebDesignDW.glencoe.com**.

(Page 477) ✓ **Reading Check** Use the `<A href></A>` tag to identify the location of an audio file.

(Page 477) **Reading Focus** Text boxes, radio buttons, check boxes, pull-down menus, and text areas are all form fields that can be added to a Web site using HTML.

(Page 477) **You Try It** **Activity 17B Add Text Boxes Using HTML** Students enter the provided HTML code to add text boxes to a Web page. Use the Solution File noted in this chapter's Planning Guide.

(Page 478) **You Try It** **Activity 17C Add Radio Buttons and Check Boxes Using HTML** Students enter the provided HTML code to add radio buttons and check boxes to the form they created in Activity 17B. Use the Solution File noted in this chapter's Planning Guide.

(Page 479) **You Try It** **Activity 17D Add a Pull-down Menu Using HTML**
Students enter the provided HTML code to add a pull-down menu to the form they created in 17C. Use the Solution File noted in this chapter's Planning Guide.

> **Teaching Tip**
> In You Try It activity 17D, students insert options for Visa and American Express into the form they are creating. Remind students that credit card numbers are important personal information that should not be published or exchanged in class.

(Page 480) **You Try It** **Activity 17E Add a Text Area Using HTML** Students enter the provided HTML code to add a text area and Submit and Reset buttons to the form they created in the previous activities. While the Submit button will not function, students can test the form's Reset button.

(Page 480) ✓ **Reading Check** When the amount of text the user enters exceeds the space provided in the text area, the control automatically displays a scroll bar that allows the user to scroll the text up and down, or left and right.

(Page 480)	**Reading Focus** CSS are used to modify form elements by entering code into an HTML document.

You Try It **Activity 17F Use CSS to Style a Form** Students use CSS to style a form in an HTML document. Use the Solution Files noted in this chapter's Planning Guide. *(Page 480)*

> **Teaching Tip**
> When students copy the code in You Try It Activity 17F, they will be copying a `method` attribute. Explain to them that a `method` attribute in a form tag tells the form how the data should be sent for processing.

(Page 481) ✅ **Reading Check** Form elements can be modified in an HTML document by using CSS.

ASSESS

(Page 481) **Section 17.1 Assessment Answers**

Reading Summary
Use the Reading Summary to help students review and reinforce the important points of the section.

What Did You Learn?
1. Students' definitions should be in their own words, but based on the information found in the section and in the book's glossary.
2. In both cases, the user selects only one option from the list of choices.
3. The `<SELECT></SELECT>` tag set defines the pull-down menu. The `<OPTION></OPTION>` tag set defines each option in the pull-down menu list.

Critical Thinking
4. Companies could use the information to create a mailing list or to register the visitor for benefits such as a free newsletter.
5. Both radio buttons and check boxes show visitors all the choices available to them. Radio buttons require visitors to select only one option, while check boxes allow visitors to select as many options as apply.

Apply It!
Use HTML Attributes With your supervision, students will visit a Web site to learn more about HTML attributes that affect the appearance of form components. A suggested site for students to visit is **www.w3.org/TR/html401/interact/forms**.

CHAPTER 17

CLOSE

Using HTML Code to Create a Form Tell the students they are the Web designer for a site that is taking a survey of high school students about which courses should be required and which should be optional. (Alternatively, you may choose a different area of inquiry, or let the students choose their own.) Have them create a form using HTML and add the following:

- appropriate text boxes
- appropriate radio buttons
- appropriate check boxes
- a pull-down menu and text area

Have them view the form in a Web browser and make any necessary corrections.

(Page 482)

Careers & Technology

WHAT DOES A WEBMASTER DO?

Answers to Tech Check

1. Reports may be written or oral. They should display a good understanding of the requirements of the Webmaster's job and the steps required to prepare for one. Students may be able to contact Webmasters by going to a specific Web site and looking for the Webmaster information often listed on the bottom of the home page. Sometimes it can be found under links labeled "About Us" or "Contact Us." Large corporate sites usually do not link to one particular Webmaster, so those may be more difficult to use for finding contacts. When using the Internet, students should be supervised at all times.

2. Students' answers will vary, but should reflect an understanding of the Webmaster's role as a project manager, business manager, human resources manager. To carry out these responsibilities, a Webmaster may be required to demonstrate skills in leadership, asset management, time management, teamwork, customer relations, and communications.

CHAPTER 17

SECTION 17.2 ADDING INTERACTIVITY USING SCRIPTING
(Pages 483–486)

FOCUS

Reviewing Scripting Languages In Chapter 10, students were introduced to the concept of scripting languages, and given some examples of these languages. Since this section focuses more on the actual code needed to produce results using scripting languages, reviewing the contents of Chapter 10 at this time will be helpful.

(Page 483)

Focus on Reading

Read to Find Out

Use the Read to Find Out feature to focus student reading. Hold a quick starter discussion to find out what your students already know.

Key Terms Online

Key term definitions and activities are available online at **WebDesignDW.glencoe.com**.

Reading Strategy Answer

Students can find the information for this activity throughout this section. Students' diagrams should look similar to this example:

Client-side scripts
- Transfer to user's computer along with HTML code
- Executed by user's Web browser

Make Web pages dynamic

Server-side scripts
- Transfer the output to the user's computer as a Web page
- Executed on the Web server

TEACH

Understanding JavaScript Elements As with the previous section, students may have a hard time understanding how the provided code in You Try It activity 17F actually leads to the results observed in Figure 17.10. Explain what makes different parts of the code "events," "conditional statements," and so on. This will give students a better understanding of these terms and how these elements come together to make a JavaScript work.

Unit 5 Advanced HTML 449

CHAPTER 17

Answers to Section 17.2 Captions and Activities

(Page 483) **Reading Focus** A client-side script is designed to be transferred to the user's computer along with the HTML code.

(Page 483) **Activity 17.2** For additional information about different types of scripts, have the students visit **WebDesignDW.glencoe.com**.

(Page 484) **Activity 17G Create a Rollover Button Using JavaScript** Students learn how to create a rollover button using JavaScript by entering the provided source code. Use the Student Data Files and Solution Files noted in this chapter's Planning Guide.

> **Teaching Tip**
> Before starting You Try It Activity 17G Step 1, have students create a new folder named **rollover**. Then, have them open the folder and create a new folder named **images**.

(Page 485) **Reading Check** An event handler defines the action that will occur when an event takes place.

(Page 485) **Figure 17.11** The name of the applet embedded in the code is myApplet.class.

(Page 485) **Reading Focus** A server-side script transfers scripting language output to a user's computer as a Web page.

(Page 486) **Reading Check** CGI stands for the Common Gateway Interface.

(Page 486) **Reading Focus** An HTML validator can be used to identify potential problems in coding.

(Page 486) **Reading Check** Alert statements are most useful to Web developers during the testing phase.

ASSESS

(Page 486) ### Section 17.2 Assessment Answers

Reading Summary

Use the Reading Summary to help students review and reinforce the important points of the section.

What Did You Learn?

1. Students' definitions should be in their own words, but based on the information found in the section and in the book's glossary.

2. Client-side scripts are transferred to the user's computer to be executed by the browser. Server-side scripts execute on the Web server and display the results in the user's browser as a Web page.

3. The `<script></script>` tag set allows you to add JavaScripts to your Web page. The `<applet>` tag tells the Web browser where to locate Java applets.

Critical Thinking

4. Answers may include that copying scripts makes the complex job of programming easier and reduces the chance of errors.

5. Answers will vary but may include: registration forms for various events or benefits, forms that users can complete to locate specific information on the site or to learn more about a particular historical event, or even a JavaScript counter that marks the number of days since a particularly significant event occurred.

Apply It!

Explore HTML Web Sites With your supervision, students will explore online JavaScript tutorials and write a paragraph summarizing a new fact or technique they learn. Suggested sites are **www.w3schools.com/js** and **www.webreference.com/js**.

CLOSE

Researching Scripting Languages This section points out that rollover buttons and Web-based forms (that users fill out and then submit to the server) are some of the features that can be produced using scripting languages. Have students do research to find out what other features and effects can be added to Web sites through the use of scripting languages. They may use Chapter 10 as a starting point, but should also do research of their own. Have them make a list, write a report, or create a chart illustrating their findings. Students may work alone or in groups.

CHAPTER 17 Answers to Chapter Review

The Chapter Review covers a wide range of student knowledge. Due to time constraints, students may not be able to complete every activity in the Chapter Review. Select the activities that are appropriate for your class needs and resources.

(Page 488) ## After You Read

Find Your Study Method Successful students monitor their study habits and understand what helps them learn and how to improve when things go wrong. Help students to consciously think about how to learn. Encourage them to keep a learning log to record the methods they use to study and test results. From this they can look for patterns to determine which study methods are most effective.

(Page 488) ## Reviewing Key Terms

1. Radio buttons allow users to select only one item from a list.
2. Another term for an option button is a radio button.
3. The similarities and differences between check boxes and radio buttons are that they both allow users to interact with the site. However, radio buttons allow the users to select only one item from a list, and check boxes allow the user to select multiple items.
4. The pull-down menu uses the `<SELECT><SELECT>` tag set.
5. A scroll bar allows a user to review what he or she has typed in a text area.
6. *Events* are triggered by a user's action or by the computer system.
7. JavaScript is the scripting language Web developers use to develop client-side scripts.
8. Server-side scripts are transferred to the user's Web browser with the HTML code.

(Page 488) ## Understanding Main Ideas

9. Interactive elements make Web pages dynamic, which helps keep users' interest and attention. Interactive elements also provide a way for a Web site to gather and dispense information that is customized for the individual user.
10. An animated GIF is a sequence of GIF images stored in one file with specific information about how long the images will appear before the next image replaces it. This image transition-delay value gives the user the sense of motion that creates the animation.
11. The tag set used to insert both audio and video files is the `<A href></A>` tag.
12. The tag and type attribute used for text boxes are `<INPUT>` and `type="text"` for the attribute.
13. The HTML tags and attributes are as follows:
    - `<INPUT></INPUT>` is the basic tag set used for radio buttons and check boxes. The `type` attribute indicates either radio or checkbox.
    - The `<SELECT></SELECT>` tag set defines the pull-down menu, while the `<OPTION></OPTION>` tag set defines each option on the menu. The `value`

Answers to Chapter Review CHAPTER 17

attribute is used with the `<OPTION></OPTION>` tag set to assign a number value to each option on the menu.

14. Both are written to perform a variety of programming tasks that make Web pages dynamic. JavaScripts are included in the HTML code for a page, while Java applets reside outside the HTML code and are located by the browser using the `<APPLET>` tag.

(Page 488) ## Critical Thinking

15. An event is something that causes an effect to occur in response to a user action or a computer system action. The event handler is the response to the event. For example, an event could be clicking the mouse and its event handler is a change of image for a rollover button.

16. CGI scripts may be used to create Web-based forms, such as order forms, for the user to fill out. The information from the user is stored in a database.

17. Students' answers will vary. Sound files could include a theme song that will be associated with the soft drink, the sound of someone opening a can of the soft drink, or a celebrity endorsing the soft drink. An animated GIF could show a can or a bottle of the soft drink being opened or drunk.

18. Students should recommend either radio buttons or a pull-down menu, because only one city should be selected. With 10 cities, a pull-down menu would make the registration form appear less cluttered.

19. It is a server-side script. The database that supports the e-commerce site is set up to store the relevant information. When a user returns to the site, the Web server accesses the database, formulates the wish list based on previous choices by the user, and generates a Web page based on this information.

20. Scripting languages are similar to HTML and other markup languages in that they give computer instructions about how and when to display information. Scripting languages use more complex programming code to direct the computer. This complexity creates interactive elements that make Web pages dynamic.

21. Answers can include examples such as a mouse event (like a mouse over) that triggers the button to display a new image and play a sound. An event handler then responds to the code and determines what action will occur based on the event type. Next, a function call is included within the anchor tag surrounding the button. A conditional statement then determines the position of the cursor and then plays the appropriate sound. Last, the mouse button is returned to its original appearance.

(Page 489) ## Command Center

22. **Ctrl + F** = Open Find dialog box
23. **F3** = Find next
24. **Ctrl + H** = Open Find and Replace dialog box

CHAPTER 17 Answers to Chapter Review

Standardized Test Practice

The correct answer is A. Advise students to read the answers carefully for statements that contradict each other (such as A and C). They can deduce that one of those statements is most likely true, and then re-read the paragraph to determine the answer.

Have students use the book's Web site **WebDesignDW.glencoe.com**.

- **Study with PowerTeach** Encourage your students to use the Chapter 17 PowerTeach Outline to review the chapter before they have a test.
- **Online Self Check** These quick five-question assessments may be used as an in-class activity, a homework assignment, or test review.

(Page 490) ### Making Connections

Social Studies—Create a Survey Form Students locate a list of personality traits in a psychology book and use the list to create a survey form (students can also search for a list online). The form asks for the person's birth order. (Students should use radio buttons or a pull-down menu.) The form also lists personality traits. People select the personality traits that apply. (Students should use check boxes.)

(Page 490) ### Standards at Work

NETS-S 3 Debug Scripts Students work with a partner to research the advanced options that Dreamweaver provides for debugging scripts and HTML code. Students then create a Web page that contains a JavaScript. You should either provide students with the JavaScript to be used or allow them to locate a JavaScript from the Internet. After testing the page, students remove one line of the script, recording the information deleted. The partner then debugs the code. Advise students to use a browser to check whether the JavaScript works as expected or not.

(Page 491) ### Teamwork Skills

Convert a Printed Form into an Electronic Form Students work in small groups to plan and create an electronic form based on a printed form. If possible, bring in a number of examples for students to choose from. Encourage students to select a form that is not too complex. Many registration forms have a reasonable number of fields. Students should identify opportunities to include pull-down menus that cannot be included on printed forms. Discuss the advantages of using preset options over text areas for items such as the state in which people live.

(Page 491) ### Challenge Yourself

Create a Dictionary of Terms The World Wide Web Consortium's site is **www.w3.org**. The validator can be found at **validator.w3.org/about.html**. Students create a dictionary of five terms that are new to them. You may want to compile all the student dictionaries into a class dictionary.

Answers to Chapter Review — CHAPTER 17

You Try It — Skills Studio

(Page 492)

1. **Create a Web Page with Audio in HTML** Students locate or create two related audio files. They write a short story or poem that incorporates these audio files. To save time, students may also start with a poem or story that they like and then find or create the audio files. Students write the HTML code that will display the short story or poem and play the audio files. Encourage students to proofread their work and test the page in a browser to make certain the sound files play properly.

2. **Create a Ticket Order Form** Students use the form illustrated to create an HTML version. Students may change any items on the form example to customize their form. Students should proofread and test their form. Remind students that the form will not submit and process data, but that they can test the Reset button.

Web Design Projects

(Page 493)

1. **Create a Survey Form** Students create an online form that allows parents to give input about the types of camps they would like to see offered. A list with check boxes will allow parents to select as many camps as they desire. If students only want parents to select one camp, then they should use radio buttons. Be sure that students include a way for parents to suggest other types of camps (this can be done by including a text area). The forms should include basic contact information so that the camp can build its contact list.

2. **Use JavaScript to Add a Submit Button** Students add functionality to the survey form created in Web Design Project 1, by adding the HTML code and JavaScript needed to include a Submit button. The specific codes are provided. Students must key them correctly. Encourage them to use debugging techniques if the Submit button does not appear on the page as expected. Again, remind students that, although they are adding functionality to the Submit button, the button still will not work since the site has not been published and cannot process user data.

UNIT 5

(Page 494)
BUILDING 21ST CENTURY SKILLS

Project 1 Problem Solving: Use HTML and JavaScript

Students use HTML to create a Web page that advertises customer service. Students type the JavaScript provided in the text into the HTML document. To determine which greeting visitors will receive, students need to replace "INSERT text here" with their own greeting. The rest of the HTML document includes an unordered list of services available and a table that asks and answers three common questions that the customer service group receives. Students may also add code to change the background and font colors.

Project 2 Communication Skills: Create a Community Services Web Site

Students create a frames-based site using HTML that describes the services available in their community. Students plan and create a simple logo for the community that will appear on the site's home page. Students build the content pages, the container page, and the link bar page. Students test the site in a browser and debug the code as needed.

(Page 495)
BUILDING YOUR PORTFOLIO

The Portfolio projects are ongoing activities that build upon the material in the unit. By the end of the course, the students should have work samples that show every stage of their knowledge development. Explain to students how to save their samples as hard copies, online copies, or on personal disks.

Create a Feedback Form

Students select a Web site that they have created during the course and add a feedback form to it. Students should work in Code view to create the form.

Students add two check box questions, one radio button question, and a text area for comments. Students also add code to make the feedback form consistent in look and feel with the rest of the site.

Students update the site's navigation structure so that the feedback form is accessible from the site's home page. Students test the form and how it fits into the site in a browser, making changes as needed.

Students create screen shots for their portfolios. They should also make an electronic copy of the finished product. This copy may replace the copy of the site that was saved earlier, or students can save the revised site under a different name.

The instructions also suggest publishing the site to the school or class Web site. Have students complete this part of the project if you have a Web server available and allow access to students. Use Dreamweaver's built-in FTP capabilities or a standalone FTP program to transfer files.

PART 3

Reproducibles and Visual Aids

Graphic Organizers

What Are Graphic Organizers?..........................458

Why Use Graphic Organizers?..........................458

Using the Reading Strategy Organizers in the Classroom...459

Using Graphic Organizers Effectively..................459

Graphic Organizer Library

Graphic Organizer Library Overview....................460

Graphic Organizer 1: Main Idea Chart..................465

Graphic Organizer 2: K-W-L-H Chart....................466

Graphic Organizer 3: Web Diagram......................467

Graphic Organizer 4: Tree Diagram.....................468

Graphic Organizer 5: Venn Diagram.....................469

Graphic Organizer 6: Matrix...........................470

Graphic Organizer 7: Table............................471

Graphic Organizer 8: Pyramid Table....................472

Graphic Organizer 9: Fishbone Diagram.................473

Graphic Organizer 10: Horizontal Time Line............474

Graphic Organizer 11: Problem-Solution Chart..........475

Graphic Organizer 12: Cause-Effect Chart (Option 1)...476

Graphic Organizer 13: Cause-Effect Chart (Option 2)...477

Graphic Organizer 14: Chain-of-Events or Flowchart....478

GRAPHIC ORGANIZERS

WHAT ARE GRAPHIC ORGANIZERS?

Graphic organizers are visual representations of written material. Charts, graphs, diagrams, and maps are all examples of graphic organizers. The use of graphic organizers promotes critical reading and thinking. In addition, writing information in a visual or an illustrated way helps students clarify and categorize data for easier recall. Using graphic organizers also helps students see connections among parallel or related facts. Finally, many teachers believe that having students list information in a graphic organizer makes learning more fun than just taking notes in the traditional way.

WHY USE GRAPHIC ORGANIZERS?

In each chapter of the student textbook, Reading Strategy Organizers, like the one shown below, appear at the beginning of each section. Use these graphic organizers to:

◆ Set a purpose for student reading.
◆ Help students organize and understand important material as they read.
◆ Provide a visual way for students to reinforce what they read.
◆ Prepare students for tests or quizzes.

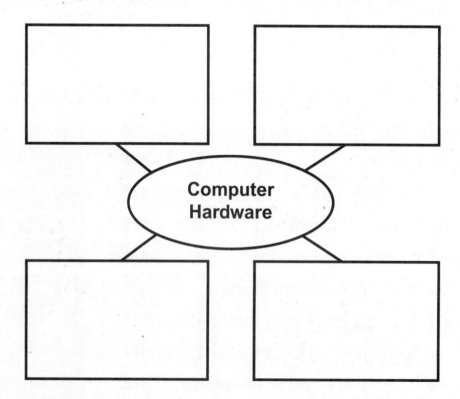

GRAPHIC ORGANIZERS

Using the Reading Strategy Organizers in the Classroom

◆ Print the Reading Strategy Organizer PDF files (organized by chapter). These are:
  - Available on the Teacher Resource CD bound into the back of this Resource manual.
  - Also available at the Online Learning Center Web site at **WebDesignDW.glencoe.com**.

◆ Give a copy to each student when you assign the section.

◆ Have students follow the directions and fill in the information.

◆ You may need to complete the first few organizers with students if they are not familiar with the graphic organizers.

◆ Alternately, students can hand draw each organizer on their own papers and write their answers.

Once students are comfortable filling in the organizers on their own, you may wish to use the other organizers provided on the following pages to help students focus their reading, take notes, and reinforce new knowledge.

Using Graphic Organizers Effectively

The graphic organizers provided in this section are intended to help students take notes and organize information when preparing oral reports and research projects.

◆ Before requiring students to complete an activity, describe the purpose of the particular graphic organizer.

◆ Demonstrate how to use the textbook and prior knowledge to fill in information for the various parts of the graphic organizer.

◆ Provide opportunities for students to work in groups as well as individually when completing the graphic organizers, which will teach students to analyze the graphic more closely.

◆ After students have completed an activity, discuss the responses as a class. This will help students learn to revise their thought processes and better clarify the organization of the graphic organizers.

GRAPHIC ORGANIZER LIBRARY

GRAPHIC ORGANIZER LIBRARY OVERVIEW

There are 14 reproducible graphic organizers provided in this section. Each type of organizer is best suited for a specific kind or purpose of presentation. For example, one type of organizer may be better suited to categorize information sequentially; another to compare and/or contrast; a third to describe, support, or exemplify a main idea; and so on. The following information will explain for what purpose each of the graphic organizers is best suited.

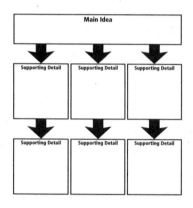

Graphic Organizer 1: Main Idea Chart

This type of graphic organizer is helpful when you want students to find the main idea of a paragraph or section, and then to analyze the reading further for more information that exemplifies and/or supports that main idea.

Graphic Organizer 2: K-W-L-H Chart

The K-W-L-H chart is used to activate students' prior knowledge and interest before they read as well as to set a purpose for reading. This chart asks for student feedback on what they Know already, what they Want to find out, what they Learned, and How they can learn more.

GRAPHIC ORGANIZER LIBRARY

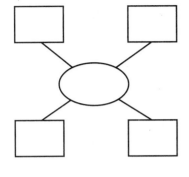

Graphic Organizer 3: Web Diagram

Web diagrams are often used to help students identify one central idea and organize related information around it. Students must determine the broad categories that should be listed in the outer parts of the web. Then students must determine what is relevant factual material and group this data into the appropriate related categories.

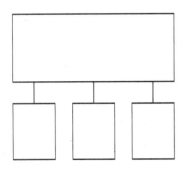

Graphic Organizer 4: Tree Diagram

A tree diagram is based upon the traditional "family tree" organizational graphic. Students are required to record how subordinate facts or statements are related to one another and to a larger, unifying statement. Tree diagrams may also be utilized as a main idea/supporting details type of graphic organizer.

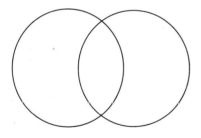

Graphic Organizer 5: Venn Diagram

Venn diagrams are used to compare and contrast information or to show similarities and differences among various objects or subjects. The Venn diagram consists of two or more overlapping circles. Differences are listed in the outer parts of the circles. Similarities are described where the circles overlap. Venn diagrams are especially helpful in displaying similarities and differences at a glance.

GRAPHIC ORGANIZER LIBRARY

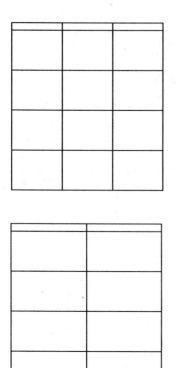

Graphic Organizers 6 and 7: Matrix and Table

Matrices and tables are used to organize or categorize information or to make comparisons among categories. A matrix is used to compare multiple items, while a table is used to compare two items. The items to be compared are listed along the left side of the table's rows, and the general features are listed across the top of the table before filling in the cells with facts or supporting information. Graphic Organizer 7 may also be used as a storyboard.

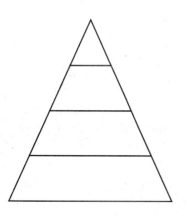

Graphic Organizer 8: Pyramid Table

A pyramid table is very effective for organizing information in a majority/minority or general-to-specific manner. A pyramid table can also be used to list details or facts leading up to a climax or culminating event.

GRAPHIC ORGANIZER LIBRARY

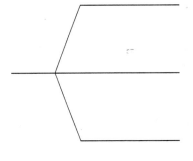

Graphic Organizer 9: Fishbone Diagram

The purpose of a fishbone diagram is very similar to that of a main idea/supporting details chart. A main idea statement or category is written on the single line to the left. Supporting facts, examples, or subcategories are written on the lines to the right. In many cases, a third set of lines can be generated and attached to the subcategories with additional information or facts.

Graphic Organizer 10: Horizontal Time Line

Time lines are used to list important dates in chronological order. Horizontal time lines require students to analyze information by sequencing events. Time lines also require students to determine baseline dates and to be cognizant of the "backward" nature of B.C. chronology.

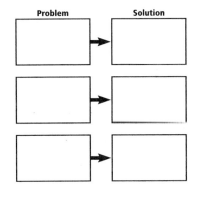

Graphic Organizer 11: Problem-Solution Chart

The purpose of this type of graphic organizer is to help students streamline the steps involved in recognizing a problem and utilizing problem-solving skills. The problem-solution chart may be best suited for group discussion after the teacher has explained an event or action. Students may then describe or predict the problem, after which they may brainstorm multiple solutions and possible results of those solutions.

Part 3—Reproducibles and Visual Aids **463**

GRAPHIC ORGANIZER LIBRARY

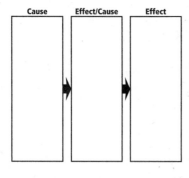

Graphic Organizers 12 and 13: Cause-Effect Charts

This type of organizer helps students analyze information by identifying cause-and-effect relationships. In some cases, students may be required to identify a sequence of a cause and its effect, which becomes the cause of yet another effect. In other cases, students will identify separate causes and their effects (see Graphic Organizer 13).

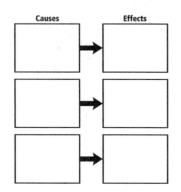

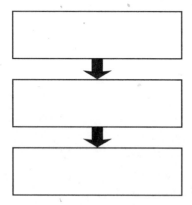

Graphic Organizer 14: Chain-of-Events or Flowchart

A chain-of-events, or flowchart, asks students to organize and interpret information by sequencing the stages of an event. This type of graphic organizer can also be used to describe the actions of a character or group, or the steps to be followed in a procedure.

Name _____ Date _____ Class _____

Graphic Organizer 1: Main Idea Chart

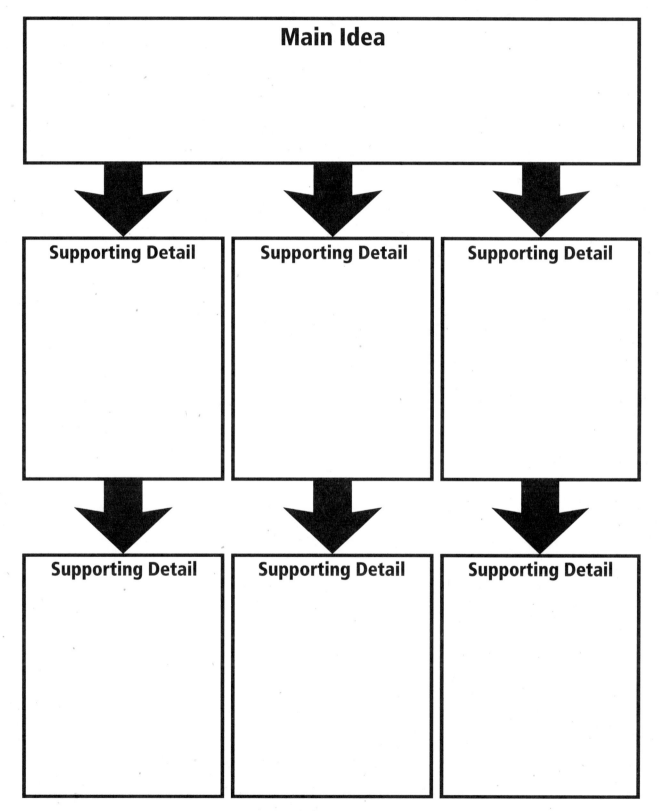

Part 3—Reproducibles and Visual Aids   465

Name _____ Date _____ Class _____

Graphic Organizer 2: K-W-L-H Chart

What I Know	What I Want to Find Out	What I Learned	How Can I Learn More

Name ———— Date ———— Class ————

Graphic Organizer 3: Web Diagram

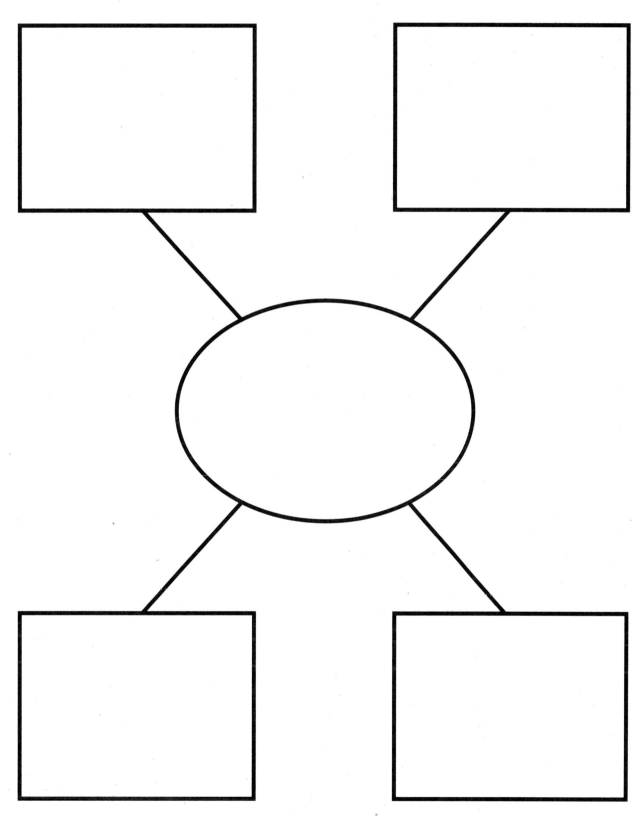

Part 3—Reproducibles and Visual Aids

Name _____ Date _____ Class _____

Graphic Organizer 4: Tree Diagram

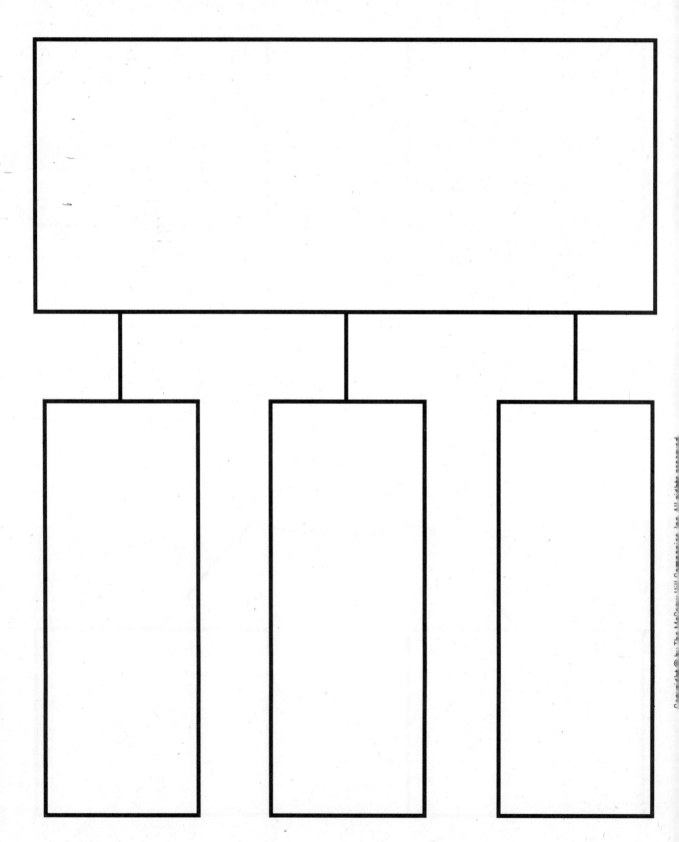

468 Teacher Resource Manual—*Introduction to Web Design Using Dreamweaver*

Graphic Organizer 5: Venn Diagram

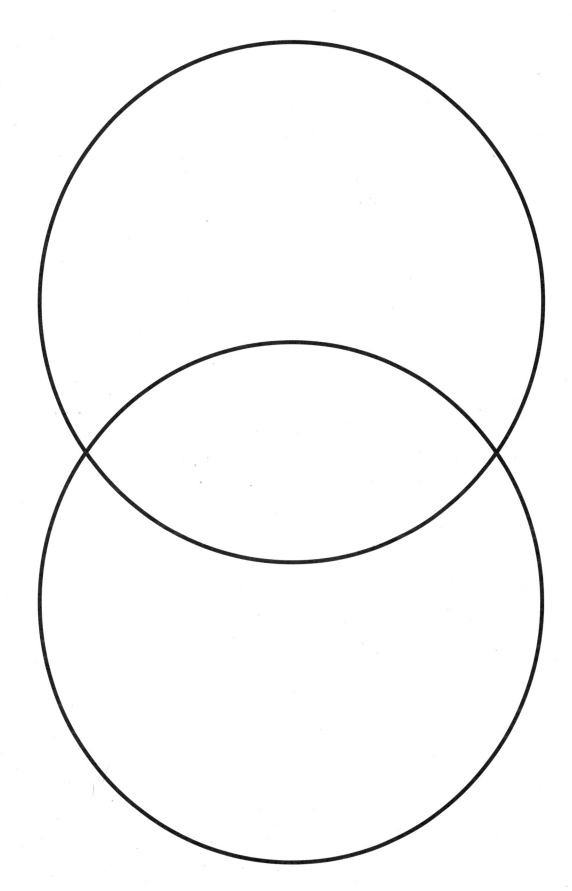

Name _____ Date _____ Class _____

Graphic Organizer 6: Matrix

Name _____ Date _____ Class _____

Graphic Organizer 7: Table

Name _____ Date _____ Class _____

Graphic Organizer 8: Pyramid Table

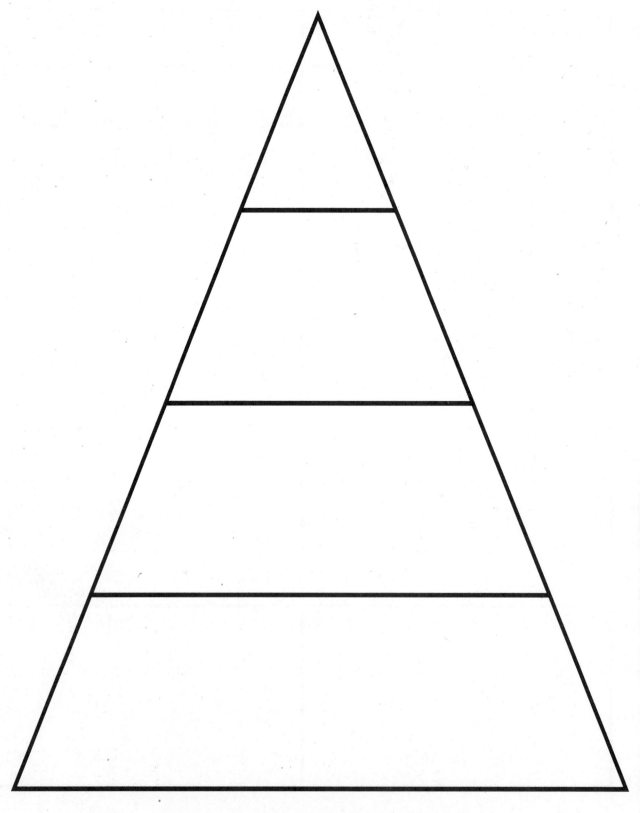

Name ——————————————— Date ——————————— Class ———————

Graphic Organizer 9: Fishbone Diagram

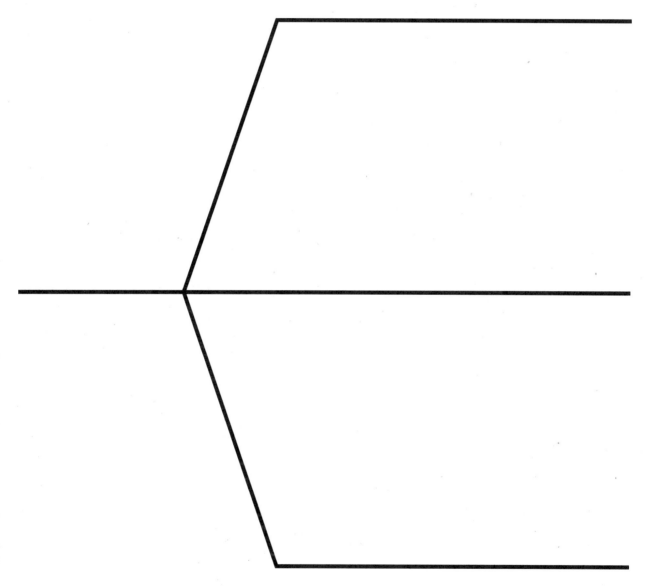

Name _____ Date _____ Class _____

Graphic Organizer 10: Horizontal Time Line

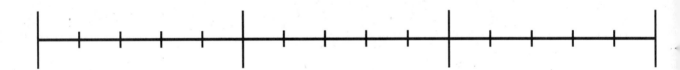

Name ———————————— Date ———————— Class ————

Graphic Organizer 11: Problem-Solution Chart

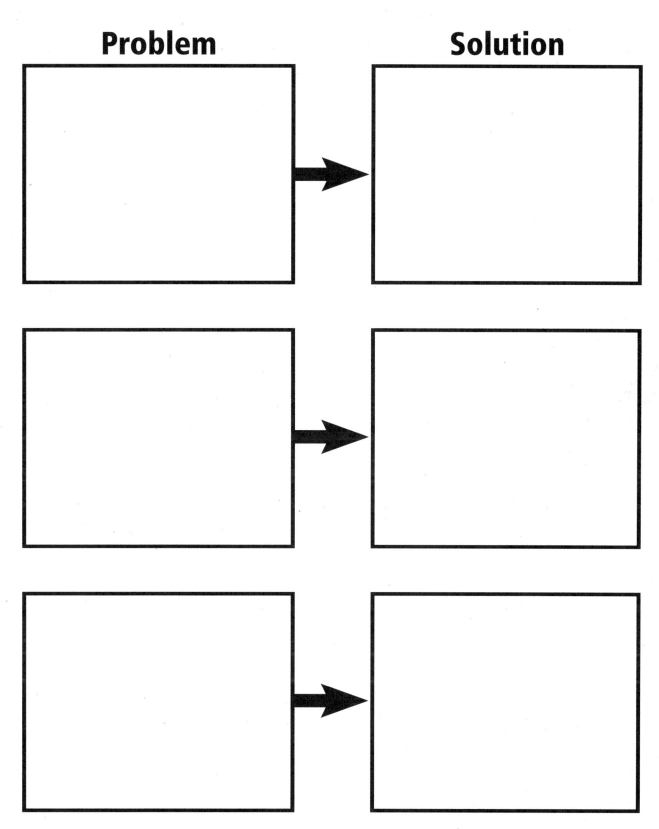

Part 3—Reproducibles and Visual Aids   475

Name _____ Date _____ Class _____

Graphic Organizer 12: Cause–Effect Chart (Option 1)

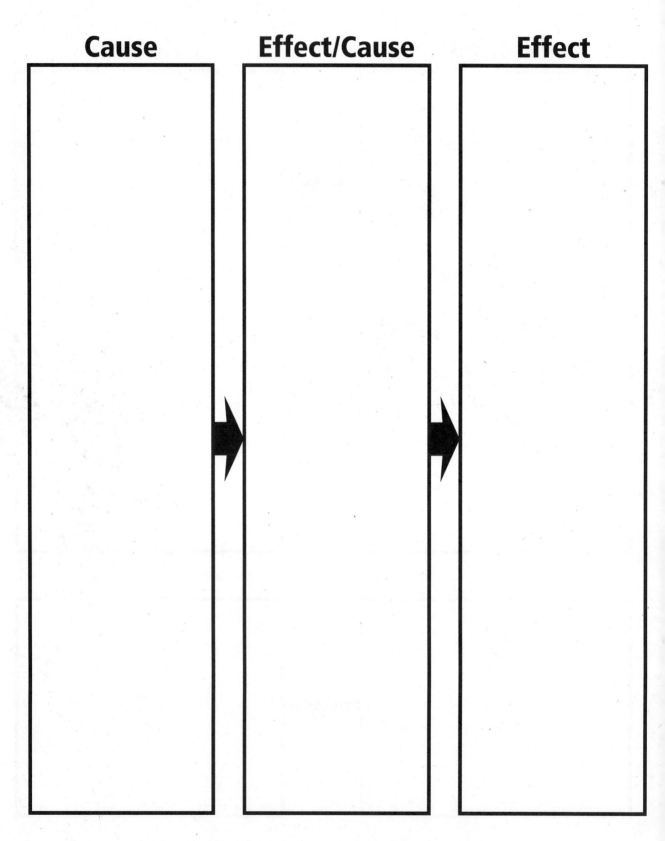

476 Teacher Resource Manual—*Introduction to Web Design Using Dreamweaver*

Name _____ Date _____ Class _____

Graphic Organizer 13: Cause–Effect Chart (Option 2)

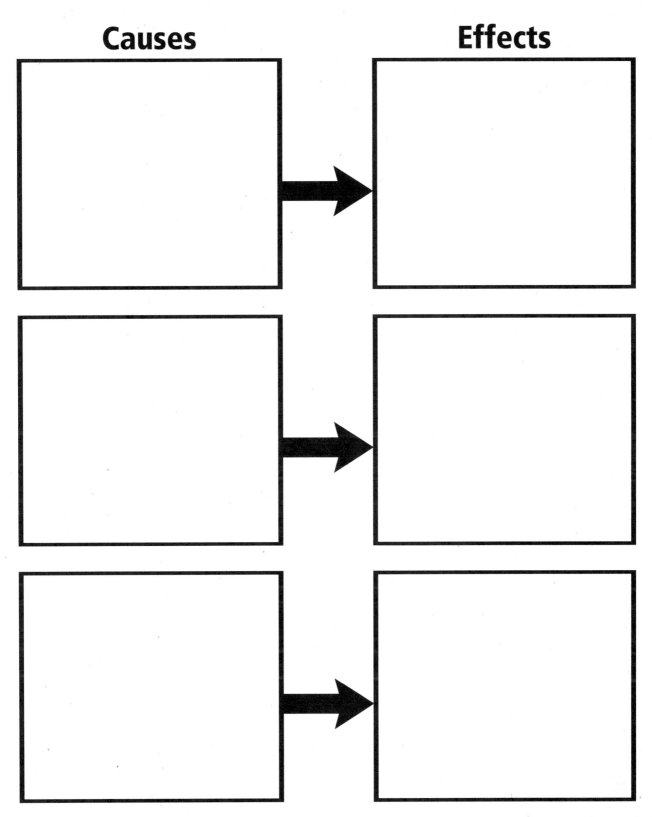

Part 3—Reproducibles and Visual Aids 477

Name _____ Date _____ Class _____

Graphic Organizer 14: Chain-of-Events or Flowchart

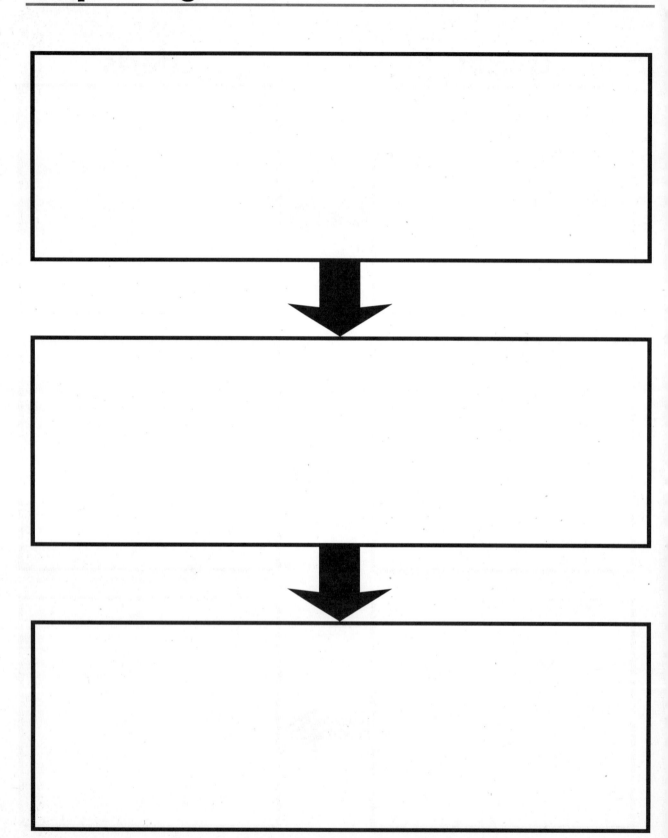

478 Teacher Resource Manual—*Introduction to Web Design Using Dreamweaver*

PART 4

PowerTeach Presentations, *ExamView*®, and TechSIM™ Interactive Tutorials

PowerTeach User Guide 480
   PowerTeach Presentation Information 480
   Installation and Startup Instructions 481

***ExamView* User Guide** 484
   ExamView Pro Test Generator Software Information...484
   ExamView Components 484
   Installation and Startup Instructions 487

TechSIM™ Interactive Tutorials User Guide 490

POWERTEACH USER GUIDE

POWERTEACH PRESENTATION INFORMATION

The Teacher Resource CD contains 17 PowerTeach Outlines—one PowerPoint presentation for every chapter of *Introduction to Web Design Using Dreamweaver*. Each presentation includes important headings, figures, and key terms that students will encounter while using the textbook. PowerTeach Outlines for every textbook chapter are also available for download or viewing in a browser on the Online Learning Center at **www.WebDesignDW.glencoe.com**.

Using Presentations in the Classroom

The following suggestions may help you use the PowerTeach Outlines in the classroom.

- Using PowerTeach, you will never lose track of transparencies in front of the class and spend valuable minutes getting them back in order.
- You may wish to show students only part of the presentations at a time. For example, view the section on social, ethical, and legal issues before students learn how to create a one-page Web site.
- Students may also use the presentations on their own for independent study.
- If your school has a wireless mouse for your computer (or other means of advancing slides in a PowerPoint presentation), you can circulate around the classroom as you teach. This will allow you to focus on an individual student's work and deal with problems before a student falls too far behind.
- Even if your class does not have a wireless mouse, you will only need to return to your computer to advance the presentation one slide at a time with one keystroke. You will not be tied to the computer as you go through a procedure in front of the class.
- The PowerTeach Outlines are intended to supplement your presentation of the material in the textbook. They are not designed as a substitute for the text or for your guided classroom teaching.

Ultimately, these PowerTeach presentations can make your job easier, accelerate learning, and allow for more individualized teaching.

INSTALLATION AND STARTUP INSTRUCTIONS

Setting Up Your Equipment

Before you begin using PowerTeach Outlines, check your equipment connections. To use PowerTeach, you will need a computer (see System Requirements below), PowerPoint software or PowerPoint Viewer software, and a projector or large screen monitor capable of displaying high-color images. Make sure your monitor is set to high-color mode.

System Requirements

Verify that your computer meets or exceeds the hardware and software requirements listed below. Check your PowerPoint user manual or **www.microsoft.com** to check the system requirements for your version of PowerPoint.

WINDOWS

- IBM PC or 100% compatible computer
- 486 or higher processor
- 8 MB of RAM
- 4X CD-ROM (or faster)
- VGA or higher-resolution video monitor *(SVGA, 256 colors recommended)*
- Mouse
- Printer *(optional, but recommended)*
- Microsoft PowerPoint 97 or later, or PowerPoint Viewer
- Windows 95 or later

MACINTOSH

- Any PowerPC processor-based, Mac OS-compatible system
- 120 MHZ processor recommended
- 16 MB of RAM *(32 MB recommended)*
- 4X CD-ROM (or faster)
- VGA or higher-resolution video monitor, supporting 256 colors and 640x400 or greater resolution
- Mouse
- Printer *(optional, but recommended)*
- Microsoft PowerPoint 98 or later, or PowerPoint Viewer
- Apple System 7.5 or later

Loading the Presentations

The PowerTeach files have not been compressed; therefore, they can be run directly from the CD-ROM. In most cases, the PowerTeach Outlines will run faster if loaded on your hard drive. If you load the presentations on your hard drive, you may have to organize them in a separate folder.

Running a Presentation with PowerPoint

The best way to run a PowerTeach presentation is with PowerPoint software. The following instructions assume that PowerPoint is located on your hard disk, and that the extension ".ppt" is recognized by your computer as a PowerPoint file.

1. Insert the Teacher Resource CD into your CD-ROM drive. If the CD does not start automatically:
   - (For Windows) double-click on the My Computer icon on your desktop, and then on the icon for your CD-ROM drive. Next, double-click on the **StartUp** file.
   - (For Macintosh) double-click on the CD icon on your desktop. Then, double-click on the **StartUp** file.
2. Click on the **Chapter PowerTeach Outlines** link.
3. For the Chapter PowerTeach Outline you wish to view, click the Chapter name. (This should automatically start the presentation.) Depending on your software configuration, you may need to change the *View* option to *Slide Show* to run the presentation as a slide show.

Navigating Between Slides

Next Slide	Previous Slide
◆ Right arrow key	◆ Left arrow key
◆ Down arrow key	◆ Up arrow key
◆ Page Up key	◆ Page Down key
◆ Right Arrow button on screen	◆ Left Arrow button on screen
◆ Space bar	
◆ Click left mouse button	

Running a Presentation with PowerPoint Viewer

If you do not have PowerPoint, you can go to the Microsoft Web site to download a free PowerPoint Viewer. Visit **www.microsoft.com**, or if you are a Mac user, visit **www.microsoft.com/mac**. Once this Viewer has been installed, follow these directions:

1. Start the PowerPoint Viewer program.
2. Click the pop-up menu and navigate to the Teacher Resource CD.
3. Choose the PowerTeach Outline folder and then the Chapter PowerTeach you wish to view.
4. When you start a presentation, you will see an opening slide. Click the *Forward* button to proceed to the next slide.
5. From the *Contents* (or Main menu) slide, you can access almost all of the PowerTeach resources. While viewing a presentation, click the navigation button to view the slide. Click the *Help* button for step-by-step instructions.
6. To end the presentation, click the *Exit* button or press the *Esc* (escape) key.

Customizing a Presentation

The PowerTeach Outlines were created using Microsoft PowerPoint (Windows). If you wish, you can customize any of the presentations using PowerPoint 97 (or a later version). Follow the steps provided in your PowerPoint user manual or in the online *Help* system that is part of the PowerPoint program.

Troubleshooting Tips

If you experience problems using PowerTeach Outlines, refer to the troubleshooting tips in the *Help* system. A comprehensive list of potential problems is provided along with suggested solutions. To access this information, start a presentation and click on the *Help* button. Select *Microsoft PowerPoint Help* and type in your question.

ExamView USER GUIDE

ExamView PRO TEST GENERATOR SOFTWARE INFORMATION

ExamView Pro Test Generator Software allows you to generate ready-made and customized objective tests using multiple choice, true/false, fill-in-the-blank, and essay questions. The questions cover all chapters in the text.

Components of the *ExamView* Pro Test Generator Software include:

- *ExamView* Pro Test Generator Software User's Manual (Windows/Macintosh)
- *ExamView* Pro Test Generator Software (Windows/Macintosh)

The CD software contains the testbank generator program that lets you retrieve the questions you want from the chapter testbanks and print tests. Answers to all questions are provided in the testbanks. The software also lets you edit and add questions as needed.

Site License

Your adoption of this textbook entitles you to site-license duplication rights for all components of the *ExamView* Pro Test Generator Software with the restriction that all copies must be used within the adopting schools. This license shall run for the life of the adoption of the accompanying text.

Using the Testbank

Before you begin, follow the directions in the *User's Manual* on the CD to make backup copies of the software. Then, set up your computer and printer and configure the software, following the instructions. The *User's Manual* contains all the instructions on how to use the software. Refer to this manual as needed to preview and select questions for your tests.

> ### Software Support Hotline
> Should you encounter any difficulty when setting up or running the programs, contact the Software Support Center at Glencoe Publishing between 8:30 A.M. and 6:00 P.M. Eastern Time. The toll-free number is **1-800-437-3715**. Customers with specific questions can contact us via the Internet at the following e-mail address: **epgtech@mcgraw-hill.com**.

ExamView COMPONENTS

ExamView Pro is a test generator program that enables you to quickly create printed tests, Internet tests, and computer (LAN-based) tests. The program includes three components: Test Builder, Question Bank Editor, and Test Player. The **Test Builder** includes options to create, edit, print, and save tests. The **Question Bank Editor** lets you create or edit question banks. The **Test Player** is a separate program that your students can use to take online (LAN-based) tests or access study guides.

Test Builder

The Test Builder allows you to create tests using the QuickTest Wizard or to create a new test on your own. Use the Test Builder to prepare both printed and online tests or study guides.

- *If you want ExamView to select questions randomly from one or more question banks,* choose the *QuickTest Wizard* option to create a new test. Then, follow the step-by-step instructions to (1) enter a test title, (2) choose one or more question banks from which to select questions, and (3) identify how many questions you want on the test. The QuickTest Wizard will automatically create a new test and use the Test Builder to display the test on screen. You can print the test as is, remove questions, add new questions, or edit any question.

- *If you want to create a new test on your own,* choose the option to create a new test. Then identify a question bank from which to choose questions by using the *Question Bank* option in the **Select** menu. You may then add questions to the test by using one or more of the following selection options: *Randomly, From a List, While Viewing, By Criteria,* or *All Questions.*

Question Bank Editor

The Question Bank Editor allows you to edit questions in an existing publisher-supplied question bank or to create your own new question banks. Always use the Question Bank Editor if you want to change a question permanently in an existing question bank. If you want to make a change that applies only to a particular test, create a new question or edit that question in the Test Builder.

A question bank may include up to 250 questions in a variety of formats, including multiple choice, true/false, modified true/false, completion, yes/no, matching, problem, essay, short answer, case, and numeric response. You can include the following information for each question: difficulty code, reference, text objective, state objectives, topic, and notes.

Online Testing (LAN-based versus Internet)

The *ExamView* software allows you to create paper tests and online tests. *ExamView* includes many features that let you customize an online test. You can create a test for a specific class, or you can prepare a study guide for anyone to use. Using the Online Test Wizard, you can schedule a test or allow it to be taken anytime. As your students work on a test, *ExamView* will scramble the question order, provide feedback for incorrect responses, and display a timer if you selected any of these options.

The program provides two distinct online testing options: **LAN-based** testing and **Internet** testing. The option you choose depends on your particular testing needs. You can choose either option to administer online tests and study guides.

The **LAN-based** testing option is designed to work on a local area network server. To take a LAN-based test, students must have access to the Test Player program included with the *ExamView* software. The Test Player is a separate program that lets your students take a test or access a study guide at a computer. You can copy the test or study guide along with the Test Player software onto your local area network. Then students can take the test at computers connected to your server.

ExamView USER GUIDE

The **Internet** testing option provides a computerized testing solution for delivering tests via the Internet or an intranet. This option is great for making sample tests and study guides available to students at home. Students do not need any other program (unlike the LAN-based option). When your students take a test, the results are automatically sent to you via e-mail.

You can publish an Internet test to your own Web site, or you can use the *ExamView* Internet test-hosting service. If you subscribe to the *ExamView* test-hosting service,[1] you can publish a test directly to the Internet with just a few simple steps. Students will have immediate access to the tests that you publish and you can get detailed reports. For more information on the Internet test-hosting service, visit the **www.examview.com** Web site.

As you work with the *ExamView* test generator, you may use the following features:

- An interview mode or "wizard" to guide you through the steps to create a test in less than five minutes
- Five methods to select test questions
    - Random selection
    - From a list
    - While viewing questions
    - By criteria (difficulty code, objective, topic, and others–if available)
    - All questions
- The capability to edit questions or to add an unlimited number of questions
- Online (Internet-based) testing
    - Create a test that students can take on the Internet using a browser
    - Receive instant feedback via e-mail
    - Create online study guides with student feedback for incorrect responses
    - Include any of the twelve question types
- Internet test-hosting[1]
    - Instantly publish a test to the *ExamView* Web site
    - Manage tests online
    - Allow students to access tests from one convenient location
    - Receive detailed reports
    - Download results to your gradebook or spreadsheet
- Online (LAN-based) testing
    - Allow anyone or selected students to take a test on your local area network
    - Schedule tests
    - Create online study guides with student feedback for incorrect responses
    - Incorporate multimedia links (movies and audio)
    - Export student results to a gradebook or spreadsheet

---

1. The Internet test-hosting service must be purchased separately. Visit **www.examview.com** to learn more.

- A sophisticated word processor
  - Streamlined question entry with spell checker
  - Tabs, fonts, symbols, foreign characters, and text styles
  - Tables with borders and shading
  - Full-featured equation editor
  - Pictures or other graphics within a question, answer, or narrative
- Numerous test layout and printing options
  - Scramble the choices in multiple choice questions
  - Print multiple versions of the same test with corresponding answer keys
  - Print an answer key strip for easier test grading
- Link groups of questions to common narratives

INSTALLATION AND STARTUP INSTRUCTIONS

The *ExamView* Pro Test Generator Software is provided on CD. The CD includes the program and all of the questions for the corresponding textbook. The *ExamView* Player, which can be used by your students to take online (LAN-based or Internet) tests, is also included.

Before you can use the test generator, you must install it on your hard drive. The system requirements, installation instructions, and startup procedures are provided below.

System Requirements

To use the *ExamView* Pro Test Generator or the online test player, your computer must meet or exceed the following minimum hardware requirements:

WINDOWS

- 100% PC-compatible Pentium computer (120 MHz or faster)
- Windows 98, Windows 2000, Windows XP (or a more recent version)
- Color monitor (VGA-compatible)
- CD-ROM drive
- Hard drive with at least 10 MB space available
- 16 MB available memory *(32 MB memory recommended)*
- A mouse (or a compatible pointing device)

MACINTOSH

- PowerPC Macintosh (120 MHz or faster)
- System 8.6, System 9.2, or OS X (10.2 or later)
- Color monitor (VGA-compatible)
- CD-ROM drive
- Hard drive with at least 25 MB space available
- 16 MB available memory *(32 MB memory recommended)*
- A mouse (or a compatible pointing device)

For PCs and MACs, Netscape 4.0/Explorer 4.0 (or a more recent version) and an Internet connection are required to take or publish an Internet test. System 8.6 (or a more recent version) is also required for MAC users.

ExamView USER GUIDE

Installation Instructions

Follow these steps to install the *ExamView* test generator software. The setup program will automatically install everything you need to use *ExamView*.

WINDOWS

Step 1
Turn on your computer.

Step 2
Insert the *ExamView* disc into your CD-ROM drive.

Step 3
Click the **Start** button and click **Run**.

Step 4
Click the drive letter that corresponds to the CD-ROM drive on your computer and double-click the file titled **setup.exe** (e.g., d:\setup.exe).

Step 5
Follow the prompts on the screen to complete the installation process.

View or Print the *ExamView* Pro User Guide by clicking the drive letter that corresponds to the CD-ROM drive on your computer (e.g., d:). Double-click to open the file titled **Manual**.

MACINTOSH

Step 1
Turn on your computer.

Step 2
Insert the *ExamView* disc into your CD-ROM drive.

Step 3
Open the installer window, if necessary. It may open automatically.

Step 4
Double-click the installation icon to start the program.

Step 5
Follow the prompts on the screen to complete the installation process.

View or Print the *ExamView* Pro User Guide by double-clicking the CD icon on the desktop. Double-click the file titled **Manual**.

The Getting Started section explains the options used to create a test and edit a question bank.

Startup Instructions

After you complete the installation process, follow these instructions to start the *ExamView* test generator software.

Step 1
WINDOWS: Click the **Start** button on the Taskbar. Click the **Programs** menu and locate the *ExamView* Test Generator folder. Click the *ExamView* Pro option to start the software.

MACINTOSH: Locate and open the *ExamView* folder. Double-click the *ExamView* Pro program icon.

Step 2
The first time you run the software, you will be prompted to enter your name, school/institution name, and city/state. You are now ready to begin using the *ExamView* software.

Step 3
Each time you start *ExamView,* the Startup menu appears. Choose one of the options shown.

Step 4
Use *ExamView* to create a test, or to edit questions in a question bank.

Using the Help System

Whenever you need assistance using *ExamView*, access the extensive *Help* system. Click the **Help** button or choose the **Help Topics** option from the **Help** menu to access step-by-step instructions from more than 150 Help topics. If you experience any difficulties while you are working with the software, you may want to review the troubleshooting tips in the user-friendly *Help* system.

TechSIM™ USER GUIDE

The Glencoe TechSIM™ Interactive Tutorials can help students learn more about file management, e-mail, system settings, and the Control Panel. The tutorials allow a safe, self-contained environment for students to explore the Windows desktop and Explorer, Microsoft Outlook, and the Windows Control Panel.

USING TechSIM™ INTERACTIVE TUTORIALS

The interactive tutorials can be used to further students' understanding of the selected topics while allowing them to gain hands-on practice. For example:

- **TechSIM A: File Management** If the computers in your classroom or lab use different versions of operating systems, then use the TechSIM™ Interactive Tutorials to allow all students to practice using Microsoft Windows. The skills taught in this series of tutorials can easily be applied when students use other operating systems, including Macintosh systems or even future versions of Windows. You may want to use this tutorial when students learn about file management in Chapter 2.

- **TechSIM B: E-mail** Students can also learn how to use Microsoft Outlook to send e-mail without having Outlook software installed on their machines. You may want to use this tutorial when students learn about e-mail in Chapter 3.

- **TechSIM C: System Settings and the Control Panel** Students can learn how to change settings in the Control Panel tutorials without actually changing any settings on their own computers. You may want to use this tutorial when students learn about system settings in Chapter 2.

INSTALLATION INSRUCTIONS

TechSIM™ Interactive Tutorials can be used on a PC or a Mac. The interactive tutorials can be accessed directly from the *Introduction to Web Design Using Dreamweaver* Online Learning Center at **WebDesignDW.glencoe.com** or they can be installed from the TechSIM™ Interactive Tutorials CD (available separately). (Note: If you install the tutorials from the CD, Internet access is *not* required.)

In order to view and run the TechSIM™ Interactive Tutorials (online or once installed from CD), you will need to have the **Macromedia Flash Player** installed on each computer using the tutorials. The Flash Player is available at no charge from the Macromedia Web site at **www.macromedia.com**.

SOFTWARE SUPPORT

For specific information about how to install the tutorials from the CD-ROM, refer to the instructions provided with the CD. If you have lost your CD or it is not working properly, contact Glencoe Software Support Center at Glencoe/McGraw-Hill between 8:30 A.M. and 6:00 P.M. Eastern Time. The toll-free number is **1-800-437-3715**. Customers with specific questions can also contact us at the following e-mail address: **epgtech@mcgraw-hill.com**.

PART 5

Complete Correlations to Standards

ISTE NETS-S Correlations **492**
    National Technology Standards for Students 492
    NETS-S Correlations to Textbook 493

SCANS Correlations **505**
    SCANS Competencies for Students................. 505
    SCANS Correlations to Textbook................... 506

NETS-S CORRELATIONS

Every chapter in the student textbook has been correlated to ISTE's NETS-S standards and performance indicators for students. Chapter correlations appear in each Chapter Answer Key in Part 2 of this manual and on the Online Learning Center at **www.WebDesignDW.glencoe.com**. For your convenience, the following pages provide comprehensive correlation charts so you can quickly see where each performance indicator and standard is met throughout the textbook.

NATIONAL TECHNOLOGY STANDARDS FOR STUDENTS

The NETS-S are divided into six broad categories:

1. Basic operations and concepts
2. Social, ethical, and human issues
3. Technology productivity tools
4. Technology communications tools
5. Technology research tools
6. Technology problem-solving and decision-making tools

Each of the six categories listed above is aligned to the performance indicators. Textbook correlations for all of the performance indicators are supplied on the following pages. The related NETS-S standard is given in parentheses after the performance indicator. For a full list of the NETS-S and performance indicators, see pages 6–9 in Part 1 of this Manual. To find out more about ISTE and the NETS-S, please visit **www.iste.org**.

NETS CORRELATIONS

NETS Performance Indicator
1. Identify capabilities and limitations of contemporary and emerging technology resources and assess the potential of these systems and services to address personal, lifelong learning, and workplace needs. (NETS 2)

Textbook Correlation	
Chapter 1	Critical Thinking (10, 14, 19, 26, 28), Go Online (18), Standards at Work (30), Web Design Projects (33)
Chapter 2	Critical Thinking (42, 46, 58), Go Online (39, 43), Apply It! (46), Making Connections (60), Standards at Work (60), Challenge Yourself (61)
Chapter 3	Critical Thinking (70, 88, 90, 91), Tech Check (83), Teamwork Skills (93), Web Design Projects (95)
Chapter 4	Critical Thinking (101, 108, 114, 122, 125), Building 21st Century Skills (130)
Chapter 5	Critical Thinking (139, 145, 154)
Chapter 6	Critical Thinking (165, 170, 176, 182, 184), Tech Check (166)
Chapter 7	Critical Thinking (201, 209, 212, 213)
Chapter 8	Critical Thinking (227, 235, 242, 244, 245), Tech Check (236), Making Connections (246), Challenge Yourself (247)
Chapter 9	Critical Thinking (256, 264, 268, 270), Apply It! (264, 268), Challenge Yourself (273)
Chapter 10	Critical Thinking (288, 291, 298, 300, 301), Apply It! (281, 291, 298), Tech Check (282)
Chapter 11	Apply It! (319), Go Online (321), Critical Thinking (326), Challenge Yourself (331)
Chapter 12	Critical Thinking (346, 352, 356), Apply It! (353), Making Connections (360), Standards at Work (360), Challenge Yourself (361)
Chapter 13	Critical Thinking (369, 374, 379, 384, 386, 387), Apply It! (369, 374, 384), Tech Check (370), Challenge Yourself (389)
Chapter 14	Critical Thinking (397, 403, 409, 414, 416, 417), Apply It! (397), Tech Check (404), Challenge Yourself (419)
Chapter 15	Critical Thinking (427, 432, 436, 438, 439), Apply It! (427, 436), Tech Check (428), Making Connections (440), Challenge Yourself (441), Web Design Projects (443)
Chapter 16	Critical Thinking (454, 461, 466, 468, 469), Tech Check (455), Challenge Yourself (471)
Chapter 17	Critical Thinking (481, 486, 488, 489), Apply It! (481, 486)

NETS CORRELATIONS

NETS Performance Indicator
2. Make informed choices among technology systems, resources, and services. (NETS 1, 2)
Textbook Correlation

Chapter 1	Quick Write Activity (4), Critical Thinking (1), Web Design Projects (33)
Chapter 2	Apply It! (42), Critical Thinking (42, 46, 58, 59), Standardized Test Practice (59), Standards at Work (60)
Chapter 3	Apply It! (70), Tech Check (83), What Did You Learn? (88), Critical Thinking (91), Teamwork Skills (93), Web Design Projects (95)
Chapter 4	Critical Thinking (125), Building 21st Century Skills (130), Building Your Portfolio (131)
Chapter 5	Critical Thinking (145, 151, 154), Apply It! (151)
Chapter 6	Critical Thinking (165, 170, 176, 182, 184, 185), You Try It (170), Apply It! (170), Teamwork Skills (187)
Chapter 7	You Try It (193, 194, 195, 196, 199, 208), Critical Thinking (182, 201, 209, 213), Apply It! (209)
Chapter 8	You Try It (230, 233, 234, 238, 240), Critical Thinking (227, 235, 242, 244, 245), Apply It! (227, 235, 242), Making Connections (246), Teamwork Skills (247), Skills Studio (248), Web Design Projects (249)
Chapter 9	Critical Thinking (256, 264, 268, 270, 271), Apply It! (256, 264, 268), You Try It (260, 262, 266, 267), Making Connections (272), Standards at Work (272), Teamwork Skills (273), Skills Studio (274), Web Design Projects (275)
Chapter 10	Critical Thinking (281, 291, 298, 300, 301), Tech Check (282), You Try It (284, 285, 286, 288, 293, 297), Apply It! (291, 298), Standards at Work (302), Teamwork Skills (303), Skills Studio (304), Web Design Projects (305), Building 21st Century Skills (306), Building Your Portfolio (307)
Chapter 11	You Try It (325), Critical Thinking (319, 328, 329), Challenge Yourself (331), Skills Studio (332), Web Design Projects (333)
Chapter 12	Critical Thinking (346, 352, 356), Apply It! (353), Standards at Work (360), Teamwork Skills (361), Challenge Yourself (361)
Chapter 13	Critical Thinking (369, 374, 379, 384, 386, 387), Apply It! (369, 374, 379, 384), Tech Check (370), Challenge Yourself (389)
Chapter 14	You Try It (396, 411, 412), Critical Thinking (397, 403, 414), Apply It! (403, 414), Tech Check (404), Teamwork Skills (419), Challenge Yourself (419), Skills Studio (420), Web Design Projects (421)
Chapter 15	Critical Thinking (427, 432, 436, 438, 439), Apply It! (427, 432, 436), Making Connections (440), Teamwork Skills (441), Web Design Projects (443), Building 21st Century Skills (444), Building Your Portfolio (445)

NETS CORRELATIONS

NETS Performance Indicator (cont'd)
2. Make informed choices among technology systems, resources, and services. (NETS 1, 2)

Textbook Correlation	
Chapter 16	Critical Thinking (454, 461, 466), Apply It! (454, 461), Making Connections (470), Standards at Work (470), Teamwork Skills (471), Challenge Yourself (471), Web Design Projects (473)
Chapter 17	Critical Thinking (481, 486, 488, 489), Apply It! (481, 486), Making Connections (490), Standards at Work (490), Teamwork Skills (491), Building 21st Century Skills (494), Building Your Portfolio (495)

NETS Performance Indicator
3. Analyze advantages and disadvantages of widespread use and reliance on technology in the workplace and in society as a whole. (NETS 2)

Textbook Correlation	
Chapter 1	Quick Write Activity (4)
Chapter 2	Quick Write Activity (34)
Chapter 3	Tech Check (83), Critical Thinking (88), Web Design Projects (95)
Chapter 4	Tech Check (115), Making Connections (126)
Chapter 5	Tech Check (152)
Chapter 6	Quick Write Activity (160), Tech Check (166), Critical Thinking (184)
Chapter 7	Quick Write Activity (190)
Chapter 8	Tech Check (236)
Chapter 9	Critical Thinking (271)
Chapter 10	Tech Check (282)
Chapter 11	Go Online (321), Critical Thinking (326)

Part 5   Complete Correlations to Standards

NETS Performance Indicator (cont'd)

3. Analyze advantages and disadvantages of widespread use and reliance on technology in the workplace and in society as a whole. (NETS 2)

Textbook Correlation

Chapter 12	Go Online (349, 351), Critical Thinking (352)
Chapter 13	Plan Ahead (381)
Chapter 14	Tech Check (404), Making Connections (418)
Chapter 15	Tech Check (428), What Did You Learn? (436), Challenge Yourself (441)
Chapter 16	Tech Check (455)
Chapter 17	Quick Write Activity (474)

NETS Performance Indicator

4. Demonstrate and advocate for legal and ethical behaviors among peers, family, and community regarding the use of technology and information. (NETS 2)

Textbook Correlation

Chapter 1	Critical Thinking (10)
Chapter 2	Challenge Yourself (61)
Chapter 3	Quick Write Activity (64), Tech Check (83), Go Online (84), Apply It! (88), Critical Thinking (88, 90), Standards at Work (92)
Chapter 4	Building Your Portfolio (131)
Chapter 5	
Chapter 6	Quick Tip (174)
Chapter 7	Tech Check (210)

NETS Performance Indicator (cont'd)

4. Demonstrate and advocate for legal and ethical behaviors among peers, family, and community regarding the use of technology and information. (NETS 2)

Textbook Correlation

Chapter 8	Quick Tip (229), Standards at Work (246)
Chapter 9	Apply It! (256), Critical Thinking (264), Teamwork Skills (273), Web Design Projects (275)
Chapter 10	Tech Check (282)
Chapter 11	Standards at Work (330)
Chapter 12	Go Online (349, 351), You Try It (349), Critical Thinking (352), Challenge Yourself (361), Skills Studio (362)
Chapter 13	Critical Thinking (369)
Chapter 14	Making Connections (418)
Chapter 15	Tech Check (428), Go Online (435), Section Assessment (436), Challenge Yourself (441), Web Design Projects (443)
Chapter 16	Plan Ahead (459), Critical Thinking (469)
Chapter 17	Building 21st Century Skills #2 (494)

NETS Performance Indicator

5. Use technology tools and resources for managing and communicating personal/professional information (e.g. finances, schedules, addresses, purchases, correspondence). (NETS 3, 4)

Textbook Correlation

Chapter 1	Tech Check (20), Web Design Projects (33)
Chapter 2	You Try It (49, 51, 52, 55), Critical Thinking (59), Web Design Projects (63)
Chapter 3	Apply It! (70), You Try It (86), Teamwork Skills (93)

NETS Performance Indicator (cont'd)

5. Use technology tools and resources for managing and communicating personal/professional information (e.g. finances, schedules, addresses, purchases, correspondence). (NETS 3, 4)

Textbook Correlation

Chapter 4	Teamwork Skills (127), Building 21st Century Skills (130)
Chapter 5	Quick Write Activity (134), Tech Check (152)
Chapter 6	Tech Check (166), Standards at Work (186), Challenge Yourself (187), Skills Studio (188), Web Design Projects (189)
Chapter 7	Web Design Projects (217)
Chapter 8	
Chapter 9	Making Connections (272), Standards at Work (272), Web Design Projects (275)
Chapter 10	Skills Studio (304), Web Design Projects (305), Building 21st Century Skills (306)
Chapter 11	You Try It (317, 325), Web Design Projects (333)
Chapter 12	You Try It (343), Apply It! (346, 353), Skills Studio (362)
Chapter 13	You Try It (373, 377, 382), Making Connections (388), Skills Studio (390), Web Design Projects (391)
Chapter 14	Apply It! (397)
Chapter 15	Standards at Work (440), Building Your Portfolio (445)
Chapter 16	Web Design Projects (473)
Chapter 17	Tech Check (482), Skills Studio (492), Web Design Projects (493)

NETS Performance Indicator

6. Evaluate technology-based options, including distance and distributed education, for lifelong learning. (NETS 5)

	Textbook Correlation
Chapter 1	Go Online (10, 18), Critical Thinking (10), Web Design Projects (33)
Chapter 2	Go Online (39, 43)
Chapter 3	Go Online (66, 84), Web Design Projects (95)
Chapter 4	Tech Check (115), Building 21st Century Skills (130)
Chapter 5	Go Online (140, 146)
Chapter 6	Quick Write Activity (160), Go Online (164, 167), Tech Focus (166)
Chapter 7	Go Online (192, 198)
Chapter 8	Go Online (228, 239), Tech Check (236)
Chapter 9	Go Online (254, 261)
Chapter 10	Go Online (278, 292), Tech Check (282), Building Your Portfolio (307)
Chapter 11	Go Online (313, 321)
Chapter 12	Go Online (349, 351)
Chapter 13	Go Online (367, 372), Web Design Projects (391)
Chapter 14	Go Online (396, 401)
Chapter 15	Go Online (424, 435), You Try It (427)
Chapter 16	Go Online (452, 460), Tech Check (455)
Chapter 17	Go Online (477, 483)

NETS CORRELATIONS

NETS Performance Indicator	
7. Routinely and efficiently use online information resources to meet needs for collaboration, research, publications, communications, and productivity. (NETS 4, 5, 6)	
Textbook Correlation	
Chapter 1	Go Online (10, 18), Tech Check (20), Challenge Yourself (31), Skills Studio (32), Web Design Projects (33)
Chapter 2	Go Online (39, 43), Apply It! (46), Making Connections (60), Standards at Work (60), Teamwork Skills (61)
Chapter 3	Go Online (66, 84), Tech Check (83), You Try It (76, 81), Apply It! (77, 88), Making Connections (92), Standards at Work (92), Skills Studio (94), Web Design Projects (95)
Chapter 4	Go Online (100, 111), Building 21st Century Skills (130), Building Your Portfolio (131)
Chapter 5	Go Online (140, 146), Tech Check (152), Standards at Work (156), Web Design Projects (159)
Chapter 6	Go Online (164, 167)
Chapter 7	Go Online (192, 198), Teamwork Skills (215), Building 21st Century Skills (218)
Chapter 8	Tech Check (236), Go Online (228, 239), Standards at Work (246), Web Design Projects (249)
Chapter 9	Go Online (254, 261), Apply It! (256, 264, 268), Teamwork Skills (273), Challenge Yourself (273), Skills Studio (274), Web Design Projects (275)
Chapter 10	Go Online (278, 292), Apply It! (291), Tech Check (282), Challenge Yourself (303), Building Your Portfolio (307)
Chapter 11	Go Online (313, 321), Apply It! (319, 326), Making Connections (330), Challenge Yourself (331), Skills Studio (332)
Chapter 12	Go Online (349, 351), Apply It! (352), Tech Check (347), Standards at Work (360), Teamwork Skills (361)
Chapter 13	Go Online (367, 372), Apply It! (369, 374), Critical Thinking (374), You Try It (377, 382), Standards at Work (388), Teamwork Skills (389), Challenge Yourself (389), Web Design Projects (391)
Chapter 14	Go Online (396, 401), Apply It! (397), Tech Check (404), You Try It (401), Making Connections (418), Challenge Yourself (419), Skills Studio (420)
Chapter 15	Go Online (424, 435), You Try It (427), Apply It! (427, 432, 436), Tech Check (428), Teamwork Skills (441)
Chapter 16	Go Online (452, 460), Tech Check (455), Making Connections (470)
Chapter 17	Go Online (477, 483), Apply It! (481, 486), Tech Check (482), Standards at Work (490), Challenge Yourself (491)

NETS Performance Indicator

8. Select and apply technology tools for research, information analysis, problem-solving, and decision-making in content learning. (NETS 4, 5)

Textbook Correlation

Chapter 1	Go Online (10, 18), Tech Check (20), Standards at Work (30), Web Design Projects (33)
Chapter 2	Apply It! (42), Making Connections (60), Standards at Work (60), Web Design Projects (63)
Chapter 3	Tech Check (83), Apply It! (77), Standards at Work (92), Challenge Yourself (93), Web Design Projects (95)
Chapter 4	You Try It (102, 104, 106, 107, 108, 110, 112, 113, 117, 118, 120, 122), Apply It! (108, 114, 122), Skills Studio (128), Building 21st Century Skills (130), Building Your Portfolio (131)
Chapter 5	Go Online (140, 146), You Try It (143), Tech Check (152), Standards at Work (156)
Chapter 6	Go Online (164, 167), Apply It! (176), Standards at Work (186), Challenge Yourself (187), Skills Studio (188), Web Design Projects (189)
Chapter 7	Go Online (192, 198), Making Connections (214), Standards at Work (214), Teamwork Skills (215), Challenge Yourself (215), Skills Studio (216), Web Design Projects (217), Building 21st Century Skills (218), Building Your Portfolio (219)
Chapter 8	Go Online (228, 239), Tech Check (236), Apply It! (235), Making Connections (246), Teamwork Skills (247), Challenge Yourself (247), Web Design Projects (249)
Chapter 9	Go Online (254, 261), Standards at Work (272), Teamwork Skills (273), Skills Studio (274), Web Design Projects (275)
Chapter 10	Go Online (278, 292), Apply It! (291, 298), Tech Check (282), Web Design Projects (305), Building 21st Century Skills (306), Building Your Portfolio (307)
Chapter 11	Go Online (313, 321), You Try It (325), Making Connections (330), Challenge Yourself (331), Skills Studio (332)
Chapter 12	You Try It (337, 349), Apply It! (346, 352), Tech Check (347), Teamwork Skills (361), Challenge Yourself (361), Skills Studio (362), Web Design Projects (363)
Chapter 13	Apply It! (369, 374), Critical Thinking (374), Teamwork Skills (389), Challenge Yourself (389), Web Design Projects (391)
Chapter 14	Go Online (396, 401), You Try It (396, 411, 412), Apply It! (397), Tech Check (404), Making Connections (418), Standards at Work (418), Challenge Yourself (419), Skills Studio (420), Web Design Projects (421)
Chapter 15	You Try It (427, 430, 434), Apply It! (427, 436), Tech Check (428), Standards at Work (440), Teamwork Skills (441), Skills Studio (442), Web Design Projects (443), Building 21st Century Skills (444)

NETS CORRELATIONS

NETS Performance Indicator (cont'd)	
8. Select and apply technology tools for research, information analysis, problem-solving, and decision-making in content learning. (NETS 4, 5)	
Textbook Correlation	
Chapter 16	Go Online (452, 460), Tech Check (455), Making Connections (470), Standards at Work (470)
Chapter 17	Go Online (477, 483), Apply It! (481, 486), Tech Check (482), Standards at Work (490), Challenge Yourself (491)

NETS Performance Indicator	
9. Investigate and apply expert systems, intelligent agents, and simulations in real-world situations. (NETS 3, 5, 6)	
Textbook Correlation	
Chapter 1	You Try It (13, 23, 25), Tech Focus (20), Skills Studio (32), Web Design Projects (33)
Chapter 2	Skills Studio (62), Web Design Projects (63)
Chapter 3	You Try It (74), Apply It! (77), Skills Studio (94), Web Design Projects (95)
Chapter 4	Quick Write Activity (96), Skills Studio (128), Web Design Projects (129)
Chapter 5	You Try It (139, 147), Apply It! (145), Challenge Yourself (157), Web Design Projects (159)
Chapter 6	You Try It (172, 174, 175, 178, 179, 180, 181), Web Design Projects (189)
Chapter 7	You Try It (193, 195, 196, 199, 208), Skills Studio (216), Web Design Projects (217), Building 21st Century Skills (218), Building Your Portfolio (219)
Chapter 8	You Try It (230, 233, 234, 238, 240), Apply It! (235), Web Design Projects (249)
Chapter 9	You Try It (260, 262, 266, 267), Web Design Projects (275)
Chapter 10	You Try It (293, 297), Standards at Work (302), Skills Studio (304), Web Design Projects (305), Building 21st Century Skills (306), Building Your Portfolio (307)
Chapter 11	You Try It (325), Challenge Yourself (331), Skills Studio (332), Web Design Projects (333)

NETS Performance Indicator (cont'd)

9. Investigate and apply expert systems, intelligent agents, and simulations in real-world situations. (NETS 3, 5, 6)

Textbook Correlation

Chapter 12	You Try It (337, 343, 344, 345), Challenge Yourself (361), Skills Studio (362), Web Design Projects (363)
Chapter 13	You Try It (373, 377, 382)
Chapter 14	Apply It! (403, 414), Skills Studio (420), Web Design Projects (421)
Chapter 15	You Try It (427, 430, 434), Applying Skills (436), Web Design Projects (443)
Chapter 16	Making Connections (470), Skills Studio (472), Web Design Projects (473)
Chapter 17	You Try It (476, 477, 478, 479, 480, 484), Tech Check (482), Apply It! (486), Web Design Projects #1 (493)

NETS Performance Indicator

10. Collaborate with peers, experts, and others to contribute to content-related knowledge base by using technology to compile, synthesize, produce, and disseminate information, models, and other creative works. (NETS 4, 5, 6)

Textbook Correlation

Chapter 1	Tech Check (20)
Chapter 2	Tech Check (47), Teamwork Skills (61), Web Design Projects (63)
Chapter 3	Teamwork Skills (93)
Chapter 4	Teamwork Skills (127), Building 21st Century Skills (130)
Chapter 5	Teamwork Skills (157)
Chapter 6	Standards at Work (186), Teamwork Skills (187)
Chapter 7	Teamwork Skills (215), Building 21st Century Skills (218), Building Your Portfolio (219)

NETS CORRELATIONS

NETS Performance Indicator (cont'd)
10. Collaborate with peers, experts, and others to contribute to content-related knowledge base by using technology to compile, synthesize, produce, and disseminate information, models, and other creative works. (NETS 4, 5, 6)

Textbook Correlation	
Chapter 8	Teamwork Skills (247)
Chapter 9	Teamwork Skills (273)
Chapter 10	Teamwork Skills (303), Building Your Portfolio (307)
Chapter 11	Tech Check (320), Skills Studio (332)
Chapter 12	Making Connections (360)
Chapter 13	Tech Check (370), Teamwork Skills (389)
Chapter 14	Making Connections (418), Teamwork Skills (419)
Chapter 15	Tech Check (428), Teamwork Skills (441), Challenge Yourself (441), Building Your Portfolio (445)
Chapter 16	Tech Check (470), Teamwork Skills (471)
Chapter 17	Tech Check (482), Standards at Work (490), Teamwork Skills (491), Building Your Portfolio (495)

SCANS CORRELATIONS

Every chapter in the student textbook has also been correlated to SCANS (Secretary's Commission on Achieving Necessary Skills). Correlations for each chapter appear in the Chapter Answer Keys in Part 2 of this manual and on the Online Learning Center at **www.WebDesignDW.glencoe.com**. For your convenience, the following pages provide comprehensive correlation charts so you can see where each performance indicator and standard is met throughout the textbook.

SCANS COMPETENCIES FOR STUDENTS

SCANS are divided into Foundation Skills (Basic Skills, Thinking Skills, and Personal Qualities) and Workplace Competencies:

Foundation Skills: Basic Skills

- Reading
- Writing
- Mathematics
- Listening and Speaking Skills

Foundation Skills: Thinking Skills

- Creative Thinking
- Critical Thinking
- Problem-Solving Skills

Foundation Skills: Personal Qualities

- Responsibility
- Self-Esteem
- Sociability
- Self-Management
- Integrity
- Honesty

Workplace Competencies

- Resources
- Interpersonal Skills
- Information
- Systems
- Technology

For a full list of the SCANS competencies, see pages 4–5 in Part 1 of this manual. To find out more about SCANS, please visit **http://wdr.doleta.gov/SCANS/**.

SCANS CORRELATIONS

SCANS Foundation Skills
Basic Skills: Reading

Textbook Correlation	
Chapter 1	Before You Read (5), Focus on Reading (6, 11, 15, 21), Reading Strategies (6, 11, 15, 21), After You Read (28), Standardized Test Practice (29)
Chapter 2	Before You Read (35), Focus on Reading (36, 43, 48), Reading Strategies (36, 43, 48), After You Read (58)
Chapter 3	Before You Read (65), Focus on Reading (66, 71, 78, 84), Reading Strategies (66, 71, 78, 84), After You Read (90), Standardized Test Practice (91)
Chapter 4	Before You Read (97), Focus on Reading (98, 102, 109, 116), Reading Strategies (98, 102, 109, 116), After You Read (124)
Chapter 5	Before You Read (135), Focus on Reading (136, 140, 146), Reading Strategies (136, 140, 146), After You Read (154), Standardized Test Practice (155)
Chapter 6	Before You Read (161), Focus on Reading (162, 167, 171, 177), Reading Strategies (162, 167, 171, 177), After You Read (184), Teamwork Skills (187)
Chapter 7	Before You Read (191), Focus on Reading (192, 198, 202), Reading Strategies (192, 198, 202), After You Read (212), Standardized Test Practice (213)
Chapter 8	Before You Read (223), Focus on Reading (224, 228, 237), Reading Strategies (224, 228, 237), After You Read (244)
Chapter 9	Before You Read (251), Focus on Reading (252, 258, 265), Reading Strategies (252, 258, 265), After You Read (270), Making Connections (272)
Chapter 10	Before You Read (277), Focus on Reading (278, 283, 291), Reading Strategies (278, 283, 291), After You Read (300)
Chapter 11	Before You Read (311), Focus on Reading (312, 321), Reading Strategies (312, 321), After You Read (328)
Chapter 12	Before You Read (335), Focus on Reading (336, 342, 348, 353), Reading Strategies (336, 342, 348, 353), After You Read (358)
Chapter 13	Before You Read (365), Focus on Reading (366, 371, 375, 380), Reading Strategies (366, 371, 375, 380), After You Read (386), Standardized Test Practice (387)
Chapter 14	Before You Read (393), Focus on Reading (394, 398, 405, 410), Reading Strategies (394, 398, 405, 410), After You Read (416)
Chapter 15	Before You Read (423), Focus on Reading (424, 429, 433), Reading Strategies (424, 429, 433), After You Read (438), Standardized Test Practice (439)
Chapter 16	Before You Read (449), Focus on Reading (450, 456, 462), Reading Strategies (450, 456, 462), After You Read (468)
Chapter 17	Before You Read (475), Focus on Reading (476, 483), Reading Strategies (476, 483), After You Read (488), Standardized Test Practice (489)

SCANS Foundation Skills

Basic Skills: Writing	
Textbook Correlation	
Chapter 1	Quick Write Activity (4), Section Assessments (10, 14, 19, 26), Tech Check (20), Chapter Review (28–33)
Chapter 2	Quick Write Activity (34), Section Assessments (42, 46, 56), Making Connections (60), Chapter Review (58-63)
Chapter 3	Quick Write Activity (64), Section Assessments (70, 77, 82, 88), Chapter Review (90–95)
Chapter 4	Quick Write Activity (96), Section Assessments (101, 108, 114, 122), Chapter Review (124–129)
Chapter 5	Quick Write Activity (134), You Try It (139), Section Assessments (139, 145, 151), Tech Check (152), Chapter Review (154–159)
Chapter 6	Quick Write Activity (160), Section Assessments (165, 170, 176, 182), You Try It (165), Tech Check (166), Making Connections (186), Chapter Review (184–189)
Chapter 7	Quick Write Activity (190), Section Assessments (197, 201, 209), Teamwork Skills (215), Chapter Review (212–217), Building 21st Century Skills (218), Building Your Portfolio (219)
Chapter 8	Quick Write Activity (222), Section Assessments (227, 235, 242), Chapter Review (244–249)
Chapter 9	Quick Write Activity (250), Section Assessments (256, 264, 268), Tech Check (257), Chapter Review (270–275)
Chapter 10	Quick Write Activity (276), Section Assessments (300–305), Building 21st Century Skills (306), Building Your Portfolio (307)
Chapter 11	Quick Write Activity (310), Section Assessments (319, 326), Chapter Review (327–333)
Chapter 12	Quick Write Activity (334), Section Assessments (341, 346, 352, 356), Tech Check (347), Standards at Work (360), Chapter Review (358–363)
Chapter 13	Quick Write Activity (364), Section Assessments (369, 374, 379, 384), Tech Check (370), Challenge Yourself (389), Chapter Review (386–391)
Chapter 14	Quick Write Activity (392), Section Assessments (397, 403, 409, 414), Chapter Review (416–421)
Chapter 15	Quick Write Activity (422), Section Assessments (427, 430, 434), Tech Check (428), Challenge Yourself (441), Chapter Review (437–443), Building 21st Century Skills (414), Building Your Portfolio (445)
Chapter 16	Think About It (447), Quick Write Activity (448), Section Assessments (454, 461, 466), Chapter Review (468–473)
Chapter 17	Quick Write Activity (474), Section Assessments (481, 486), Tech Check (482), Chapter Review (487–493), Building 21st Century Skills (494), Building Your Portfolio (495)

SCANS CORRELATIONS

SCANS Foundation Skills		
Basic Skills: Mathematics		
Textbook Correlation		
Chapter 1	Making Connections (30)	
Chapter 2	Apply It! (42), Standardized Test Practice (59)	
Chapter 3	Teamwork Skills (93), Web Design Projects (95)	
Chapter 4	Building 21st Century Skills #1 (130)	
Chapter 5	Apply It! (145), Challenge Yourself (157)	
Chapter 6	Tech Check (166), Standardized Test Practice (185)	
Chapter 7		
Chapter 8	Apply It! (227), Critical Thinking (245), Making Connections (246), Challenge Yourself (247)	
Chapter 9	What Did You Learn? (264), Web Design Projects (275)	
Chapter 10	Standardized Test Practice (301)	
Chapter 11	Making Connections (330), Challenge Yourself (331)	
Chapter 12		
Chapter 13	Critical Thinking (386), Web Design Projects (391)	
Chapter 14	You Try It (396), Challenge Yourself (419), Skills Studio (420)	
Chapter 15	Apply It! (427)	
Chapter 16	Challenge Yourself (471)	
Chapter 17		

508 Teacher Resource Manual *Introduction to Web Design Using Dreamweaver*

SCANS Foundation Skills

Basic Skills: Listening and Speaking

Textbook Correlation

Chapter 1	Tech Check (20)
Chapter 2	Tech Check (47), After You Read (58), Challenge Yourself (61), Web Design Projects (63)
Chapter 3	Teamwork Skills (93), Web Design Projects (95)
Chapter 4	Teamwork Skills (127)
Chapter 5	Teamwork Skills (157)
Chapter 6	Tech Check (166), Teamwork Skills (187)
Chapter 7	Teamwork Skills (215), Building 21st Century Skills (218), Building Your Portfolio (219)
Chapter 8	Teamwork Skills (247)
Chapter 9	Before You Read to Succeed (251), Tech Check (257), After You Read (270), Making Connections (272), Teamwork Skills (273), Web Design Projects (275)
Chapter 10	Teamwork Skills (303)
Chapter 11	Tech Check (320), Skills Studio (332)
Chapter 12	Making Connections (360), Teamwork Skills (361)
Chapter 13	Tech Check (370), Teamwork Skills (389)
Chapter 14	Making Connections (418), Teamwork Skills (419)
Chapter 15	Tech Check (428), Making Connections (440), Teamwork Skills (441), Challenge Yourself (441)
Chapter 16	Tech Check (455), Teamwork Skills (471)
Chapter 17	Standards at Work (490), Teamwork Skills (491)

SCANS CORRELATIONS

SCANS Foundation Skills	
Thinking Skills: Creative Thinking	
Textbook Correlation	
Chapter 1	Think About It (3), Quick Write Activity (4)
Chapter 2	Quick Write Activity (34)
Chapter 3	Quick Write Activity (64)
Chapter 4	Quick Write Activity (96), Building Your Portfolio (131)
Chapter 5	Think About It (133), Quick Write Activity (134)
Chapter 6	Quick Write Activity (160), Making Connections (186), Web Design Projects (189)
Chapter 7	Quick Write Activity (190), Teamwork Skills (215), Challenge Yourself (215), Web Design Projects (217), Building 21st Century Skills (218), Building Your Portfolio (219)
Chapter 8	Think About It (221), Quick Write Activity (222), Teamwork Skills (247), Web Design Projects (249)
Chapter 9	Quick Write Activity (250), Making Connections (272), Standards at Work (272), Teamwork Skills (273), Web Design Projects (275)
Chapter 10	Quick Write Activity (276), Standards at Work (302), Teamwork Skills (303), Web Design Projects (305), Building 21st Century Skills (306), Building Your Portfolio (307)
Chapter 11	Think About It (309), Quick Write Activity (310)
Chapter 12	Quick Write Activity (334)
Chapter 13	Quick Write Activity (364), Standards at Work (388), Web Design Projects (391)
Chapter 14	Quick Write Activity (392), Teamwork Skills (419), Web Design Projects (421)
Chapter 15	Quick Write Activity (422), Making Connections (440), Building 21st Century Skills (444)
Chapter 16	Think About It (447), Quick Write Activity (448), Making Connections (470), Web Design Projects (473)
Chapter 17	Quick Write Activity (474), Making Connections (490), Standards at Work (490), Teamwork Skills (491), Challenge Yourself (491), Web Design Projects (493), Building 21st Century Skills (494)

SCANS Foundation Skills

Thinking Skills: Critical Thinking

Textbook Correlation

Chapter 1	Think About It (3), Critical Thinking Activities (10, 14, 19, 26), Tech Check (20), Web Design Projects (33)
Chapter 2	Critical Thinking (42, 46, 56, 58, 59), Tech Check (47), Standards at Work (60), Challenge Yourself (61), Web Design Projects (63)
Chapter 3	Critical Thinking (70, 77, 82, 88, 90, 91), Tech Check (83), Teamwork Skills (93), Web Design Projects (95)
Chapter 4	Critical Thinking (101, 108, 114, 122), Making Connections (127), Teamwork Skills (127), Building 21st Century Skills (130)
Chapter 5	Critical Thinking Activities (139, 145, 151), Standards at Work (156), Teamwork Skills (157), Challenge Yourself (157), Web Design Projects (159)
Chapter 6	Critical Thinking Activities (165, 170, 176, 182), Tech Check (166), Standards at Work (186), Teamwork Skills (187), Web Design Projects (189)
Chapter 7	Critical Thinking Activities (197, 201, 209, 212, 213), Tech Check (210), Making Connections (214)
Chapter 8	Think About It (221), Critical Thinking (227, 235, 242, 244, 245), Tech Check (236), Making Connections (246), Challenge Yourself (247)
Chapter 9	Critical Thinking (256, 264, 268, 270, 271), Tech Check (257), Challenge Yourself (273)
Chapter 10	Critical Thinking (281, 291, 298, 300, 301), Tech Check (282), Challenge Yourself (303)
Chapter 11	Critical Thinking (319, 326, 328, 329), Tech Check (320), Standards at Work (330), Teamwork Skills (331), Challenge Yourself (331), Web Design Projects (333)
Chapter 12	Critical Thinking (341, 346, 352, 356, 358, 359), Tech Check (347), Making Connections (360), Teamwork Skills (361), Challenge Yourself (361), Web Design Projects (363)
Chapter 13	Critical Thinking (369, 374, 379, 384, 386, 387), Tech Check (370), Making Connections (388), Teamwork Skills (389), Challenge Yourself (389), Web Design Projects (391)
Chapter 14	Critical Thinking (397, 403, 409, 414, 416, 417), Tech Check (404), Making Connections (418), Standards at Work (418), Teamwork Skills (419), Challenge Yourself (419), Web Design Projects (421)
Chapter 15	Critical Thinking (427, 432, 436, 438, 439), Tech Check (428), Standards at Work (440), Teamwork Skills (441), Challenge Yourself (441), Web Design Projects (443), Building 21st Century Skills (444), Building Your Portfolio (445)
Chapter 16	Critical Thinking (454, 461, 466, 468, 469), Tech Check (455), Standards at Work (470), Teamwork Skills (471), Challenge Yourself (471), Web Design Projects (473)
Chapter 17	Critical Thinking (481, 486, 488, 489), Tech Check (482), Making Connections (490), Standards at Work (490), Teamwork Skills (491), Web Design Projects (493), Building 21st Century Skills (494), Building Your Portfolio (495)

SCANS CORRELATIONS

	SCANS Foundation Skills
	Thinking Skills: Problem Solving
	Textbook Correlation
Chapter 1	Making Connections (30), Teamwork Skills (31)
Chapter 2	Apply It! (42), Tech Check (47), Standards at Work (60), Web Design Projects (63)
Chapter 3	Challenge Yourself (93), Web Design Projects (95)
Chapter 4	Apply It! (101, 108, 114, 122), Skills Studio (128), Web Design Projects (129–131)
Chapter 5	Teamwork Skills (157), Challenge Yourself (157), Skills Studio (158), Web Design Projects (159)
Chapter 6	Apply It! (165), Teamwork Skills (187)
Chapter 7	Web Design Projects (217)
Chapter 8	Standards at Work (246), Web Design Projects (249)
Chapter 9	Apply It! (256), Teamwork Skills (273), Web Design Projects (275)
Chapter 10	Standards at Work (302), Skills Studio (304), Web Design Projects (305)
Chapter 11	Tech Check (320), You Try It (325), Skills Studio (332), Web Design Projects (333)
Chapter 12	Critical Thinking (358, 359)
Chapter 13	Apply It! (379), Critical Thinking (386, 387), Teamwork Skills (389), Web Design Projects (391)
Chapter 14	Apply It! (403, 414), Challenge Yourself (419)
Chapter 15	Standards at Work (440), Web Design Projects (443), Building 21st Century Skills (444)
Chapter 16	Standards at Work (470), Challenge Yourself (471)
Chapter 17	Standards at Work (490), Building 21st Century Skills (494)

SCANS Workplace Competencies

Resources: Manage time, money, materials, facilities, human resources

Textbook Correlation

Chapter	
Chapter 1	Command Center (29)
Chapter 2	Apply It! (42), Command Center (59), Standards at Work (60)
Chapter 3	Tech Check (83), Command Center (91), Web Design Projects (95)
Chapter 4	Command Center (125), Building 21st Century Skills (130)
Chapter 5	Quick Write Activity (134), Tech Check (152), Command Center (155)
Chapter 6	Tech Check (166), Command Center (185)
Chapter 7	Command Center (213), Web Design Projects (217)
Chapter 8	Command Center (245)
Chapter 9	Tech Check (257), Command Center (271), Standards at Work (272)
Chapter 10	Command Center (301), Building 21st Century Skills (306)
Chapter 11	You Try It (317, 325), Critical Thinking (319, 324, 328, 329), Command Center (329), Web Design Projects (333)
Chapter 12	You Try It (343), Apply It! (346), Critical Thinking (358, 359), Command Center (359), Web Design Projects (363)
Chapter 13	You Try It (377, 382), Command Center (387), Skills Studio (390), Web Design Projects (391)
Chapter 14	You Try It (396), Apply It! (397), Command Center (417)
Chapter 15	You Try It (427), Command Center (439), Standards at Work (440), Web Design Projects (443)
Chapter 16	Command Center (469)
Chapter 17	Tech Check (482), Command Center (489)

SCANS CORRELATIONS

SCANS Workplace Competencies

Interpersonal: Work on teams, teach others

Textbook Correlation

Chapter 1	Teamwork Skills (19), Tech Check (20)
Chapter 2	After You Read (58), Teamwork Skills (61), Web Design Projects (63)
Chapter 3	Apply It! (70), Teamwork Skills (93)
Chapter 4	Teamwork Skills (127), Building 21st Century Skills (130)
Chapter 5	Teamwork Skills (157)
Chapter 6	Standards at Work (186), Teamwork Skills (187)
Chapter 7	Before You Read (212), Teamwork Skills (215), Building 21st Century Skills (218)
Chapter 8	After You Read (244), Teamwork Skills (247)
Chapter 9	Before You Read (251), After You Read (270), Teamwork Skills (273), Web Design Projects (275)
Chapter 10	After You Read (300), Teamwork Skills (303), Building Your Portfolio (307)
Chapter 11	Think About It (309), Quick Write Activity (310), You Try It (317, 325), Critical Thinking (319), Tech Check (320), Teamwork Skills (331), Skills Studio (332)
Chapter 12	Quick Write Activity (334), Making Connections (360), Teamwork Skills (361)
Chapter 13	Tech Check (370), Critical Thinking (386, 387), Teamwork Skills (389)
Chapter 14	Teamwork Skills (419)
Chapter 15	Teamwork Skills (441)
Chapter 16	Applying Skills (461), Teamwork Skills (471)
Chapter 17	Standards at Work (490), Teamwork Skills (491)

SCANS Workplace Competencies

Information: Acquire, evaluate, organize, maintain, interpret, communicate and use computers to process information.

Textbook Correlation

Chapter 1	Apply It! (10, 14, 26), Go Online (10, 18), You Try It (13), Command Center (29), Standards at Work (30), Challenge Yourself (31), Web Design Projects (33), Skills Studio (32)
Chapter 2	Go Online (39, 43), Apply It! (42, 46, 56), Tech Check (47), You Try It (49, 51, 52, 55), Command Center (59), Teamwork Skills (61), Skills Studio (62), Web Design Projects (63)
Chapter 3	Go Online (66, 84), Apply It! (70, 77, 82, 88), Tech Check (83), You Try It (74, 76, 81, 86), Command Center (91), Making Connections (92), Teamwork Skills (93), Challenge Yourself (93), Skills Studio (94), Web Design Projects (95)
Chapter 4	Go Online (100, 111), Tech Check (115), Command Center (125), Making Connections (126), Standards at Work (126), Teamwork Skills (127), Challenge Yourself (127), Skills Studio (128), Web Design Projects (129), Building 21st Century Skills (130), Building Your Portfolio (131)
Chapter 5	You Try It (139, 143, 147, 149, 150), Apply It! (139, 151), Go Online (140, 146), Command Center (155), Making Connections (156), Standards at Work (156), Teamwork Skills (157), Challenge Yourself (157), Skills Studio (158), Web Design Projects (159)
Chapter 6	You Try It (165, 172, 174, 175, 178, 179, 180, 181), Apply It! (165, 170, 176, 182), Go Online (164, 167), Tech Check (166), Command Center (185), Making Connections (186), Standards at Work (186), Teamwork Skills (187), Challenge Yourself (187), Skills Studio (188), Web Design Projects (189)
Chapter 7	Go Online (192, 198), You Try It (193, 195, 196, 199, 208), Apply It! (201, 209), Command Center (213), Standards at Work (214), Teamwork Skills (215), Challenge Yourself (215), Skills Studio (216), Web Design Projects (217), Building 21st Century Skills (218), Building Your Portfolio (219)
Chapter 8	You Try It (230, 233, 234, 238, 240), Critical Thinking (227, 235, 242, 244, 245), Apply It! (227, 235, 242), Tech Check (218, 230), Go Online (228, 239), Command Center (245), Making Connections (246), Standards at Work (246), Teamwork Skills (247), Challenge Yourself (247), Skills Studio (248), Web Design Projects (249)
Chapter 9	Go Online (254, 261), Critical Thinking (256, 264, 268, 270, 271), Apply It! (256, 264, 268), You Try It (260, 262, 266, 267), Command Center (271), Making Connections (272), Standards at Work (272), Teamwork Skills (273), Challenge Yourself (273), Skills Studio (274), Web Design Projects (275)
Chapter 10	Go Online (278, 292), Apply It! (281, 291, 298), You Try It (284, 285, 286, 288, 293, 297), Critical Thinking (281, 291, 298), Command Center (301), Making Connections (302), Standards at Work (302), Teamwork Skills (303), Challenge Yourself (303), Skills Studio (304), Web Design Projects (305), Building 21st Century Skills (306), Building Your Portfolio (307)

SCANS CORRELATIONS

SCANS Workplace Competencies (cont'd)

Information: Acquire, evaluate, organize, maintain, interpret, communicate and use computers to process information.

Textbook Correlation

Chapter 11	Go Online (313, 321), Apply It! (319, 326), You Try It (325), Critical Thinking (328, 329), Command Center (329), Making Connections (330), Standards at Work (330), Challenge Yourself (331), Skills Studio (332), Web Design Projects (333)
Chapter 12	Go Online (349, 351), You Try It (337, 338, 339, 343, 344, 345, 349, 355), Critical Thinking (346, 358, 359), Apply It! (343, 352), Tech Check (347), Command Center (359), Making Connections (360), Standards at Work (360), Teamwork Skills (361), Challenge Yourself (361), Skills Studio (362), Web Design Projects (363)
Chapter 13	You Try It (377), Apply It! (369), Command Center (387), Making Connections (388), Challenge Yourself (389)
Chapter 14	Go Online (396, 401), You Try It (396, 401, 406, 407, 408, 411, 412), Critical Thinking (397, 403, 409, 414, 416, 417), Apply It! (397), Tech Check (404), Command Center (417), Making Connections (418), Standards at Work (418), Teamwork Skills (419), Challenge Yourself (419), Skills Studio (420), Web Design Projects (421)
Chapter 15	Go Online (424, 435), You Try It (427, 430, 434), Critical Thinking (427, 432, 436, 438, 439), Apply It! (427, 432, 436), Tech Check (428), Command Center (439), Making Connections (440), Standards at Work (440), Teamwork Skills (441), Challenge Yourself (441), Skills Studio (442), Web Design Projects (443), Building 21st Century Skills (444), Building Your Portfolio (445)
Chapter 16	Go Online (452, 460), You Try It (453, 459, 464, 465), Critical Thinking (454, 461, 466, 468, 469), Apply It! (454, 461, 466), Tech Check (455), Command Center (469), Making Connections (470), Standards at Work (470), Teamwork Skills (471), Challenge Yourself (471), Skills Studio (472), Web Design Projects (473)
Chapter 17	Go Online (477, 483), You Try It (476, 477, 478, 479, 480, 484), Critical Thinking (481, 486, 488, 489), Apply It! (481, 486), Tech Check (482), Command Center (489), Making Connections (490), Standards at Work (490), Teamwork Skills (491), Challenge Yourself (491), Skills Studio (492), Web Design Projects (493), Building 21st Century Skills (494), Building Your Portfolio (495)

SCANS Workplace Competencies

Systems: Understand, monitor, correct, improve, design systems.

Textbook Correlation

Chapter	
Chapter 1	Teamwork Skills (31), Web Design Projects (33)
Chapter 2	Tech Check (47), Skills Studio (62), Web Design Projects (63)
Chapter 3	Skills Studio (94)
Chapter 4	Web Design Projects (129), Building 21st Century Skills (130), Building Your Portfolio (131)
Chapter 5	Apply It! (145), You Try It (150), Making Connections (156), Teamwork Skills (157), Challenge Yourself (157), Skills Studio (158), Web Design Projects (159)
Chapter 6	You Try It (169, 178), Apply It! (170), Standards at Work (186), Teamwork Skills (187), Skills Studio (188)
Chapter 7	You Try It (193, 195, 196, 199, 208), Apply It! (197, 201, 209), Standards at Work (214), Challenge Yourself (215)
Chapter 8	You Try It (230, 233, 234, 238, 240), Skills Studio (248), Web Design Projects (249)
Chapter 9	Teamwork Skills (273), Skills Studio (274), Web Design Projects (275)
Chapter 10	You Try It (284, 285, 286, 288, 293, 297), Teamwork Skills (303), Challenge Yourself (303), Web Design Projects (305)
Chapter 11	Skills Studio (332), Web Design Projects (333)
Chapter 12	You Try It (337, 344, 345), Apply It! (343), Skills Studio (362), Web Design Projects (363)
Chapter 13	You Try It (373, 377, 382), Teamwork Skills (389), Skills Studio (390), Web Design Projects (391)
Chapter 14	You Try It (401, 411, 412), Skills Studio (420), Web Design Projects (421)
Chapter 15	You Try It (430, 434), Teamwork Skills (441), Building 21st Century Skills (444), Building Your Portfolio (445)
Chapter 16	You Try It (453, 459, 464, 465), Tech Check (455), Skills Studio (472), Web Design Projects (473)
Chapter 17	Web Design Projects (493), Building 21st Century Skills (494)

SCANS CORRELATIONS

SCANS Workplace Competencies

Technology: Select, apply, maintain, and troubleshoot technology.

Textbook Correlation

Chapter 1	You Try It (13, 23, 25), Go Online (20), Standards at Work (30)
Chapter 2	Go Online (39, 43), You Try It (49, 51, 52, 55), Apply It! (42, 46, 56), Standards at Work (60), Skills Studio (62), Web Design Projects (63)
Chapter 3	Go Online (66, 84), Apply It! (70, 77, 82, 88), Tech Check (83), You Try It (74, 76, 81, 86), Making Connections (92), Challenge Yourself (93), Skills Studio (94), Web Design Projects (95)
Chapter 4	Go Online (100, 111), You Try It (102, 104, 106, 107, 108, 110, 112, 113), Apply It! (101, 108, 114, 122), Challenge Yourself (127), Skills Studio (128), Web Design Projects (129), Building 21st Century Skills (130), Building Your Portfolio (131)
Chapter 5	Go Online (140, 146), You Try It (143)
Chapter 6	You Try It (169, 172, 174, 175, 178, 179, 180, 181), Go Online (164, 167), Apply It! (170), Standards at Work (186), Challenge Yourself (187), Skills Studio (188), Web Design Projects (189)
Chapter 7	Go Online (192, 198), You Try It (193, 195, 196, 199, 208), Apply It! (186, 193), Making Connections (214), Standards at Work (214), Challenge Yourself (215), Skills Studio (216), Web Design Projects (217), Building 21st Century Skills (218), Building Your Portfolio (219)
Chapter 8	You Try It (230, 233, 234, 238, 240), Apply It! (227, 235, 242, 244, 245), Go Online (228, 239), Making Connections (246), Teamwork Skills (247), Challenge Yourself (247), Skills Studio (248), Web Design Projects (249)
Chapter 9	Go Online (254, 261), Apply It! (256, 264, 268), You Try It (260, 262, 266, 267), Making Connections (272), Standards at Work (272), Teamwork Skills (273), Skills Studio (274), Web Design Projects (275)
Chapter 10	Go Online (278, 292), You Try It (284, 285, 286, 288, 293, 297), Apply It! (291), Standards at Work (302), Teamwork Skills (303), Challenge Yourself (303), Skills Studio (304), Web Design Projects (305), Building 21st Century Skills (306), Building Your Portfolio (307)
Chapter 11	Go Online (313, 321), Challenge Yourself (331), Skills Studio (332)
Chapter 12	Go Online (349, 351), You Try It (337, 338, 339, 343, 344, 345, 349, 355), Apply It! (343, 352), Skills Studio (362), Web Design Projects (363)
Chapter 13	You Try It (373, 377, 382), Go Online (367, 372), Teamwork Skills (389), Challenge Yourself (389), Skills Studio (390), Web Design Projects (391)
Chapter 14	Go Online (396, 401), You Try It (396, 401, 406, 407, 408, 411, 412), Apply It! (397), Tech Check (404), Standards at Work (418), Skills Studio (420), Web Design Projects (421)

SCANS Workplace Competencies (cont'd)	
Technology: Select, apply, maintain, and troubleshoot technology.	
Textbook Correlation	
Chapter 15	Go Online (424, 435), Apply It! (427, 436), You Try It (430, 434), Teamwork Skills (441), Skills Studio (442), Web Design Projects (443), Building 21st Century Skills (444), Building Your Portfolio (445)
Chapter 16	Go Online (452, 460), You Try It (453, 459, 464, 465), Apply It! (454), Tech Check (455), Making Connections (470), Teamwork Skills (471), Challenge Yourself (471), Skills Studio (472), Web Design Projects (473)
Chapter 17	Go Online (477, 483), You Try It (476, 477, 478, 479, 480, 484), Apply It! (481, 486), Tech Check (482), Making Connections (490), Standards at Work (490), Teamwork Skills (491), Challenge Yourself (491), Skills Studio (492), Web Design Projects (493), Building 21st Century Skills (494), Building Your Portfolio (495)

CREDITS

SCREEN CAPTURE CREDITS

Abbreviation Key: MS = Screen shots used by permission from Microsoft corporation.

© 2005 McGraw-Hill companies, **19;** © 1983–2005 MS Explorer, **18, 21;** © 1997–2004 Macromedia® Dreamweaver® MX 2004, All rights reserved. **20, 21;** © 2005 USA TODAY, a division of Gannett Co. Inc., **21;** © 2005 Museum of Modern Art, **21.**